# THE
# BLACK JOKE

The True Story of One Ship's Battle
Against the Slave Trade

## A. E. ROOKS

SCRIBNER

New York  London  Toronto  Sydney  New Delhi

Scribner
An Imprint of Simon & Schuster, Inc.
1230 Avenue of the Americas
New York, NY 10020

First Scribner hardcover edition January 2022

SCRIBNER and design are registered trademarks of The Gale Group, Inc.,
used under license by Simon & Schuster, Inc., the publisher of this work.

For information about special discounts for bulk purchases,
please contact Simon & Schuster Special Sales at 1-866-506-1949
or business@simonandschuster.com.

The Simon & Schuster Speakers Bureau can bring authors to your live event.
For more information or to book an event, contact the Simon & Schuster Speakers Bureau
at 1-866-248-3049 or visit our website at www.simonspeakers.com.

Manufactured in the United States of America

1   3   5   7   9   10   8   6   4   2

Library of Congress Cataloging-in-Publication Data has been applied for.

ISBN 978-1-9821-2826-5
ISBN 978-1-9821-2828-9 (ebook)

Image credits: pp. 15, 42, 57, 78, 141, 192, 204, 231, 243, 294: © National Maritime Museum,
Greenwich, London; pp. 30–31, 60–61, 118–21, 144–45, 168–69, 196–97, 206–7,
252–53, 270–71, 282–84, 296–97: Published by the National Archives,
Kew (Digital Microfilm Project). Sourced from Henry B. Lovejoy, dir., Liberated Africans,
https://liberatedafricans.org (accessed 2021); and p. 165: digitally sourced from the Medical
Heritage Library (contributed by King's College London, Foyle Special Collections Library).

For my father, who always wanted this,
and my mother, who made it possible

# CONTENTS

# AUTHOR'S NOTE

The most difficult voice to hear in the history of the transatlantic slave trade is that of the enslaved themselves. Often, people are barely individuated—for all historical intents, just one more body caught up in the morass of profit motives and policy decisions whose personal history we'll never know.

When *Black Joke* captured a slaver, the ship was sent to Freetown for trial; if condemned, the enslaved on board were formally freed, which is to say transferred to the jurisdiction of the British Crown as colonial subjects. The Liberated African registers from Sierra Leone give us the names of these people, their ages, and a bit of physical description—height, usually, but also sometimes scarring and ritualistic markings. Historians have been able to use these details to trace the tribal origins of some of them, to better illuminate the journey that brought them to Freetown, but when compared to the information that's available about the life of, say, the commodore of the Squadron, it's not much at all.

But it is something, and though many of their voices may not have survived in the historical record, in this way, their identities did. Though reproducing every relevant page of the register was not an option, after every chapter in which a slave ship was captured, the first pages of the Liberated African register for that ship are included here. It feels like somehow both the most and really the least I could do, but it's what we have.

Since even these records would not have been accessible to me during a pandemic without the work of archivists, historians, and librarians, I would like to especially thank Henry Lovejoy and the Liberated Africans project (https://liberatedafricans.org/), the National

Archives, Kew (Digital Microfilm Project), and the Sierra Leone Public Archives for the efforts toward education, digitization, and preservation that made the inclusion of these images possible.

And while we're on the subject of institutions that made what you'll see possible, the rest of the pictures herein are available courtesy of the National Maritime Museum in Greenwich, London, with special thanks to Beatrice Okoro, for patiently walking me through the process.

# THE
# BLACK JOKE

# AN INTRODUCTION

Beware, beware, the Bight of Benin,
there's one comes out where fifty went in.
—Sea shanty

The fire made for a beautiful sunset. The screams of sailors and slavers were a memory. The terrible cacophony of the cargo over which they'd struggled had also gone silent. It was as if the flames consumed not just ship timbers but sound; stillness had settled where the breeze of the sea refused to let the smoke rest, despite the crowds of people the blaze had drawn to the harbor. If evidence remained of the lives lived on board the now-empty vessel, it went up with the pungent smell of the burning decks, and the acrid scent of charred wood and whitewash accompanied the crack and snap of sparked beams. Naturally, the ship had been looted first, everything of value removed. The western coast of Africa was not a place where stores and sails would go to waste; what could not be used would be sold or traded by the same people who'd destroyed one of the finest Baltimore clippers ever to sweep across the open sea.

It wasn't the first time this notorious ship, the *Black Joke*, had been laid bare. Only five years previously, it had been a legendary slaver making quick work of a terrible job, with a reputation for being too fast to ever be caught—but one fortuitous night it had been. Repurposed from horrific duty to a higher calling and outgunned for much of its career, *Black Joke* nonetheless set about capturing slavers in the same waters it had so recently cruised for human chattel—and persevered. In a world where news traveled in months, rather than minutes, the slaver-turned-hunter was famous in both incarnations,

1

renowned in battles, outmaneuvering ships of every nation until its precipitous end. Those bearing witness to that demise knew that this time there would be no next chapter, no last-minute reprieve. This was irrevocable. It was not the sort of conflagration from which one arose.

Toasted by its peers and enemies alike upon its destruction in 1832, it's possible people wept upon hearing the news of *Black Joke's* ignoble end. Certainly the free Black population of Freetown, looking on from afar, would have saved the ship if they could have. The *Black Joke* had seized thirteen slave ships in its short life as an enforcer of abolition, but by many accounts, the tally in human lives spared bondage, at least in the immediate sense, was much greater. Setting aside the wider impact of the chilling effect created by *Black Joke's* mere presence on the water—which wasn't insignificant— while the ship was active, approximately a quarter of all the enslaved who arrived at Freetown to be officially liberated arrived care of this single ship and its crew. The crew on board included everyone from eager teen sailors (as young as thirteen) to grizzled veterans, in a diversity of ethnicities that demonstrated the incredible reach of the still-growing British Empire. A symbol to the whole of the West Africa Squadron (WAS) to which it had briefly belonged, the *Black Joke* had found and, at least temporarily, freed at least three thousand people. A figure to compare with how many the ex-slaver had itself brought to bondage, to be sure, but overall, barely a drop in the ocean of lives lost to the trade.

But how had it come to this? For four years, the *Black Joke*, itself a captured vessel, manned by a rotating crew, plagued by illness, dogged by bureaucracy and pirates, nonetheless sailed as the scourge of traffickers, releasing thousands of the enslaved from the cramped decks of ships flying flags from dubious diplomatic partners. Its captains and commanders had cracked slaver codes, discovered secret trade routes, and brought home the kind of prize ships that could change a man's life, and perhaps even his station. It had navigated shoals corporeal and political—whether off the coast of western Africa or ensconced in the Admiralty House in London, both were surpassingly treacherous. As those made rich from the sale of human flesh lifted a glass to a common enemy's downfall, speculation must've raged regarding who or what had destroyed the most celebrated thorn in the Atlantic slave trade's side.

To answer this question requires a deeper exploration of the transatlantic slave trade than many of us, especially in the United States, ever encountered in school. If your education was anything like mine, what we learned about the slave trade as children and teens—if we learned much of anything at all—can be distilled into two broad statements: it was extremely unpleasant, and it ended before the Civil War. Beyond these limited understandings, many seem to believe that after bans were enacted ... sometime in the 1800s, slave trading came to a mostly natural end.

Nothing could be further from the truth.

Despite its short tenure in the service, the journey of what would eventually become His Majesty's Brig *Black Joke* and its crew touched on nearly every aspect of this frequently overlooked chapter in the popular history of the abolition of slavery. If one begins with the ship's history as a slaver and its unlikely capture, to follow in the *Black Joke*'s outsize wake is to discover a ready microcosm of a difficult transition period for Britain. From biggest slavery profiteer before the turn of the nineteenth century to the most vociferous proponent of abolition soon thereafter—all while attempting to drag the rest of the world with it for reasons both high-minded and pragmatic—decades of British interventions in the slave trade, for good and ill, are reflected in *Black Joke*'s genesis, incredible campaign, and ultimate end.

In the oft-ignored era post-dating Napoléon and predating Victoria, the *Black Joke*'s crew, fortunes, and failures can be linked to not only the global evolution of the slave trade, but the demise of the Age of Sail, the increasing steam behind the Industrial Revolution, and the rise of Pax Britannica. However, this is not just a story of big ideas and global changes. The daily tensions and privations faced by the crew and their captured prizes—particularly in a time when the West Africa Squadron (also known as the Preventive Squadron) was arguably the most dangerous post in the British Royal Navy— reveal courage and suffering, greed and folly, all against the backdrop of one of the greatest blights on humanity's collective history. The actions undertaken by these sailors may have occurred on salt-crusted rigging or below enemy decks sluiced with blood, but they had the potential for far-reaching and explosive repercussions on the international diplomatic stage and for the cause of abolition as a whole.

The *Black Joke*'s voyage in the contemporary imagination went much further than its patrol. As we struggle to dismantle racist and colonialist legacies today, the *Black Joke*'s journey demonstrates that battles for freedom have never been short, uncomplicated, or without sacrifice—though they are, conversely, easily forgotten. Far from dying a slow, if mostly natural, death, the slave trade had to be actively dismantled over many years of tense maneuvers in storms both political and nautical, and if British sailors had a hand in it, so, too, did Africans, enslaved and free, as well as ardent abolitionists, politicians both reluctant and enthusiastic, and collaborators the world over.

This is not, however, yet another narrative in which Britain mostly saves the day. The history of the *Black Joke* (and certainly that of the Royal Navy) resists such simplistic assessment. Far from a story of unmitigated White Saviorism, this is a complex history with few uncomplicated heroes, even when writ as small as a single ship in a much-larger landscape. The slave trade, the fits and gasps of its final decades, the aftermath—the choices made then have filtered into every facet of our modern world; the *Black Joke*'s cruise is still in the food we eat and clothes we wear, it is still in the land we live on or occupy, it is in our wars and our peace and our borders and our economy and how cultures the world over grapple with legacies of colonialism and racialized violence. The repercussions of the transatlantic slave trade surround us, still. Regardless of which side of the Atlantic we live on, the reverberations of centuries of human trafficking and the turbulent decades encompassing the fight to finally end it are still felt now; it is in reading and writing about escaping the slave trade that one realizes that the legacy of the slave trade and its abolition is yet inescapable.

In our current political climate, one of tense negotiations and tenuous alliances in the face of an increasingly shrill White supremacist movement, perhaps these lessons from an untidy history, gleaned from a battle for justice that was waterlogged and dirty, nuanced and treacherous, can help in navigating society's way to better shores. Though one ship alone could never hope to stop the proliferation of slavery, to read the history of the *Black Joke* is to wonder if its example could have, to wonder why its success couldn't be replicated, to wonder further at the avarice, inefficiency, and moral relativism that frequently scuttled even the best efforts to halt the flow of the enslaved across the Atlantic. So much more could have been done decades sooner to effectively police the transatlantic slave trade. Hundreds of thousands of lives might have been spared the lash or saved outright had intrigue and ineptitude not created a scenario in which the greatest navy on earth somehow fielded a woefully understaffed fleet to contend against the flood of slavers pouring from so many ports.

Even a ship without peer, when situated in a military bound by distant bureaucracy, on a coast known for deadly maladies, in waters rife with hostility, was poorly equipped to cope with the sheer magnitude of the task set before it. This tiny ship of fifty or so men was Britain's reflection on troubled water—an image of morality and principle, regularly disrupted by waves of indifference to and profit from the trade in human chattel. As the embers of the *Black Joke* crumbled near Sierra Leone, one thing was clear: the Royal Navy would never contain its like again.

# CHAPTER ONE

*Henriqueta*
September 1827,
569 enslaved people

It was a ship with a reputation, and rumors of its speed might have been the only thing, in 1827, that sailed across the ocean faster than it did. American built, small timbered, lean, and by all accounts beautiful, the ship was masterfully crafted, and its sleek hull snuck through the deep night—quick, yet cautious. As it headed inexorably toward the equator and open ocean, its low profile was sunk lower still into the lapping waves by the weight of the bodies tightly packed belowdecks. Though it was a prime prize for many who might seek to claim the ship by right, might, or both, its captain nonetheless sped confidently through the warming September waters off the coast of Lagos, where he'd packed over five hundred then-shackled people into an impossibly small space. They would, soon enough, be in northeastern Brazil, a region under the yoke of centuries of sugar cultivation. They were bound for Bahia.

João Cardozo dos Santos might almost have felt sorry for his mostly still cargo. Were it not for British interference, their journey would at least be markedly shorter. The detours required by British treaties added weeks to the trip—his last had been forty-nine days—but did little to stop the trade; if the British supposedly cared so much for the enslaved, why make the inevitable worse? As for him, surely he minded the additional weeks on board, certainly he minded the farce of British diplomacy that had held his nation hostage to what he must have thought a fool's bargain, yet despite the money at stake, the penalties, the dangers, Cardozo dos Santos probably sat on deck unbothered. After all, he'd dealt with pirates and other slavers—what was the British navy to him, a man steering a ship he didn't own, carrying cargo that (perhaps with a few exceptions) did not belong to him, flying the recently crafted flag of his nascently independent country?

Despite the fact that Brazil had formally separated from Portugal a mere five years prior, in 1822, its dominance as a market for the slave trade remained unsurpassed. By the time the nation formally abolished slavery—over sixty years after Captain Cardozo dos Santos's soon-to-be much less quiet night—approximately 44 percent of enslaved people shipped to the Americas from Africa would have arrived, toiled, and, if dubiously fortunate, survived for more than a few short years working on the vast sugarcane, rice, tobacco, and cotton plantations or in gold and diamond mines across Brazil's territory. In contrast to the United States, which had nominally ended the practice of importing newly enslaved people after a congressional ban on slave trading went into effect in 1808 and thus relied heavily on "natural increase" (enslaved reproduction) to replenish the unpaid force on whose back the wealth of the nation rested, Brazilian slaveholders often found it more expedient to instead simply work their human property to death and buy more. Part of the reason for this difference may have been the nature of the work, as both sugar production and mining were notoriously difficult, onerous labor and thus thought to be inappropriate, if not impossible, for most women to perform. Brazilian slave markets thus demanded a substantially higher proportion of male enslaved Africans, and the ratios of the enslaved population, near 80 percent men to 20 percent women in some areas, made import, as far as slave holders were concerned, the only viable mechanism of sustaining Brazil's booming agricultural economy. The fact that the work was deadly, well, that simply meant import was very good business.

Slavery itself, not just land and resources, made men (and occasionally women) rich, and though Captain Cardozo dos Santos didn't have an ownership stake in this voyage, it's probable he was aiming to in the future. This was his seventh time captaining his current berth, the *Henriqueta*, a ship so fine it may well have been built for an emperor, for the only like craft sold in the era, originally named the *Griffin*, was purchased either by or for Pedro I of Brazil in 1825. The *Henriqueta's* previous six trips to this part of Africa, the Bight of Benin, had each been a resounding economic success, and the pretty little ship hiding unimaginable horrors, the same one cruising ever closer to safe passage under the cover of night, had already delivered over three thousand newly enslaved Africans to its home port, Salvador de Bahia, the region's capital, profiting its owner, Jose de Cerqueira Lima, approximately £80,000, over £8.5 million (nearly $11 million) in 2020. Extraordinarily rich and socially prominent with it, de Cerqueira Lima was, perhaps even more than his employee, likely supremely unconcerned with the fate of the *Henriqueta*. The wealthiest and most famous slave trader of his era in all of Brazil, which is saying something in a time when well over forty thousand (and rapidly rising) Africans were trafficked each year to that country, de Cerqueira Lima was a busy man with business, with parties, with politics—he was serving as a city councilman that year—and this ship was just one of a fleet of at least a dozen slavers reaping him handsome, if blood-soaked, profits.

And besides, he had insurance. No matter that missions such as the *Henriqueta's* had been rendered illegal via laws enacted under pressure from Britain, first under Portuguese rule and then as independent Brazil, de Cerqueira Lima and his ilk were so powerful that they were able to protect their interests in vessels purpose-built for illegal trade, even specifically insuring them against capture by the Royal Navy right in the policy. Though *Henriqueta* called Salvador home, the ship was insured by an outfit in Rio; few in power anywhere in Brazil were eager to obey treaties forced on them by a foreign empire bloated with economic might, and this, Cardozo dos Santos knew, suited his employer just fine. Him, too, truth be told—he'd only risked capture once in this, arguably the fleetest of ships, and that had been bad luck more than anything else. The second time he and this ship had made this voyage, the *Henriqueta* had been spotted loading shackled Africans at Lagos, and was either reported by the nearby American schooner *Lafayette*, or the slaving brig was being abetted by the schooner, yet was nonetheless found by the Royal Navy's HMS *Maidstone*. If the former, since Americans had also built Cardozo dos Santos's ship and most like it, the captain wasn't sure why they feigned disdain when coming across them at their business on the water, but it hadn't mattered. He had outsmarted them the usual way.

A simple, if tedious, solution worked nearly every time: Cardozo dos Santos ordered his crew to off-load any of the enslaved already on board, with haste, then waited to sit through the "inspection" by the British. After whatever cumbersome tub they had on patrol had finally lumbered to harbor, the captain presented them a ship devoid of human cargo, and even if the chains sat in plain view on what was very obviously a slave deck, regardless of whether coffles of the enslaved stood packed in barracoons within sight of the harbor, or even at the docks themselves, there was nothing the English could do. No enslaved on board, no crime. Then he and his crew would idle a while longer to ensure the English were well away—a few days perhaps, though it could be weeks, even months—a respectable period of time, time spent drinking and eating and, in his case, making pleasant conversation with the locals who mattered. Then upon reloading the enslaved under cover of night, they aimed the *Henriqueta* straight for the open ocean, hurrying toward the equator (and away from British jurisdiction) at full sail. The Royal Navy ships were old, often repurposed warships, lots of guns, but achingly slow for the task to which they'd been set. Though the *Maidstone* had waited for them, again, it hadn't mattered; if it had been a real chase, Cardozo dos Santos had barely noticed, and he'd arrived in Salvador, only slightly delayed and cargo very much intact, without even a good story to show for the patrol's efforts.

Yes, business was good, excellent even, despite the fevers, the heat, the rain, the ruthless competition, and the incessant meddling of England, embodied in its slow and infrequently spotted West Africa Squadron. If one could not hear the cries or smell the stink, the former, at least, lessening as the hour eased past midnight and exhaustion claimed his captives, it was peaceful on board one of the most prolific slavers on the coast—until a voice rang out over the slick deck in the still night, and the captain started, refocusing on the horizon. There, suddenly, another ship had leaped into view and was rapidly closing.

*Leaped* might have been pushing it, but the much-bulkier silhouette of the HMS *Sybille* was certainly putting on its fair share of speed despite being everything the *Henriqueta* quite deliberately was not. Designed by the famous French naval engineer Jacques-Noël Sané, the *Sybille* had been in service since 1792 and seen plenty of action, including its own initial capture by the British HMS *Romney* just three years after being launched from Toulon. Having been in service to the Royal Navy for the next thirty-three years, *Sybille* was now a little more antiquated, more liable to show its age and wear. Though the *Hébé*-class frigate was four times larger than its quarry with nearly eight times the complement of sailors and dozens more guns, the firepower and French proportions that had once served it well in the Napoleonic Wars here, when compared to those of its nimble American-built target, simply made it heavy and more ill-suited to its duty: no less than the eradication of the Atlantic slave trade.

*Sybille* was not without its advantages, even in these seemingly mismatched circumstances. Both the ship's crew and its commander, the recently arrived Commodore Collier, had plenty of experience with pirates, many of whom sailed smaller, more maneuverable ships, more akin to the *Henriqueta* than those he commanded as an officer of the Royal Navy.

Just a scant decade earlier, in 1818, Francis Augustus Collier had been recalled into active service to combat a "piratical scourge" in the

Persian Gulf, which is to say quell local resistance to British economic colonialism. This "resistance" at the time took the form of tolls that the family controlling the area, the al-Qawasim, charged all ships doing business in the Gulf, money the British had no interest in paying, which eventually prompted some raids of British vessels. However, rumors of supposed piracy (and attendant Arabic barbarism) had almost certainly been vastly overblown by the British East India Company in an effort to provoke just this sort of military response. The validity of the assignment was of little interest to anyone back in London at the time; of greater import, Collier's first command of a squadron—and the resulting effort to quell opposition to British regional intervention—had been a resounding success. A career navy man who'd thus far earned his promotions while on service in the West Indies, Collier's creativity, diligence, ability to command, and willingness to order the complete eradication of entire harbors until little was left but smoldering ruin were credited by some with functionally eliminating the practice of piracy from an entire geographic area.

This seems like less of a feat when the history of regional "piracy" was as short as it was exaggerated, but given that the British informal empire in the Gulf can be dated to the treaty forced out of this ruinous campaign (and lasted deep into the twentieth century), the significance of the action can't be overstated. International parties and the British commander of the land operation, Major General William Kier Grant, heaped praise on Collier's "zealous, cheerful, and active" leadership, without which the campaign might have failed. Awards for distinguished service followed soon after—the Order of the Lion and Sun from the Persian sovereign (though the Foreign Office disallowed Collier's wearing of it), and the Cross of the Legion of Honor, the highest class of France's top military honor, from then Louis Philippe (III), Duke (of) Orléans, cousin to the king (and later king himself). Back at home, however, the Admiralty's reaction to Collier's resounding success had been substantially more tepid. Through a sleight of bureaucratic hand based on his not yet being of flag rank, aka an admiral, Collier, already a Companion of the

Order of Bath for previous service, was denied the knighthood those involved thought he unquestionably deserved. Though other British naval officers present for the campaign would be knighted for their valor, Collier would never receive any official recognition from his own government for his success in the Persian Gulf. A man who was as courageous as he was frequently uncompromising, Collier seems to have not always been uniformly beloved by his superiors. For him to be promoted to commodore of an overseas squadron, however, some in the Admiralty must have suspected that if any man could turn an impossible naval task into a foregone inevitability, or at least make a good showing, it was the one at the helm of the *Sybille*. Moral imperatives aside, this was a job, and Collier was determined to finally make an example of the loathsome *Henriqueta*.

Collier's habit of doing things right, regardless of whether they made him popular, probably divided opinion—for instance, he regularly petitioned his superiors on behalf of his men, but was known to be a strict disciplinarian, and this in the days of severe, even deadly, corporal punishment. Collier was unambiguously good at his job and came from a solid naval lineage, in both family and patronage. He had been hand-selected by none other than Admiral Horatio Nelson, among the greatest naval heroes Britain had ever produced, who had remained Collier's patron until Nelson's untimely death in the Battle of Trafalgar in 1805. Nelson had, it cannot be overstated, been a *massive* fan of Collier's, ever since he'd encountered a ten-year-old Francis on the streets of Bath in 1798, smartly dressed in naval uniform, and with a child's eagerness to adventure.

Though many in the Royal Navy joined the service young, Collier's initially rapid ascension was a reflection of his connections, his precociousness, and the times in which he lived. He'd been born in 1788 to a recently established naval family, as his father, Vice Admiral Sir George Collier, had risen from middle-class origins to great success harassing the American colonists in their war for independence. Sir George, much like his son, had been known as a man of great initiative, with a talent both for command and for annoying his superiors with his forthright opinions; he'd been vocal in his opinion that the American war was unwinnable as it was being managed, which made him enemies among those then in power in the navy. Sir George was an unconventional man: he used his spare time in the Americas adapting theatrical works; spent his life challenging superiors, possibly to the detriment of his career; spent his political capital on oppositional positions in Parliament; and last, though certainly not least, spent his actual capital securing a divorce—Francis, one of his father's seven children, was the product of Sir George's *second* marriage. Divorce, though not completely unheard of in the eighteenth century, was an uncommon and often embarrassing experience, as the willful dissolution of a marriage required a literal act of Parliament to accomplish and could only be granted for adultery. Though not solely the province of the aristocracy, divorce was an expensive process, and only about 325 occurred during the 150-plus years these acts were required. Sir George's ability to secure one in 1772, even before his most successful tours of duty in the colonies and resulting honors, speaks volumes to just how far the senior Collier had already risen, even before the peak of his career (and about the problems that existed in his first marriage).

Sir George's second marriage, to Francis's mother—Elizabeth Fryer, a wealthy merchant's daughter from Exeter—was presumably a happier affair, but it, too, was eventually cut short. By the time Sir George's naval career had begun to recover from his foray into politics, enough to merit two promotions in just two years after over a decade of waiting, the newly minted vice admiral's health failed so suddenly that he was forced to resign the active command he'd spent his life seeking. The senior Collier left his ship in January of 1795 and was dead by April, only a year after his seven-year-old son entered his first ship's books (or list of personnel). Signing up for naval service at an exceptionally young age was a common practice to gain an advantage in time served for the naval experience required of officers, though boys so young rarely served on board any Royal Navy vessels bound for distant harbors. So when Nelson encountered a

Engraving of Sir George
Collier (© NMM).

Watercolor of Sir Francis
Collier (© NMM).

previously unknown lad that fateful morning in Bath—who, if he'd resembled his father at a young age, would have shown the promise of a "middle stature"; "well made and active"; with an "open and manly" countenance and "complexion fair"; his hair light and his eyes blue and beaming with intelligence—whatever he'd found remarkable about the boy Francis Collier's demeanor was not a function of long experience or family name. The recently promoted admiral had an eye for the man he thought young Francis might become, not merely the circumstances into which he'd been born.

Sunny disposition, keen intelligence, or just awfully snappy in a uniform, whatever ineffable quality it was Collier had, Nelson, always on the lookout for talent to add to his ships' complement, found himself entirely taken with the lad, and upon learning that Francis's father had also been an admiral of some skill, the soon-to-be hero of Britain sought permission to call on Francis's mother at the family's residence in Bath.

Perhaps if it had been after Nelson's greatest fame, rather than before, Lady Elizabeth Collier wouldn't have hesitated. Sir George had been dead for three years now, and after all, both Francis and her oldest son, also named George, were already enlisted in the navy. It wasn't even particularly unusual for a family to allow their son to go to sea with what was essentially a stranger; earlier in the century two vicar's sons, Alexander and Samuel Hood, would eventually go on to become feted admirals and peers of the realm after a carriage accident brought then Captain Thomas Smith to the boys' home for the night while awaiting repairs—the younger boy, Alexander, leaving for sea almost as soon as the captain did. Perhaps lively and cheerful Francis, such a joy to be around that the very sight of him arrested high-ranking strangers and passersby, was simply his mother's favorite. Perhaps she was scared for the child's life, as Nelson, who happened to be home in England because he was recuperating from having lost his right arm in a defeat to the Spanish at the Battle of Santa Cruz de

Tenerife, would have been a stark reminder of how deadly life at sea could be. No matter the cause, Lady Elizabeth took more than a little convincing, including several additional letters, visits, and assurances from Nelson, to give her son up to the admiral's custody, and with it active service, that same year. (Given that Nelson's correspondence for the next few years would include written updates regarding young Francis's progress and prowess to the boy's mother, one imagines Lady Elizabeth's eventual assent came with some strings attached.)

If she was concerned for Francis's well-being, Lady Elizabeth must've felt downright prescient when the first action her ten-year-old son saw was the famous Battle of the Nile in 1798. The long, pitched, and ultimately decisive night engagement; creative tactics; and impressive head injury to his new mentor, Nelson, surely must have made an impression as Collier, who in later letters preferred "Frank," adjusted to life at sea. In 1803, when the Peace of Amiens collapsed after only one year, ending the brief respite from open hostilities between French and British—and, at some point or another, seemingly every other major and minor European—powers, Collier found himself on the front lines of British colonial interests in the West Indies. Then a lieutenant so freshly minted that he'd had to carry blank promotion papers from England to be signed upon his arrival—despite Nelson's insistence to Earl St. Vincent, First Lord of the Admiralty, Collier simply wouldn't have served enough time to rise in the ranks until his transport to the Caribbean had concluded—Collier had been all of fifteen years old when he'd arrived at the Leeward Islands Station in April of 1803; war resumed in May. The teen who'd arrived to his berth on the HMS *Osprey* was not an inexperienced youth, but a war veteran who'd already served with Nelson and Sir Charles Ogle and, once on board, quickly earned distinction as a reliable and courageous leader of men. Perhaps, like his father, he was more vocally opinionated than his superiors would prefer, but if this was a defect, it was one many saw as outweighed by Collier's growing reputation as the kind of man who, twenty-five years later, could jump-start a lackluster campaign—exactly what he'd been tasked to do as the captain of the *Sybille* and the commodore of the West Africa Squadron.

The West Africa Squadron could use whatever help it could get. By the time Collier arrived in 1827, the Squadron had existed in some fashion for nearly two decades, but it hadn't been robustly supported during either of them. Some would much rather see the recently minted commodore fail, likely more due to animus to the mission rather than the man. Despite England's having abolished the slave trade in 1807, the battle to do so had been highly divisive both in Parliament and throughout the nation, in no small part because a great deal of the British economy directly depended on either the ongoing enslavement of Africans or on the products the practice produced. From the moment John Hawkins took the less than laudatory distinction of being England's first slave trader in the mid-1500s until abolition of the trade, it's estimated that English slavers had shipped approximately 3.1 million enslaved Africans to ports scattered throughout the Americas, and at least four hundred thousand of those individuals never survived the journey. Gradual moves toward abolition in 1799 restricted the British trade to three ports in England proper—Liverpool, Bristol, and London—and Glasgow in Scotland participated heavily as well, but by this point the now British Empire had dominated the slave trade for at least the previous century and had already been immeasurably enriched by human bondage. Beyond the coin made in the sale and trade of the enslaved, the British Empire created via colonization relied on the labor Africans provided to not merely function, but to economically survive.

While the United States had violently exited the British domain decades before *Sybille* sailed the ocean, England remained intricately invested in the cotton trade as a leading manufacturer of cloth, and in distant holdings such as Jamaica and Barbados, colonial governments ruled over a fractious plantation class that demanded enslaved labor to keep up with the world's insatiable craving for sugar. The imperial reliance on sugar cultivation had been a crucial aspect of England's participation in what is also known as the triangular trade and was a likely root of much of the skepticism many had regarding *Sybille*'s (and the rest of the Squadron's) larger mission. If some higher-ups within the British government and Captain Cardozo dos Santos agreed on one thing, it was that both thought it unlikely that England could continue its present economic dominance without the ongoing existence of slavery. Enslaved people produced the raw materials that English industrialism consumed to create products often used to trade for more enslaved people—by the end of the eighteenth century, at least half of the ships transporting the approximately eighty thousand newly enslaved each year were of British extraction. Those who welcomed responsibility for the presence of the *Sybille* were either less fatalistic or more ethically driven, but there was no altering the plain historical fact that European slave trading had existed on the western coast of Africa for centuries and, at the outset of the nineteenth century, constituted upward of 75 percent of total regional exports. For England's economy to survive a collective bout of moral reckoning, it was imperative that the rest of the world's powers also give up the sale of human beings—without a global shift in attitude, or at least law, Britain would have lost its primacy in the market without creating perceptible change regarding slavery.

One could not simply ban a major industry and expect that to be the end of it, especially since incentives to disregard the new law were both plentiful and lucrative; such a massive shift in policy would have to be enforced. Given the inherent maritime element of a transatlantic trade, it makes sense that Parliament would turn to the Admiralty (in conjunction with the Colonial Office) to see its will carried out, but there were more reasons than water to merit the Admiralty's involvement. When the abolitionist push at the highest levels of government began in earnest in the 1780s with a comprehensive fact-finding mission, it was slavery's impact on the Royal Navy, not Africans, that ultimately cracked open the door to serious consideration of the movement's ultimate goals. It had long been taken for granted that seamen unassigned to one of His Majesty's ships might seek their paycheck from the private sector—England had the largest merchant marine in the world undergirding its powerhouse economy, alongside everything else—and the slave trade was widely regarded as just one of several licit ways to make a living at sea. If it was more dangerous to engage human cargo rather than bales or barrels of freight, well, a job was a job, even risking pay in weaker West Indian currency, and sailors readily switched between seafaring industries. At slaving's peak in Britain, as many as 130,000 British sailors may have worked in the trade. What piqued the Privy Council's interest, however, was abolitionist Thomas Clarkson's discovery, after the examination of over twenty thousand muster rolls (lists of ships' personnel), that the slave trade was not just some mildly riskier business—a fifth of the *crew* of a slaving vessel could be expected to die on a round-trip voyage, usually from illness, though overzealous punishment from slaver captains and enslaved uprisings claimed their share of lives, too. On top of that another fifth, though not dead, would likely be rendered unfit for service as far as the Royal Navy was concerned, be it through incapacitating illness or disability, or parting ways with the slaver on foreign shores partway through the trip.

A yearly 40 percent hit to a large sector of the available manpower with sailing experience had the Admiralty's attention because, as was the way of things at the time, war with France was both recently concluded and on the horizon. It was the Treasurer of the Navy who proposed gradual abolitionism in 1792, and though an end to the British slave trade wasn't promulgated for another fifteen years, it was the navy that would ultimately be tasked with making the new law reality. That is not to say that it was a priority. By 1807, war with France was very much back on, and the Admiralty wasn't willing to give much in the way of resources or thought to preventing the slave trade. Though some back in England used the next few years to transition to licit trade, others—particularly in the cities most profiting from slavery—tried to circumvent the new law in a variety of ways, from shifting to foreign investments in the slave trade to attempting to fly foreign flags on their slavers to avoid detection. British participation tapered, but by no means ceased, in the wake of An Act for the Abolition of the Slave Trade's going into effect in 1808; espe-cially in the early years, slave trading was likely hampered more by European conflict than by any nascent preventive efforts. As for the navy, it made a number of early captures in the West Indies, which was already a theater in the war against Napoléon, but the first ships sent to patrol the western coast of Africa the first year the law could be enforced weren't even a squadron—they were instead listed as "on particular service," a designation for Royal Navy vessels that were unassigned to an official squadron or station. It would take several years for a formalized West Africa Squadron to come into being, and it rarely contained more than six assigned ships in any given year, a fact Collier's arrival on the *Sybille* would not fundamentally change. All the while, the slave trade continued almost apace as other nations rapidly filled the gap in the market Britain had (mostly) left.

Thus, aged, comparatively cumbersome, and not really suited to the task at hand, HMS *Sybille* typified the force of the British will to end slavery, and clearly it was a populace divided. Though a more comfortable berth than smaller ships, the *Sybille* and its peers in the West Africa Squadron were frequently outclassed by slavers in speed and maneuverability, and the talents of the Squadron's crews and command were repeatedly called on to make up for shortcomings that seemingly only increases in budget (or perhaps more precisely, political favor) could remedy. But the merchants and politicians of England weren't on this ship—Francis Collier was, and he was de-termined make headway where his predecessors had not, no matter how much opposition he had at home or across the water. The com-modore had a job to do, and he had the men to do it, but he needed more ships, faster ships. Ships like the *Henriqueta*.

At deadly cross-purposes, it's possible, even probable, that at an-other time, in a different place, the *Henriqueta* might have evaded the Squadron's hunt; it obviously had before. Cruising off the shores of the Bight of Benin at midnight, *Sybille* had been lucky to spot the low-slung brig in the darkness, recently laden and just leaving harbor. Just as lucky was the fresh breeze that rose in the tropical night as the crew crowded on sail in pursuit. Most fortunate of all, however, might have been that Captain João Cardozo dos Santos was assured of the unparalleled speed of his slaver. Certain of his ship's escape, unafraid of risking capture, the captain attempted to get windward of the *Sybille*, ordering *Henriqueta* to cut across the bow of the larger frigate. The spray disappeared into the night as the crew of the slaver executed its daring move toward an irony-rich freedom, putting on as much sail as could safely be filled by the brisk wind.

Had Cardozo dos Santos simply tried to flee as he had before against the *Maidstone*, relying on the passage of time as much as *Henriqueta*'s speed, he might have managed to clear the equator and, with it, any obligation a Brazilian brig might have to English authority. When he instead attempted to get upwind, bringing the slaver dangerously near its foe, the *Henriqueta*'s risky path and the *Sybille*'s able sailing—due in no small part to the abilities of the latter's first lieutenant, William Turner, who had already served a commission on that ship—put the brig directly in sight of *Sybille*'s gunners. With the easy practice born of veterans of the Napoleonic Wars, they fired their bow chasers, skipping heavy balls of cast-iron shot off the water and into the slave ship's rigging, destroying sails and masts while (they hoped) sparing the lives trapped belowdecks. In the darkness, *Henriqueta* had come far too close; though the *Sybille*'s size was a detriment in some respects, it also allowed the frigate to carry far more in the way of armament than that mounted by its small, seemingly indefatigable quarry. More men, more firepower—the frigate's guns flashed above the depths and into the darkness until the smaller brig had no hope of flight and was forced to surrender to boarding from armed British sailors. One of the most notorious ships in the slave trade was on her way to a new identity, while young First Lieutenant Turner had just helped capture the ship that would alter his course forever.

Even after capture, a slave ship still held perils for all who'd encountered it. A captured ship accused of slave trading could not be left to it own devices. A crew from the *Sybille* would have to steer the *Henriqueta* to judgment by the Mixed Commission, established for the purpose, again by treaty, in Freetown, Sierra Leone. Commodore Collier was by no means unfamiliar with at least some of the risks he'd be asking of every sailor assigned to man the slaver's final journey. He'd seen action against French privateers in the Napoleonic Wars and, while assigned to the *Osprey*, had served on prize crews in the Caribbean. There, within two months of his arrival, the teenage Collier had led landing parties of seamen and marines in support of British territorial control in the Caribbean, and within six months he found himself at the head of a prize crew of perhaps a dozen men tasked with escorting the French privateer *Ressource* into custody. Prize crews, while they left ships shorthanded, could serve several Royal Navy purposes at once. The most obvious is that they were necessary to preserve custody of captured bounty before legal disposition, which often took place in specific locations that might be far out of the way of the capturing vessel's normal patrol, such as Freetown, the home of one of three Courts of Mixed Commission tasked with the adjudication of slaving ships. As an internal naval matter, being placed at the head of both ship and crew provided valuable experience to promising young officers—conversely since, depending on the circumstances, prize ships could reach their destinations several months and several hundred miles distant from the navy ship whence the crew came, those crew members who were less than promising could effectively be reassigned to another, closer HMS vessel, making the prize crew an efficient mechanism to make problem sailors someone else's problem.

It's not known whether Collier's prize crew was of the fractious sort, but it seems rather unlikely given what happened once he took the helm of the *Ressource*. Though he had not led the party that boarded and captured the vessel he now guided, when the crew spotted yet another privateer, the *Tremuse*, young Francis, who had clearly never lacked initiative, didn't hesitate. The French ship had a complement of forty-five sailors, but undeterred, Collier and his tiny crew took that vessel as well, spreading themselves even more thinly among all the tasks that had to be accomplished to keep two captured ships' crews subdued, as well as both boats afloat and aimed in the correct direction. Many prize ships were often less fortunate, or less well manned. Though some simply took an inordinate amount of time to complete otherwise short journeys due to navigational or structural issues, others succumbed to disease, insurrections from captured crews, or even rebellion from the enslaved population on board, for whom one captor was much the same as another. However, when *Osprey*'s prize crew eventually arrived at the Vice Admiralty court for adjudication, the talented young lieutenant's gamble paid off impressively; if issues with recognition later dogged the future commodore's career, this time his actions on the *Ressource* and *Tremuse* likely provided the next logical step toward his advancement up the ranks, as Collier returned to the *Osprey* soon to become its first lieutenant.

So, better than most, Commodore Collier, who now faced a subdued *Henriqueta*, knew that his choice of prize crew was important, particularly if he wanted to ensure this vessel would be available to redeploy as soon as possible. Though Lieutenant Turner may have seemed like a logical choice, Collier likely needed him aboard *Sybille*—losing a prize was one thing, but capable personnel were, due to the conditions of service in the West Africa Squadron, considerably more valuable and, in some ways, even more easily lost. So instead the dubious honor of guiding the slaver to Freetown fell to an Admiralty mate named Frederick Mather. In the WAS, the groups of sailors known as prize crews frequently consisted of as few as nine or ten men assigned to take possession of a slave ship, as well as its surviving crew and all the enslaved, and navigate the journey to their day in court in Sierra Leone. Due to the need to stay close to the coast for safety reasons and given that the trip to Freetown went against the ideal currents and winds, what could have been a quick (for the time) three-week trip had the potential to become a voyage of several months. The crews were necessarily small because WAS ships needed the personnel, but the job of caring for the malnourished and dehydrated human cargo, ensuring that a noncooperative enemy crew stayed imprisoned, and sailing the ship shorthanded was an exhausting one.

There was good reason it was difficult for the enslaved Africans to tell the difference between slaver and nominal liberator—in their quest to maintain order, prize crews frequently rechained captives, continued to ration water and food, and used whips and floggers as incentive and punishment. Though it's true that more than one of these smaller crews had succumbed to rebellion from their slaver prisoners or from the recently enslaved themselves, the real danger constantly stalking the decks of all ships was a variety of deadly maladies that respected neither skin color nor nationality. The conditions on slave ships exacerbated what was already a serious risk of illness; unlike navy vessels, which were cleaned more regularly and weren't overcrowded, the slave trade's demand for maximum profits created conditions that murdered the very people it commodified. Collier's predecessor atop the West Africa Squadron, Commodore Bullen, had been so appalled at the conditions he'd found on a slave ship captured in May of that year, a few months before Collier's arrival, that he felt compelled to detail the horrors in a letter to the Secretary of the Admiralty:

> *The putrid atmosphere emitting from the slave deck was horrible in the extreme, and so inhuman are these fellow creature dealers, that several of those confined at the farther end of the slave-room were obliged to be dragged on deck in an almost lifeless state, and wasted away to mere shadows, never having breathed the fresh air since their embarkation. Many females had infants at their breasts, and all were crowded together in a solid mass of filth and corruption, several suffering from dysentery, and although but a fortnight on board, sixty-seven of them had died from that complaint.*

Having released as many people from the slave deck as the upper deck would allow, the *Henriqueta* was said to be so crowded with naked bodies on the prize crew's voyage to Freetown that a captive African fell overboard in the night and no one noticed until morning. The overcrowding was also illegal, as in just 1824 Brazil had, at least on paper, changed the permissible ratios of people to ship tonnage to make the slave trade more "humane." While three years earlier, under Portuguese rule, Captain Cardozo dos Santos would have been permitted as many as 600 enslaved people crammed into a space significantly smaller than *Henriqueta's* roughly ninety-by-twenty-six-foot frame, in 1827 that number should have dropped to a licensed capacity of 490 . . . yet 569 enslaved people had been embarked in Lagos into a seemingly impossible space. Though Brazilian authorities seemed distinctly uninterested in consistently enforcing these changes—at least if the rest of Jose de Cerqueira Lima's extensive fleet of slavers was anything to go by—this gave the *Henriqueta* the rather common distinction of being illegal both at home and abroad. Lest any laws remain unbroken on the voyage in between, Cardozo dos Santos had been carrying double passports at the time of the ship's capture, the better to obscure where he'd purchased the Africans on board and thus circumvent Brazilian treaty obligations while maximizing profits.

Upon arrival in Freetown—the moans and wails of the sick and dying inescapable, crawling with all manner of insects and pests, and literally stinking of every conceivable guilt as it sat in the harbor, as the "excessively disagreeable and oppressive" reek of the "dense mass of human beings was suffocating" to those who boarded even after the slaver anchored—the *Henriqueta* was soon ready to be tried in court. Back in 1808, when the nations of Europe were in global conflict, a Vice Admiralty court had been established in Sierra Leone to adjudicate the fates of captured enemy slave ships; these courts presided over maritime crimes, prize cases, and the occasional commercial conflict. However, at least when it came to prizes, the advent of peace had necessitated an increasingly complicated spate of treaties to accomplish what the expedient of war no longer provided—an international right of search and, with it, the ability to police the seas. By the time of *Henriqueta*'s trial, the judicial body in Freetown had evolved into one of three Courts of Mixed Commission—the other two were in Rio and Havana—specifically impaneled with a multinational slate of judges to represent the interests of all concerned nations while adjudicating such matters. (At least in theory they were multinational; in actuality, the commissioners in Sierra Leone were usually uniformly British due to the difficulty of getting a non-British national to accept a posting in Freetown, which, as a somewhat recently established colony, was considered a backwater.) The Brazilian brig's purpose and location when apprehended were difficult to dispute; *Henriqueta* was rapidly condemned as a slaver by the court and, as was the custom, put up for auction. Commodore Collier, fresh off success and with permissions in hand, wasted no time, using £900 of his own money to acquire what would eventually become the pride of the Squadron on January 5, 1828.

Jose de Cerqueira Lima almost certainly took the loss with equanimity. He'd lost ships to the British before and would go on to lose several more—it was just the risk one ran in this business. He continued to be a prominent and influential citizen, eventually becoming a justice of the peace with a home so extravagant that it would later officially house provincial presidents and Bahia's governors. And besides, de Cerqueira Lima, although the biggest at the time, was just one of a number of high-profile Brazilian slave traders, and one of hundreds, even thousands, of those who owned or invested in a boat engaged in the involuntary shipping of enslaved people worldwide. As little satisfaction as there is in knowing that de Cerqueira Lima had a long and prosperous life as a pillar of the community despite any economic setbacks inflicted by the Royal Navy, it mirrored the state of things in Brazil in the late 1820s. The global abolition of the slave trade was a stutter-step process officially commenced by Britain in 1807, but it had only been a dream nominally acceded to by Brazil in 1826. The latter nation insisted on a gradualist approach to abolition that was meant to be strengthened by existing and progressively more stringent laws until Brazil abandoned the market altogether in 1830, but acquiescing to the British had had an unintended side effect on the market that had made reality far less satisfying.

Given these conditions—questionable political will, lax enforcement, reluctant partnerships, and massive profits to be potentially had by anyone willing to break the law—it's unsurprising that at the time of *Henriqueta*'s capture, the slave trade remained rampant. In Brazil, at least, the panic created by the prospect of the abolition of the slave trade spurred massive investment in procuring new enslaved laborers that might not be available for much longer, increasing the demand for trafficked persons. But if de Cerqueira Lima and his captain Cardozo dos Santos—who, though technically liable for his part in the transaction, would, like so many other slaver captains, walk free, if missing a ship and several hundred people who should not have belonged to him or anyone in the first place—embodied the desires of some to cling to slavery and their continuing ability to be successful at exploiting it (current setback notwithstanding), then the ship they lost came to represent quite the opposite. The transition from American shipbuilding worthy of royalty to Brazilian slaver to Royal Navy vessel was not always a smooth one. The small brig would come to symbolize new methods and ideas for fighting slavery, heralding the possibility that a moral and ethical disgrace global in scope and centuries in the making could actually be fought and quickly dismantled, piece by piece.

The battles over change that marked this span of years weren't limited to a single brig. A spreading fervor for a radically different future could be found in government, nationhood, and ideology, and with it, a growing will to abandon at least some aspects of the past to progress. So it was fitting that the new year and the new owner had yielded the *Henriqueta* one more major change—a new name. In early 1828, rechristened and repurposed, the now *Black Joke*, for let it not be said that Collier lacked a sense of humor, embarked on a campaign of harassment of slave traders that arguably no single ship had ever, or would ever, match. The *Henriqueta* had personally delivered 3,040 enslaved people to Bahia's markets. Though the lives shattered and lost on the way to Salvador and on Brazil's plantations could never be recovered, it would be up to the *Black Joke* and its crew to make whatever amends for the past, and changes to the future, the little brig with the legendary speed could accomplish. This transition from slaver to liberator would pace Britain's larger struggle to abolish the trade in the face of a cavalcade of obstacles and obstruction from within and without the empire, but not without cost. Though the *Black Joke* had been created suddenly, birthed out of redemptive opportunity and sheer force of will, the circumstances that would lead to its destruction were already in motion.

Portuguese Brig "Henriqueta" Register of Slaves Natives of Africa
captured on board the said Vessel by His Majesty's Ship Sybille
Francis Augustus Collier CB. commander and Emancipated by Decree
of the British and Portuguese Court of Mixed Commission on the
29 day of October 1827; the said Brig having been pronounced liable

| No | Names | Sex | Ag | Stature ft | In | Descriptions |
|----|-------|-----|-----|----|-----|-------------|
| 11397 | Ayah | Man | 27 | 5 | 7 | cuts on the face & CC on left Breast |
| 11398 | Bankolay | , | 27 | 5 | 6 | cuts on the face and body |
| 11399 | Okolay | , | 26 | 5 | 10 | do & CC on left Breast |
| 11400 | Chuboloo | , | 28 | 5 | 7 | do & body — do — |
| 11401 | Odochinnah | , | 29 | 5 | 9 | Cut all over |
| 11402 | Epinno | , | 32 | 5 | 7 | Cuts on the face & CC on left breast |
| 11403 | Gpraiddaymee | , | 26 | 5 | 11 | Cut all over — do — |
| 11404 | Elollah | , | 27 | 5 | 9 | — do. — do |
| 11405 | Elookobu | , | 24 | 5 | 8 | Cuts on face — & CC on right breast |
| 11406 | Oguisu | , | 26 | 5 | 8 | do & CC on left breast |
| 11407 | Meedayhing | , | 29 | 5 | 9 | Cuts all over & CC on left breast |
| 11408 | Osugbah | , | 28 | 5 | 6 | Cuts around middle of body & — do — |
| 11409 | Ebagbay | , | 32 | 5 | 9 | — do — do — do — |
| 11410 | Olokay | , | 18 | 5 | 4 | Cuts all over & CC on left breast |
| 11411 | Aynah | , | 21 | 5 | 5 | cuts on both shoulder & left Arm & CC on left breast |
| 11412 | Egbay | , | 20 | 5 | 4 | cuts on face & breast & CC on left breast |
| 11413 | Ayenah | , | 19 | 5 | 3 | cuts all over — do — |
| 11414 | Edowoo | , | 21 | 5 | 5 | — do — do — |
| 11415 | Madda | , | 25 | 5 | 5 | — do — do — |
| 11416 | Cudjoo | , | 44 | 6 | 0 | Cuts on face & CC on left breast |
| 11417 | Kodonnah | , | 27 | 5 | 4 | — do — do — do — |
| 11418 | Chackiroy | , | 23 | 5 | 3 | Cuts all over do — do — |
| 11419 | Gubook | , | 21 | 5 | 5 | — do — |
| 11420 | Dimday | , | 29 | 5 | 10 | Cut on face & CC on left breast |
| 11421 | Chackay | , | 26 | 5 | 4 | Cuts on breast & Belly — do — |
| 11422 | Maddoo | , | 27 | 5 | 2 | Cut all over — do — |
| 11423 | Fattirah | , | 21 | 5 | 3 | Cuts on face & Breast — do — |
| 11424 | Kittam | , | 27 | 5 | 1 | — do — & CC on left breast |
| 11425 | Diggekay | , | 28 | 5 | 6 | CC on left Breast |
| 11426 | Atodoo | , | 24 | 5 | 3 | Cut on face, breast & Belly & S on back of right shoulder |
| 11427 | Ellarko | , | 29 | 5 | 3 | do. do & CC on left breast |
| 11428 | Bahsamo | , | 25 | 5 | 4 | Cuts on the face — do — do — |

Register, Henriqueta

liable to condemnation by the said Commission on the same day, for
having been at the time of capture engaged in the illicit traffic in Slaves—

| No. | Names | Status | Ap.t | Stature ft. in. | Description |
|---|---|---|---|---|---|
| 11429 | Wookahnee | Man | 27 | 5 3 | Cut on face & body & CC on left breast |
| 11430 | Mahtillahyah | " | 29 | 5 9 | Cut all over — & do — do — |
| 11431 | Ogobee | " | 26 | 5 3 | — do — do — do — |
| 11432 | Sadahtoo | " | 27 | 5 5 | — do — do — do — |
| 11433 | Ojoo | " | 26 | 5 6 | do — do — do — |
| 11434 | do | " | 28 | 5 6 | — do — do — do — |
| 11435 | do | " | 29 | 5 9 | — do — do — do — |
| 11436 | Sallahtoo | " | 24 | 5 5 | — do — do — do — |
| 11437 | Addam | " | 26 | 5 7 | CC on left breast |
| 11438 | Ocher | " | 30 | 5 5 | Cuts all over & CC on left breast |
| 11439 | Quireehbee | " | 27 | 5 6 | Cuts on the face — do — do — |
| 11440 | Odoso | " | 27 | 5 5 | Cut all over — do — do — |
| 11641 | Olummanee | " | 23 | 5 5 | — do — do — do — |
| 11642 | Shguoboo | " | 29 | 5 5 | — do — do — do — |
| 11443 | Ahdaytayge | " | 25 | 5 2 | Cuts on face & left arm & do — do — |
| 11444 | Sados | " | 26 | 5 8 | Cut all over — & do — do — |
| 11445 | Dayguguay | " | 27 | 5 4 | — do — do — do — |
| 11446 | Ahmusee | " | 28 | 5 4 | — do — do — do — |
| 11447 | Mahmah | " | 27 | 5 4 | — do — do — do — |
| 11448 | Bahkay | " | 28 | 5 5 | Cut on face & Breast |
| 11449 | Azahtimboo | " | 24 | 5 3 | Cuts all over & CC on left breast |
| 11450 | Danganneah | " | 29 | 5 6 | Cut on the temples & Breast |
| 11451 | Bahkay | " | 26 | 5 6 | Cut all over & CC on the left breast |
| 11452 | Ojoroo | " | 28 | 5 10 | — do — do — do — |
| 11453 | Abah | " | 26 | 5 7 | Cuts on the face & CC — do — |
| 11454 | Brimah | " | 27 | 5 2 | Cut on Breast & left arm & CC on left breast |
| 11455 | Mahnah | " | 28 | 5 3 | CC on the left breast |
| 11456 | Mahgannah | " | 23 | 5 5 | Cut all over & CC on left breast |
| 11457 | Mahmah | " | 35 | 5 7 | Cut on face & Breast & do — do — |
| 11458 | Alley | " | 26 | 5 4 | Cut all over |
| 11459 | Ahkeykah | " | 28 | 5 3 | — do — & CC on left breast |
| 11460 | Landlatoo | " | 36 | 5 7 | Cut on breast. do — do — |

# CHAPTER TWO

*Gertrudis* (aka *Gertrudes*; Eng.: *Gertrude*)
January 1828,
155 enslaved people

Collier's choice of name was perhaps even more tongue-in-cheek than modern sensibilities might suggest and may not have been referring to current understandings of Blackness at all. *Black Joke*, now a seemingly obvious reference to the *Henriqueta*'s rather abrupt change in mission, was then most commonly known as either the titular object of a bawdy jig, or the type of lewd humor of which it was generally representative. Dating back to at least 1730, the extant verses—and there are many—celebrate, at great length and in increasing detail, the nether regions of an unnamed comely British woman, she "with a black joke, and belly so white." The song and its variations were still so popular that this new *Black Joke* wasn't even the first ship with that name to serve—between hired crafts and nicknames, at least two *Black Jokes* had been on the water in recent memory. The brig didn't even have the distinction of being the only *Black Joke* sailing in 1828, as a notoriously unmerciful pirate, Benito de Soto, had just that past year participated in a mutiny on board the slave ship *Defensor de Pedro* and, upon succeeding in taking the slaver and killing both the old and the newly elected captains, renamed his ill-gotten ship *Burla Negra*, or "Black Joke." This transition was as meaningless as the *Henriqueta*'s had been dramatic—in 1824, Britain enacted a law stating that slavers had committed "felony, piracy and robbery, and should suffer death without benefit of clergy and loss

33

of lands, goods and chattels as pirates, felons and robbers upon the seas ought to suffer," but no British slaver was ever prosecuted under it, so men like de Soto were merely the most obvious and vicious examples of a veritable ocean full of pirates and "pirates" engaged in similar business. For the purposes of the West Africa Squadron, well, they all looked alike. Call him a slaver or a pirate—the job title would have made little difference to de Soto as he was, quite avidly, both— either way, he'd immediately set about pillaging any ships unfortunate enough to meet him, preferring to brutally execute the crews he encountered rather than take on prisoners or additional sailors, capturing any enslaved on board for further maltreatment and eventual sale.

Whether or not all the possible meanings were intentional, sharing a name with a dirty tune or a prolific and ruthless pirate ship and slaver, albeit in a different language, was the least of the *Black Joke's* potential controversies as it began its new career. The very existence of ex-slaver tenders in the West Africa Squadron was a point of contention for many of those at the top of the Royal Navy's hierarchy. The tender system, in which a nonmilitary craft is introduced to the force and, in cases such as this, is understood to be simply part of an existing Royal Navy vessel, was not new at the time of *Henriqueta's* capture and remains ongoing today. Traditionally, tenders are smaller than their military counterparts and are often used as supply ships, running vital goods—such as munitions and food—from shore. All the previous naval crafts officially named *Black Joke* were tenders in this traditional sense.

What Collier wanted to do with this new *Black Joke* was rather different, but it certainly wasn't precedent shattering. The previous commodore of the West Africa Squadron, Charles Bullen, initiated the practice of deploying tenders on active cruise, rather than as mere support vessels, and vigorously advocated that the Squadron make as much use of former slaver tenders as the Admiralty and Navy Board would permit. Getting this particular ship for his first tender must have felt to Collier like a fitting final salute to Bullen's time in the WAS. After all, HMS *Maidstone*, which had almost captured

Cardozo dos Santos and his sleek brig on the *Henriqueta*'s second voyage, was Bullen's own flagship, and Commodore Bullen—by this point more than three months departed from the coast of Africa for a much-needed rest back in England—if not remotely successful in dealing anything resembling a death blow, had left quite a wake. Having sailed off toward an eventual appointment to the Navy Board as Commissioner of the Navy for Pembroke Dockyard, several promotions, and eventual knighthood, Charles Bullen, who also had the distinction of having been a captain at Trafalgar under Nelson, had been the third commodore in the West Africa Squadron's official existence, and during his three-year tenure, British sailors had liberated approximately ten thousand enslaved people. Collier, another of Nelson's protégés, would have not just appreciated, but heeded, Bullen's advice and experience.

Bullen had recognized that tenders in the WAS could do quite a bit more for their mission than merely carry supplies. Freed from the requirements that the Napoleonic Wars, various revolutions, and budgetary wrangling had placed on Royal Navy craft of the era— meaning many of the WAS vessels were older, repurposed warships by design and necessity—"tender" status potentially allowed for the slave ships the British were already capturing to be acquired cheaply, removed from circulation in the slave economy, and ultimately used against their former compatriots in human trafficking. However, what should have been an obvious win-win-win was undoubtedly complicated by the uncharted and, frankly, murky waters into which Britain's foray into bully pulpit diplomacy had cast the WAS. Was the capture of a slaver by a tender even legitimate? No less than the foreign secretary himself, George Canning, had recently had to craft a letter clarifying the official English stance on this point of maritime law. The situation precipitating Canning's involvement had been initiated by Commodore Bullen, who, realizing that it might be better to ask forgiveness than permission, used the wide latitude sheer distance from the Admiralty back in England granted him to put the tender question to the test.

Back in November of 1826, the *Hope*, a former slaver now tender to Bullen's *Maidstone*, captured the slave ship *Nicanor* as it departed Little Popoe (modern-day Aného, Togo). Though the capture had been an unmitigated success and was in every other manner done in deference to Britain's treaty obligations, the propriety of the *Hope's* actions turned on an outwardly minor technical point. Tenders, not officially independent ships in their own right, did not then as a matter of course carry the requisite paperwork (copies of those self-same treaties) that would empower them to capture slavers—those papers were reserved for Royal Navy vessels. Yet the unique nature of service in the WAS necessitated creative solutions, and Bullen was reasonably certain this one might be effective. Before the somewhat innovative strategy of exploiting the legal status of tenders to put more ships to sea capturing slavers could be put into wider use, however, it would have to be legitimated. This wasn't a question of using foreign vessels—England was already much in the habit of repurposing any ships the nation captured to whatever end might best suit. The problem was that, given that extant treaty obligations granting Britain the right to search the ships of other nations had been hard enough to come by, and with foreign "partners" constantly trying to wriggle out of the already agreed-upon terms, clearly few outside of Britain were looking to willingly cede even more potential power to police to an already swaggering nation, demonstrably keen to throw its weight around internationally.

For the foreign secretary, widely regarded as one of the most brilliant politicians and orators of his age and at this job for the second time, the reluctance of his international peers to accede to any terms that might have a meaningful impact on the trade probably made the answer easy, or at least easier, to settle on. George Canning would eventually go down in history as one of the first European politicians to understand the import of recent revolutionary affairs in South America and can be directly credited for helping bring about the independence and recognition of several new Latin American countries, including Brazil, as well as forcing fellow colonizing empires Spain and Portugal to recognize their former holdings as nations in their own right. This work had allowed England to weaken its European rivals while reaping the benefits of newly accessible markets across the ocean, but though the treaties were signed and the ink mostly dry, the geopolitical landscape remained precarious. Canning, a vocal proponent of abolition, readily realized that the Squadron had a hard enough go of it without being hamstrung by unstipulated details like what sorts of British ships were allowed to capture slavers, and with the weight of hastily compiled precedent, he came down firmly on the side of Bullen's interpretation of maritime law, writing:

> *I have received your [dispatch] [. . .] in which you call my attention to the Case of the "Nicanor," captured and condemned for illegal Slave-trade. The peculiarity of this Case was, that the Slave-trader was captured by a Vessel acting [ . . . ] as a Tender to His Majesty's Ship "Maidstone." On this point I have to acquaint you, that, by a Communication from the Admiralty, it appears that it would be contrary to all the Regulations of His Majesty's Naval Service, to consider the Tenders as in any way distinct from the Ships to which they belong; and I have further to state to you, that it is the opinion of His Majesty's Law Officer that you have acted properly in the Case referred to, and that you should continue to act on the same principle in future Cases. I have also to acquaint you, that, for the more fully carrying of this principle into effect, the Lords of the Admiralty have given orders, that the respective Officers commanding the Tenders in question should each be furnished with the signed Instructions required by the Treaties for the repression of the Slave-trade.*

In short, Canning asserted that since tenders were a part of the Royal Navy ship directing their actions, the authority a Squadron vessel had to detain slavers should theoretically transfer to the tenders beneath them. Sure, any ship making captures for slave trading was supposed to be in possession of its own signed copies of the treaty papers, not unlike the letters of marque carried by privateers, and would going forward. But if said tender was officially indistinct from the ship to which it was assigned—and as such wouldn't have been carrying its own papers regardless—then when it caught a slaver, by the transitive property of Britain's say-so and as a matter of legal fiction, Canning decreed that it was essentially the same as if the Royal Navy ship that supervised it had done the deed.

The appeal of such a shift in policy had to be obvious to those who, like Canning, were supportive of the WAS efforts in the Atlantic. Building new ships was expensive and time-consuming, especially during the dawning of the era of Pax Britannica. The Napoleonic Wars had only just ended in 1815, and the Royal Navy's prize for decades of (mostly) successful war-making on multiple fronts across the globe would be several more decades of aggressively militaristic "peacemaking" on multiple fronts across the globe. The relatively recent conclusion of the wars in Europe had left a sufficient glut of sailing personnel that the practice of press gangs, or roving bands of men involuntarily conscripting their fellows into the Royal Navy, had ceased by 1815 (which is to say, not in time to prevent the War of 1812, which had been sparked in part by increasingly strenuous objections to the pesky British tendency to impress American nationals). New ships, however, were not in like supply. While some of the fleet had been rendered unfit or outright destroyed by the incessant confrontations marking the turn of the nineteenth century, those that could be repaired and salvaged would soon again be scattered across the globe, this time as self-appointed referee rather than open combatant.

The end of this age of warfare precipitated an altogether different kind of decimation within the Royal Navy. Up until quite recently the British government's largest (and most expensive) employer, the massive fleet of 1812, with 543 ships and over 130,000 men, employed only 20,000 just five years later. Alongside the navy's diminished capacity came a diminished role in the affairs of the empire it had helped secure, and the once-powerful political forces supervising the Admiralty and the Navy Board were steadily declining in influence and might. The unsteadiness of the new normal created by these rapid changes was amplified by fear. Though Britain's economic position was strong and would gain as the century progressed, the cessation of the slave trade had many concerned that even more sailors, those employed in the merchant marine, would also be put out of work. Among the more prosperous set, recent uprisings in the colonial holdings, not to mention the end of costly and protracted wars with Napoléon et al., had many in government and in trade deeply concerned as to whether the English economy could weather such a commitment to moral indignation. And now a much reduced and likewise divided navy had been tasked with enforcing it all.

In the era of the *Black Joke*, when much of Europe and the Americas was approaching the twilight of what would come to be known as the Industrial Revolution, a zenith of an altogether different, and in some ways antithetical, historical moment was also taking place. The Age of Sail, dating from the mid-sixteenth to mid-nineteenth centuries, had seen the domination of maritime pursuits as vital components of robust statehood, and though enormous navies and colossal warships may have been on their way to passé, the particular demands of slavery in the 1820s and '30s meant the wind was still full for shipbuilders who knew how to put on the speed. Shipbuilding had been just as susceptible to the energy of the era as any other trade, and *Henriqueta* and its slaver kith had readily proved in most every encounter that ships built to contain human cargo were much speedier than warships. The Royal Navy had just had reasonable success in several wars and clearly wasn't hurting for decent ships—the class of French frigates to which the *Sybille* belonged, in particular, was so popular a design that the Royal Navy had fifty-four near copies finished or under construction by 1831. While smaller than the towering ships of the line that dominated in Nelson's day, these new frigates being turned out over a decade after the wars had concluded were still fairly large, and though capable of reaching speeds up to thirteen knots, they were primarily built to send and withstand volleys from similarly structured opponents. Successful innovations in the types of smaller wooden vessels that would make up the bulk of the Squadron were not yet forthcoming, either.

The War of 1812, as it's known in the United States—apparently in Britain this conflict doesn't merit an appellation as it was only one of several fronts—had prompted a rather different response from American shipbuilders. In deference to the realities of costs, crew size, and available armament, the use of privateers had become a necessary expedient in the conflicts with Britain, and American shipwrights turned their attention to crafting progressively faster ships capable of evading British enemies at sea, sturdy enough to take a fight, or flight, on open and betimes storm-battered waters. As the war progressed, increasing numbers of American privateers took to harassing the British frigates, and the world couldn't help but notice that, quiet as it had been kept, the former colonies were steadily putting out arguably the best ships on the water. Beautiful, seaworthy, well-formed, and, above all, wickedly quick, the fastest of these privateers were capable of reaching twenty-one knots, almost double the speed of the frigates. Just as fast as the famous clipper ships popular almost a half century later and hardy, it's no surprise that, after the war, the American privateers became a model for slavers—they shared many of the same needs, and the same builders. Over the years, the "race-horse beauty" of American slave ship design evolved through the shipyards of the northeastern United States to an epicenter in the Chesapeake (Baltimore) region, which, though not exactly places normally associated with the wholesale embrace of slavery today, both made use of and were integral to the transatlantic slave trade in the eighteenth and nineteenth centuries.

Many Americans, despite the foreign slave trade being banned in 1808, remained perfectly happy to do business with anyone willing to buy ships, and slave brokers were eager indeed. The period after the war saw continued innovations in shipbuilding, and prohibitions notwithstanding, the 1820s debuted the kind of purpose-built slave ships Bullen and now Collier would face off the coast of Africa; unfortunately for the WAS, the British suppression efforts of the previous decade were already strongly influencing their design. Indeed, every facet of the slave trade was considered in the creation of a ship. Slavers couldn't be too large, as a massive profile against the horizon would make them obvious targets for the Royal Navy, and besides, new restrictions on the trade meant that it was difficult to purchase sufficient quantities of human beings in any one market, and even with an undermanned patrol, attempting two ports simply wasn't worth the risk. And there was a minimum size, too. To turn a profit, traders, wholly untouched by the moralizing sentiments of the day, performed a nasty calculus. There were several ways to be murdered on a slave ship—presuming one wasn't raped, beaten to death, or thrown overboard for "disobedience" (or to set an example) by a crew member, claustrophobic conditions limited the air supply, fostered unmitigated filth, and propagated disease. Prosperous slave traders had an eye for the bottom line, not human suffering, and each of thousands of voyages was a horrific negotiation between the number of Africans who could be unreasonably crammed into a space and how quickly those same Africans would die from the conditions of that space and the voyage. The most profitable slave ships ranged from sixty to a hundred feet, and with room at a premium—and decent care viewed as an unnecessary expense—a certain percentage of loss of life was not only acceptable but expected to maximize profits.

The obscene money to be made meant that those commissioning new ships in the 1820s were capable of funding the creation of craft perfectly suited to the trade in size and seaworthiness, all with particular attention to the specific climates, routes, and even the individual harbors where a vessel would likely make port. None of this care for craftsmanship was extended toward the comfort of those captured and detained.

Allowing for the limited space available for enslaved, crew, and supplies required for oceanic travel, the slave deck was near uniformly less than five feet in height, often three feet or lower in practical headroom, and situated at or near the waterline, making it difficult to keep dry.

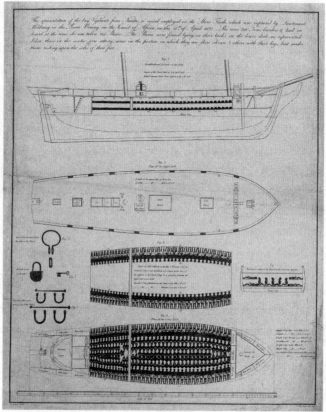

Plan of slave ship *Vigilante* (© NMM).

Grated hatches let in some air because it could be presumed that the enslaved would spend at least sixteen hours a day held below, but provided no relief from the heat, particularly on days when the temperature on even the upper deck surpassed ninety degrees. Suffocation and heat-related deaths were common killers, and though many deadly illnesses also attended the decks of slave ships, there was no dedicated treatment area beyond moving the ill from the slave deck to a section of the main deck, where they often shared what little space there was with the sleeping hammocks of the crew. Thought was usually given to the construction of a barrier to separate the enslaved by perceived gender, though this may have been less for propriety's sake—rape was prevalent, and any number of enslaved women would disembark on the other side of the Atlantic pregnant—and more to allow the crew a place to retreat in the event of an uprising.

Despite this multitude of humanitarian flaws, the attention given to their speed and armament ensured that purpose-built slavers were, as a rule, simply better suited to the theater of conflict in which they and the West Africa Squadron found themselves. The slavers, compared to British ships built in England, or those that had been acquired from other nations in previous wars, had additional features that commended their use to the Royal Navy, at least once they had been captured, tried, and condemned. Had the Admiralty been more considered about and less resistant to the notion, had they purchased former slavers rather than only grudgingly accepting them when pressed, they would have found that these ex–slave ships were much cheaper to put into use than the products of England's best shipyards. At auction, the slavers were as little as a tenth, even a twentieth, of the cost of building a ship in England, and that doesn't include getting it to the coast of Africa. Even with the cost of refitting slave ships to serve in the Royal Navy, the WAS could have been creating and sustaining a force that might have been capable of effectively patrolling the coasts of Africa and would have been able to replenish itself without committing substantial additional resources. After a vessel had been worn out through service, it still had uses. The materials on board could be repurposed, and through the process of "removing the lines," particularly well-designed craft would be dismantled, and the elements of their construction documented, enabling them to be copied and replicated and thus availing the navy of any of the latest innovations in shipbuilding abroad.

Commodore Bullen had been moderately successful using tenders and had made no bones about how vital he felt they could be for the Squadron's mission: they were cheaper, they were better designed for the service in question, they were best equipped to capture ships like themselves, and the Royal Navy had an established history of both using tenders and adding ships to the fleet via capture. And yet the Admiralty continued to refuse to enthusiastically back their use. Given all the positives, this vacillation seems rather senseless, but there were some valid drawbacks. Though Canning's letter had made it clear that it was acceptable to use tenders to capture slavers—ideally while possessed of the proper paperwork—no policy mandated, or even much governed, their use in this way. This is most obvious when one recalls that it was not the Royal Navy who was buying these tenders—officers were. And it was not up to the Admiralty to adjudicate what was a legitimate capture—that's what the Mixed Commission was for. Once suspected slave ships were brought to Freetown (or Rio or Havana), both they and members of their crews were examined before a court meant to be composed of a panel of judges representing all treaty-partnering nations. Since Freetown was considered a pestilential, undeveloped hinterland by citified Europeans and South Americans—if an extraordinarily scenic one—no judges particularly wanted to go there, meaning the Mixed Commission in Sierra Leone had thus far exclusively contained British judges. As a result the court also had the highest rate of condemnations, and if so judged, the slave ship was auctioned off to the highest bidder, some of whom were naval officers like Collier or Bullen, while others were proxies for slave traders looking to secure quality, gently used shipping at an extremely low price. The Admiralty did not provide a budget for the acquisition of additional vessels to officers already assigned a berth on one of His Majesty's ships; any ships so purchased did not just become recognized members of the Squadron simply due to being owned by a captain. Given the nature of WAS service, it was entirely possible, even likely, that when an officer returned to England after a tour was completed, he would simply auction off any tenders he owned to the highest bidder ... who was usually a slave trader. Rather than become vigilant about the disposal of former slave ships, the Admiralty had instead recently issued commands that officers be discouraged from making such purchases at all—any benefits weren't worth the risk of scandal.

No matter the outward political situation, for the moment the men of the Navy Board and the Admiralty retained near-complete control of internal policy. Before leaving England, Collier had felt the political winds and seen that the attitude toward tenders from the higher-ups was lukewarm at best and rapidly cooling—and whether or not he gave a damn about optics, the new commodore was by now adept at the political gamesmanship success the Royal Navy demanded. To that end, Collier secured permission to buy such a ship *before* he left England, and as such, before the Admiralty began to actively discourage their acquisition. So when a marvelous specimen had all but presented itself scant months after he arrived in Sierra Leone, he could move to follow Bullen's advice as quickly as the adjudication process would allow. Given that Collier had caught the *Henriqueta* almost as soon as he arrived and purchased it immediately thereafter, the acquisition occurred well before his superiors would have had a chance to change their minds and communicate any increased restrictions on the tender policy to the Squadron on the coast—his expedient, plus £900, had worked. Further, since the Admiralty had already agreed months earlier to furnish a tender of Collier's with its own set of official treaty papers should he nab a suitable one, the *Black Joke* would have the distinction of becoming the first tender in the West Africa Squadron that could unquestioningly legally cruise for slavers entirely independent of its parent ship, presumably with the understanding that Collier would be kind enough not to embarrass the navy by allowing the ship to fall back into a slaver's hands.

Those who topped the Royal Navy's command structure were responsible for every aspect of the administration of an organization that was still, even recently diminished, a major force in British political and cultural life and identity. For these men—and they were all men—safeguarding the reputation of the navy was of paramount concern. Indeed, reputation and moral standing were much on everyone's mind, as this was an era when the power of perception had diplomatic stakes as well. At the time, Britain was leaning heavily on its mercantile power to force other nations to acquiesce to England's newfound morality in regard to slavery, or at least the slave trade, which it had itself outlawed in 1807. This move wasn't universally popular by any stretch of the imagination—at one point Liverpool was one of the richest slave-trading ports in the world—and if selling the notion on the home front in England was difficult, convincing historical rivals like France, Spain, and Portugal to give up one of the most lucrative trades in the world frequently seemed next to impossible, while forcing many of their own colonists in places like Jamaica to do so was a pipe dream. Both slavery itself and indentured servitude were very much still legal in the British Empire—only the buying, selling, and shipping of the enslaved was forbidden. Maintaining the tide of rectitude that had given rise to the WAS and supported its mission on the home front necessitated positive public opinion. The more strident abolitionists would not brook the thought of Britain doing anything that might facilitate the trade, even as an afterthought or by-product. Diplomatic matters abroad likewise required Britain's dealings to appear beyond reproach—powers in other nations already looked askance on English intentions toward slavery, and lest years of interminable meetings ultimately come to naught, any hint of backroom dealings and external profit motives had to be righteously snuffed out.

This need to keep up appearances was balanced by the colossal amount of economic power Britain could access. Many treaty negotiators had found the power of the purse to be the most compelling of the available diplomatic strategies. Agreements between England and Portugal, and England and Spain, both involved direct monetary payouts in exchange for concessions that would allow the Royal Navy the right to search suspected slavers and seize the guilty, as well as grant the newly established Courts of Mixed Commission the power to judge those so captured. Complicating matters, these treaties frequently had to be renegotiated, whether in light of newly discovered implementation problems, or due to an acute case of national reorganization, as both the Spanish and Portuguese empires were at that time in an ongoing process of spectacular collapse.

The revolutions that caught the winds as the *Black Joke* cruised were not just metaphors for sea change in industry and economics; there were also quite literal revolutions happening with what must have seemed like startling frequency all over the globe. When the colonizers and the colonized rose up against their shared imperial overlords, together or independently, it meant that Britain had to provide inducements to remain at the bargaining table to not just the French, American, Spanish, Portuguese, and Dutch state representatives, but also to the new governments of any recently liberated holdings. Loath to lose any progress in regulating the slave trade, British negotiators were required to craft these additional agreements with a mind to both the desires of the new nation and the previously stipulated obligations of its former rulers.

The *Henriqueta*'s capture, for instance, was governed by the terms Britain had ratified with two recognized foreign powers. Brazil, formerly of Portugal, had agreed to abolish the slave trade three years after the date of the mutual ratification of its treaty with Britain in 1827. However, because the nascent Brazil had desperately needed English recognition of its independence to strengthen its position and ensure its economic survival, it had also been obliged by this new treaty to honor Portugal's previous agreements with Britain in regard to the abolition of the slave trade. Although these terms had been settled even before Brazil's formal existence, in 1810, 1815, and 1817—and in the face of plenty of resistance from wealthy Brazilians—the British had made it clear that the simple expedient of revolution could not be used to allow colonies-turned-nations to evade the restrictions on the slave trade that had previously governed them. (Given the resistance to regulation the English faced in their own Caribbean territories, it's fair to assume they were particularly uninterested in the kind of precedent *that* might set.) Since Portugal was restricted to trading the enslaved below the equator, by subsequent agreement so was Brazil, for three years from the ratification, and after that date, in 1830, the international trade became wholly illegal and equivalent to piracy. This meant the *Henriqueta*, which was flying Brazilian colors in 1827—after the treaty was signed but before full abolition of the trade went into effect—but boarding enslaved people in Lagos (above the equator), was, in contravention of the previous *Portuguese* commitments inherited by Brazil, acting illegally, and thus subject to legitimate capture by the British.

If this sounds confusing, it was, extraordinarily so, and was perhaps nowhere more evident than on the decks of the ships tasked with enforcement. Since different vessels were potentially party to a potpourri of treaties, WAS ships had to judge each encounter with fresh eyes and potentially radically different rules. While power moves on the world stage dictated which countries' ships the Squadron could rightfully detain where, a different kind of ruthless practicality ruled the waves. Tricks, feints, and treachery surrounding the nationality of a ship, its port of origin, its destination, its rig, its cargo, and even the national identity of the crew were so commonplace as to be the norm. Many sailing captains (not just the slaving ones, and not just the merchant ones) were willing to lie, and lie boldly, about who they actually were if they felt the situation required it. Frequently they would take every available precaution to tailor their deceptions to both context and foe; given that lives, not just livelihoods, often depended on it, they tended to be proficient. Due to the existence of privateers—state-sanctioned pirates—even vessels involved in legitimate trade had reasons to deceive, the means and props to do so, and plenty of practice.

If Collier wanted a ship that would make proverbial waves, the kind that might increase support for the campaign at home and change attitudes toward tenders in Whitehall (Admiralty) and Somerset House (Navy Board), just one mile apart in London, he knew he would need a smart, bold, and resourceful lieutenant as its captain. That WAS service was not exactly in a popular location might have been a hindrance when opportunities for advancement were plentiful—say, during a war—as many serving in the Squadron from England could barely tolerate the heat and climate (and certainly not without complaint):

*Freetown and its vicinity [. . .] has a most pleasing appearance, and notwithstanding that its climate is so pernicious to European constitutions, the most prejudiced must grant that the scenery here is magnificently picturesque. The wide confluence of the Sierra Leone river with the sea, resembles a smooth and extensive lagoon, bounded on one side by the low, woody [. . .] shore, on the other by the verdant and gentle acclivity on which the town is situated, the [background] of which, gradually ascending, terminates in a semi-circular range of moderate side hills, forming a sort of amphitheatre, decorated with lofty trees and richly foliated shrubs; while every spot of the ascent, here and there studded with neat country seats, presents to the delighted eye a picture of the most agreeable character.*

Despite the weather, the recent downsizing and long-established system of patronage (or what was then known as interest) meant loads of hungry and capable young officers and their patrons were clamoring for any service that might increase the latter's influence by moving the former up the ranks. This is not to say that capability and character didn't matter; they very much did, particularly in a workplace in which one's coworkers were not only constant companions, but potentially vital to the survival of the entire crew. It's just that whom a lieutenant knew could be as crucial for promotion as what he knew, which had been standardized, or who he was as a man and an officer. The quality, speed, and, perhaps above all, independence of the *Black Joke* would make its captaincy an excellent opportunity for young officers suddenly confronted with a dearth of wars to fight to demonstrate why they deserved promotion. As a tender, *Black Joke* would be led by a lieutenant, the rank below commander and post-captain. And post-captain was arguably the most difficult rank to achieve in the Royal Navy.

In modern nomenclature a post-captain would, most recognizably, be the captain of a ship. In the Royal Navy of the early mid-nineteenth century, there were lots of potential ways for a lieutenant, and even the occasional petty officer, to end up at the helm of a vessel—death or incapacitation of the appointed captain not least among them—and some ships weren't viewed as large enough to merit such a senior officer; thus, the rank was distinct from the duty. Many post-captains didn't have continuously active commands throughout their career; especially in those days, there were always more officers than berths to contain them. It was also one of a few positions that could not be achieved through what was, in most other cases, an issue of seniority and paperwork. Time could advance the rank of long-serving post-captains and admirals. It was a matter of an exam to make a lieutenant of, ostensibly, any man with the requisite experience and competence. Good patronage could advance the common sailor and young gentleman alike through the noncommissioned ranks and the junior officer corps. However, it took all three—time, patronage, the lieutenant's exam, plus assignments to captain appropriately size ships and a bit of the winds of fate besides—to advance a man to lieutenant, through the rank of commander, and, ultimately, to post-captain.

Though clearly merit mattered, the ongoing impact of patronage on advancement in the Royal Navy cannot be overstated, and this kind of internal political reckoning would have been at the forefront of Collier's mind when selecting who would command the *Black Joke*'s first outings. Despite that many of the realities of naval life were in flux with both the times and several somewhat rapid-fire political changes that would continue to impact Admiralty policy well into the next decade, the role of patronage was deeply entrenched, and had been only somewhat liberalized by the comparative relaxing of class distinctions within the navy's officer corps in the eighteenth century. Though it may seem that such a system was guaranteed to encourage the advancement of the well-connected over the best suited, in practice, the system's pervasiveness and the participants' mutual dependencies kept it rather perversely honest. Senior officers, as patrons, and junior ones, as followers, relied on one another for influence and advancement. Too, it was often thought that the characteristics of a senior officer would inexorably, via the slow osmosis of a long time

at sea, rub off on those beneath him. If an admiral promoted or recommended someone who subsequently did poorly in his duties, the
admiral's ability to secure promotions for his other protégés would
suffer, and future lieutenants would not choose to align with an officer who could not help their career, no matter how famous or how
senior. These professional ties were so closely bound that the sudden
death or fall from grace of the senior half of this symbiosis could
and often did completely destroy the career of nearly every junior
man known to follow him—even if the latter had been stationed half
the world away and had had nothing to do with any of it. Collier,
as a protégé of Nelson's, would have known this risk intimately—if
Nelson hadn't been a hero of the realm for the ages, his notorious
personal life and untimely death could've decimated Collier's bud-
ding naval career, and there was no guarantee that the open secrets
swirling around Nelson hadn't already had a detrimental impact.

In the postwar years, demand for promotions within the navy far
outstripped the supply of available commissions, and given that every
senior officer was expected to have his own loyal coterie of younger
men, it would have been understood that Collier's own protégés were
likely at the front of the queue for any of his major staffing needs.
After securing positions for those who were already in his own circle,
Collier could then dispense such positions as he had left among those
recommended to him in streams of letters by and between other powerful senior officers (who had their own followings to consider). As
commodore for the West Africa Squadron, Collier was particularly
well equipped to engage in this quid pro quo by post. The commanders of overseas squadrons weren't obliged to wait for the Admiralty's
dispensation before naming someone to a new position—the mail
simply took too long to meet the immediate needs and rapid turn-
over of a fleet on active duty. Since it was expected that the powers
that be in the Admiralty would ratify their decisions after the fact,
the commodores—whether they were post-captains with temporary
authority or had already "obtained their flag" as rear admirals—had
the simple ability to promote men, meaning that if patronage and

advancement defined the market of power, commodores were nearly as flush with the backroom coin of the Royal Navy as those at the top of the hierarchy. Even being appointed to such an independent station speaks to how trusted Collier, then still a post-captain, was among his superiors as a man of sterling character and commitment, as he now possessed not just the power to make and break the careers of his subordinates, but the followings of his peers.

The opportunities for prize ships made a promotion to commodore as lucrative as it was powerful and would have required some substantial "interest" to achieve in and of itself, so it's possible that Collier owed someone, maybe several someones, consideration for his current post and, with it, due attention to any of their personnel requests. Nonetheless, respect for the sotto voce mechanisms of naval patronage was so well established that in reality Commodore Collier could have his pick among his or anyone else's best men without raising too many Admiralty eyebrows, provided they happened to be in proximity. Not the type to leave anything to chance if he could help it, however, Collier had once again come prepared. Much like his preemptively requested official copies of the treaties that would enable an as-yet-unpurchased tender to independently sail for an as-yet-unimagined international renown, the commodore had simply brought his as-yet-unpromoted choice for the captaincy of what was once little more than a plan—now manifested in a smart, swift brig—with him from England. Twenty-five-year-old Lieutenant William Turner would actually have known Collier's recently commissioned vessel even better than his boss did, as this was Turner's second berth on *Sybille*, the first having been as a mere midshipman five years earlier. Now the extraordinarily popular wine merchant's son from Portsmouth would be serving as the new brig's captain.

Given that Collier's reputation would be bound to the success of the Squadron, it's probable that Turner was one of Collier's own followers, someone the commodore was certain he could trust to represent both his superior and the Squadron well, even unsupervised.

Though Turner wasn't notably young for a man of his rank, he hadn't joined the Royal Navy until he was thirteen or fourteen, years older than many of the young men of the gentlemen's class with whom he had to compete. Born wealthy (for a commoner, anyway) on his father's increasingly profitable gentleman's-farm-cum-manor, the Elms, in Bedhampton, a village near Portsmouth, young Turner had probably felt some pressure to join the family business before choosing the navy. He'd signed up in 1816, despite the fact that the end of the Napoleonic Wars the year before had likewise spelled an end to the complications involved in procuring French wines, profiting legitimate purveyors like his father, and in a city with a centuries-long reputation for heavy drinking. Having grown up surrounded by comfort, scampering across over twenty acres of bucolic meadows, tall elms, and mature fruit trees to the sounds of the elder William Turner's constant improvements to the family's country estate—the father would add a "brew house, a wash house with a mangle room, a granary, a barn, a four stall stable, open cow ranges and a piggery, as well as coal, wood and pigeon houses," all before his son's eighteenth birthday—the future lieutenant would have been able to contrast his home life with the sight of many of the impoverished residents of Bedhampton crowding the poorhouse as they struggled in the grip of an economic downturn. Likewise, Turner could not have missed the industry around which much of Portsmouth's cultural, economic, and political life turned—shipping, and, more specifically, the bustling navy dockyard, then the largest known industrial complex in the entire world, directly and indirectly fueled the businesses of many of Portsmouth's wealthiest residents, including his father's.

Portsmouth's inextricable connection to the navy might have been a reason for his father to support, rather than bemoan, William's decision not to follow him into the wine business. Turner the elder was well-known and well-off, but class barriers in nineteenth-century England were notoriously impermeable—perhaps he saw his son's service as a new avenue for upward mobility and encouraged it accordingly. The Royal Navy's officer corps was one of the few venues in which a man could forever alter the class of his birth, which made it an attractive option for those young men blessed, it seemed, with everything in life but sanctioned nobility to continue to progress their families socially. Given that Turner quickly passed his lieutenant's exam (with its math and navigational requirements) and rapidly became beloved by those he knew in the service, it would probably have been evident from his youth that he was a bright and friendly lad, demonstrably capable of eventually handling his father's business even at a relatively young age. No matter, as Turner's choice had instead brought him, as a first-class volunteer and soon midshipman, on board the HMSs *Scamander*, *Vengeur*, *Queen Charlotte*, *Sybille*, and *Romney*—not the same *Romney* that had originally captured the *Sybille* from the French, as that would just be too poetic for historians to hope for—before this, his second and suddenly rather brief return to the *Sybille*'s quarterdeck as first lieutenant. As a member of the crew that had taken the *Henriqueta*, but not one of the men escorting the brig on the three-week jaunt back to Freetown, the disposition of the *Black Joke* must've constantly circled Turner's mind. To get what would be his first command in experience if not in job title within four scant months of his arrival—and at the helm of such a ridiculously fast ship, some unknown Baltimore shipwright's best work, the sort almost guaranteed to see the kind of action that could merit promotion—that was just the kind of luck to which William Turner had likely been accustomed his whole life.

Despite accusations to the contrary, Freetown's harbor, where both Turner and the *Henriqueta* awaited their destined union, wasn't the worst place to idle. It was, as mentioned, a beautiful landscape and natural harbor tucked into impressive hills, and the settlement itself, after multiple decades of uneven administration, finally seemed to be on steady (if admittedly colonialist) footing. It was still a site of conflict, particularly in the battle between those in favor of and opposed to abolition, but by the end of 1827, this was primarily a war of words. Despite a lack of cohesive planning that had consistently plagued colonial Sierra Leone since its inception, it now had a population of over fifteen thousand, over half of which were Africans who'd been removed from slave ships, and the colony engaged in trade both local and distant. There were schools and churches aplenty, as well as newspapers, distinct neighborhoods, and adjacent villages; the city could boast fairs and holidays featuring rowing and wrestling competitions and "sky rocket" displays, social clubs, amateur theatricals, horse racing, public dinners, and all-night dancing. Despite hand-wringing to the contrary, the death rate didn't seem much higher for Europeans than in other, similarly situated, tropical locales—and regardless, as one White resident was quick to point out, Sierra Leone hadn't been founded for Europeans, but for repatriating Africans, many of whom seemed better suited to the climate than their paler counterparts. Far from the disorganized and ill-fated arrival of the first settler colonizers back in the eighteenth century, and despite the complaints of those who felt it still lacked the amenities available in longer-established ports, the harbor where the young lieutenant idled had things to recommend it over months at sea.

After the trial's conclusion, transferring from the *Sybille* to the *Black Joke* with a small crew and a small boat—one of *Sybille*'s, its purpose to further gild the legal fiction that the brig was a mere extension of the frigate, no matter how far apart the two sailed—Turner and company would have seen, as they approached, a sleek, low-sided, two-masted brig with "very raking ends" that cut a distinct profile. (*Rake* simply refers to the angle of something, in this instance a not-uncommon adjustment in clippers to perfect a ship's buoyancy, balance, and/or motion through the water.) At its longest, the new tender was ninety feet, ten inches, measured across the gun deck, at its widest, twenty-six feet, seven inches, and by all accounts it was "a most symmetrical specimen of naval architecture." Put in perspective, if these dimensions were squared off, the *Black Joke* would have been less than twenty-five hundred square feet for approximately fifty people, and the little brig was far from square; back when it was *Henriqueta*, those raked ends, plus the additional storage spaces at either end of the ship, meant an even smaller slave deck, into which over ten times that number of bodies were unwillingly wedged with barely room to breathe, much less move.

But if it was the same ship in body, it was now much altered in name, purpose, and populace. On board were grizzled ratings like Richard Holt and William Fielder, each over fifty, all the way to adolescent boys like George Martin. Turner was also joined by fellow promotion hopefuls Edward Lyne Harvey and Edward Harris Butterfield, both mates aspiring to make the coveted leap to lieutenant (and with it, an officer's commission and guaranteed half pay when not assigned a berth). After what was probably an especially thorough cleaning, it must have felt auspicious that their first outing was both unremarkable and yet astonishing in its speed. Collier had spent two days in Sierra Leone in early January, officially purchasing the *Henriqueta* at auction on January 5, 1828, and the ink was scarcely dry on the bill of sale when, seven days later, the crew of the *Black Joke* captured a Spanish schooner bound for Cuba, *Gertrudis*, only forty-eight hours laden with human cargo from Gallinas, both a river and a region spanning modern-day Liberia and Sierra Leone. It's not that finding a slave trader near the Gallinas was unusual; the river and islands of its estuary were liberally sprinkled with stations for the sale of the enslaved, and the area had traded in people, and only people, for as long as many a British naval officer could remember. It was odd because ships of the Squadron usually spent months cruising for any prey, much less treaty-suitable prey, and the *Black Joke* had barely even existed for a week before capturing its first slaver. Making it odder still was that Gallinas in the 1820s had as its most prominent slave trader a British citizen and ex–army officer named John Ouseley Kearney, whose contacts in Freetown, insofar as possible, kept him abreast of the Squadron's every movement. Perhaps more than any other illicit harbor in the vicinity, Gallinas should have been prepared for "unexpected" visits from the Royal Navy. To find and successfully capture such a prize, with human cargo loaded yet none dead, so close to the Gallinas and so quickly—it just wasn't normal.

It would be easy to suppose that any surprise factor, and thus the

Detail. H.M. Brig 'Black Joke,' tender to HMS 'Sybille' and prizes [...]
'Providentia,' [...] 'Vengador' [...] 'Presidente' [...] 'El Hassey' [*sic*]
'El Almirante' and [...] 'Marianna'
(© NMM).

*Black Joke*'s success at the expense of the *Gertrudis*, may have turned on the ship's recent transition and unmistakable profile. Given the turnaround between sale and sail, it's unlikely that Turner's crew had had time to do much of anything but clean, make their best attempt to arrange their new berth to Royal Navy specifications, and hit the open water. The *Black Joke* was unmistakably a purpose-built slaving vessel; it was the size of a slaver, rigged like a slaver, gunned like a slaver, and moved like a slaver. More akin to a racing yacht than an English frigate, nothing about the craft would have seemed out of place in the waters of the Gallinas. Certainly, *Black Joke* was probably better looking and of higher quality than most of the ships that might have found their way to that unfortunate port, however, but for any British colors it may have been flying, it would have blended. On the other hand, Turner had recently been sailing alongside the *Sybille* and HMS *Esk*, a vessel whose service on the coast was ending just as *Black Joke*'s began. In this part of the world, nothing about a brig traveling with a frigate and a ship-sloop was low profile.

No, perhaps unsurprisingly, it was the speed. After his ship was spotted, Francisco Sans, captain and owner of the slaver, tried everything he could think of to shake off the British patrol, even tossing his own guns overboard to drop *Gertrudis*'s weight and enable its flight, and though he'd managed to pull away from *Sybille* and *Esk* easily enough, *Black Joke* had instead steadily gained, and gained, and gained, chasing the *Gertrudis* for twenty-four hours straight until Sans was forced to surrender. The tender was just a much-faster offering than any slave trader had come to expect from the WAS, and Sans, who had nothing with which to adjust to the new reality confronting him, soon found his ship taken with little fuss. Worldly in the manner of most illicit vessels, *Gertrudis* had first been an American schooner before eventually hoisting the flags of Spain and Brazil, and was originally named *Julia* before being purchased by Sans, a Spaniard, for $5,000. While the order for the captives on board and ownership of them fell to his partner in the venture, Isidro Romagoza of Havana, their presence on his boat at this location meant

Sans and his ship were quite obviously guilty of violating Spain's treaties with England. The ship would be condemned by the Mixed Commission just three weeks later, and all 155 enslaved people on board—80 of whom were children—were processed into Freetown. Though they couldn't have known it then, once the slaver was sold at auction (and likely after having changed owners a few more times), *Gertrudis* would harbor in Freetown again just a year and a half later, captured this time as the Brazilian schooner *Ceres*. Such a disheartening end—really, continuation—for the *Black Joke*'s debut capture highlights the quixotic expectations regarding the WAS mission. In the moment, however, the whole affair had been a wild success for Turner and the rest of the tender's crew from outset to nominal conclusion and likely could not have done more to cement Collier's confidence in his choice. But, as every sailor knows, luck can change.

Spanish Schooner "Gertrudis". Register of Slaves. Natives of Africa captured
on board the said Vessel by His Majesty's Ship "Sybille" & Francis Augustus
Collier CB Commander and Emancipated by Decree of the British and
Spanish Court of Mixed Commission on the 2nd day of February 1828. the
said Schooner having been pronounced liable to Condemnation by the said

| № | Names | Sex | Age | Stature Ft. In. | | Description |
|---|-------|-----|-----|-----|-----|-------------|
| 12020 | Doalloo | Man | 27 | 5 | 5 | Tattooed on the Back |
| 12022 | Quarree | " | 23 | 5 | 0 | do + do and Breast |
| 12023 | Frah | " | 22 | 5 | 2 | do all over Body |
| 12024 | Indammah | " | 26 | 5 | 2 | do on the Back |
| 12025 | Rahbanjo | " | 29 | 5 | 6 | Cuts on right Arm & Tattooed on Back |
| 12026 | Bannah | " | 25 | 5 | 7 | Tattooed on right Arm |
| 12027 | Brahhumah | " | 26 | 5 | 4 | Cuts on Face and right Arm |
| 12028 | Dowahjarroe | " | 21 | 5 | 1 | Tattooed on the Back |
| 12029 | Rombah | " | 27 | 4 | 9 | No marks |
| 12030 | Warhah | " | 29 | 5 | 3 | Tattooed on the Back |
| 12031 | Bahye | " | 29 | 5 | 0 | Cuts & Tattooed on left Arm |
| 12032 | Bahnee | " | 28 | 5 | 8 | A scar on left Jaw |
| 12033 | Bashkahbye | " | 30 | 5 | 7 | Cuts on Temples & Cheek & Tattooed on Body |
| 12034 | Romay | " | 27 | 5 | 0 | Tattooed on left Arm |
| 12035 | Rahtombo | " | 28 | 5 | 4 | do all over Body |
| 12036 | Dyboo | " | 29 | 5 | 6 | do do do |
| 12037 | Dammeyi | " | 26 | 5 | 5 | do on the Back |
| 12038 | Fjauh | " | 16 | 5 | 3 | A scar on left Cheek |
| 12039 | Ingobay | " | 27 | 5 | 6 | Tattooed on Back & cuts on left Arm |
| 12040 | Malahah | " | 35 | 5 | 3 | do do |
| 12041 | Wonee | " | 22 | 5 | 8 | No marks |
| 12042 | Consignar | " | 26 | 5 | 3 | do |
| 12043 | Oudoh | " | 29 | 5 | 4 | Tattooed on Belly Back & cuts on right Arm |
| 12044 | Myah | " | 19 | 5 | 3 | No marks |
| 12045 | Sarrah | " | 27 | 5 | 7 | Tattooed on the Back |
| 12046 | Fahyarrah | " | 24 | 5 | 4 | do do Belly and right Arm |
| 12047 | Dollah | " | 25 | 5 | 4 | No marks |
| 12048 | Faraybludder | " | 29 | 5 | 5 | Tattooed on Breast and Belly |
| 12049 | Dowse | " | 22 | 5 | 2 | do do do and Back |
| 12050 | Moodoo | " | 21 | 5 | 4 | do Back and right Arm |
| 12051 | Frauh | " | 23 | 5 | 2 | do do |
| 12052 | Bah | " | 26 | 5 | 4 | No marks |

Register, Gertrudis

Commission on the same day for having been at the time of capture engaged in the illicit Traffic in Slaves.—

| No. | Name | Sex | Age | Stature F. In. | Description |
|---|---|---|---|---|---|
| 12053 | Warree | Man | 26 | 5 3 | Tattooed on Back |
| 12054 | Indolay | " | 9 | 5 8 | do — both Arms & Belly |
| 12055 | Fowdennay | " | 28 | 5 8 | do — right Arm |
| 12056 | Kahwonnee | " | 27 | 5 4 | do — Breast & Belly |
| 12057 | Howe | " | 18 | 5 3 | Letter 8 on right Shoulder |
| 12058 | Dowarros | " | 30 | 5 3 | Tatt. on Breast & Belly & picked with small Pox |
| 12059 | Alyah | " | 34 | 5 9 | Tattooed on Body |
| 12060 | Heindoh | " | 27 | 5 3 | do — left Arm |
| 12061 | Buninah | " | 28 | 5 6 | do all over Body |
| 12062 | do | " | 27 | 5 7 | Cuts on Breast and Back |
| 12063 | Pandahwondl | " | 26 | 5 4 | do — Back and left Arm |
| 12064 | Kahmoo | " | 25 | 5 9 | do — Breast and Back |
| 12065 | Gaybah | " | 26 | 5 4 | No marks on Arms |
| 12066 | Sombyeyah | " | 29 | 5 2 | Tattooed on right Arm No marks |
| 12067 | Bayshay | " | 29 | 5 4 | do — right Arm |
| 12068 | Howree | " | 30 | 5 5 | do — Back & under each Arms |
| 12069 | Salbah | " | 35 | 5 7 | No marks |
| 12070 | Bubloh | " | 27 | 5 5 | do |
| 12071 | Zuyeway | " | 28 | 5 1 | Tattooed on Back and Belly |
| 12072 | Dyeyah | " | 27 | 5 5 | do — Arms, Breast, Belly & Back |
| 12073 | Yahkoo | " | 31 | 5 4 | do — Back & cuts on right Arm |
| 12074 | Yegbay | " | 26 | 5 4 | do — do |
| 12075 | Yoahroo | " | 29 | 5 0 | do — right Arm |
| 12076 | Ingolay | " | 23 | 5 2 | do — Back |
| 12077 | Koyandee | " | 29 | 5 7 | do all over Body |
| 12078 | Yekkhay | " | 34 | 5 6 | Cuts down forehead |
| 12079 | Cumikhoah | " | 28 | 5 5 | No marks |
| 12080 | Perpah | " | 26 | 5 0 | Tattooed on Breast, Belly, and Back |
| 12081 | Gehbong | " | 37 | 5 8 | No marks |
| 12082 | Dyeyah | " | 47 | 5 0 | do |
| 12083 | Bhyyew | Woman | 27 | 5 4 | Cuts on Back & Tattooed on both Arm |
| 12084 | Cumbah | " | 26 | 5 0 | Tattooed on left Arm |

# CHAPTER THREE

*Providencia* (aka *Providentia*; Eng.: *Providence*)
April 1828,
0 enslaved people

For the crew of the *Black Joke* to be consistently successful, they would have to regularly find appropriate quarry—no small task. Between 1827 and 1832, well over a thousand slave voyages would vie for profits and historical ignominy crossing the Atlantic. The pool from which the Squadron could actually fish, however, was much smaller.

Other than the brief respite provided by the aforementioned Treaty of Amiens, between the French Revolutionary Wars (aka the Wars of the First and Second Coalitions) and the Napoleonic Wars (the Third to Seventh Coalitions), Britain had battled with various European powers from 1793 to 1815, and the Royal Navy had featured prominently in many of the island nation's victories. Indeed, a prolonged series of wars among numerous countries in which allies and enemies had been interchanged as readily as sails— except for, generally, that historical enemy France—had created a rather unique set of global conditions, and British politicians were determined to take advantage. Given how comparatively well positioned Britain was in the postwar years, it's not difficult to compass the logic behind the machinations. Arguably no combatant came out of the years following the turn of the nineteenth century in better shape than England. Not sharing a land border with any of its wartime rivals helped, but decades of both internal and external conflict had also sapped, to varying degrees, the economic strength of traditional continental powers such as the Portuguese, Spanish, Dutch, and, naturally, French empires, even as postwar territorial concessions and colonial realignments—as well as robust revolutionary sentiment—eroded many imperial aspirations these governments may have still harbored. By stark contrast, though attitudes in Britain were slowly turning away from the sort of "formal" control of territorial possessions requisite for the mercantilist mindset, the shift toward free trade allowed for imperialist economic coercion in the Persian Gulf, China, Latin America, and elsewhere, such that the number and strategic value of England's overseas interests actually *increased* as the nineteenth century progressed.

A proliferation of British bases of military and economic operation was only one facet of the deeply enmeshed relationship between the Royal Navy and national economic interests, but it was an important one. Negotiations following the long-awaited peace of 1815 granted the English what must have seemed like, to the average citizen, a seriously random list of territorial concessions and recognized claims, not at all commensurate with the scale of their perception of British triumph. Though a list of these acquisitions—including Heligoland, Malta, the Ionian Islands, Ascension, Mauritius, the Seychelles, Ceylon, Malacca, St. Lucia, Tobago, Guiana, plus assent to British holdings in Africa as far north as the Gambia and as far south as Cape Town—seems at first to be a rather scattershot smattering of islands and inlets, their value to the Royal Navy, and thus the English economy, would soon demonstrate the canny rationale undergirding these choices; at least one member of the Admiralty would later assert that quality bases were second only to men and ships in underpinning British naval superiority. From these diverse ports, the Royal Navy would have a base capable of comparatively rapid response just about anywhere on the globe (but for the Pacific Ocean). Ready, worldwide military deployment might seem like a strange goal for peace talks, but then, Pax Britannica wasn't destined to be a particularly peaceful era. Unsurprisingly, other governments seeking to reimagine the world after Napoléon were deeply suspicious of British motives, concerns that, through the excellent looking glass of hindsight, managed to somehow be both well-founded and misplaced. True, England was about to unequivocally eclipse all its rivals, entering a period of global dominance the likes of which the world has never again seen, and undoubtedly the Royal Navy was a primary mechanism through which this aim would be realized. However, the unfolding geopolitical drama that would resolve into the long "peace" of nineteenth-century Britain was not to be decided by pitched battles between massive fleets. It was trade and treaties—and perhaps the occasional, proverbial "whiff of grapeshot"—not large-scale military maneuvers, that would steer the course of the future.

Well, and pirates. Though what historians now consider the golden age of piracy ended well before an officially constituted West Africa Squadron was a gleam in anyone's eye, the waters were nonetheless rife with predation in the early 1800s. While the end of the wars had precipitated a particular rise in nefarious activity in the Caribbean and Mediterranean, the economic impact of the disruption of maritime trade by illicit vessels could be felt the world over. During the previous conflicts, many of these aquatic aggressors had been privateers, distinct from pirates, their actions against merchant ships sanctioned by an often-distant government. The letters of marque these privateers carried distinguished them from pirates and protected them from interference so long as they kept their (piratical in everything but name) activity to enemies of the state they represented. Revolutions in Latin America meant privateers would continue to be in play, but given that the large European powers were ostensibly now at peace—at least with one another—it would be in much smaller numbers than seen the previous years. Those ships that wished to continue the lucrative business of robbery at sea could, in the main, no longer seek the shield of the nation-state (and that's if they even desired it)—privateers may have been the tools of some, but pirates were the bane of nearly all. The obvious losses measured in goods, ships, and lives stolen at sea were only part of a colossally destructive economic picture; it's impossible to reckon how much was also lost due to the cost of protective measures, such as extra crew, more weaponry, insurance, and so on. What's indisputable was that with the conclusion of war came fewer opportunities for privateers and an increase in piratical activity, with extraordinary economic impact. In 1815, a working resolution seemed difficult to find.

It was obvious to those gathered in Austria that the resurgent pirate situation was going to require vigorous policing of the open seas. But where, oh where, could a maritime force of sufficient size, strength, budget, and political incentive be found? The majority of those attending the Congress of Vienna in 1814–15 were uninterested in looking to England, least of all many of the English themselves. British representatives had come to the negotiations bound by heightened public pressure to, among other things, secure concrete measures to eradicate the global slave trade from Africa, not piracy; in fact, the Barbary Coast piracy that most agitated the continental powers had frequently served British trade interests rather well. The abolitionist sentiment that continued to mount even after England's legislative abandonment of the slave trade in 1807 had surged before the meetings in Vienna, when campaigners presented the government with petitions containing well over a million signatures demanding support at the Congress of Vienna for universal cessation of slave trading. A stated belief in the manifest injustice of the trade (and by extension, slavery itself) may have pervaded many of the intellectual and diplomatic circles of the various representatives to the Congress—and scientific justifications for inequality referencing the innate inferiority of the Black race entire had not yet reached their future popularity—but British diplomats were surely sailing against the wind. Even those continental representatives who'd witnessed the clamor against the trade in London firsthand when they visited the city in the lead-up to the Congress suspected that, whatever the motives of the populace, the English government's drive to restrict the trade was born of national self-interest, not altruism.

Britain's rivals were generally more interested in taking advantage of the window of profit left open by its abandonment of the slave trade, not in joining in the country's potentially economically disastrous moralism. Denmark had been the first European power to abolish the slave trade in 1792, though the law wasn't in effect until 1803, while the United States enacted legislation and began enforcing bans against the slave trade at around the same time that Britain itself did, in 1807 and 1808. Britain already had some leverage in their relationship with the Dutch, so inducing an end to the trade from the Netherlands had been a relatively simple matter in 1814 before the Congress began. Bringing other slave-trade profiteers to the table would take substantial inducement, more than a little time, and substantive proof of Britain's willingness to deploy its navy for humanitarian intentions that *wouldn't* profit it . . . which is to say that if England was so keen to police the sea, as far as other European powers were concerned, England could start by doing something about those damn Barbary pirates. After all, if Britain couldn't be compelled by the prospect of "white slavery" much closer to home, how was anyone to trust this newfound antislavery political attitude that extended much farther abroad, and to Africans to boot? Never mind that the practices of the Barbary Coast were not akin to the chattel slavery to which the African populace was subjected across the Atlantic, nor that the number of European captives had dwindled to perhaps a few hundred a year by this time in the nineteenth century, or that these captives were regularly ransomed, rather than sold, back to Europe—either Britain was opposed to the slave trade or it wasn't. Opting to be demonstrative, England would send a detachment of ships to eradicate the Barbary pirate problem in 1816 and, with that action, would by fits and starts embark on an international policing mission that, if somewhat thrust upon it, would nonetheless come to typify the role of the Royal Navy in the coming age.

Gestures, even grand ones, were not going to be enough to force the Portuguese, Spanish, and French to capitulate, nor to meaningfully change the international suspicion of English motives. Though the British walked out of the Congress of Vienna with a signed declaration decrying the slave trade as "repugnant to the principles of humanity and of universal morality," asserting that "the public voice in all civilized countries calls aloud for its prompt suppression," and "declaring the wish of [the signatories'] Sovereigns to put an end to a scourge which desolates Africa, degrades Europe, and afflicts humanity," it was worth about as much as the vellum it was inked on. The declaration had little to say on either timetable or methodology for bringing about its pronouncements. Nations were mostly left to themselves to determine "the period at which each particular power may definitively abolish the trade," with the addition that "the period for universal cessation must be the subject of negotiation between the powers concerned"—those still directly profiting from and sanctioning the slave trade, and England—and that "no proper means for accelerating that period are to be neglected." However, neither were any means for accelerating that period enumerated. Unlike with the Netherlands and Denmark, whose share of the slave trade had already slowed to a trickle when they moved to abolish, or the United States, where hereditary enslavement and the practice of regularly trafficking both women and men meant its unpaid labor needs could now readily be met by "natural increase" and a robust domestic slave trade, sudden British abolition left a market vacuum that Portugal, Spain, and their soon-to-be-independent colonial holdings in the Americas were positively aching to fill. Persuading the two cash-strapped empires to give up so much potential profit—a move sure to be deeply unpopular when some of their richest citizens were slave-trafficking profiteers—was going to take seriously lucrative incentives.

Aware that collective discussions for universal abolition of the trade could well come to naught, Britain's representatives at the Congress had met with their opposite numbers from Portugal and Spain, continuing negotiations for bilateral treaties that had been ongoing since 1807 and 1808, respectively, and that would extend long past the Congress of Vienna's conclusion. The diplomatic approach taken with both nations during the war had been similar, and with similarly lackluster results—Portugal had paid lip-service-by-treaty to British enforcement of trade abolition in 1810 and 1813 with no tangible progress toward enforcement, and Spain had done even less. This time, the Congress, one of the most consequential gatherings the continent had ever seen, the meeting that reapportioned Europe and swaths of the world besides, had, when it came to the slave trade, yielded little more than more high-minded and ultimately worthless commitments. Now that it was over, and the threat of Napoléon no longer imminent, neither Portugal nor Spain saw any reason to simply acquiesce to British demands.

It wasn't until a year or a few later, when Britain added money to the deal, that the gears finally began to meaningfully turn, as both Portugal and Spain were in increasingly desperate and expensive bids to retain their Latin American colonies. After signing yet another series of empty promises in 1815 in Vienna, Portugal, it was finally agreed in 1817, was to be paid £300,000 (almost £26 million today), have the remainder of a £600,000 war debt to England cleared (about £480,000 in money still owed, or about £41.5 million today), all with additional payments to come. In exchange, Portugal agreed, among other things, that trade north of the equator would be abolished; that a Portuguese law would be enacted to punish those who continued to trade in slaves in violation of the treaty; that the Portuguese flag could not be used as cover; that vessels above this line could be boarded, searched, and, if applicable, detained by the British; and that a Court of Mixed Commission to adjudicate the fates of these ships would be established in Sierra Leone. (Brazil, when seeking recognition of its independence almost a decade later, would agree to be governed by this treaty.) Likewise Spain—£400,000 up front and more in the future, and in return, the slave trade would be abolished north of the equator forthwith (decreed by the king of Spain in 1817), south of the equator and from all "Spanish dominions" at the end of May in 1820, and Britain would have the right to seize and detain ships that would be tried in a Court of Mixed Commission to be established in Cuba. These concessions might have been more meaningful if Portugal (and by extension, Brazil) couldn't access slave trading south of the equator and if Cuban slavers had not worked with a complicit Spanish colonial government to subvert the intention of the agreements—really, if either government had had any intention of stringently, or even halfheartedly, enforcing anything they'd just agreed to.

The situation with France was even worse. Even at the Congress of Vienna, abolitionist demands were tepidly received by the French delegation, in no small part because anti-English sentiment was running particularly high after the French defeat. Just as popular opinion at home forced British representatives to seek an end to the trade, French delegates felt pressured to not concede to British machinations, high-minded or no. French suspicion regarding British motives was rampant from the most enlightened salon to the cheapest newspaper; there was perhaps nothing in which France was less interested than granting the Royal Navy the right to search French ships for literally any reason. France did, nevertheless, agree to the declaration at the Congress and was willing to state publicly that the traffic in the enslaved should end. By 1817, the king of France had decreed that any ship attempting to land enslaved people in a French colony was subject to confiscation (presumably by the Crown), but France was not yet ready to abolish the trade, nor "withdraw the protection of its flag" from slave traders, nor make any other move to prevent human trafficking from Africa.

The next decade of international relations would see a frustrated Foreign Office stymied by readily exploited legal loopholes and repeatedly pushed to demand assistance, or at least the end of active subversion, from England's supposed treaty partners and "enlightened" foreign frenemies in its efforts to end the slave trade. As made hopelessly clear by the example of France, crucial to all of this wrangling was the "right of search," or, under what specific circumstances the Royal Navy could board, search, detain, and potentially confiscate ships suspected of illegally transporting human cargo for condemnation by the Mixed Commission. (Unsurprisingly, when it came to countries England didn't consider its equal—diplomatically, racially, or otherwise—"right of search" was rapidly becoming a nonnegotiable feature of British foreign relations.) It wasn't as if some in the British delegation hadn't tried to forestall this problem by formally suggesting an international naval force at the Congress of Vienna, and again at the Congress of Aix-la-Chapelle in 1818, and again the next year, but the notion had never gained much traction in European circles and was a nonstarter in the United States, given that it had recently fought a war in part over this very issue. So even with nominal partners, by 1828 perhaps the only thing that was clear was that, for all the effort spent garnering paper support and fragile concessions, Britain was basically alone on the waters if it wanted to stop the slave trade.

And there was so *much* water. The Royal Navy had, in essence, been charged with enforcing England's abolition of the trade since the 1807 ban had been conceived. The text of the act makes it clear that the drafters were far less concerned with how Africans from all parts of the continent arrived at coastal ports already bound for enslavement across the Atlantic than their oceanic disposition thereafter:

> *All Ships and Vessels, Slaves or Natives of Africa, carried, conveyed, or dealt with as Slaves, and all other Goods and Effects that shall or may become forefeited for any Offence committed against this Act, shall and may be seized by any Officer of His Majesty's Customs or Excise, or by the Commanders or Officers of any of His Majesty's Ships or Vessels of War.*

Any such action on the part of the Royal Navy would, in the years immediately following abolition of the slave trade, remain generally subsumed to the war effort—despite the massive size of the wartime force, there weren't ships available to create a dedicated patrol. As early as January of 1808, HMS *Derwent*, a brig-sloop, successfully detained two American slavers off Cape Verde, but no one in Freetown was sure what was supposed to happen next. Clarifications and increased stringency would be forthcoming . . . eventually, but in the interim, those tasked with enforcement—such as the *Derwent*, its frigate companion HMS *Solebay*, and the entire colonial government of Sierra Leone, such as it was—simply made do against what must have felt like an indefatigable adversary. In 1811, as Parliament realized that the slave trade would not just taper off under the weight of semi-collective British disapprobation, a new act elevated slave trading from a misdemeanor (punishable by a fine that a successful voyage could readily cover) to a felony (replete with potential transport to Australia). This change did have some effect, particularly among British nationals, but quite a few slave traders were, on account of not being British, not subject to British law and, regardless, were not the sort to scruple the legality of their actions any more than they had the morality of them. Naively, it seemed, many of England's abolitionists, and at least some politicians, had expected the eradication of the trade to be a relatively simple endeavor that would pave the way to abolition of slavery itself, imagining it would take a scant few years, perhaps. Slavers, in large part, simply contrived new methods to evade condemnation, even if captured; though the increase in penalty was a deterrent in some cases, the lure of astronomical returns on investment still brought enslavers, daily, to the coasts of Africa. Just throwing the Royal Navy at the problem sounded like an easy fix, but substantively addressing the complexity and entrenchment of the slave trade across the Atlantic would actually take decades of bilateral negotiations hand in glove with unilateral action.

England may not have come out of the Congress of Vienna with much in the way of abolitionist partnerships, but the power to police international waters, even in a limited capacity, would ultimately change the face of the world and make the era in which *Black Joke* sailed possible. By the time other nations sanctioned England's efforts to police the slave trade in 1815—or at least didn't directly oppose them—and the Admiralty chose Captain Sir James Lucas Yeo to lead the newly recognized force, Royal Navy vessels had been patrolling the waters of the coast in search of illegal slave traders for several years under the rules of war. These Royal Navy ships had been "on particular service" since 1808, and in that guise there had already been three commodores—Edward Columbine (1809–11), Frederick Irby (1811–13), and Thomas Browne (1814–15). Yeo would be the last of these early commodores. This first group had had success capturing several illicit traders, though it wasn't difficult when slaver captains could easily boast of seeing "no less than eighty" like-missioned vessels headed in the same direction the day they sailed from Havana. Yeo's assignment, refashioned in the wake of diplomatic negotiations, was deceptively straightforward:

> You are hereby required and directed to put to sea, in the ship you command, as soon as she shall in all respects be ready to sail, and proceed without delay to the coast of Africa, for the purpose of visiting the several British forts and settlements on that coast and rendering them such assistance and protection as you may find them to require.
>
> You are to repair in the first instance to Sierra Leone. . . . In proceeding down the coast you are diligently to look into the several bays and creeks on the same between Cape de Verd [sic] and Benguela, particularly on the Gold Coast, Whydah, the Bight of Benin, and Angola, in order to your seizing such ships or vessels as may be liable thereto, under the authority of the several Acts of Parliament prohibiting the slave trade (abstracts or copies of which we herewith inclose for your information and guidance); and you are to use every other means in your power to prevent a continuance of the traffic in slaves and to give full effect to the Acts of Parliament in question.
>
> With regard to the conduct to be observed towards the Portuguese ships and settlements, we send you herewith copies of two treaties between this country and Portugal, signed at Vienna on

*the 21st and 22nd of January 1815, and we hereby strictly require and direct you to govern yourself according to the instructions and stipulations contained therein.*

Simple enough, it would seem, but for a few, rather important, considerations. First, the Squadron was tiny; for several months in 1815 the Royal Navy had had no ships stationed to the coast at all. Now, beyond his own ship, HMS *Inconstant*, Yeo would be joined by *Princess Charlotte*, the single serviceable colonial schooner still left in Sierra Leone—which was, in fairness, still actively harassing slavers with enthusiasm—HMS *Bann*, which actually departed the coast ere Yeo arrived, and eventually HMS *Cherub*, manned by the transferred crew of the *Bann*. That's it. And little help would be forthcoming. Internationally, the Dutch and Spanish fleets had been decimated by war, the United States made sympathetic noises while providing little tangible support, and the Portuguese and French, occupied by internal political strife and external profit, were as yet uninterested. Domestically the situation was little better. While Yeo's understanding was that a small squadron would follow him to the coast, the powers that be in England made an eleventh-hour choice to send those ships to St. Helena to guard Napoléon instead. Even that minimal assistance would not be forthcoming from home.

Adding insult to rapidly accruing injury, Yeo's minuscule force was tasked with reining in the trade from Cape Verde—the actual cape, not the islands off the coasts of Senegal and Gambia—to the Benguela River in Angola, over *three thousand miles* of coastline. The "several bays and creeks" he was meant to patrol while making this cruise were nigh on innumerable, and while navigable for the smaller-framed slaving vessels, they were extraordinarily treacherous (if not outright impossible) for the Royal Navy's sometimes much-larger ships, which had to detach small boats to perform this work; natural harbors, areas that were both protected from the worst weather and waves the ocean had to offer and deep enough for ships to anchor, were almost entirely confined to the major slaving rivers. The unreasonable nature of the Admiralty's expectations did dovetail with a larger purpose, as 1815 had also seen the beginning of a monumental and ultimately successful effort to survey and accurately map the seas and then, in contravention of historical practice, practically give the information away to anyone who wanted it. However, accurate maps are the work of years, so all this meant for Yeo in the present, and the *Black Joke* in the not-too-distant future, was that the hazard-ridden and absurdly long stretch of coast the Squadron was meant to police was both perilous and less than thoroughly charted.

Logic dictated that at least some of the Admiralty's instructions would have to be more honored in the breach, and over these early years, it seems the Squadron rarely bothered with the farthest reaches of its assigned watch, largely confining its patrol to the middle two thousand miles, from off the coast of what is now Conakry, Guinea, to present-day São Tomé and Principe/the Gabon Estuary. Even after British efforts to geographically restrict the trade via treaty began to have some impact over the coming years, thus allowing the Squadron to better focus on slaving distribution hubs, sailing was further impeded by the capricious winds that could suddenly appear in the tropical environs, as well as an ever-contrary current that ran from west to east and had long confounded sailors in the region. These additional factors could readily lengthen a two-week cruise along the coast to over five, just to go back the way they'd come. Yeo, who'd had bouts with debilitating fevers and "overwork" in the past, would die from illness on his return trip to England (by way of Kingston) in 1818, at just thirty-five, well before the increasingly formalized Squadron could become more effective. Honestly, it's debatable whether there really was a Squadron as such until after Commodore Sir George Collier (no relation to the *Sybille*'s Francis Augustus) replaced Yeo on the coast. By 1819, the Admiralty had seen fit to provide Sir George Collier with six Royal Navy ships, still bound to cruise from Cape Verde to Benguela, but here the size of the Squadron would again stall. While the quantity of enslaved people being exported from Africa would precipitously rise from at least forty-eight thousand in 1815 to a postwar peak well over a hundred thousand in 1829, the number of ships the Royal Navy fielded to suppress the trade from West Africa would remain near stagnant all the way through 1832.

Almost ten years and three commodores later, when the *Black Joke*, freshly rechristened, embarked on its new mission under Francis Collier in 1828, the vision for the Squadron was less than clear. Opponents to the original abolition act in England had declared the goal of eradicating the slave trade practically impossible, the policy forthcoming from the polity hadn't helped, and the outlook seemed bleak. Even including the new tender, the ships of the West Africa Squadron were outnumbered by slave traders by almost thirty to one the previous year. Though the Royal Navy was, in the aggregate, notably low-cost, plenty of folks back in England were less than enthused about the West Africa Squadron's mission, method, or both and were not eager to continue to subsidize its efforts to the tune of anywhere from £60 million to £100 million per year.

So, though the expansive scope of the Squadron's assigned territory would remain constant, additional help, in the form of military vessels of any available national extraction or substantially improved charts, would not be immediately forthcoming; domestic enthusiasm in Britain was complicated, and foreign enthusiasm practically nonexistent. The ships being sent from England were not ideally suited to the job at hand. And that was only the surface—these were just the issues to be reckoned with before anyone in the Squadron even stepped foot on a slaver.

Though the view was not altogether rosy, the West Africa Squadron continued to adapt, and it's not difficult to see why both Bullen and Francis Collier were keen to develop the use of tenders on the coast. As the Squadron evolved, each successive commander learned more about what measures it would take to patrol these waters with any appreciable success. This preservation of institutional knowledge, along with the kind of training only experience can provide, was a key component of the Royal Navy's overall success. England's geographic reality in relation to that of other European powers meant that the nation had historically had a greater investment in sea power, rather than land power, and the recent military actions across the globe had only strengthened that model. This investment meant that, compared to other navies or pirate ships, the Royal Navy usually held the advantage in tactics, gunnery, seamanship, and discipline. As a result, those back in Whitehall expected His Majesty's ships to win, even when outmanned and outgunned—a normal state of affairs on the African coast when combating ruthless slavers and pirates who were willing to kill for money.

Then why bother to cruise at all? As incentive to ensure the most commitment with the least oversight, the Admiralty held out the possibility of promotion and the potential to earn prize money. Simply waiting around ports, as opposed to cruising for opponents, would have diminished everyone's chances at both—in a peacetime navy that was much reduced in size, if not public stature, where the promotion ladder was congested and opportunities few, berths were both deeply valuable and difficult to come by, at least for officers. Showing initiative (and being successful) could set men apart from equally long-suffering peers waiting for promotion in parts of the world with a lot less potential for action. And given that only 3 percent of the Royal Navy's personnel were serving off the coast of West Africa in the late 1820s, not to mention that, at higher rankings, as few as one in ten officers were fully employed at all, a berth in the WAS could be both career making and purse filling for men able and willing to make the most of the opportunity. Besides, the closer a slaver was to port, the easier it was for its captain to run back to shore and disembark their human chattel, waiting until Royal Navy ships were out of sight again before setting sail.

So, after the capture of *Gertrudis* at the beginning of 1828, the *Black Joke*, like all ships of the WAS, cruised. And cruised. And cruised. The territory the Squadron was meant to monitor had been divided at first into four sections, then into three: Senegal to

Sierra Leone; Sierra Leone to Cape Coast, Ghana; Ghana to the Bights, and with them, the equatorial line dividing legal and illegal slave trading. Each area was assigned to particular vessels, much like servers at a restaurant; not only did this practice make the whole endeavor more manageable, it also helped prevent squabbles over the pursuit of prizes. Though a ship might have orders to report to Freetown, be due for a "wood and water" resupply in Fernando Pó, need to rest and refresh in Ascension, or have some other such task that required a specific destination, there was also a lot of just . . . sailing around, up and down the coast. Of the three patrols, the Bights, farthest south and most subject to calm winds and strange currents, was the least suited to a native-born Englishman's constitution, but did have the benefit of plenty of potential prizes, particularly near the Bonny and Calabar Rivers, and naturally, it was here that the little brig found itself for several months as the winter passed into spring. To increase their chances of finding a ship that could not

View of Clarence Cove, Fernando Pó (© NMM).

just be caught, but successfully condemned, officers and sailors alike trolled for information about where such ships might be loading and when they planned to depart—both conversations ashore and with other ships they encountered could prove fruitful. Opportunities for gossip notwithstanding, this constant patrol was, more often than not, rather boring.

However, it was not idle. In the spring of 1828, the *Black Joke* had forty-three men on board: mostly seamen, but also including Royal Marines, midshipmen, Kroomen, an assistant surgeon, and Lieutenant Turner himself. They would have been divided into two, possibly three, watches, and given that the running of a ship is a twenty-four-hour operation, one watch was on duty at all times, the sound of bells echoing, like clockwork, in their ears. Each assigned watch lasted four hours, but for two watches of two hours, called dogwatches, from 4:00 to 8:00 p.m., with the time marked by a bell every half hour; one watch was eight bells, and then the count reset. A two-watch system would mean that, when a ship was at sea—which in the case of the *Black Joke* was nearly all the time—no one rested for more than four hours. Sleeping, when done, was accomplished in hammocks strung in spaces as small as fourteen inches wide per man, assigned and usually alternated by watch to provide more space and always stored away in the morning. Being roused for one's watch was not a gentle affair, as the boatswain's mates might just as readily resort to canes as loud shouts. If it was the beginning of the day, the deck would be scrubbed while the cook finished breakfast, usually served at 7:00 a.m. After eating, there would be ship maintenance or possibly drills. Accurate navigation required the sun be sighted at noon and its location noted, followed by an hour- to hour-and-a-half-long lunch (or "dinner"), the largest (and longest) meal of the day, when all watches could eat communally. More work for one watch, then dinner (or "supper") at four, the two dogwatches, and finally "the watch was set" at eight. At this point, Lieutenant Turner would retire to the designated captain's quarters, likely leaving his boatswain, Harvey, or Butterfield, in charge of the watch on duty. The night watch was less onerous in many respects—the ship had to be steered and the lookout kept, but other than for the occasional trimming or reducing of sails, men could, for the most part, relax during these late hours. Depending on how kind Harvey was, and how much he trusted them to be ready at a moment's notice should the need arise, he may have even let portions of the watch sleep on deck.

The Black Jokes—the crew of a ship was referred to, in the collective, by the ship's name, no matter how strange it might sound to the modern ear—might go weeks without any other company but the sharks that ominously swam alongside the brig. The ship rarely put into port because empty slavers couldn't be condemned and doing so risked illness unnecessarily. Due to the patrols, slave traders were now in the habit of boarding the enslaved at night, so, if near a likely port or inlet, the *Black Joke* might find a spot, perhaps thirty, forty miles from shore, and wait in the darkness, hoping to be in position to pounce at first light should a ship appear. So it went, day after day, unless, suddenly, "Sail ho!" pealed out, goading the crew to quick and well-rehearsed action. The lucky sailor who'd raised his voice would receive an £8 bonus—a month's pay and more for everyone but Turner and the assistant surgeon of the *Sybille*, Coates, who acted as chief medic for the tender, and nothing to sneeze at for them, either—but first, the ship had to prove to be a genuine slaver.

If most of the crew's time at sea was an orgy of repetition, in this moment just about anything might happen. Turner, taking up his scope, would sight the vessel—since the mast was the first thing to appear above the horizon, it could take some time to see those particular characteristics of a vessel's profile and movement (the rigging, size, shape, and speed) that might mark a slaver. During this time, the senior midshipman, or mid, called, "All hands!"—summoning anyone who might be belowdecks, and all the while the *Black Joke* itself was in motion, too, already having altered its course toward what was usually a short-lived mystery. Not every craft off the coast of Africa, particularly as Britain moved to replace its previous returns from the slave trade with agricultural exploitation rather than

human trafficking, was a slave trader. While readily observable outward physical signs were key in attempting to identify potential enemies at sea, they weren't foolproof. But presuming that far-off mast
didn't belong to a legitimate merchant ship or a fellow Royal Navy
vessel, things could get exciting rather quickly.

And all of these things, from the labyrinthine treaty agreements
to the duplicitous slave traders, factored into Turner's dilemma on
the spring night that the *Black Joke* first sighted the *Providencia*,
roughly forty miles southwest of Principe. It was early April 1828,
at about 2:00 a.m., when the shout came—"Sail ho!" An extraordinarily keen-eyed sailor on the *Black Joke* had noticed, in the far
distance, an unidentified brig. Someone, possibly Harvey himself,
roused Turner, calling him to his scope, and whatever the lieutenant
saw must have kindled his suspicion. As the helmsman laid in the
direction, seamen swarmed in a beautifully executed riot of movement, setting all available sail to catch every scrap of wind as the
pursuit laid on. Still, the "hurry up and wait"—or perhaps more precisely "wait and hurry up"—current that steered the experience of
service in the Squadron was inescapable. Once a course had been
set, one still had to wait hours to catch up to and hail that distant
ship; even if the winds were with one's craft, as they were that early
April morning, there was yet more waiting. Arriving swiftly and before daybreak, as the *Black Joke* soon did, could only save so much
time. They'd need sunlight before the next move could commence.

It was a question of flags, and the simplicity of the task belied the
difficulty of the circumstances. All of those treaties Turner had in
the *Black Joke*'s possession were useless if the ship waiting across the
water could make a credible claim to being from any nation where
the particulars of this precise moment—including the unknown
vessel's current latitude, claimed point of departure, stated destination, supposed nationality, and the nature of its cargo—exempted it
from the Royal Navy's jurisdiction. Of the over two hundred slaving
ships leaving the coast of Africa each year in the late 1820s, just over
10 percent are recorded as sailing under French or US flags. Since

neither government had succumbed to British pressure to recognize a (nominally) mutual right of search, no treaty on board the *Black Joke* (nor anywhere else in the world) would let Turner legally search a ship under those colors, much less take one. Not every slave captain had access to the resources to acquire fake flags and the requisite papers to accompany them, but if Turner's potential adversary raised the unembellished and solid-white flag of France's Bourbon restoration, or the already distinctive flag of the United States (if with twenty-four stars, rather than fifty), his quarry could not be searched at all, and any lost sleep was for naught. The rest of the other nearly 90 percent of slave-trading ships that are known to have sailed that year claimed association with Portugal or Spain, the precise governments for which Turner had a boatload of applicable treaties . . . that clearly enough said that such ships could only be fruitfully searched and detained, location and itinerary permitting. Now, any slaver claiming Dutch extraction was a viable target regardless of where it was found, but Dutch vessels were scarce on the water during this period. Admittedly, one of those had been apprehended by *Sybille* less than a fortnight previous, but the odds of this unknown ship making it easy for Turner by flying a Dutch flag were quite slim.

All of this presumes that the flag being raised was accurate. It should not be surprising that those who valued profit above life and human dignity were also not above lying their entire faces off— and in every conceivable fashion and manner, with every means available—if it would prevent the WAS from capturing and condemning the illicit wealth imprisoned in their ship. One practice was to have one or two persons of the nationality the ship claimed always in the crew, or even as the captain, able to lend a native speaker's veneer of truth to the lie of the vessel's actual affiliation. Some would carry multiple commissions from various nations and simply destroy the set that could get them condemned during any chase that might ensue. Some would, like *Henriqueta* had, fake the papers that showed where they had come from and where they were going or have multiple sets, both accurate and inaccurate, to show the patrol depending on the slave trader's position relative to the equator. In other instances, like a macabre comedy trope, slaver captains would simply pretend not to speak English at all, daring their opponents to take the gamble of capturing them. This was a very real gamble—if a captain in the WAS erroneously captured a ship that was not subsequently condemned by the Mixed Commission in Freetown, he was *personally* liable for the costs and damages of his mistake; neither Parliament nor the Admiralty would indemnify the individual enforcers of its national will against reasonable error for another several years, no matter how difficult to fathom the actual rules of engagement remained.

Even the liability question was disturbing—if the *Black Joke* erred in detaining a ship, who would be liable, Turner, the captain in all but rank, or Collier, *his* captain? Remember, the *Black Joke* was a tender, not an official Royal Navy ship, and Turner had arrived in Sierra Leone as first lieutenant of the *Sybille*, serving on the *Black Joke* essentially at the commodore's pleasure. The *Black Joke* was administratively inseparable from the frigate it served, and Turner must've recognized that his mistakes would also be Collier's mistakes, that if Turner failed, it would reflect poorly on the man who safeguarded his career and potentially hit him in the purse as well. The precedents to be found in those first years of preventative activity in the area could not have been heartening—part of all that money Britain had bribed Portugal and Spain with to get an enforceable agreement had specifically been named as redress for slave ships illegally captured and detained under misinterpreted versions of older treaty agreements. On the other hand, the precedents also weren't necessarily relevant—as Bullen's letter to Canning the year before clearly demonstrated, the legal and administrative questions brought to the surface by tenders could hardly be called settled law.

WAS officers were just as incentivized to not make mistakes as slavers were to slip out of their reach, and perhaps few more so than Turner, born to a commoner (if a rich one) in an age when "lowborn" officers had all but disappeared from active service. It had become so unlikely, in the much-contracted postwar Royal Navy, for someone such as a wine merchant's son to even become a lieutenant, much less a first lieutenant in command of his own ship, that William Turner's trajectory was already an exceptional occurrence, even if he never advanced any further. Of course, anyone who'd managed to come that far usually wasn't interested in resting on whatever laurels and half pay he'd managed to accrue—advancement through the officers' ranks was accompanied by sizable increases in income. It had also been one of the very few mechanisms of social mobility that existed during this period in England; if Turner ever wanted to become something his society recognized as more than his father's son, he would have to succeed.

Success against the slave trade required a certain degree of pragmatism, and pragmatism required more flags than the one to which Turner's service was pledged. Which is probably the rationale, though certainly not the how, behind why an officer in His Majesty's Royal Navy, commanding a vessel of that navy, just so happened to have several flags of his own, only one of which would have been a Union Jack.

As the two ships faced off, a strange, if altogether expected, vexillological dance commenced. The light of day saw Turner raise the British flag, and in response, the mystery ship hoisted the Red Ensign—a civil, rather than military, flag used to indicate a British merchant or passenger ship—and moved to a spot within earshot on the *Black Joke*'s weather beam, or the side of the ship facing the wind. As the two ships approached each other, the still-unidentified ship brought down the Red Ensign and hauled up another, now identifying itself as Spanish. Since flag shenanigans were a regular occurrence, this behavior was, if suspicious, not inherently evidence of shady piratical dealings or enslaved people on board. Once within hearing distance of Turner and his speaking trumpet—vintage megaphone—the Spanish (for he was actually Spanish) captain seemed reasonable enough, perfectly happy to send an officer to the *Black Joke* to explain his ship's presence off the coast. This offer accepted, almost immediately the captain changed his mind, saying he would still gladly send over men, if only Turner could send over a boat, as the Spaniard had "no boat that could swim." Turner, ever obliging, sent Harvey and two other men in a small craft over to the other ship, but rather than being joined by one or more from the Spanish vessel, the three men were forced to board the Spanish ship in what was beginning to look an awful lot like the prelude to a hostage situation. Easing the tension slightly, once the smaller boat had been vacated, an officer from the other ship and five of his fellows promptly hopped in and rowed back to the *Black Joke*. Once on board the English brig, Turner politely greeted the new arrivals, but the Spanish officer was having none of it. He identified his ship as the *Providencia*, a privateer commissioned against any ship of the South American states and, in what must have seemed like an odd turnabout, immediately demanded to see the *Black Joke*'s identification papers.

This isn't quite as strange as it might first appear. In most respects the *Black Joke* very much *looked* like a slaver, due to the undeniable fact that it had been one, and there were those on the seas who could yet recognize it, visually, from its days as the *Henriqueta*; news still traveled slowly enough that not everyone may have been aware that the distinctively built brig had made the transition to legitimate waters. If it had still been a slaver, illegally flying British colors over twenty years after the nation abolished the trade, the same treaties Turner had in his possession might likewise have empowered the *Providencia*, if it was truly officially sanctioned, to detain the *Black Joke*, rather than vice versa—it was a *mutual* right of search, after all, even if only the Royal Navy much bothered. That the *Black Joke* was staffed by British sailors also wouldn't have evidenced much to the Spanish officer. It cannot be presumed that the crew of the *Black Joke* looked stereotypically "English"—in the eighteenth century, at least, the sailors of the Royal Navy were a far more diverse bunch than is imagined in the present day; the expansion of Britain's global aspirations could, in many ways, be seen in the diversity of faces that graced its navy. Not only was the crew almost certainly not racially or ethnically homogenous—even setting aside the ubiquitous Kroomen—in 1828 only commissioned officers in the Royal Navy had any sort of stipulated regular uniform; seamen provided their own clothes. English sailors certainly had a rather specific (and sometimes flamboyant) cut to their proverbial jib—a phrase just moving from the maritime lexicon to the popular one in the 1820s, as a jib was a triangular sail and its positioning was often used, aptly enough, to identify the nationality of a ship—but it wasn't as if the Royal Navy had a universal, or even universally recognizable, uniform. The *Providencia* officer's claim to suspect the *Black Joke* of being a Colombian privateer wasn't per se unreasonable, given the difficulty distinguishing Royal Navy seamen from those of other nations, or from the average pirate.

It wasn't even a stretch. Britain's Foreign Office was very much involved in what was going on, revolutionarily speaking, in South America, and despite a professed neutrality, it didn't exactly seem to be backing the Spaniards or Portuguese as the two empires fought to retain their colonial holdings. A number of British sailors who'd found themselves out of work when the Royal Navy downsized after 1815 had joined the naval effort for South American liberation, perhaps most famously the semi-disgraced yet unquestionably brilliant Lord Thomas Cochrane, the Sea Wolf, who had just left South America at the end of 1827 to assist Greek liberation from the Ottoman Empire, but only after helping organize and lead both the Chilean and Brazilian navies in successful rebellion against their Spanish and Portuguese overlords, respectively. So the fact that Turner was claiming to represent the Royal Navy was nice and all, but one can't exactly blame the *Providencia*'s designated representative for seeing an Englishman in an officer's blue coat leading a small and somewhat diverse crew aboard what very much appeared to be a particularly fine slaver and nonetheless having his suspicions.

Turner complied with this demand, unwilling to hazard the lives of his men on the other ship, and showed the officer the *Black Joke*'s commission. As the parley progressed, it was soon discovered that there should be a quick way to settle all of this. The *Providencia* said it had already been boarded by a WAS ship just forty-eight hours prior—and not just any ship, *Sybille* itself. Apparently a thirty-eight-gun frigate flying the commodore's broad pennant had been a lot less questionable—or less easy to argue with—than a slick little brig with a single gun, so when boarded, the *Providencia* showed Commodore Collier a seemingly authentic commission from the king of Spain, and Collier had signed the back in acknowledgment. Collier's signature was also, naturally, all over the *Black Joke*'s own paperwork, both its commission and orders to cruise. It should have been a relatively simple matter to compare documents, ensure the signatures were authentic, retrieve Harvey and his companions, and go on their merry ways, no worse for the wear. However, the Spanish officer wanted to accomplish this comparison on *his* ship, rather than *Black Joke*—after all, that's where the *Providencia*'s papers were, and why make the extra trip?

Turner, who was no fool, didn't like where that was headed at all, and though he was also under orders to be as courteous as possible in the execution of his duty, he was not going to just ship his commission off with potentially disreputable strangers and hope it came back. So the young lieutenant refused and opted instead to keep his own hostages—the Spanish officer, and two of his shipmates, would be staying on the *Black Joke* until the matter was sorted. Unsatisfied but less abrasive than his underling, the captain of the *Providencia* called out again and gently insisted that, as an alternative, Turner could send over fifteen more men, that he would likewise send fifteen of the *Providencia*'s complement back, then both ships could reconvene at Prince's Island (modern-day Principe) to sort all of this out once and for all. Otherwise, the captain would be forced to take action. This was the last straw for Turner, as it was now abundantly clear that being polite was getting him nowhere. The *Black Joke* had only forty-three men aboard, and three of them were already on the other vessel, while the larger, fourteen-gun *Providencia* looked to have roughly double the number of sailors. A straight exchange of so many men may have looked fair on its face, but it would crucially disadvantage the former while negligibly impacting the latter. Put another way, had the lieutenant agreed, he would have had only twenty-five men on his ship to contend with eighteen Spanish "hostages," several of whom would be busy sailing the ship to Principe, while his men on board the *Providencia* would remain greatly outnumbered by their Spanish counterparts. Besides, Turner knew that his orders were authentic; if there was to be any dispute, the fault would lie with the Spanish documentation, which, though Harvey may have had a chance to glimpse during this discussion, his captain, still on the *Black Joke*, had not.

So Turner, without hesitation, refused. And the *Providencia*, until now the picture of cooperation, immediately fired a broadside directly into the *Black Joke*. Clearly regard for the lives of the hostage Spaniards on board the English ship had come second to a different motive, because the two ships, so recently close enough to parley, now moved into clear and deadly opposition. Thinking quickly, Turner ordered his crew to take up a position on the bow of the *Providencia*, thus making *Black Joke* harder to hit while preserving his own field of fire, and an extended combat ensued. Despite facing fourteen twelve- and twenty-four-pounder Spanish carriage guns to their one long eighteen-pounder on a pivot and—possibly because they had *not* forgotten that three of their fellows were on the enemy ship—primarily armed with grapeshot, the Black Jokes refused to yield to their larger foe. Grapeshot consisted of canvas bags tightly packed with small balls of iron; when paired with excellent gunnery, its subsequent spray, akin to that of a giant shotgun, could be used to devastating effect on an adversary's rigging while minimizing loss of life on and belowdecks. Taking out the rigging, rather than firing into the body of the ship, was always an important consideration when attempting to rescue the enslaved without killing them, especially if the ship was to be subsequently condemned for additional prize money. (Not every sailor in the WAS personally agreed with the mission, but all certainly agreed with the money.) The same technique now came in handy when attempting to both survive the sudden attack and not kill their hostaged compatriots.

For two hours, the *Black Joke* staved off the *Providencia*, firing grapeshot charge after charge from their lonely eighteen-pounder, slowly but systematically dismantling the rigging of the larger brig. Though Turner's maneuvering and the crew's labors had been genuinely exceptional, the unvarnished reality was that the average Royal Navy vessel had better equipment and was perceptibly better at aiming than their average opponent, regardless of nationality. Many historians attribute the difference to a longer tradition of professionalism in the Royal Navy—and a lot more practice—but whatever the rationale, the Black Jokes showed the truth of it that day. By the time the Spaniards waved the flag of truce, the *Providencia* had been nearly unrigged, its previously complex structure of ropes and sails almost entirely dismantled or destroyed. Though *Black Joke* had sustained notable damage to its own rigging, cuts to the sails and the like that would want repairing, it was largely unharmed, as were the long-suffering Harvey and his fellows. The three men had, it turned out, been in more danger from their surroundings than their shipmates on the *Black Joke*; on several occasions members of the crew of the *Providencia* had attempted to kill all of them—only the interventions of the Spanish captain, ever calm, had kept them alive long enough to see a return to the *Black Joke*.

This wasn't the reason, however, that Turner ultimately let the *Providencia* go on its way, even after the unprovoked attack. Quite simply, he had to. Even if the Spanish ship had proved much more pirate than privateer, thin as the line was between them, it certainly did not have enslaved people on board; the Black Jokes who'd been there could confirm that. The ship's commission had looked legitimate enough that Collier really had signed it—British papers later recounting the incident would state as fact that the *Providencia* had been boarded by the *Sybille* only two days earlier—but no matter how bogus its commission may have been, a ship had to have the enslaved on board to be validly captured under Anglo-Spanish treaties. It could have been much, much worse. The *Black Joke* had sustained some damage, but not a single casualty, not even a man wounded. Though after the encounter the *Providencia's* captain had refused to say how many of his eighty-seven men "of all nations" had been lost, Harvey reported that, at the least, several men had been wounded and some likely killed. The proof of this came soon enough—after capitulating, the *Providencia* lowered its flag to half-mast and commenced to bury its dead. Turner's leadership had saved the day, as far as the home front was concerned—the *Hampshire Telegraph* wrote, "Too much encomium [praise] cannot be given to Lieut. Turner, for his intrepidity and judgment on the occasion."

When the full accountings reached England's shores, the Admiralty agreed. While the Admiralty expected a degree of naval superiority from all its officers, Lieutenant Turner's gallantry against the pirate—for that's how the *Providencia* would ultimately be remembered in contemporaneous British accounts—had demonstrated excellent judgment in a fraught situation and exceptional courage in the face of a much more powerful foe. Though he didn't know it yet, Turner had earned his much-coveted promotion to commander, and more besides. Commodore Collier was so impressed by Turner's action that the commodore had a sword worth £220, over a year and a half of a lieutenant's sea-pay, presented to Turner upon his receipt of his promotion back in England, and engraved:

A token of respect and regard from Commodore Collier, the Captain, officers, and ship's company of H.M.S. Sybille, to Capt. Wm. Turner, for his zeal and gallantry while Lieutenant-commanding the Black Joke tender.

And Turner wasn't alone. Edward Lyne Harvey, who'd maintained his equanimity throughout the entire affair, was also promoted, from mate to lieutenant, moving him from the ranks of the senior-most petty officers to the commissioned class. But as yet, neither Harvey nor any of the other men on the *Black Joke* were aware of the new circumstances their victory had wrought, changes that would eventually find soon-to-be-commander Turner replaced at the helm. For now, flush with victory, if a little worse for the wear, the *Black Joke* sailed on, in search of a prize it could keep.

# CHAPTER FOUR

*Vengador* (aka *Vingador, Vincedor,* Eng.: *Avenger*)
May 1828,
645 enslaved people

*Presidente* (aka *President,* Eng.: *President*);
*Hosse* (aka *Nosse, Josse*)
August 1828,
0 enslaved people

*Zepherina* (aka *Zeferina*)
September 1828,
218 enslaved people

Six weeks after encountering the *Providencia*, on May 16, 1828—hardly any length of time at all when cruising the coast—the *Black Joke* would find its next chance. If the *Providencia's* antics had been emblematic of the many issues that made effective service on the coast such a complicated affair for the West Africa Squadron, the experience capturing the brig *Vengador* was the complete opposite . . . yet still somehow just as emblematic of the complications for captains and everyone else. The *Vengador*, despite mounting eight guns, didn't even put up a fight; if a single shot was fired, there appears to be no record of it. The *Black Joke* approached, and Miguel

Netto, captain of the suspected slaver, opted to heave to rather than attempt to fight an unexpected—and unexpectedly nimble—foe. Wary, Turner probably waited for *Vengador* to back, or lower, all of its sails, lest he send a boat to board the slaver only to have it rapidly reset all sails and hie off into the horizon at the precise moment *Black Joke* was least equipped to give chase, but no such tricks were forthcoming. *Vengador*, its hold tightly crammed with the bodies of 645 people, simply capitulated.

Given that many ships in the Bights and beyond, slavers or not, were obviously willing to fight a lot harder for a much smaller potential profit, this may seem like a curious end to what would otherwise be a rather brief anecdote. After all, the *Providencia* hadn't even embarked any enslaved, yet had engaged in a deadly two-hour gun battle; *Gertrudis* had, just five months before, led Turner and his men on a not-so-merry chase for an entire day just to forestall the surrender of 155 people, less than a quarter of those carried by the *Vengador*. While infrequent, relatively uneventful captures were more the norm than the *Black Joke*'s once and future service history would seem to evidence, it's possible some contributing factors were at work in Netto's lack of resistance. One problem might have been that not just Netto's cargo, but also a significant minority of his crew, were in bondage. Of the *Vengador*'s complement of forty-five sailors, fourteen of them were *also* enslaved and were listed as such in the slaver's *rôle d'équipage* (muster roll, or the list of the crew on a ship). Though this wasn't unusual, perhaps Netto didn't like his odds if nearly a third of his own sailors might be inclined to seize the opportunity—and with it, potentially their own freedom—and side with the British forces.

Briefly traversing ever further into the morass that is supposition and hindsight, Netto may also have sailed with the understanding that he was to offer no resistance to the Squadron if escape didn't seem feasible. In this instance, escape was unlikely because a vessel—even one made for speed, like a purpose-built slaver—weighed down, whether by licit goods or stolen lives, didn't have much chance of getting away from a counterpart lacking a like burden, much less one faster than most any other ship of the era. Escape was potentially unimportant because the *Vengador* was likely insured, easily replaced, and probably one of many in a fleet, as it was almost certainly owned by a man already deeply intertwined in the *Black Joke's* own history—the *Henriqueta's* previous owner, the still-rich and still-powerful Jose de Cerqueira Lima. Though de Cerqueira Lima had lost what was arguably his fastest ship, he'd nonetheless continued to seek the lucre of a filthy business with his fleet of slavers—it's quite possible he already recognized *Henriqueta's* forced defection as more anomaly than trend. (Since it was the only other known ship of his in this period to be captured with the enslaved on board, this would have been an unfortunately accurate assessment.) Perhaps in deference to his burgeoning political career, and with a tacit nod to Britain's ongoing diplomatic involvement in Brazil specifically and South America generally, the prominent slave trader sought to avoid the appearance of flagrantly violating Brazil's treaty agreements, no matter how resentfully borne, by capitulating quietly and avoiding any further inquiry into the ship's actual ownership. Almost certainly, though, de Cerqueira Lima had assurance, even beyond simple indemnification, that his losses would be minimal should *Vengador* be captured.

He was likely covered in the obvious way, in that slavers continued to insure themselves against the efforts of the WAS, despite the rising costs. This may have helped ease de Cerqueira Lima's mind, if not his bottom line alike, but one has to imagine the *Vengador's* own history (and what it said about its likely fate) could have been at least as warm a comfort. The slaver was going to be condemned by the Mixed Commission in Freetown, of this there was little doubt. Not only was Netto clearly above the equator with enslaved people on board, those individuals must've been loaded at Lagos, given where Turner found the slave ship, while the *Vengador's* passport clearly stated its destination as Cabinda, a slaving port south of the line. Sure enough, when the *Vengador* arrived in Sierra Leone in June—

escorted by the *Black Joke*, unusual for prize ships—the Mixed Commission found the slaver to be in violation of its otherwise authentic Brazilian passport, and further, that the entire voyage had been planned to that end, with premeditated intent to contravene the treaties regarding where the enslaved could be purchased. The judges made their determination with corroboration from Netto and his mate on the *Vengador*, testimony they seem to have provided without reservation or concern for the stated penalties for slave traders to be found in the Anglo-Brazilian treaties—namely, banishment to Mozambique for five years if one was an officer—likely because these punishments were, for all intents and purposes, never applied.

But the saga of the *Vengador* did not end there, just as it had not begun when the *Black Joke* came upon the slaver two days out from Lagos. Netto's ship had also been rechristened; it was once known as the *Principe de Guine* and had been captured with "considerable bloodshed" by Bullen's pathbreaking tender, the *Hope*, in August of 1826, only a year previous to the *Black Joke's* own capture as *Henriqueta*. Once captured, the then *Principe de Guine* was auctioned off and sold to Commodore Bullen for use as a tender, and upon leaving the coast, he sold that ship, along with *Hope*, at auction once again, as was the custom. The vessel was purchased by a foreign buyer, likely a proxy, who subsequently transferred ownership to someone in Bahia, presumably Jose de Cerqueira Lima's slave-trading outfit. In short, the once *Principe de Guine* had been captured, sailed back to Freetown, tried, condemned, auctioned to Bullen, repaired, possibly used as a tender by the navy for a few months, sold again, sailed to Brazil, and, embarking from Rio, was back to the coast with a new captain as the *Vengador* in time to be recaptured by the *Black Joke* in the Bight of Benin roughly twenty months later, in May of 1828.

If this, then, had truly been the end of it, it would still be more than enough to call into question the system by which the Royal Navy disposed of its slaver tenders. Alas, it most definitely was not. Collier, realizing how untenable this all was, addressed a letter to

Croker, Secretary of the Admiralty, later that year, in early December, recounting what is, for this narrative, the final disposition of the *Vengador*. It may sound as frustratingly familiar now as it must have been to Collier. After the slaver was condemned the second time around, it was again auctioned, this time to a recent arrival named Mr. Brockington, who'd come from Santos, a Brazilian port north of Rio, with the specific intention of buying slave ships. Brockington, a British national and thus prohibited from the trade, was either the business partner to or agent of the American consul in Rio, and he successfully purchased three ships, including the *Black Joke's* first two prizes, *Gertrudis* and *Vengador*. Brockington then did everything he could to get out of Freetown as quickly as possible, before, one imagines, anyone started asking any incriminating questions. The most expeditious way to clear the coast of Africa was under the British flag, given the presence of the Royal Navy, and to this end Brockington hoisted same on the *Vengador*, but by law, for a ship to fly a British flag it had to have a certain number of British sailors crewing the boat. Undeterred, Brockington hied off on his new purchase himself, even calling in favors from prominent British nationals in Sierra Leone to get the requisite number of Englishmen on board to legitimize his actions, and sailed for Brazil, along with his other purchases. To whom the now ex-*Vengador* was eventually sold is unclear, but what it unequivocal is that, by the time of Collier's frustrated missive less than six months later, it was back on the coast of West Africa *again*, for the third time (and with a third name) in as many years. Now in the guise of the *Perseverance*—who knows if the irony was intended—this recycled slaver had become, as Collier disgustedly pointed out, "a most notorious Vessel" under its new name.

Lest this read like an unfortunate anomaly, it's instructive to look at the rest of Collier's letter, because here the quagmire created by the Admiralty's policy on the disposition of the slave ships becomes maddeningly obvious. Getting directly to the point, Collier opens with:

*Sir,*

*I have to state to you, for the information of His Royal Highness the Lord High Admiral, that most of the Slave-vessels that are captured and sent here [Freetown] for condemnation, are again purchased by Agents here and sent to the Brazils.*

Given that Brazil had filled much of the void left by Britain in the brisk business of human trafficking, the implications were clear, and Collier knew it. Seeking to press home the extent of the problem, he didn't restrain his exasperation to the *Vengador* incident, detailing the disposition of another slave trader, the *Esperanza*. The commodore's frustration leaps off the page, even almost two hundred years later. Truly, one sympathizes, because get this: the *Esperanza* was formerly known as . . . the *Hope*.

While it's true that *esperanza* does literally mean "hope" in Spanish, the problem was much more complicated than a case of duplicate names. Just a month before the *Black Joke* came upon the *Vengador*, on April 13, 1828, the *Sybille* detained an empty slaver, the Portuguese schooner *Esperanza*, captained by Jose Rios. Rios had already been condemned as a slaver captain the year before, in March 1827, by none other than Bullen's flagship, the *Maidstone*, the same ship that had captured the *Hope* (under the name *Hoop*—it was originally of Dutch extraction). After that judgment, Rios had been free to go despite his crime, and evidently it hadn't been difficult to find another berth. He wouldn't fare any better this time. Though the *Esperanza* had been empty when it was captured, it, like the *Vengador*, was awfully far north to be loading the enslaved in Cabinda, to the tune of nine hundred miles in the wrong direction. Rios claimed to have accidentally become very, very lost—obviously no one believed him—and the ship was condemned and slated for sale at auction. So far, so reasonable. *Esperanza* was sold in June to a landed British resident of Sierra Leone, William Henry Savage, Esq., who shamelessly rehired the twice-condemned Rios—and the remaining slaver crew of the *Esperanza*, plus a bonus Englishman to serve as a figure-head captain—and promptly attempted to sail the ship out of Sierra Leone and back to Brazil. *Black Joke* was also in Freetown's harbor, having just accompanied the *Vengador* to its date with the Mixed Commission, and recognizing what was about to happen, Lieutenant Turner (for his promotion would not be official for another two weeks) refused to let the schooner leave.

Even if it had been nominally purchased by a British national, everyone familiar with the trade was well aware that condemned ships sent back to Brazil fared much the same as their captains—they continued to go about their business. (Namely, enslavement.) It was also clear that this had been the *Hope*. Savage, protesting mightily to anyone who might listen, even had the unmitigated gall to make the connection explicit, likely referring to the now *Esperanza* as the *Hope* in letters in an effort to distance the vessel from its extraordinarily recent slaving past. (It may not have helped his argument to remind everyone that his new purchase had been a tender of the Royal Navy that had, with alacrity, found itself back on the wrong side of the law and history.) He wasn't hiring an (almost) exclusively Brazilian crew to staff a slaver, of course not, he just wanted to help "to take away the whole of the Brazilians from this Place, under an expressed and written direction from the Brazilian Ambassador to myself, to do all in my power on behalf of their Subjects, until the arrival of a more authenticated Personage." In these letters, Savage, the picture of innocence and cooperation, swore he would be happy to "make any concession" to satisfy Turner's suspicions (which Savage implied were manifestly unreasonable) and thereby expedite the *Hope/Esperanza/Hope*'s departure . . . except for giving up its armament, which Savage contended would simply be too difficult and potentially deleterious to the vessel to remove. Not content to merely blow smoke, Savage ended his June addressing complaints to both the lieutenant governor of Sierra Leone (via his private secretary, Lieutenant Maclean) and Collier's own prize agent in Sierra Leone, the Honorable Kenneth Macaulay, asking the latter to intervene "as a particular favor" since "as Agent to Commodore Collier, [his] opinion must have great weight with Lieutenant Turner."

An agent in this case meant prize agent, and men like Macaulay acted on behalf of naval personnel to make arrangements for the sale and disposition of prize ships, as well as their gear and any licit cargo that may have been on board, and became ridiculously rich on a percentage of the profit. Given that the *Black Joke*'s prizes were, in effect, the *Sybille*'s prizes, Kenneth Macaulay—who was not just an agent at the firm Macaulay and Babington (not the named partner, that was his cousin, famous abolitionist and previous colonial administrator Zachary Macaulay), but also one of Freetown's most prominent businessmen and public citizens—was the prize agent for both Collier and Turner in Sierra Leone. Accordingly, he stepped in to help Turner get the matter settled, brokering a meeting between Turner and Savage the morning of June 30 at Macaulay's residence, just one day after he'd received Savage's note. It would turn out to be a good thing for Turner that Macaulay had taken such active involvement. Sometime between June 30 and July 1, most likely at that very meeting, it seems that a portion of the *Hope/Esperanza/Hope*'s documentation as a former slaver was provided to Turner; Turner, in turn, was to redeposit this paperwork with Henry Rishton, the acting colonial secretary of Sierra Leone, on July 1, which he did. The next day, Rishton fired off a letter to Macaulay, in which he accused Turner of only returning a portion of what he'd been given, adding that what had been returned was so "mutilated" that Rishton couldn't possibly tender the documents to the lieutenant governor in their "present state"; perhaps, at least, Macaulay had the missing papers? Collier's agent wasted no time nipping this accusation of impropriety at the root:

> Neither myself, nor any connected with the "Sybille," or "Black Joke," have any of the "Hope's" Papers in our possession. To the very extraordinary charge you bring against Lieutenant Turner,

*I beg leave to give the most unqualified denial; the 2 Licences al-
luded to were delivered to Lieutenant Turner, in my presence, in
the very same state and condition they were forwarded to you. He
did not "mutilate" them, neither did he take the Bill of Sale, and
the other Documents away.*

The crux of the issue was money. Even if Turner knew he wasn't
wrong about Savage's plans for the *Hope/Esperanza/Hope*, he
couldn't afford the risk of standing his ground on a charge of "illegal
navigation" without Collier present to back him, both administratively and financially, in the event Savage sued for recompense and
won. So the lieutenant, under intense pressure as Savage called in
favors around town, felt obliged to compromise. In order to leave
Freetown's harbor, Turner had Savage sign two documents, oaths
assuring the reader and posterity that he was the owner of the *Hope*,
as opposed to a middleman laundering a dirty ship; that he was willingly surrendering the ship's previous papers from its return to slave
trading, "so professing to give to the said Schooner 'Hope' a British
character," which is to say change the national identity of the ship
to English, with the attendant regulations vis-à-vis the slave trade
that would accompany such an affiliation; and that he would also
dismantle and store any guns on board and give up the *Hope's* gun
carriages (how the guns were mounted to the ship) entirely. Perhaps most important to Turner, Savage further agreed to indemnify
Turner and any of his men from actions they had already taken to
prevent his departure, as well as release any claim he might have
against Turner *or Collier*, their heirs and assigns, etc., for the de-
tention of the schooner in the harbor and any expenses related to
both that and the compromises agreed upon to secure the *Hope's*
release. Answering the question of fiscal responsibility for mistakes
prompted by *Black Joke's* previous encounter with *Providencia*, it's
clear from this incident that the commodore would be jointly liable
if his tender's captain erred in judgment, and the cost of restitution
could be steep enough to bankrupt those Royal Navy officers whose

eagerness outstripped their personal pocketbooks. So Turner, reluctant to the last but out of options, was forced to let the *Hope* sail. One can only imagine his misgivings—and annoyance—as he watched the ship disappear, once again, from Freetown's harbor to Brazil's distant shores. The reality of service on the coast was discouraging, as circumstances constantly conspired against success, and efficiently doing one's duty for king, country, and, depending on one's sentiments, the literal soul of humanity—for such was the rhetoric back in abolitionist circles in England—was unreasonably difficult.

Which ultimately brings the tale back to Collier's letter to his superiors in December of 1828. The commodore shared his protégé's frustration, and more, because now Collier could say with certainty that Turner had been smart, appropriately reactive, and, above all, *absolutely correct* back in early July when he'd claimed the *Esperanza/Hope* was headed back to the slave trade, and further, that this problem, writ large, would continue to make the Squadron's mission on the coast nigh impossible. That fall, the *Esperanza*—for Collier refused to even dignify Savage's previous dissemblance by using the name *Hope*—had, sure enough, been spotted once again in the Bight of Benin, just come from Ajuda and loaded with "upwards of 300" enslaved people, a scant three months after the practical realities of Admiralty policy had effectively forced Turner to either let the ship go or risk penury. Including a signed affidavit from a witness who would swear to seeing the *Esperanza* filled with the enslaved in October, Collier begged the Admiralty to, at the least, seek cases against Savage, Brockington, and men like them as British nationals participating in the slave trade, and one gets the distinct impression that Collier would have had no problem with the notion of shipping all such facilitators to Australia on the first available boat. Though the commodore's letter and the evidence he included were duly passed up the chain from the Admiralty to the Foreign Office, there's no evidence that any specific punishments came of Collier's efforts.

Again one wonders why the Royal Navy itself refused to commit to purchasing tenders. A fleet of repurposed slavers would have been a cheap and effective way to increase the size of the Squadron, and the navy's representatives in the field—or in this case, at sea— like Bullen and Collier, could clearly see that such supplementation was necessary if the Admiralty intended to keep the West Africa Squadron to six to eight official navy vessels. However, counterintuitive though it may seem, the custom at the time was to allow officers to purchase ships for use in the Royal Navy's service, retain a portion of the profits derived from those vessels if they captured prizes, and wash their hands of whatever happened next, including the disposition of those ships once an officer left his service on the coast. The Royal Navy was so reluctant to spend its own funds that captains even had to pay for the expenditures (such as supplies) generated by the transport of a prize back to Freetown when they initially captured it! Only if officers had the economic wherewithal and a requisite need might they buy that prize themselves. This itch was not, or at least not always, merely a question of creating a stronger fighting force. Some in the WAS—like Captain William Fitzwilliam Owen, administrator of the outpost at Fernando Pó—were discovering, first, that the acquisition of prizes could be a lucrative sideline and, second, that the most expedient way to catch some slavers was to buy one.

This language of "prizes" was not a purposeful distancing mechanism—ships captured under similar circumstances, whether in war or peace, had been called prizes long before suppression followed oppression to Africa. What is obscured by this shorthand, though, is that in the Squadron, the most lucrative and desirable of prizes could be more accurately described as dozens to hundreds of terrified people in straits beyond dire and the suffocating, disease-ridden hell in which they suffered and often died—and not just at the hands of slavers. The Royal Navy's own disciplinary system was, in this era, no stranger to the whip; it's entirely unsurprising, if still horrifying, that there are accounts of prize crews resorting to such means on the very people they were sailing to "liberate." Prize crews might also, in the name of order on deck, attempt to shove all of the enslaved back into the claustrophobic pit they'd just escaped, resorting to violence if the crews felt it warranted. Sexual assault of enslaved women (as no one was officially liberated until the ship was actually condemned by a Mixed Commission) was sufficiently common that one officer suggested the level of "impropriety" as a rationale for a policy cutting or denying prize crews their daily allotment of alcohol as prescribed by the Victualling Board. To be captured by the Royal Navy was almost certainly better than the alternative—how much better is an entire discussion unto itself—but that truth can't absolve its sailors of any crimes against humanity they committed against those they ostensibly sought to free.

Though sometimes the enslaved might have had a difficult time differentiating between the behaviors of the slavers and the Squadron, the far more universal problem was neglect. Prize duty created a lot of work for Royal Navy seamen on board both the victor and the captured vessel—both would be operated shorthanded for the duration of the prize ship's trip to adjudication in Freetown, and on the prize ship, the crew also had to feed and provide rudimentary medical care to the enslaved and the slaver's crew, combat the illnesses that were more prevalent on slaving ships, and ensure that the crew of the slave trader didn't connive a way to retake the ship, a not infrequent occurrence. It wasn't remotely unheard of that prize crews and the ships they sailed simply disappeared, and whether these disappearances were due to insurrection from the captured crew, an uprising of the enslaved on board, or severe weather such as tornadoes at sea might never be discovered. If the slaver actually arrived in Sierra Leone, it still had to face judgment, by no means certain, that the ship had been legally detained—only then could a prize earn back the direct and indirect costs of capturing it and bringing it to court. What made the expense, labor, and potential pitfalls worth it—especially if a sailor was not particularly devoted to the cause of abolition—was the opportunity to substantially supplement his income from the Royal Navy. It was rare, but a particularly valuable prize could be economically life-changing for those who'd helped capture it. The sources of that money were one-quarter of the proceeds from the recovery and sale of the ship and its contents (or "salvage"), and a £10 per person flat rate the WAS ship collectively received as a bounty for each enslaved person recovered and liberated (or "head money"). Though this rate per head was actually much lower than the scale the suppression effort had begun with—£60 per man, £30 per woman, £10 per child had proved unsustainable by 1824—and would drop again to £5 per enslaved person in 1830, between money and the comparative ease of condemnation, it's clear why ships with human cargo on board were an ideal prize, no matter the risk.

That's, of course, presuming that the men could get the money to which their work entitled them. Agents like Macaulay were necessary precisely because, having gone through the harrowing process of getting a prize to the Mixed Commission, sailors in the Royal Navy still had to plead, cajole, berate, and provide ample paperwork before the Treasury would actually dispense prize money. Adding insult to serious annoyance, if an officer who owned a tender (and only officers could afford such an expense) left service on the coast for the shores of England, the expense of transporting any purchased ships back to England remained with the man who bought it, no matter how much valuable service the vessel had provided. Since this was not often believed an endeavor worth the cost to even those who could afford to buy such a ship, these repurposed slavers were most frequently put back up for auction. And though restrictions were supposedly in place as to who could purchase them, slave traders in the Americas found it farcically easy to entice an entirely different breed of agents, friendly to slavers, to act as fronts and get ships back to Brazil, where they could be repaired, renamed, issued a new passport, and sailed right back out to enslave once more. Men such as Brockington and Savage earned their money as temporary owners at best—their real job was to funnel vessels lost to the slave trade right back into it, thereby erasing much of what suppression was meant to accomplish. Stories like the *Vengador*'s surely made many leery of using and maintaining tenders that could well become slavers once again—it was a scandal waiting to happen, and Collier's letter could not be entirely ignored . . . but it could be put aside. The commodore had bitterly complained in 1828, yet meaningful orders requiring that any ships purchased for the service had to be sold to the Royal Navy or scuttled would not arrive until the mid-1830s, and it would be even longer before the Admiralty disavowed the practice of allowing officers to buy tenders at all, ensuring all ship purchases and dispositions went through official channels. In the interim, for Collier's entire command of the WAS, not only was this loophole wide open, but the enterprising slaver could, via proxy, even purchase slave-trading vessels via Lloyd's of London (a particularly popular option from a prize-money perspective), a body that still exists today as an insurance underwriter (and which has apparently only just begun to grapple with its intimate ties to the slave-trading industry). Clearly, a variety of economic considerations, from international trade agreements to the disposition of secondhand ships, contributed to the perception that ending the slave trade might be a Sisyphean task.

Unfortunately for the commodore, back when the *Black Joke* made its quick capture of the *Vengador* in 1828, this recycling of slaving vessels wasn't even close to Collier's most pressing problem. At present, WAS ships resupplied in Freetown, though plans constantly seemed to be percolating to move that depot to Fernando Pó, where opponents to the mission and/or very existence of Sierra Leone had been advocating it be put for years now. On May 13, back when *Sybille* first brought the *Esperanza* into Freetown, the commodore found the WAS ships *Primrose*, *Clinker*, and *Plumper* docked and aimlessly waiting in the harbor. This was not entirely unusual for *Plumper*, which had a defective copper bottom and an arguably even more wanting captain—one who'd supposedly been put to pasture over a decade previous, replete with a note from the Admiralty to never give him a ship again (so either powerful friends or one hell of an administrative error there)—but *Primrose*, a ship-sloop under

Captain Griffenhoofe, was the most successful nontender in the entire Squadron. What's more, they'd all seemed to have been there for a while. The captains, far from neglecting their duties, informed Collier that the supply chain had fallen apart . . . somewhere, and the WAS stores onshore were empty—no one could safely leave until they resupplied, meaning every WAS ship that sailed into the harbor was stuck in Freetown until the problem was resolved. Collier couldn't have been happy to then see the *North Star* sail into the harbor two weeks later—this meant that every single Squadron vessel but for *Black Joke* was effectively trapped in Sierra Leone.

One might think that such an event might incline Collier to favor a move to Fernando Pó, which maintained a brisk trade with the metropole in its own right due to extensive lumber exports and had the support of a vocal contingent back in England, but pretty much no one in Freetown wanted the change, the commodore very much included. That island had its own potential deficits, not the least of which being that Captain Owen, who ran the settlement there, was the closest thing Collier had to a nemesis on the coast and had been the same to Bullen before Collier. As such, the commodore was extremely disinclined to go that route unless forced to by command. (And the feeling between the two men was entirely mutual, though Owen would have welcomed the traffic.) So the *Black Joke* was, for close to a month, the only Squadron ship on the entire coast doing any patrolling whatsoever. (Captain Owen had his own tenders that also remained active, but since he was acting way beyond his orders from the Admiralty in doing so, they were not actually part of the West Africa Squadron.) Once the supply chain issue was resolved, the *Sybille*, eager to get back out to sea, had departed by the time Turner arrived with the *Vengador* to a port now empty of Squadron ships, just in time to try to stop *Esperanza/Hope* from heading back to Brazil. But Collier, frustrating though he would find it six months later, had just left, and since there was nothing Turner could do once it was decided to let Savage proceed, the *Black Joke* took advantage of the (finally) refilled stores and also headed back out to cruise. The crew could not have known that their string of relatively easy and mostly bloodless victories was about to come to an end.

It was close to two months later, on an afternoon in late August, when the *Black Joke*, on orders to deliver messages to the *Primrose* and take a gander at what folks might be getting up to near Ouidah, sighted a suspicious brig and two schooners near "Whydah Roads." By this time, rumors of the *Black Joke*'s legendary speed and exploits had spread among slave traders, and Turner, attempting to stay as incognito as possible, was flying a Brazilian flag. Still, he must've wondered if his disguise might be working slightly *too* well when the three ships, far from avoiding an encounter, weighed anchor and sailed straight for him—the larger schooner heavily armed and clearly signaling the others as they came. Figuring out whether these were slavers, pirates, or something else entirely—and with it, what their intent and next move might be—became more and more pressing as the leading ship closed. Of course, for the purposes of the law, there was no difference. Pirates were not as plentiful as they had been throughout the previous two centuries, but were part of the upsurge in dangerous maritime activity that occurred when the slave trade became an illegal market. Piratical activity, on the other hand, had exploded due to a legal shift, as earlier in the 1820s, both Britain and the United States had opted to erase the legal distinction between slave trading and piracy. (As the disposition of *Vengador*, *Esperanza*, and other slaving crews demonstrated, a de facto difference—particularly in punishment and sentencing if caught—nonetheless remained.) Obviously both (now) operated illegally on water, but one reason for the change was more particular—since most pirates didn't discriminate between profiting from the seizure of inanimate goods and living people in bondage, all it took for a pirate to become a slaver was the capture of a vessel with people, rather than goods, to seize and ultimately sell. As slave ships were some of the most valuable craft to be found at sea, the line between the pirate and the slaver was often already nonexistent.

The larger schooner was precisely one such, a notorious pirate and sometime privateer that had been wreaking havoc to such an extent that slavers likely sought to avoid both it and *Black Joke* in equal measure. Over the summer of 1828, the *Presidente* had terrorized practically everyone it had come across, flying virtually every available flag in pursuit of bounty. The two ships accompanying the large schooner, the brig *Hosse* and the smaller schooner *Marianna*, were previous victims of the pirates. The captain of the *Hosse*, Juan Maria Evangelista, would later testify that the *Presidente* had, in contriving to board his vessel, identified itself as American, but when he went aboard the *Presidente* to show its captain, Prouting, papers identifying both himself and his vessel as Portuguese (and thus not subject to American authority), Prouting replied, "Never mind flags; you shall keep aboard all night, and tomorrow we will see what we can do." Based on its cargo, Evangelista was sailing a supply ship, not a slave trader, though nonetheless one owned by notorious Ouidah slaver Francisco Félix de Souza, also known as "Cha Cha," possessed of an empire of flesh and agony so sprawling he had an entire fleet of like ships to supply the barracoons he kept stocked with the enslaved up and down the coast of western Africa. It didn't matter. By the time Evangelista left Captain Prouting's cabin, the entire crew of the *Hosse* was in shackles. Evangelista soon found himself likewise confined—though in the gun room with some freedom of movement about the ship, rather than in irons, as befitting his station as a captain. That had been August 26. On the twenty-seventh, around 2:00 p.m., hearing someone shout, "A vessel in sight!," Evangelista made his way above deck on the *Presidente*; though he was quickly hurried back down to the gun room, he did later see the *Presidente* hoist a French flag, though he'd seen it flying the flag of Buenos Aires that very morning (not to mention the Stars and Stripes the day before).

Commander Turner, now that his promotion was approaching six weeks official, caught little of this initial action because, though it had been seen, the *Black Joke* hadn't sighted the *Presidente* in return until 4:00 p.m., and when, an hour later, the unidentified ship closed to a distance of half a gunshot, it flew no identifying colors at all. Making sail and tacking back inshore, the *Presidente* hoisted a French flag—this was the moment Evangelista caught. Turner mirrored the probably-not-French ship's movements until, after an hour and a half, Prouting tired of the charade—he'd decided the *Black Joke* was definitely Brazilian, and, what's more, quite possibly a supply ship loaded with gold bullion, bound for Gibraltar and rumored to be in the vicinity. From its position on the little brig's lee quarter, the *Presidente* let off a shot and switched its flag to that of Spain. Turner, assuming the *Black Joke* had already been recognized, struck the Brazilian flag and raised British colors, setting his sails to make moves. The *Presidente* fired again, this time joined by the two ships still trailing it, but the *Black Joke*, unfazed, pressed closer, then closer still, now a pistol shot away, then half that. Close enough to talk, or at least trumpet, Turner called, "Schooner, ahoy!" and attempted to hail the lead ship once, twice, thrice. He wouldn't get a fourth chance.

The only answer the *Black Joke*'s hails got was a massive broadside from all seven of the *Presidente*'s guns. Whether Prouting genuinely initially believed the *Black Joke*'s British flag to be yet another ruse was a legal question to be answered another day, but he, and several other crew members of the *Presidente*, were irrefutably British nationals and so fully subject to the jurisdiction of the empire (as represented by the *Black Joke*) whether they were pirates or slavers or hapless souls who had, all unwittingly, just fired on one of His Majesty's ships. Evangelista tried to point this out; he'd been allowed to briefly observe the initial chase, and though night had closed in fast, the moon was bright, and the Portuguese captain was quite familiar with the ships that sailed this coast. Evangelista *knew* that was the *Black Joke*, which he mentioned to the sailor who'd been guarding him in the gun room, and as the message worked its way to the captain, dread and deadly commitment followed. Attacking a Royal Navy ship as a British national was treason; the penalty, death by hanging. And the damage had already been done. Far from changing

Prouting's mind, the unwelcome news Evangelista bore meant there was no turning back. "I don't care a curse!" the doomed pirate captain cried. "As soon as they come near me, I'll fight them like hell!" Shouts of assent rose up from the deck, another sailor rallying his fellows with "Never mind flags[!] Everybody I find on the coast I shall rob! We'll try to take that brig because she has a great deal of money!" Prouting agreed, "She is a damned fine brig, has but one gun, will do very well for us, and I *must* have her."

The *Presidente* was wrong in one crucial respect—though still outmanned and outpowered, the *Black Joke* now had *two* guns and returned the broadside. Collier had, just days before, given the *Black Joke* a twelve-pounder carronade from *Sybille's* own launch, now mounted on a traversing carriage and ready to make things a bit more lively. Still, three opponents to one weren't good odds, even for a ship and crew of the *Black Joke's* caliber, especially given that the *Presidente* was heavily armed with seven guns, had two additional vessels and their armament as support, and boasted a crew that was noticeably experienced at taking ships. It was also clear that, of the piratical cohort, the *Presidente* was the fastest—and this gave Turner an idea. Even as the other ships closed to assist, the Black Jokes applied every bit of skill they had to maneuver the tender the hell away from the immediate danger of being that close to a ship full of pirates. Slipping free, *Black Joke* stood off, keeping its distance, and Prouting gave chase. Through the evening, Turner and his crew ran, fighting to stay just out of range and returning fire high, hoping to hit the *Presidente's* sails or masts, while pushing the two support ships off the pace.

Soon the fighting slowed, then stopped altogether. Hours passed, and as the sound of cannons ceased and the moon rose ever higher, Turner steadily drew Prouting farther and farther from his other ships. And then finally, close to midnight, it happened. *Presidente* had appeared on the *Black Joke's* weather quarter, and it was all alone— not another sail in sight. This was the moment the Black Jokes had sailed hours to reach. As the call of beating drums brought nearly the brig's entire complement on deck, Turner tacked the ship, bringing the *Black Joke* into close quarters, but the *Presidente* was as practiced as he'd feared, and for over an hour, the two ships circled, neither able to get quite close enough to board the other, and both seemingly running out of time. Prouting broke first, setting all of the schooner's sails to run, likely with the hopes of reconvening with his other ships quickly enough to turn about once more and bring their full power to bear on the little brig. Now it was the *Black Joke's* turn to give chase, and as the brig poured on every ounce of speed it had, it became clear which vessel the slavers should truly fear to come across. The *Presidente's* crew was admittedly ruthless, willing to murder every enemy on board if it was expedient. But before anyone could get killed, they'd have to get caught, and here *Black Joke* excelled.

It was past four in the morning, a full twelve hours since the *Black Joke* had sighted the *Presidente*, when the navy ship finally caught up to the pirate, and though he could see the sails of his support in the distance, Prouting knew he had to make a stand. Rounding on the *Black Joke*, Prouting sent off another broadside, which was returned and then some. One suspects it was now Turner and the Black Jokes who were impatient with this fight—surely tired, and there was still a boarding to accomplish—and their cannons bore that out, as they stuffed each gun almost to the brim with every variety of ammunition they had to hand, lined up with muskets, successfully ran alongside the *Presidente*, and fired everything they could at it all at once. Making a daring move, Turner pressed his advantage and immediately ordered nearly everyone to board the *Presidente*, leaving only three sailors on the *Black Joke*, two of them boys and one with his hands full minding the suddenly empty ship. Despite the fact that both vessels were sailing at over seven knots—roughly eight miles per hour—over shark-infested ocean, the Black Jokes made the leap over the *Presidente's* low rail with cutlasses at the ready, throwing themselves at men with nothing to lose armed to greet them with pikes, battle-axes, and the sailor's swords known as hangers. One last shot of the guns had accompanied the crew of the *Black Joke* in their fearsome rush to the opposite deck, and it was a beauty. The *Presidente's* boom shattered from the impact, its rigging cut and sails crashing to the deck, killing the sailor at its wheel. In the confusion, Prouting, desperate, called an order to fire the long guns into the oncoming horde, but his last order made little difference; in the short, pitched fight that ensued, he died, along with at least five of his men, for a total of over thirty wounded or killed.

The *Presidente's* crew surrendered once Prouting died, but the *Black Joke* had suffered its first battle casualty: the gunner's mate had been killed in the rush of boarding. Though the *Presidente* had no enslaved on board and was clearly not in the area to purchase its own enslaved, having much preferred to take someone else's ill-gotten trade, the loss was not entirely in vain. Upon searching Prouting's cabin, Turner discovered a logbook of secret codes employed by pirates throughout the area, and when the *Hosse* finally did catch up the next morning, having missed the battle entirely—the other ship, *Marianna*, was nowhere to be found—Turner used these codes to signal them from the pirate ship's deck, as if the *Presidente*, if worse for the wear, had won the day. Trusting the signals, the pirate crew holding the *Hosse* closed to the battered *Presidente*, and the *Black Joke* made easy work of reuniting Evangelista with his ship.

And then, as was the way of service on the coast, things got complicated. The *Presidente* was a pirate ship flying the flag of Buenos Aires (and everywhere else) with a mostly British and American crew, while the *Hosse* was a slaver supply ship with a Portuguese captain and Portuguese papers, owned by a resident slave trader known to supply Bahia, and the third (still-missing) ship might not have been a slave trader per se, either, and was reputedly Spanish to boot. The *Presidente*, barely seaworthy, was wrecked on its voyage to Freetown, though the entire prize crew of Black Jokes survived; the British crew members of *Presidente*, at least, would be on their way to England to be tried as pirates in criminal court at the Surrey County Sessions House on Horsemonger Lane. The *Hosse* was also taken back to Freetown for adjudication, and though it didn't precisely qualify as a slaver, it was deemed a Portuguese ship taken by pirates, so the *Black Joke* was credited with rescuing it and awarded salvage. The crew of the *Hosse* was equally free to go back to supplying slavers, but for Captain Evangelista—he would instead be taking the trip back to England as a court witness to testify against the surviving members of the *Presidente's* crew. He and the alleged pirates would be traveling on Collier's least favorite ship, *Plumper*, undeniably too worn-out to continue in the Squadron and finally being sent back home for an overhaul. And they would have one more, unexpected, traveling companion—Commander Turner, also acting as a witness at the trial back in England, would join the motley assemblage headed back to get their day in court. But before leaving, while *Presidente* was breaking up and as its prize crew and captives made their way to Freetown, where the disposition of *Hosse* would be determined, William Turner, ever the overachiever, would take one more ship at the helm of the *Black Joke*. Because complications were the way of things in the WAS, he wouldn't get any recognition for it.

It was the *Primrose*, not *Sybille*, as represented by the *Black Joke*, that would be credited with what was arguably Turner's last capture, but determining who was ultimately responsible for bringing in the *Zepherina*, and as a result how the prize money should be apportioned, resulted in a case that went all the way to the High Court of the Admiralty. The morning of September 14, thirty miles south of Lagos, lookouts on *Primrose* sighted what appeared to be a laden slave ship bound for Brazil. Accordingly, Captain Griffenhoofe ordered pursuit. While *Primrose* was probably the fastest and most nimble of the nontenders—certainly, during Collier's tenure, the most successful—it had not been designed primarily for speed, and it showed; though ably handled, and despite the best efforts of the crew over the course of the next six hours, the Squadron ship just couldn't manage the necessary knots to catch the slaver as it sped ever closer to the equator. Enter the *Black Joke*, quite literally. At three in the afternoon, Turner and his crew appeared on the horizon heading in the opposite direction, and quick on the uptake as usual, the little brig immediately joined the chase. At this point, the *Zepherina* had to decide which ship it had the best chance against, and the captain changed course, heading toward the *Primrose*. By 6:00 p.m., the *Black Joke* had effectively herded the slaver to within a half mile of *Primrose*, and Griffenhoofe seized the moment and fired. As a consequence, one imagines, of having just been shot at, *Zepherina* struck its colors and surrendered to the *Primrose*. Both Royal Navy vessels then approached, both boarded the slaver, and both contributed members to the prize crew that brought the ship and its enslaved cargo to Freetown.

So why not share the credit, and with it the bounty, equally? Given the way the chase had been going, there was no dispute that, had the *Black Joke* not arrived and had Turner not reacted as quickly as he did, the *Primrose* might never have caught *Zepherina*. There was even an established rule for just such a scenario:

> . . . [The] Order in Council of the 30th of June 1827, for the distribution of such captures [. . .] directs, "that all rewards for arrests and seizures made by tenders employed by the order of the Lord High Admiral, or of the commissioners for executing that office for the time being, or by boats or officers belonging to and detached from H.M. ships and vessels, are to be shared by the officers and men of the ship or vessel to which such boats or officers belong, in the same manner as if the seizure was made by the said ship or vessel."

The problems, as the court saw them, were twofold. First, the *Black Joke* wasn't the "actual captor" of the *Zepherina*. *Primrose* saw the slaver first, *Primrose* spent more time (as in, all day) chasing it, *Primrose* fired the only shots, and the slaver surrendered to the *Primrose*. At best, the *Black Joke* had been a "joint captor," never mind the fact, which the court admitted, that had the tender not appeared, the *Zepherina* might well have sailed free and cleared the equator to waters in which the Squadron had no jurisdiction. Second, the *Black*

*Joke* wasn't actually the *Sybille*, no matter how well recognized and deeply entrenched the legal fiction. The practical support the ships could have offered the *Primrose*, had the situation become sticky, was very different—what the *Black Joke* lacked in armament was compensated for by its speed and handling, while the bigger, slower *Sybille* had more guns than the *Black Joke* could ever hope to fit on its comparatively tiny deck. Prize money in joint captures was apportioned by the amount of "force" each ship contributed to the seizure. While being fast enough to compel the *Zepherina* to change course had been vital, it wasn't exactly what the framers of the order had had in mind. By this reasoning, the *Black Joke* should receive only a tiny portion of the bounty relative to the force it contributed to the capture. The court sympathized; since the *Black Joke* was a tender, even that comparatively paltry sum had to be distributed among the entire crew of the *Sybille* as well, and the opinion expressed the hope that there might be "some reciprocity between parties so detached" that could mitigate the disproportionate balance in the awarding of prize money. But the decision stood. The *Primrose* would remain the captor of record.

This anticlimactic capture would be both William Turner's and Edward Lyne Harvey's last on the *Black Joke*. Collier had acquired more tenders, and the now Lieutenant Harvey got a command of his own aboard the *Paul Pry*. Two months after the capture of the *Zepherina*, in November 1828, Commander William Turner transferred his life-changing brig to its new captain, Lieutenant Henry Downes. That accomplished, Turner boarded the *Plumper* for England and the trial of the pirates of the *Presidente*, and there he would be presented with the sword that Collier, on behalf of the entire crew of the *Sybille*, had gotten him in recognition of his exceptional work throughout 1828. The frigate had a lot to thank him for. On Turner's watch, the *Black Joke* had been responsible for more seizures, officially or unofficially, than any other vessel in the Squadron. The commander returned home responsible for the liberation of between approximately nine hundred and over sixteen hundred people, and due to the vagaries of Royal Navy assignments, there was no guarantee that he'd be back. It may not have helped that Turner had made enemies, too, among the slavers and their agents in Freetown. While he was gone, they got to work.

Portuguese Brig "Vengadow", Register of Slaves Natives of Africa, Captured on board the said Vessel by His Majesty's Ship "Sybille" Francis Augustus Collier CB Commander and Emancipated by Decree of the British and Portuguese Court of Mixed Commission on the 16th day

| Nº | Names | Sex | Age | Stature f. i. | Description |
|---|---|---|---|---|---|
| 12489 | Iffay | Man | 24 | 5 0 | P on right Breast and Talk on same |
| 12490 | Appah | " | 25 | 5 4 | CC on left do. & Cuts on Cheeks |
| 91 | Iyoh | " | 26 | 5 7 | P on right do. & Cuts all over |
| 92 | Obonah | " | 21 | 4 11 | Cuts all over |
| 93 | Oye | " | 24 | 5 5 | CC on left Breast, Cuts on Back & Belly |
| 94 | Chomoko | " | 28 | 5 9 | Do. Do. Cuts on face & Belly |
| 12495 | Oalayby | " | 26 | 5 5 | P on right Do. Do. Do. |
| 96 | Bojaybu | " | 23 | 5 5 | CC Do. Do. Do. Do. |
| 97 | Ifhi | " | 26 | 5 6 | CC left Do. Cuts on face & Talk on Belly |
| 98 | Amlassok | " | 25 | 5 8 | CC Do. Do. & Cuts all over |
| 99 | Agah | " | 18 | 5 3 | A Scar across the Back |
| 12500 | Ajutohday | " | 29 | 5 8 | C on right breast & Cuts on Face |
| 1 | Hudahsu | " | 28 | 5 1 | CC do. & Cuts all over |
| 2 | Lahju | " | 27 | 5 2 | P do. do. do. |
| 3 | Oguadoe | " | 26 | 5 4 | P do. do. do. |
| 4 | Ahdowayto | " | 22 | 5 5 | Cuts all over Body |
| 12505 | Ahchasolo | " | 21 | 5 3 | P on right breast, 1 Cut down Breast & Belly |
| 6 | Oyojaykah | " | 22 | 5 3 | CC on left do. & Cuts on face & Talk on Breast |
| 7 | Adaybu | " | 20 | 5 1 | C on right do. and Cuts all over |
| 8 | Lahyohu | " | 29 | 5 9 | CC on left do. do. |
| 9 | Veahlay | " | 24 | 5 5 | P on right do. & Pitt with smallpox on face |
| 12510 | Ahchu | " | 27 | 5 5 | P on do. & Cuts down Belly & Back |
| 11 | Ahbonah | " | 19 | 5 4 | CC on left do. & Cuts on face |
| 12 | Fahjoebu | " | 28 | 5 7 | P on right do. & Talk around the body |
| 13 | Songkay | " | 26 | 5 3 | CC on right do. & Cuts all over |
| 14 | Addah | " | 28 | 5 4 | P on do. & Cuts on right Arm & back |
| 12515 | Bywah | " | 22 | 5 4 | P on do. & Cuts on face, & down Belly |
| 16 | Ogorbu | " | 25 | 5 4 | Cuts down Breast, Belly and Back |
| 17 | Ochu | " | 29 | 5 6 | CC on left do. & Cuts all over |
| 18 | Do. | " | 23 | 5 8 | P on right do. 1 Cut on face Belly & Back |
| 19 | Quvahsu | " | 29 | 5 9 | CC on left do. Cuts on face, Belly & Back |
| 12520 | Efahwa | " | 26 | 5 1 | do. do. & Cuts all over |

Register, Vengador

day of June 1828 the said Brig having been pronounced liable to Condemnation by the said Commission on the same day for having been at the time of Capture Engaged in the illicit Traffic in Slaves—

| No. | Names | Sex | Age | Stature ft. In. | | Description |
|---|---|---|---|---|---|---|
| 12521 | Ojoe | Man | 28 | 5 | 3 | N. on left Arm, + Cuts all over |
| 22 | Ochaw | " | 26 | 5 | 2 | C. on " Breast + D.º |
| 23 | Ebokah | " | 23 | 5 | 1 | C. . right Arm + D.º |
| 24 | Kellanko | " | 27 | 5 | 7 | C.C. . left Breast - Cuts on face + Breast |
| 12525 | Okojobee | " | 26 | 5 | 5 | C.C. . D.º D.º Cuts on face, Breast and Belly |
| 26 | Omahlofee | " | 28 | 5 | 6 | C.C. . D.º D.º D.º |
| 27 | Ochahchonnay | " | 26 | 5 | 9 | C.C. . D.º D.º D.º |
| 28 | Ochow | " | 28 | 4 | 10 | P. . right D.º + Cuts all over |
| 29 | Daddah | " | 25 | 5 | 1 | C.C. . left D.º Cuts on face, Breast and Belly |
| 12531 | Oleggee | " | 27 | 5 | 5 | Cuts on Face, Belly and Back |
| 31 | Komahpye | " | 25 | 5 | 7 | P. on right Breast. Cuts on face, Breast + Belly |
| 32 | Annewah | " | 32 | 5 | 9 | C.C. . d.º D.º , Cuts on Belly, Arms + Back |
| 33 | Geesah | " | 29 | 5 | 6 | C.C. . left D.º + Cuts all over |
| 34 | Colow | " | 27 | 5 | 6 | . D.º . D.º + Cuts on face + Breast |
| 12535 | Oluboh | " | 31 | 5 | 5 | Cuts on the Face and Belly |
| 36 | Koshalah | " | 28 | 5 | 8 | C.C. on left Breast + Cuts on face |
| 37 | Hyenah | " | 26 | 5 | 11 | D.º D.º + Cuts all over |
| 38 | Okoyay | " | 29 | 5 | 6 | D.º D.º D.º |
| 39 | Olokoo | " | 32 | 5 | 11 | C. below the Navel. D.º |
| 12540 | Fahbulay | " | 25 | 5 | 6 | P. on right Breast. Pith with small pox on face and Cut all over |
| 41 | Wahlolee | " | 28 | 5 | 5 | C.C. on left D.º + Cuts all over |
| 42 | Giboo | " | 23 | 5 | 6 | P. . right D.º D.º |
| 43 | Okojobee | " | 34 | 5 | 10 | C. . D.º D.º D.º |
| 44 | Yhtoloo | " | 21 | 5 | 4 | P. . D.º D.º Cuts on face + Belly |
| 12545 | Ojodee | " | 29 | 5 | 11 | — D.º D.º D.º |
| 46 | Fahladay | " | 24 | 5 | 7 | C.C. . left D.º D.º + Breast |
| 47 | Molojo | " | 30 | 5 | 7 | D.º D.º + Cuts all over |
| 48 | Abesahdoo | " | 22 | 5 | 5 | P. . right D.º D.º |
| 49 | Olutahlah | " | 27 | 5 | 4 | C.C. . left D.º D.º |
| 12550 | Kelekilly | " | 26 | 5 | 6 | — D.º D.º + Tattoed all over |
| 51 | Olubisoo | " | 20 | 5 | 3 | P. . right D.º Cuts on face, breast + Belly |
| 12552 | Ahjedo | " | 25 | 5 | 10 | C.C. . left D.º D.º + a scar on the Belly |

## Brazilian Schooner "Zepherina":-

Register of Slaves, Natives of Africa, Captured on board the said Vessel by His Majesty's Ship "Primrose". Thomas Saville Griffinhoofe
Capt^n

| N°. | Names | Age | Stature F. I. | Description |
|---|---|---|---|---|
| 14,177 | Akkasee | Man 31 | 5 9 | I on right breast O on left d° Cuts on temples & Tatt^d across the body |
| 78 | Okonno | „ 22 | 5 4 | PP on D° and Cuts on face |
| 79 | Lokoway | „ 20 | 5 6 | Cuts all over |
| 14,180 | Achoh | „ 24 | 5 2 | D°. D° |
| 81 | Beyong | „ 29 | 5 4 | P on right breast & Cuts on face |
| 82 | Mallah | „ 30 | 5 9 | D° D° and Cuts all over |
| 83 | Brahoo | „ 28 | 5 4 | Tatted with I P on face |
| 84 | Olacheemee | „ 29 | 5 5 | Cuts all over. |
| 14,185 | Piyo | „ 26 | 5 4 | P on right breast |
| 86 | Monday | „ 25 | 5 6 | L D° and Cuts on face |
| 87 | Akojohee | „ 37 | 5 8 | Cut on face & Tattoed on breast |
| 88 | Landoo | „ 30 | 5 6½ | D° D° and breast |
| 89 | Ahjannoo | „ 28 | 5 2 | Tatted with I P on face & Cuts in belly |
| 14,190 | Ozah | „ 26 | 5 4 | T on left breast & Cuts on face & belly |
| 91 | Mammah | „ 24 | 5 6 | Cut on face and breast |
| 92 | Afeemee | „ 23 | 5 1 | P on right breast & Cuts on face |
| 93 | Oloomee | „ 33 | 5 7 | D° D° D° |
| 94 | Inday | „ 29 | 5 6 | Cuts all over |
| 14,195 | Mammah | „ 36 | 5 9 | P on right breast & Cuts all over |
| 96 | Pahwah | „ 40 | 5 9 | Cuts on Cheeks |
| 97 | Mammah | „ 22 | 6 . | P on right breast & Cuts all over |
| 98 | Ahlahmo | „ 25 | 5 6 | Cut on face |
| 99 | Lashee | „ 21 | 5 6 | Cut all over |
| 14,200 | Oggeday | „ 25 | 5 5 | P on right breast and Cut on face |
| 1 | Ahketto | „ 36 | 5 11 | D° D° and Cuts all over |
| 2 | Molomahlah | „ 19 | 5 5 | D°. D° and Cuts on face. |
| 3 | Lachee | „ 18 | 5 7 | D° D° and Cuts all over |
| 4 | Moday | „ 30 | 5 9 | D° D° D° |
| 14,205 | Edowoo | „ 42 | 5 2 | D° D° D°. |
| 6 | Bohallay | „ 40 | 5 4 | D° above the navel D° |
| 7 | Alowolah | „ 37 | 5 5 | D° on right breast & D° |
| 14,208 | Okadoo | „ 28 | 5 5 | O „ left D° D° |

Register, Zepherina

Esquire Commander, and Emancipated by Decree of the British
and Brazilian Court of Mixed Commission established in this
Colony of Sierra Leone, on the 9th day of December 1828. The said
Schooner having on the day aforesaid been pronounced liable to
confiscation

| No | Names | Sex | Age | Stature | Description |
|---|---|---|---|---|---|
| 14,209 | Wantam | Man | 24 | 5 5 | CC below the navel & Cuts on temples. |
| 14,210 | Hyenah | " | 26 | 5 7 | Cuts & Tattooed all over |
| 11 | Ojor | " | 22 | 5 5 | C on right breast |
| 12 | Olosahday | " | 19 | 5 1 | Cuts all over |
| 13 | Ahjai | " | 39 | 5 6 | Pitted with S Pox face & Cuts all over |
| 14 | Kamballee | " | 36 | 5 4 | P on right breast & Cuts on face and breast |
| 14,215 | Sahtoo | " | 28 | 5 4 | Do left Do Cuts on face |
| 16 | Ofonah | " | 32 | 5 6 | Do right Do Cuts on face and belly |
| 17 | Mahdotah | " | 20 | 5 2 | L left Do and Cuts all over |
| 18 | Dakambee | " | 17 | 5 7 | Cuts all over |
| 19 | Olashremee | " | 18 | 5 2½ | P above the navel and cuts all over |
| 14,221 | Robahkay | " | 19 | 5 2 | L on left breast Do |
| 21 | Chojoo | " | 33 | 5 5 | P right Do and Cuts on face |
| 22 | Ahjai | " | 18 | 5 7 | A in right Arm and Cuts all over |
| 23 | Powahlakam | " | 45 | 5 6 | Cuts all over |
| 24 | Ochoh | " | 42 | 5 4 | P on right breast & cuts all over |
| 14,225 | Ahloo | " | 27 | 5 3 | Cuts all over |
| 26 | Omatajo | " | 28 | 5 3 | Cuts all over the body |
| 27 | Moladoo | " | 16 | 5 3 | L below the right breast & Cuts all over |
| 28 | Dowo | " | 23 | 5 5 | P on right breast and Cuts all over |
| 29 | Ocholu | " | 27 | 5 7 | Do Do Do |
| 14,230 | Ahlojee | " | 18 | 5 6½ | Do below the navel and Cuts all over |
| 31 | Jahblee | " | 24 | 5 6 | Do on right breast and Cut all over |
| 32 | Lajokoo | " | 17 | 5 4 | Do Do, lost 2 fingers of the left hand. Cut all over |
| 33 | Ahehoh | " | 21 | 5 2 | Cuts all over |
| 34 | Ahehaoday | " | 39 | 5 6 | A below the navel and Cut all over |
| 14,235 | Ahfentee | " | 37 | 5 5 | P on right breast and cut on face & belly |
| 36 | Olopahday | " | 32 | 5 2 | Cuts all over |
| 37 | Chanojo | " | 29 | 5 5 | P on right breast and cut all over |
| 38 | Ojoi | " | 24 | 5 2 | Cuts on forehead |
| 39 | Agayo | " | 28 | 5 6 | Cuts on face and belly |
| 14,240 | Ahbagee | " | 24 | 5 2 | Do Do Do |

# CHAPTER FIVE

*El Almirante* (Eng.: *The Admiral*)

January 1829,

466 enslaved people

E very surviving British sailor—reputedly forty men—on the
*Presidente* went free. Turner and Evangelista both attested to the
men's violent intent and piratical acts in the Surrey County Sessions
House, a criminal court back in London with a gaol (jail) and visible
gallows adjacent, but the court found this testimony to be insufficient
evidence in the face of the pirates' argument alleging they were acting under the authority of Buenos Aires as privateers. Though the
paperwork for said commission was long expired, Buenos Aires was
indeed at war with Brazil, and the *Presidente*'s crew asserted that their
captain had been entirely justified in firing on and taking any ship
flying Brazilian colors. Since the *Black Joke* had been flying the flag of
Brazil when they first encountered it, that was that. Despite the clear
testimony regarding the *Presidente*'s flagrant disregard for maritime
agreements no matter what flag its quarry flew, as far as the magis-
trate court in London was concerned, no one could prove that the
crew of the *Presidente* didn't believe their target to be legitimate. This
was especially disheartening to many when it was discovered, during the trial, that the *Presidente* was likely the pirate ship responsible
for a recent atrocity against HMS *Redpole*, in which the captain was
shot, every member of the crew was made to walk the plank to his
death, and the ship was sunk. (Arguably the greatest trick pirates ever
pulled was convincing future generations that they were all about lov-

able antiheroes and good times.) Despite the allegations, there was no verifiable evidence of the slaughter, and the British members of the crew already in custody couldn't even be tried.

One might expect that the disposition of the "privateers" of the *Presidente* would prompt a major scandal, not a few scattered newspaper articles, but clearly not everyone in Britain was on board with ending the slave trade. Given the economic climate in England, and that slavery itself would not be outlawed in the empire until 1833, more men than just the crew of the *Presidente* still sought to profit from human chattel. Swaths of the British economy had, before the 1807 abolition, benefited both directly and indirectly from the slave trade, and not just the slavers and their agents. The Atlantic slave trade was genuinely triangular, wherein the enslaved were brought from Africa to produce raw materials in the Americas that, often enough, were processed in Britain's industrial centers into ready-made and now easily manufactured goods, such as cloth, that, until the Industrial Revolution, had cost substantially more to produce. In turn, these goods were traded, along with money, in the purchase of enslaved Africans, thus perpetuating the cycle. This meant that, though it may have appeared that some merchants, shipwrights, industrial tycoons, and the like were not intimately tied to the perpetuation of the slave trade, they very much were. These people may have publicly tolerated suppression for political or appearance reasons, but certainly not all did, and many tried to base their rationale on the impossibility of ending the slave trade, rather than the morality of allowing, even encouraging, it to continue. As one politician noted on the floor of the House of Commons as the involvement of the Royal Navy in the suppression was being debated, he had twenty reasons that such a plan was folly, and that since the first was that it was impossible, he need not detail the other nineteen.

Protesting the feasibility of the goal was not the only way British antisuppressionists sought to undermine the combined efforts of Parliament, the Foreign Office, and the Royal Navy. In the court of public opinion, many on both sides of the debate didn't bother to hide their beliefs regarding the inherent inferiority of Africans as a race. More insidiously, as the discourse surrounding slavery progressed from cause célèbre to humanitarian duty, those who profited from slavery often masked their avarice by shamelessly co-opting the language of morality for their ethically indefensible stance. The gist of the moral argument for slavery was thus: Setting aside the unchristlike behavior that was perpetuating incredible suffering and death in order to make gobs of money, was it not better to be a slave in a Christian empire than a free heathen? That maximizing profit was a chief precipitator of maximizing suffering was unsaid; that their Lord and Savior Jesus Christ had had several choice words for the proverbial "rich man" went ignored. Other antisuppressionists in England were less oblique about their economic concerns. In reality, England, a tiny island that couldn't even feed its population with what it grew at home, was on the precipice of one of the most globally dominant periods a single nation had ever seen, a position that would be strengthened, not hampered, by suppression efforts. Even the most prescient of slave-trade advocates couldn't have realized that at the time, though, and they were confounded by the prospect of upending the whole economy just because some abolitionists insisted it was the right thing to do.

The opinions of the enslaved, whether they'd rather pass their days in their homelands or experience forced conversion to the Good Book by those of dubious morality themselves, were also ignored, other than through the occasional release of an ex–enslaved person's narrative, or perhaps a quote or testimony in some particularly affecting antislavery pamphlet. Religion was an oft-used source to justify slavery, but given the extent to which many indigenous Africans sought to maintain their own religious practices, even the most disingenuous Europeans likely had an inkling what the response might be if they did ask.

In England, they could have asked, or rather listened to, their own free Black population, many of whom happened to be sailors. If not precisely a great equalizer, the sea offered opportunities to both escape slavery and earn a living; Black British and African sailors had been a relatively common sight for decades, so much so that in 1777, after accusations that British ships in the Caribbean were harboring escaped slaves, the Royal Navy had implemented a rule dictating that no more than four Black sailors could serve on the same ship at the same time in that region. It was a geographically specific rule and not observed the further away one got, in both distance and time, from the particular issues that then characterized service in the Caribbean—a quarter century later, at least ten Black men served with Collier's patron, Admiral Nelson, on *Victory* at the Battle of Trafalgar. (At some point, then, Commodore Collier had near certainly served alongside Black men.) Bristol, Liverpool, and other port cities had, by this time, long-established free Black communities that, having first agitated to end the practice of slavery in England, continued to campaign to end slavery entirely, not just the trade.

By contrast, a group happy to explore, loudly and vociferously, every conceivable objection to the end of Britain's direct involvement in the slave trade were the empire's planter-colonists in the Americas. The notable exception (and major blow) of the loss of the colonies that now formed the United States notwithstanding, Britain's holdings in the Americas, particularly the Caribbean, had expanded after the cessation of the Napoleonic Wars in 1815, and with them, the perceived colonial reliance on slavery as a means of perpetuating the ungodly profits of plantation-based economies. Jamaica's planters, in particular, had advocated loud and long against ending the British slave trade; given that abolitionists in England clearly intended such a move as a precursor to ending slavery entirely, slaveholding colonists knew the threat to their way of life was very real. England may have been slowly trending toward boasting of, if not bearing out, a hands-off approach to its empire later in the nineteenth century, but in the earlier decades, the ties between the imperial seat in England and colonial outposts in the Americas (and, increasingly, Asia) were still ones of unambiguous and near-unilateral control. Having lost the battles of the 1807 act abolishing the slave trade and the subsequent measures enacted to strengthen it, and taking the potential loss of their ill-gotten and incredibly wealthy livelihoods extremely personally, the planter classes of Jamaica and other British Caribbean holdings set about winning the war to preserve slavery.

The same phenomenon was happening in Brazil (soon to be formerly Portuguese), in Cuba (still Spanish)—basically anywhere where the entire economy, conceptualized as the creation and acquisition of European wealth, was so reliant on enslaved labor that those who benefited from slavery could not compass a world, or perhaps more aptly their pocketbooks, without it. In that last respect, the planters weren't wrong—even today, labor tends to be the most expensive part of operating a business, so with incredibly labor-intense crops such as cotton, coffee, and most notably sugar, there really was no equivalently cheap way to maintain their business model. The United States had managed it, which may have been part of the reason that its government so readily acceded, comparatively speaking, to ending the trade along with Britain; slaveholders in the United States had made a practice of purchasing almost as much female enslaved labor as male. This was feasible there in a way it could not be farther south, due in part to the geographical realities of crop cultivation in the Americas. The United States, but for its few subtropical areas (such as southern Louisiana, recently purchased alongside a third of the modern continental United States from Napoléon in 1803), did not have the climate to grow sugar—the cash crop that ruled the day that far north was cotton, produced on a massive scale to be shipped to industrial centers back in England and, increasingly, the United States' own industrial powerhouses in the northern portions of the country, where, as in England, slavery was oft banned yet nonetheless freely profited from.

Though picking cotton was backbreaking work that prematurely ended untold numbers of lives in the United States—if the conditions of enslavement, namely violent preservation of a once emergent and rapidly entrenching racial hierarchy, didn't do it first—cultivating sugar required even more physical risk and the production process was often fatal. The geography and labor required to produce these two crops would lead to the rapidly diverging systems of enslavement found in much of the United States versus farther south. In the nineteenth-century mindset, harvesting and processing cotton could be a job for any sex; harvesting sugarcane was generally presupposed to be men's work. In the United States in 1662, the then–colonial Virginia legislature had enacted laws asserting that enslavement was inheritable from one's mother, a contravention of English precedent. This legislation was soon emulated up and down the Eastern Seaboard of British North America. And so, African women could pick cotton just as efficiently as men without arousing anyone's gendered sensibilities, and, further, could be used, like so much sentient livestock, to create more enslaved people. Far from being undesirable, importing Africans who could give birth was not just a cheaper source of equivalent labor but also a potential investment in *generations* of enslaved labor, rather than a single lifetime's worth. The United States didn't *need* to keep importing the enslaved. Setting aside the parts of the country where sugar was grown, cotton didn't kill enslaved people as quickly, and when they did die, their numbers were readily supplemented by so-called natural increase, whether derived from the enslaved's own reproductive choices (such as were available) or those of slaveholders who were unabashedly "breeding" their own workforce. In the United States, slaveholders could treat the enslaved population as poorly as they wanted and, provided they were healthy enough to bear children and didn't die in large numbers, the slave economy would continue to perpetuate itself. What need had they for new Africans? Agreeing to end overt participation in the Atlantic slave trade was nothing so much as sleeves out of the United States' vest. Clearly the United States was unabashedly trading in slaves after 1807, primarily via inter- and intrastate traffic, but since this trade was almost entirely domestic, Britain had no state interest in preventing it and no jurisdiction besides.

Farther south in the Americas, where the British could more easily intervene, or interfere, sugar reigned, and sugar killed. Though many died before becoming acclimated to their new environment or were claimed by disease, sugar was tedious to sow and grueling to harvest, and it was even more dangerous to process. Cleaning cotton before the invention of the gin was onerous and backbreaking; refining sugar was a veritable orgy of ways to die. The leaves of sugarcane are sharp enough to cut, and after being harvested by machete without protective gear, the cane had to be pressed by mechanized rollers that regularly took a hand, an arm, or worse, to make juice that would boil in vats of viscous liquid that clung to the skin and burned, over fires that had to be kept going twenty-four hours a day during refining season. The state of medicine—and what knowledge there was, was rarely expended on the enslaved population—meant that even if one was "merely" maimed, rather than killed outright, one still had a high likelihood of dying from the injury. Rather than seeking to alter that manufactured reality, a system in which the average life expectancy for a mill worker was approximately seven years, slaveholders in the Caribbean and Brazil chose instead to lean all the way in—they decided that many women could not do this work (particularly harvesting) as well as men, and that if an enslaved person was quite possibly going to die anyway in short order, the most cost-effective solution was to get as much work out of them as possible before they passed on.

Thus, the extremely common practice of literally working people to death. Indifference, neglect, mismanagement, and cruelty united to reinforce a self-perpetuating labor shortage, with the practical result that, when it came to importing the enslaved in Brazil—or for sugar cultivation more broadly, many plantation owners predominately sought African men and, further, had to replace them every few years as an expected business expense. The radical gender imbalance among the enslaved population meant that domestic natural increase, even if forced, could not alleviate demand created by the wanton deaths from sugar cultivation. Though slaveholders throughout the Americas could all agree that they unequivocally needed the enslaved to maintain their economic dominance, unlike in the United States, slaveholders in Brazil and places like it—such as Jamaica—believed wholeheartedly that they also very much needed a foreign trade in the enslaved to maintain the most profitable business model.

Rather unlike the aforementioned naysaying politician—he of the twenty reasons that such a plan was "folly," foremost that it was an impossibility—in the Americas, when Britain announced in 1807 and with subsequent legislation that, in so many words, it would be ending the Atlantic slave trade not just for itself but everywhere, for everyone, forever, and all because of the principle of the thing, slaveholders very much believed that such an outcome was entirely possible and acted accordingly. That even Jamaican opposition to the measures, lucrative as the colony had been, was noted and summarily dismissed had to seem like confirmation of the worst fears of British slaveholders and traders far beyond that island's shores. The practical result was the exact opposite of what abolitionists wanted—in every place where it was known that abolition of the trade was coming, by either law or treaty, slave trading spiked. In such places as Cuba (before 1820) and Brazil (before 1830), Spanish and Portuguese holdings subject to imperial agreements with Britain, surges in human trafficking were also driven in part by industrialization, Britain's decelerating (though by no means abandoned) commitment to industries dominated by enslaved labor, and demand for the products of those industries, particularly in, of all places, Britain. Plantation owners, regardless of imperial affiliation, were in a full-blown panic to acquire as many enslaved people as possible before Britain's onslaught of anti-slave-trade treaties could come into their fullest effect. But where slaveholders and traders in the British-held West Indies had gone through this process back in 1807 when Parliament banned the trade, in Brazil, the year of reckoning was 1830. So 1829 was about to be a very busy year.

Those serving as officers and seamen in the West Africa Squadron weren't immune to the temptations of obscene wealth generated by the slave trade. As previously noted, one of the most prominent slave brokers in Gallinas, John Ouseley Kearney, was a former Royal Army officer, and though he was a particularly infamous example, he was by no means the only one. Some WAS officers, their tour completed, operated and/or captained slave ships. Even bolder was one early WAS officer who, entrusted with a prize ship to sail to Freetown, opted instead to resell the enslaved on board. Lest this paint the entire service in an unwontedly mercenary light, others in the Squadron were vocal (if paternalistic) abolitionists, not the least of whom was that pain in the sides of Commodores Bullen and Collier (the second), Captain Owen of Fernando Pó. The first Commodore Collier, George, had also been committed to the cause of ending slavery, so much so that when he committed suicide in 1824, three years after ending his tenure on the coast and three years before the second Commodore Collier entered the scene, the impact of regular contact with the extensive misery, degradation, and despair to be found on every slaver was cited as a potential precipitating cause for his ending his life. (The larger issue may have been allegations of both incompetence and cowardice during the War of 1812 charged in a then recently published history, but there seemed no doubt that exposure to the horrors of slavery had impacted his mental state, and not for the better.)

Opposing slavery did not, however, equate with what would now be considered an "anti-racist" position. Plenty of those in the Squadron—not to mention in the settlement at Freetown and England generally—opposed slavery as an immoral institution while simultaneously asserting the inferiority of the African race. Far from eschewing the trope of the "white savior," British abolitionists characterized the work of the Preventive Squadron as an extension of the will of God, and those involved in the suppression efforts, such as Captain Owen of Fernando Pó, had no problem picking up this ennobling and sanctifying language for themselves and their mission. One former governor of Sierra Leone, closing out a letter, said, "It is impossible to dismiss this narrative without reflecting on the interposition of Providence by which we were thus [enabled] to contrib-

ute to the deliverance of so large a number of our fellow creatures."
No less an esteemed personage than Lord Palmerston—who was, in
1829, approaching his 1830 debut as foreign secretary—went one
step further and would later assert that, at least in regard to finally
destroying the slave trade, "Great Britain is the main instrument in
the hands of providence." Since similar rationales would also be used
to justify Britain's exploitive colonialist policy throughout the nineteenth century, it's tempting to view such grand proclamations as
little more that pious self-aggrandizement, but at least some in the
WAS undoubtedly wholeheartedly agreed with this selfless conception of their service, as well as its meaning in a larger moral sense.

On individual ships, though, the situation could be quite different. Some free Black sailors chose service on the coast—indeed, the
Royal Navy was often thought preferable to other potential berths
at sea because one's risk of being kidnapped or captured as a "prize
Negro" was substantially lowered. (The regular contact with slavers
still meant that even postwar the chances of this weren't zero.) The
same 1777 order that had limited the quantity of Black sailors on
British ships also stipulated that, for want of personnel who would
willingly serve in the Royal Navy, the definition of "British" was explicitly expanded to include those who were British by "birth, natu-
ralization, denization [vintage permanent residency], conquest or
service" plus "any Negroes belonging to any person or persons being
or having become His Majesty's subjects," which is to say the enslaved. It's extremely difficult to know precisely how many Black seamen were in the WAS, as Royal Navy records only haphazardly, if at
all, recorded the race of its sailors, but estimates suggest that every
vessel likely had between one to four Black seamen, one of whom
was likely to be the ship's cook. This figure is not to be conflated
with the additional complement of Kroomen that served with each
ship, but added to that tally, it does make plain that WAS ships, far
from being the bastions of unrelieved Whiteness that the language
surrounding the Preventive Squadron's mission might suggest, had

at least some diversity in the number and origin of Black faces that could be found on board. (Other now-White populations, such as the Irish or those of Southern or Eastern European extraction, would have added to the contemporary perception of that diversity, as increasingly, in conjunction with the rise of scientific racism, they would be categorized as separate and/or sub-Anglo races unto themselves. Additionally, Britain's extensive contact with and interventions in the East meant it was entirely possible that sailors of Asian heritage may have served as well.)

The ability to serve, even when officially recognized as a British national, did not forestall prejudice against those of African descent. Historians can be reasonably certain that these Black sailors were usually among the seamen of the lower decks because of an ongoing and pervasive combination of race and class bias. The commissioned-officer core, downsized after the peace in 1815 drastically shrank the fleet, was already almost entirely constrained to the well-connected and wealthy, with only rare exceptions made for the exceptionally talented. Though at least some Black sailors were entirely capable of performing in such positions admirably—which the Royal Navy was certainly aware of from the war years—they were not given the same opportunities in peacetime to prove it. Additionally, as the education required to pass a lieutenant's exam was hard to come by for an impoverished White sailor, it must have been doubly so for a Black one. If aspiration to a commission was a nonstarter, one might think that at least a position among the warrant officers could be a possibility. Evidence suggests that some Black men did attempt to climb the promotional ladder in this way, where, unlike among the ranks of the lieutenants and their superiors, class should have been far less of a barrier, but in large part they were also stymied. If the Royal Navy can be said to have been operating an ostensibly "color-blind" system, individual prejudices nonetheless had institutional outcomes. If White sailors refused to respect the authority of a Black man senior to them, that man could not be an effective officer in the closed society of shipboard life, and more than one capable warrant officer had summarily been demoted, with their commanding officer's regrets, for this reason.

Where Lieutenant Henry Downes, the second captain of the *Black Joke*, stood on all this is unknown, but the logbook he kept while serving on *Black Joke* does provide some circumstantial evidence to his state of mind. In it, Downes, with painstaking effort, took the time to note English translations of common phrases in what he referred to as the "Accou" language, the most commonly spoken tongue to be found among enslaved Africans embarked from Ouidah and Badagry. Rather than treating these people as inherently sub-human, Downes made an effort to communicate with words, rather than force. Included in his list are such terms as "quickly, quickly" and "silence or you'll get punished," so one shouldn't rush to paint Downes with a saintly brush. However, given that many more of the phrases concerned not just the care of the enslaved (such as indicating illness or a need to use the facilities), but their desires—"I don't want," "I want to eat," and (this author's favorite) "I want *aguadiente* [*sic*]" (a slight bastardization of a Spanish word used generically for alcohol)—it seems that Downes was possibly more sympathetic to the plight of the enslaved than many, maybe even most, of the others in the West Africa Squadron.

He also had the time. Downes, unlike Turner, had entered the service in 1805, well before the end of the sundry wars concluded in 1815, and at the age of thirty-nine, he was probably a good ten years older than his predecessor; 1829 would mark his fifteenth year at the rank of lieutenant. Downes, it seems, also lacked Turner's brand of lightning-strike luck—rather than the mere week it took Turner to find and capture the *Gertrudis*, the seasoned lieutenant would have to wait close to four months before taking his first slaver. Perhaps as a result, his logbook is a meticulously kept trove of small tidbits about life on board the *Black Joke* and in the service of the West Africa Squadron. What immediately stands out in his account of the *Black Joke*'s many days is something Downes himself never explicitly mentions, but every WAS sailor knew: even in the midst of daring sea actions and meddling higher-ups, much of the time spent on a Squadron ship on cruise was incredibly boring—". . . Thermometer 86 degrees, no change of companions, no supplies of fresh stock except at long intervals." Patrols were long and tedious, and even *finding* quarry was often difficult—"cruising, cruising, cruising, and very unprofitably too," described one commander. If one lacked operable intelligence from sources, such as cooperative traders reporting what they'd seen on their own routes, ships were forced to resort to simply cruising several thousand miles of water, hoping to spot a ship from the right country, in the right area, preferably with enslaved people on board, but at the very least with the wrong passport (indicating slave-trading intent). While seamen had several clever methods to visually divine information about ships still several miles away, it was an incredibly inefficient way to patrol a multinational trade in thousands of people per year across dozens of ports.

The men aboard the *Black Joke*, when not at work, amused themselves while on these seemingly interminable cruises. Downes, beyond being an excellent record keeper, was an amateur inventor and artist who sketched while at sea. Others on the cruise might tell stories, sing songs, play instruments, and, perhaps, if they were literate and could afford the luxury of paper, write letters. Ships with a large enough complement might even mount plays—anything to relieve the tedium. The sailors did occasionally have a brief leave where they might seek the sexual company of women, but women of the coast were, it seems, not especially interested. St. Helena, long a British holding and then under the control of the East India Company, was, at least in Collier's estimation, the only place where sailors' advances would be appropriately welcomed. The alternative was shipboard sexual relations between men, of which the Royal Navy vehemently disapproved, going so far as to specifically prohibit sexual acts between sailors in the 29th Article of War. While a charge of "uncleanliness" or "indecency" could lead to anything from whipping to dismissal from the service to two years in solitary confinement, buggery—requiring both anal penetration and subsequent emission—carried a death sentence.

It's impossible to know whether such relations were happening on the *Black Joke*, though they did seem to be most prevalent on larger ships that could afford more private and semiprivate venues in which to couple. However, Downes certainly knew better than just about anyone else what could happen if the Admiralty found out. His last berth, over a decade prior, had been the infamous HMS *Africaine*, a thirty-eight-gun fifth-rate frigate—comparable to the *Sybille*—on which an entire homosexual subcommunity had been discovered, leading to court-martial proceedings that, between witnesses, accusers, and accused, involved fifty men, fully a quarter of the ship's complement. Downes, who'd begun his service on the *Africaine* as an acting lieutenant and had the promotion confirmed one year into the vessel's three-year tour to Asia, was one of the men called to testify at the resulting proceedings, as he had witnessed the entire affair from implosion to end. As a lieutenant, he'd sat in on the questioning that had blown open the scandal a full year before the *Africaine* returned to England, plus all the interrogatories that followed. Ultimately 10 percent of the crew, two dozen men and boys, were implicated as participants. He also stood witness on the decks of the *Africaine* as those found guilty who hadn't been sent to Newgate were punished, as two teens received 170 and 200 lashes for "unclean practices," and then as five adults and one teen were executed. Downes might even have been the man charged with, in the immediate aftermath of those executions, reading the entirety of the 29th Article of War aloud to the ship's complement; he was probably there when the *Africaine* was broken up, as if the very ship needed to be punished for the perceived sexual transgressions that had taken place on its decks.

But what Downes wasn't, despite all of this, was a snitch. Multiple people testified that flagrant sexual congress was happening all over the *Africaine* at all hours, with activity concentrated in the *entire front half* of a ship only 154 feet in length. Given that the participants—who had, in the main, mostly testified against one another—described having sexual relations, among other places, against and between guns, under tarps on the upper deck, next to hatches and in the galley, not infrequently in the broad light of day (or at least during the last dogwatch, 6:00 to 8:00 p.m., when plenty of the *Africaine*'s sailors would have been awake and milling about), it seems like all the sex would have been extremely difficult to miss, particularly for an artist as observant as the lieutenant. Events later in Downes's life seem to indicate that he was pious in the manner of his day, but he'd reported nothing against his crew and provided no evidence against the men beyond what they themselves had confessed on board during questioning in front of him and the other commissioned officers. When called before a subsequent inquiry regarding the discipline kept by the *Africaine*'s captain, Downes, along with the other lieutenants and the master, swore that discipline on board had been comparable to that of any other ship they'd served on, clearing their captain of wrongdoing. Though the phrase would have been unfamiliar, it seems clear that experience would have led Downes to a policy of "don't ask, don't tell," particularly if crew members so inclined acted surreptitiously enough, or waited until it was dark enough, for him to deliberately ignore them. Henry Downes had proven that he was a man loyal to his ship. His relationship with his crew and captain had kept his mouth shut, insofar as it could be, all those years ago, and now that *Sybille* had finally gotten him back on active duty, he'd probably used these first few months to earn the trust and respect of his new crew. Of course, all of these men would officially have been assigned to *Sybille* while serving on its tender, but even there they would have been accustomed to Turner's leadership as first lieutenant, while Downes was an altogether different man who'd yet to prove himself at the helm of the *Black Joke*.

In all these months patrolling, Downes, on orders from Collier, had been on watch for just one ship—the notorious slaver *El Almirante*, which was reputed to be back in the area and was known to have already illegally transported thousands of the enslaved to the

Americas in its sordid career. Ships of the Squadron had boarded the slaver on several occasions without success, as it had never been caught with the enslaved in hold. In mid-January 1829, the *Black Joke*, while patrolling near Lagos, came across what appeared to be several Brazilian slavers embarking Africans. Standing off the coast so as not to spook them, rumor reached Downes that one ship was actually a familiar Spanish brig nearly ready to set sail—after all his waiting and unproductive cruising, *El Almirante* had, all unexpected, made its appearance.

On the open water, rumors traveled both ways; just as Downes had heard that this brig was the one he sought, *El Almirante* had, in turn, been warned of the appearance of *Black Joke*. The former captain of *El Almirante* having died on the coast the previous October—the same time that intelligence from an unknown source of the ship's reappearance had reached Collier and prompted his orders to the *Black Joke*—Damaso Forgannes, the first mate who'd ascended to the post, could not have been less concerned about the prospect of capture. Reputed to have laughed upon hearing the news, Forgannes scoffed publicly at the ludicrous notion of the *Black Joke* capturing his vessel, continuing to openly purchase enslaved people. The reaction wasn't entirely unreasonable—*El Almirante* was an inordinately expensive ship, even for a slave trader, purpose-built and equipped with every advance in design its (undoubtedly American) shipwrights could conceive. If making a break for open water was not an option, the slaver crewed upward of eighty men and carried ten eighteen-pounders assisted by another four long nines, for a total of fourteen guns.

There was no question that the two-gunned *Black Joke*, with a crew of forty-seven plus a temporary supplement of eight men from another Squadron ship, was hugely outpowered in just about every measure. Downes, as undeterred as his opposite number on the slaver, set the *Black Joke* just out of sight of the harbor, periodically sending boats to check on the progress of the Spanish brig and make sure it continued to load human cargo, since the presence of the enslaved would be the vital evidence against *El Almirante* that might ultimately condemn it. This loading took place over the next several days, as staging and embarking the enslaved was a multistep process, but Downes had been patient this long and would not be lured into prematurely attacking a ship so close to harbor and far superior in firepower. Nor would he twiddle his thumbs; just as he had on the *Black Joke*'s long cruise, the lieutenant kept himself usefully occupied. Rather than settle in and relax until *El Almirante* made its appearance, Downes turned his nimble mind to how he could possibly secure some small advantage against such a top-of-the-line brig. Continuing to gather information soon proved worthwhile, especially when a crew member reported back to the *Black Joke* with the slaver's destination. Having thus discovered *El Almirante*'s next port, Downes spent every idle hour calculating the best way to get to the Antilles, accounting for location, currents, and season. When he emerged from his cabin, satisfied that he had charted the most likely route *El Almirante* would take, Downes ordered the *Black Joke* moved to another position outside the harbor. Still out of sight and hopeful that its captain had anticipated the correct course, *Black Joke* was as prepared as it could be. Now, truly, all they could do was wait.

On January 31, a full two weeks after the *Black Joke* finally stumbled upon the fancy Spanish brig, *El Almirante* appeared with first light. Primed as the crew aboard the *Black Joke* must've been, they immediately crowded on all sail and, catching a scant breeze, gave chase . . . but the delays weren't over. In the vital moment, after five months of searching and two weeks of waiting, the wind died. Becalmed, yet undeterred, Downes ordered sweeps (oars), and his crew set to rowing. Nine hours and thirty grueling miles later, they caught the slaver, who met the *Black Joke*'s arrival by immediately firing on it, hoisting Spanish colors, and following up their initial greeting with two broadsides. Seeing as it was now sunset and his crew was, understandably, exhausted, the ever-patient Downes resolved to wait until morning to proceed farther. For now, he was content to keep *El Almirante* in sight.

Everything about catching the Spanish brig had been difficult, and Forgannes had no intention of bucking that trend; the now captain of the slaver, no matter how well armed, was not foolish enough to simply wait for *Black Joke* to make its move. Throughout the night, *El Almirante* repeatedly attempted to close on its would-be captor, firing broadside after broadside. The tender's bulwarks were not equipped to protect its crew from the slave trader's heavy armament, so still mostly becalmed, Downes ordered the crew back to oars. For the rest of the night, far from taking the break they'd richly earned, the Black Jokes evaded the slaver by means of paddling rather than tacking sails, always just out of reach of *El Almirante*'s guns. The move was clever, effective, and utterly exhausting. By dawn on February 1, both ships were much as they had been the evening before, still becalmed less than a mile and a half from each other, and with the arrival of the sun, the fighting temporarily ceased. Clearly everyone was prepared for the coming battle, but for the duration of the hot, still morning, both crews could do little else but rest.

Just past noon, the breeze returned. Rather than run, Forgannes moved toward the *Black Joke*, still certain of victory. Downes, altering his position, wasn't intimidated—after all, his ship and crew had just spent the entire night proving they could ably outmaneuver the larger vessel. As soon as the *Black Joke* was within range of grapeshot to the aft of the slaver, Forgannes tried for another broadside. Mortal peril notwithstanding, the crew of the *Black Joke* had been waiting for this moment for months, and they responded with three cheers and two double-shotted cannons aimed directly at the slave trader's deck. For forty-five minutes the *Black Joke* held, but when it came to guns, nothing had changed—*El Almirante* had too many of them. Rather than continue when they were so clearly outmatched, and with the slaver again closing in, Downes switched tactics entirely and gave the order to bring the *Black Joke* alongside and prepare to board—

HM Brig *Black Joke* engaging the Spanish slave brig *El Almirante*
(© NMM).

When suddenly, in what must have been an annoyingly familiar turn of events, the wind died. Again.

This shift in conditions allowed Forgannes to get off a shot that could well have been deadly for everyone aboard the *Black Joke* had it been better aimed, but it went high, passing over the heads of the tender's crew. A fresh (if still light) wind fifteen minutes later allowed *El Almirante*, buoyed by the near miss and even more confident in success, to once again take the offensive and move in for another attack. The breeze wasn't much, but it was enough to give the more maneuverable ship the advantage, and Downes knew exactly which ship that was. In that moment, Downes asked every bit of skill from his crew and everything of *Black Joke*—and both delivered. The *Black Joke* successfully attained *El Almirante*'s leeward quarter, and from there it give the slaver all it could handle and then some. For twenty minutes, without pause or respite, the tender raked the quarter and stern of the slaver, and the *Black Joke* did not miss. The repeated attack to just one section of the ship created a serious risk of structural damage that, if continued, might well have rendered the slave trader permanently unseaworthy. Realizing this, *El Almirante* at last struck its colors and surrendered. No less than Commodore Collier himself, when he eventually got a chance to see firsthand the havoc his tender had wrought on the supposedly superior *El Almirante*, declared that he had "never in his life witnessed a more beautiful specimen of good gunnery."

When the Black Jokes finally boarded, they discovered that, regrettably, eleven enslaved people had been killed in the prolonged action. Among the slaver's crew, fifteen were killed and thirteen wounded; Forgannes, and every officer but the third mate, had died in the fighting. *Black Joke* had fared better, but had six wounded, two of whom would eventually succumb to their injuries. Both ships' rigging had taken extensive damage, though here, again, *El Almirante* had the worst of it. The *Black Joke* did have at least one Black, non-Kru seaman, a free African named Joseph Francis, and though he was (as expected) the cook, he'd been determined to "strike a personal blow" against the infamous slaver. During the battle, he'd got twelve feet of chain into one of the ship's guns as it was being loaded; when it was fired, "the starboard main shrouds of the slaver were cut off [. . .] as if by the single blow of an axe." Even with the damage, *El Almirante* was still a valuable prize, but there was more. One of the *Black Joke*'s officers, upon searching the slaver, discovered a large cache of gold doubloons, which would be added to the tabulation of the prize bounty, for a total cost to the owners of roughly "35,000 dollars." Of arguably more importance—at least to the Squadron, if not those still flush with battle on the *Black Joke*—was the additional discovery of cryptic letters in some kind of cipher. Less than a week later, on the sixth, *Sybille* would capture the slaver *Uniao*, which, during the chase, had been seen tossing papers, presumably in some sort of receptacle. When *Sybille* recovered the letters from the water, they, in conjunction with those found on *El Almirante*, divulged the nature and location of secret slave-trade routes to Havana, then one of the world's busiest slaving ports. They also warned other slavers that the West Africa Squadron had become an effective force, and only fast, well-armed ships could have a chance of escaping capture. *El Almirante* fit that description, but still hadn't managed to evade one particular ship on the coast. Rumors would continue to spread—the *Black Joke* was more than just another WAS ship to avoid.

It was *the* ship to avoid.

# Spanish Brig "El Almirante."

Register of Slaves Natives of Africa Captured on board the said vessel by His Majesty's Ship "Sybille" Francis Augustus Collier CB

| No. | Names | Sex | Age | Stature ft. in. | | Description |
|-----|-------|-----|-----|-----|-----|-------------|
| 16,575 | Sonnoo | Man | 30 | 5 | 4 | Cuts all over |
| | Okodepay | " | 23 | 5 | 9 | Do |
| | Ogahbee | " | 25 | 5 | 3 | Do |
| | Odonjou | " | 23 | 5 | 4 | Do |
| | Dakanday | " | 26 | 5 | 2 | Do |
| 16,580 | Odosah | " | 27 | 5 | 4 | Do |
| | Akiai | " | 21 | 5 | 3 | Do |
| | Oseke | " | 22 | 5 | 1 | Do |
| | Mahkejo | " | 27 | 5 | 5 | Do |
| | Ahidi | " | 31 | 5 | 8 | Do |
| 16,585 | Ojah | " | 23 | 5 | 5 | Do |
| | Pokoday | " | 21 | 5 | 5 | Do |
| | Adeah | " | 26 | 5 | 3 | Do |
| | Deahbee | " | 24 | 5 | 4 | Do |
| | Ozah | " | 25 | 5 | 4 | Do |
| 16,590 | Broo | " | 30 | 5 | 7 | Do |
| | Atowee | " | 31 | 5 | 8 | Do |
| | Oehee | " | 28 | 5 | 5 | Do |
| | Oshebo | " | 35 | 5 | 4 | Do |
| | Ogojobbe | " | 30 | 5 | 4 | Do |
| 16,595 | Dasomoo 1st | " | 19 | 5 | 4 | Do |
| | Do Do | " | 27 | 5 | 0 | Do |
| | Ochee | " | 26 | 5 | 4 | Do |
| | Msoo | " | 28 | 5 | 6 | Do |
| | Osoke | " | 29 | 5 | 6 | Do |
| 16,600 | Ahdabarree | " | 26 | 5 | 4 | Do |
| | Mahjechay | " | 28 | 5 | 5 | No marks |
| | Bahday | " | 23 | 5 | 6 | Cuts all over |
| | Allejay | " | 25 | 5 | 9 | Do |
| | Kimmay | " | 30 | 5 | 7 | Do |
| | Bakoo | " | 28 | 5 | 5 | Do Pitted on face with S.P |
| 16,606 | Ohojonee | " | 29 | 5 | 7 | Do |

Register, *El Almirante*

Commander, and Emancipated by Decree of the British and of
Spanish Court of Mixed Commission on the 20th day of March 1828?
The said Brig having on the day aforesaid been pronounced liable to
Confiscation and accordingly condemned by the said Commission.

| No. | Names | Sex | Age | Stature ft | in | Discription |
|---|---|---|---|---|---|---|
| 16,607 | Nahmoo | Man | 28 | 5 | 7 | Cuts all over |
| | Norrkoo | " | 29 | 5 | 1 | Do |
| | Osoo | " | 33 | 5 | 7 | Do |
| 16,610 | Odojobboo | " | 19 | 5 | 5 | Cuts on face |
| | Odorombay | " | 32 | 5 | 1 | Cuts all over |
| | Arlahboloo | " | 22 | 5 | 2 | Do |
| | Olojoo | " | 21 | 5 | 5 | Do |
| | Daboo | " | 23 | 5 | 5 | Do |
| 16,615 | Sokoyoo | " | 26 | 5 | 9 | Do |
| | Sahjohkoo | " | 28 | 5 | 4 | Do |
| | Oshoo | " | 26 | 5 | 2 | Do |
| | Ochoo | " | 28 | 5 | 4 | Do |
| | Cochoo | " | 29 | 5 | 6 | Do |
| 16,620 | Solooah | " | 27 | 5 | 3 | Do |
| | Anxdoo | " | 28 | 5 | 1 | Do |
| | Sarmjay | " | 27 | 5 | 9 | Do |
| | Addoo | " | 26 | 5 | 4 | Do |
| | Odowoo | " | 28 | 5 | 8 | Do |
| 16,625 | Bansollay | " | 27 | 5 | 6 | Do |
| | Jisomoo | " | 26 | 5 | 3 | Do |
| | Kynah | " | 30 | 5 | 8 | Do |
| | Oshoo | " | 27 | 5 | 6 | Do |
| | Ooo | " | 26 | 5 | 4 | Do |
| 16,630 | Aalay | " | 27 | 5 | 4 | Do |
| | Zuidh | " | 30 | 5 | 3 | Do |
| | Andoo | " | 27 | 5 | 3 | Cuts on face |
| | Nanday | " | 26 | 5 | 4 | Do |
| | Kannah | " | 27 | 5 | 6 | Cuts all over |
| 16,635 | Ochopay | " | 28 | 5 | 6 | Cuts on face |
| | Cholokuy | " | 27 | 5 | 3 | Cuts all over |
| | Molahday | " | 23 | 5 | 1 | Do |
| 16,638 | Osokoo | " | 27 | 5 | 3 | Do |

# CHAPTER SIX

*Carolina*

March 1829,

420 enslaved people

Once again, promotions rained down on the crew of the *Black Joke*. Lieutenant Downes achieved the rank of commander after having been a lieutenant for almost two decades. Butterfield and Slade, mates both, had already been slated for a promotion, and Thomas Le Hardy, who'd been wounded in the fight, would now join them as a lieutenant. There was more good news. After the long drought that had preceded the dramatic capture, the crew of the *Black Joke* stayed busy throughout the spring of 1829. While promotions were lovely and the conflict with *El Almirante* the stuff of legends and eventual paintings, those aboard the tender were surely relieved when the *Black Joke* managed one of its few uneventful captures, that of the Brazilian brigantine *Carolina* in the first week of March. The *Black Joke* encountered the *Carolina* less than a hundred miles from Lagos with a hold full of the enslaved, and the captain, João dos Santos, indicated that he had embarked those enslaved in Lagos, which violated extant treaty obligations. Taking the captain at his word, the *Black Joke* claimed the slaving ship as a prize, and for the *Carolina* it was off to Sierra Leone and a date with the Mixed Commission. But things were rarely easy and never simple on the coast of Africa for any ship in the WAS, and certainly not for the *Black Joke*. Captain dos Santos still had a few tricks in reserve, and though they wouldn't cost lives on *Black Joke*, his machinations would certainly cause the kind of headaches back in Freetown that tended to be contagious to London.

Upon his arrival, dos Santos, along with the *Carolina*'s cook, went through the usual proceedings, admitting that the vessel was owned by João Alvez da Silva Porta, a Brazilian slave merchant, and the enslaved were his purchases. The plot twist occurred when both suddenly swore that they had picked up their human cargo in Molembo, and for a buyer in Rio. Beyond the fact that lying about where they'd been and where they were going was endemic to slave traders, there didn't seem to be much reason for this at first—the *Carolina* had been found near Lagos, and the captain, when pressed after he'd been boarded, said the enslaved had come from Lagos, not Molembo, and he was going to Bahia, not Rio. Compounding the evidence, the passport dos Santos had for the *Carolina* was a regular commercial, rather than slaving, Brazilian passport, and it listed his destination as Onim . . . which was another name for Lagos. When questioned again by the Mixed Commission, the captain and the cook finally capitulated, admitting that, yes, as dos Santos had first revealed, he'd purchased and boarded the enslaved from Lagos. The Mixed Commission expressed some tsk-tsking at, it seemed, the particularly egregious and wholly unnecessary lies from dos Santos, and noting that they were not born the previous day, the commissioners summarily condemned the *Carolina*.

No one cared about the deception, least of all the commissioners, who, when detailing the peculiarities of the case, dismissed it out of hand, writing of dos Santos that the "perjury thus exhibited is now, we are sorry to say, become too notorious a practice to require any more particular notice from us." What did require special attention was *Carolina*'s authentic commercial passport—it was going to be a problem, and a big one. Seeking to impress upon the Admiralty back in London the depth of its concern, the Mixed Commission added to its normal summation of adjudication an alarmed letter, which read in part:

*. . . [In] this Case, proof of a new system of fraud not hitherto generally followed, but which, we have little doubt, will now be universally adopted. We allude to the abandonment by Slavers of the regular Slave Passport, and the providing themselves with simple Commercial ones. A number of Letters found on board this Vessel, all speak of the Writer sending so many Slaves to this and that person, in return for such and such goods; thus fully establishing the fact, that the "Carolina" was from the very first, destined for the Slave-trade, yet the Authorities at Rio de Janeiro scrupled not to grant her a Commercial Passport, which, had the Slaves not actually been found on board, would have screened her from Capture, and she would, on her arrival in the Brazils, have reported herself as from Molembo.*

The *Carolina*, captured though it had been, was frightening because it represented an evolution in the evasive tactics being used by slave traders, one being enacted with the blatant assistance of the highest levels of government in Brazil. The officials responsible for granting the passports all merchants departing from Rio carried knew well what strictures the Anglo-Brazilian treaty contained; Brazilian officials had been seeking ways around them for years and had tried everything from issuing double passports to slave ships, to perhaps pointedly suggesting Brazil adopt an "apprenticeship" system akin to Britain's setup between Sierra Leone and the West Indies, to insisting all judgments against Brazilian slavers in which a Brazilian commissioner had not heard the case be vacated. (A particularly ludicrous demand given that Brazil had not managed to actually send a judge to the Mixed Commission until this very year, 1828, and wouldn't have minded if its refusal to participate provided legal standing to invalidate the entire operation.) Given that this last dodge had been attempted by both the Brazilian Foreign Ministry and Judge Joseph de Paiva, the very commissioner (finally) appointed to serve in Sierra Leone, tacit, if not explicit, coordination between slave traders and members of the Brazilian government was entirely expected. British officials seemed to react to this with a hapless shrug—spurious complaints resting on improbable legal theories and questionable treaty interpretations were just a thing Brazil did vis-à-vis the slave trade, and it wasn't as if Britain was inclined to heed the objections of other nations, legitimate or no, if it didn't have to.

However, the fact that the *Carolina's* commercial passport had been authentic meant that Brazilian slave traders were attempting an entirely new technique to evade their treaty obligations, and the Mixed Commission was concerned that the powers that be in Brazil had finally hit upon a genuine loophole, one large enough to sail tens of thousands of Africans a year through. Since a slaving passport unmistakably identified the business of the ship, it had, up until now, been a relatively simple matter for the captains of the WAS and the judges of the Mixed Commission to ascertain whether a slave trader was where it was meant to be—if caught above the equator as a slaver from Spain, Portugal, or Brazil, that almost certainly meant a trip to court and, with it, the potential condemnation of one's vessel. With an official commercial passport, the type given to merchants who *weren't* slavers (which had been issued by some European governments since at least the seventeenth century), it would be impossible to tell whether a ship was or wasn't meant to be doing business above the equator unless it had enslaved on board, meaning the only way to prove illicit intent was to, as with the *Carolina*, catch someone red-handed and full-berthed. And the existence of such passports, procured through official channels, meant that, at best, officials in Salvador, Brazil, were ignorant of slave traders' lies or, at worst (and far more likely), complicit in them.

The "illegal passport" rationale had itself been a work-around of a sort, perpetrated by British officials; while a ship still couldn't be detained for having the requisite equipment for slaving without recently purchased enslaved people physically present, it could be detained for being in the wrong place with the wrong passport, even if the hold was just as empty. This had been one of the most effective ways of getting around the lack of equipment clauses in antislavery treaties, and neither the judges nor the Squadron was interested in losing what few advantages they had. With that aim in mind, the Mixed Commission floated a possible response to the incipient crisis in the text of its judgment of *Carolina*—and to the modern eye, it's absurdly obvious:

> *After this, and some of the late instances before them, [the judges of the commission] cannot but feel that their decisions must be formed, on the circumstantial Evidence of the Case, rather than on the Testimony of the Parties interested, to which no credit can be given beyond what it may otherwise receive from such Evidence.*

That it took until 1829 for someone to say, in all seriousness, that perhaps the slave traders themselves were not a reliable source of evidence and that only those statements that could be corroborated could be relied upon is, frankly, shocking. Clearly, incredible profits, professional reputations, and livelihoods were on the line for every slave trader attempting the coast—slavers had every conceivable incentive to lie as much as possible, in every manner possible, if it would get them back to Brazil or Cuba with a passel of Africans in chains. Any testimony they provided should obviously have been taken with a pillar of salt, and given that the suppression effort was already laboring under a number of external constraints, it boggles the mind that up until this point the Mixed Commission had wasted any time giving the slavers the benefit of the doubt.

Setting aside what one might consider the obvious lack of moral compass displayed by their choice of this profession—trafficking human beings into lifelong bondage—the perfidy of slave traders had already been amply demonstrated. Capturing a slave ship was no guarantee it would stay off the water—not even for a reasonable length of time, though a substantial portion of that inefficiency could be laid at the Admiralty's door in Whitehall—because, as the histories of the *Vengador* and *Esperanza* illustrated, slave traders and their agents would go to great lengths, and tell huge lies, to keep their business operations running smoothly. And sure enough, while *Black Joke* was dealing with dos Santos's dubious testimony in Freetown, the *Sybille* was busy picking up the *Hosse* . . . again. The *Hosse* had begun life as the *Trajano* and had first been captured and condemned as a slaver in 1827 when it was captained by, of all people, Jose Rios, most recently of the *Esperanza* (because when it came to slave traders on the coast in the 1820s, anything old could be new again). As was the custom, the Brazilian government had complained mightily about the *Trajano's* capture, citing it as a particularly egregious case of British overreach, and had its protestations ignored. As was also the custom, the *Trajano* was sold at public auction after condemnation by the Mixed Commission, changing hands twice before it reached the private fleet of Francisco Félix de Souza (Cha Cha), who renamed the ship the *Hosse* and procured for it legitimate Portuguese papers. Cha Cha was deploying it as a supply vessel when it was taken by the pirate/privateer *Presidente*, which was almost immediately thereafter captured by the *Black Joke*, which was awarded salvage for the *Hosse* upon depositing the ship in Freetown. Andrez Fernandez, Cha Cha's agent in Sierra Leone and one of the two buyers who'd laundered the *Hosse's* ownership the first time around, dutifully got his boss's ship back a second time. By February, now captained by Benito Torrent, the *Hosse* was replicating almost the exact path that had landed it in the clutches of *Presidente* and subsequently the *Black Joke*, carrying supplies such as tobacco and rum to Ouidah, and since no pirates were around to stop it, the *Hosse* there embarked enslaved people to transport to Bahia. This time, though, it was Torrent, not Evangelista, who had the displeasure of meeting not the tender, but its owner. Collier and the *Sybille* made short work of the capture and sent *Hosse* back to Freetown to be thrice condemned in under three years by three different WAS ships. Even *El Almirante* would be back on the water, slaving again, by the next year. This constant capture and recapture of slave ships, as unwelcome as the prospect clearly was to Collier and his captains, was the source of far greater problems than an annoyingly familiar case of severe déjà vu—each seizure carried real danger, a risk of dying orders of magnitude beyond that found in conflict. And the entire West Africa Squadron was about to see how much worse it could get.

It should be said, slave ships stank. In multiple accounts of interacting with slave-trading vessels, observers seemed unable to help but note the smell, near uniformly described as an unrelenting stench somewhere on the spectrum between inescapably noxious and unbearably nauseating. WAS search parties often used smell as evidence—Lieutenant Butterfield had once been barred from searching a ship by a recalcitrant Spanish captain and still reported that the prize should be boarded and taken because he could smell the presence of the enslaved on board—and the Mixed Commission had, too. It was a very particular, awful smell. Slave ships stank, everyone knew, because they were incredibly dirty. Slavers were cleaned far, far less frequently than the majority of their Preventive Squadron (or even licit merchant) counterparts, and while this was just one facet of the terrible conditions on board, it was a big one. For instance, on WAS ships, where the deck might be scrubbed every morning, seamen cleaned so much that it was legitimately feared that the self-imposed, or rather captain-imposed, damp conditions were increasing rates of rheumatism and tuberculosis in sailors. In 1824, the Royal College of Medicine—represented by sundry exasperated naval surgeons—recommended naval policy switched from wet scrubbing to dry scrubbing, and the incidence of both diseases dropped precipitously. In essence, seamen had been making themselves sick from overcleaning. A marine serving on board a naval vessel once got three hundred lashes after "pissing from his hammock upon the deck." Cleaning was just a fundamental element of daily shipboard life in the Royal Navy, no matter where one was stationed.

Slavers were less rigorous when it came to cleaning (though not punishment, there they excelled). The upper deck where the crew congregated was generally not scrubbed daily, and the slave deck was cleaned whenever the captain happened to decide, maybe every two to three weeks, maybe not at all for the duration of the multiweek journey, other than, if the enslaved were perversely fortunate, the bare minimum of removing the especially sick and the dead from the hold. There was usually a surgeon, but reports still detailed incidents like a corpse left to rot beneath the living and bodies dead of suffocation in the hold, or lying in pools of waste from dysentery on deck, flesh rubbed off from the motion of the ship upon the waves. Where they persisted, there was no drive to improve these conditions. This was because a certain degree of loss—dead Africans—was not just expected, but specifically calculated and built into the slave trader's estimation of the number of enslaved people that could be packed incredibly close together for weeks and still make it to the auction block in Brazil or Cuba or, hell, Jamaica (where slavery was still very much legal, despite its being a British holding). Also, certain ports were more dangerous than others; the Bight of Biafra, in particular, had the worst slave ship mortality rates of any port of embarkation in its region, though it seems doubtful anyone realized this at the time. Though there were informal networks circulating information in the form of books, pamphlets, and medical observations and findings, due to the illegal nature of the trade, medical personnel on slave ships did not have access to the same supplies and stores of knowledge as the naval surgeons stationed aboard WAS ships. And it was beyond unlikely that, absent the impetus of military regulation, something such as overcleaning would ever become a problem.

These issues, writ large, made every single slaver a potentially serious vector for disease, a ripe breeding ground for the illnesses to be found in the tropical climate (and everywhere else). Unlike the experience of indigenous peoples in the Americas and the world over, in which populations were decimated by contact with Europeans and their novel diseases, on the coast of Africa in the nineteenth century, it was the Europeans who were felled with regularity. According to one account, at Fernando Pó, which was initially meant to eventually supplant Freetown as a base of operations for both the Squadron and the Mixed Commission, "on an average [. . .] two or three of the forty or fifty whites in the settlement die weekly, and the whole of the remainder, with few exceptions, either are, or have been ill." In describing the island, another officer said:

> . . . it is about forty miles in length by twelve in breadth, with a high peak rising in the centre 10,700 feet above the level of the sea, covered with vegetation nearly to the summit. This peak is visible on a clear day, in coming from the westward, for nearly 100 miles! The island is beautifully picturesque, and about sunset presents one of the grandest objects it is possible to conceive, as the chasms in the neighbourhood of the peak afford so many splendid and varying colours when the sun is far below our visible horizon; but yet, falling with his dying lustre upon these high pinnacles, every projecting fragment reflects different bright tints, which keep constantly changing as he approaches his ocean bed. It is strange that the most picturesque spots along this coast are in general the most deadly. Sierra Leone is a beautiful grave: this spot again is almost [unrivaled] for scenery, but the air is contaminated;
>
> > "—dread pestilence, with her poison'd tongue,
> > Lurks in each breeze."
>
> The gale, which you fondly court to cool your burning brow, is the breath of destruction. It has passed over the valley of death, and comes heavy with the cold damp of the charnelhouse, to woo

*you to his court! This island, to appearance, possesses every thing desirable for a settlement. Nature has been prolific in the extreme; fertility, plenty of water, a commodious harbour, good anchorage, abounding with fish, and a good soil capable of producing any description of vegetation, offer every inducement to the settler, and promise all that he can wish for. But the curse of Africa soon finds out the unthinking victim; and ere he can reap the seed which he has sown, Death, with his unsparing scythe, cuts the slight thread of his existence.*

So the environs weren't exactly healthy for many British sailors. However, even on the cleanest Royal Navy ships sailing in the most conducive-to-the-European-constitution waters, officers and seamen were already used to the perils of typhus, scurvy, tuberculosis, cholera, all manner of sexually transmitted infections, and smallpox, though vaccination for this last was becoming more common (for Europeans; it had already been common among populations of Africans). None of those possibilities went away with duty on the western coast of Africa, where the much-warmer and positively mosquito-ridden climate was anything but welcoming to those who'd not spent their lives, or even better, generations, building up resistance. Sailing near the equator carried the additional risk of contracting malaria, yellow fever, dengue fever, and blackwater fever, as well as, to a lesser extent, yaws (a tropical skin infection), leprosy, elephantiasis, and guinea worm. (Hepatitis was also believed to be present and impacted by season and climate, as well as water quality.) And since slavers cleaned a lot less, if one were a sailor on a slave ship or on a prize crew, one could add the risk of contracting dysentery, ulcers and additional skin diseases, and ophthalmia, an eye disease that can cause temporary or permanent blindness and had been known to leave entire ships, both enslaved and crew, blind on the water, left to stumble into harbors or simply disappear, never to be heard from again. Depression, unsurprisingly, was rampant, and suicide on slave ships was not uncommon.

So the shanty "Beware, beware, the Bight of Benin, / there's one comes out where fifty went in"—if it does, as many scholars believe, refer to the risk of death from disease that stalked service on the coast—was an exaggeration, but less than one might imagine. That being said, up until this point, only twice in the history of the WAS had this propensity toward all manner of maladies exploded into a full-blown epidemic that ravaged the enslaved, the service, and the population of Freetown alike. Once was in 1823, just before the beginning of Bullen's tenure as commodore. And in a piece of extremely bad luck for *Sybille* and *Black Joke*, in particular, the other was in 1829. In the average year, the West Africa Squadron might lose roughly 5 percent of its men to disease, which was plenty. In 1829, over 25 percent of *the entire Squadron* would succumb to a terrifying malady.

*Black Joke* had departed Freetown after the condemnation of *Carolina* on April 13, and things were fine. How the outbreak had spread in Freetown's harbor wasn't immediately evident, especially in the midst of a chaos of grisly death, but from the account of James Boyle, the colonial surgeon, the first case originated in Freetown on April 21, 1829, in the colonial secretary's office. *Eden* arrived May 1, with diseased enslaved people on board. The next case in Freetown showed up in a man who'd just returned from a boat trip to the Scarcies River May 4. Chief Justice John William Bannister, who'd barely been in the colony a year, was struck fourth (finally succumbing to a relapse a few months later), the eighteen-year-old apprentice of Turner's old nemesis Savage was fifth, becoming ill May 18, the same day the *Sybille* prize crew arrived in the *Panchita*, with diseased enslaved people on board. By May 19, the sixth case in Freetown had made it to Judge Jackson's house, and five days later, *Sybille*'s prize crew was dead.

Hindsight, mostly courtesy of Boyle, provides a cohesive order of events, but that Collier would have argued that the *Eden* was the initial source of the outbreak wasn't just his animosity at work; there was a lot of evidence to point to *Eden*. The commodore's dis-

dain for Captain Owen, and particularly his disregard for regulations, was on record; Owen's ship *Eden* was, much like its captain,
unkempt by Royal Navy standards. The ship arrived between the
first and second cases in Freetown. As Boyle noted after boarding,
the *Eden* was poorly ventilated and at least an order of magnitude
filthier than ships of the Squadron under Collier's command. The
*Eden* had also taken a slaver rife with disease, but the *Eden* had
stopped in Fernando Pó, as was Captain Owen's wont, before arriving in Sierra Leone in early May. (Owen did this in part so he could
expand the workforce at the island settlement by, essentially, skimming people off the total number of enslaved to be liberated—or
not—by the Mixed Commission in Freetown. He didn't keep them
in bondage on Fernando Pó, but they also weren't exactly "freed"
through approved channels nor given much choice in where they
were now to live or how they would be employed. This was just
another of the many reasons that many distrusted William Fitzwilliam Owen.) By the time the ship had dropped anchor in Freetown's harbor, most on board were deathly ill, if not already dead.
The catastrophic decimation of *Eden*'s crew had also laid the ship's
surgeon low, and Boyle, as the colonial surgeon, was asked to look
at the conditions on the vessel and proffer treatment, an opinion
on what was killing so many men, and, hopefully, what the commodore might do about it.

Collier had already been sick more than once during his service
on the coast. His fit of letter writing in regard to the *Vengador* and
*Esperanza* in December of 1828 had been during one such episode.
The commodore, known to be a disciplinarian of the old school, undoubtedly kept a clean and well-run ship. What he couldn't fight
and did not know how to fight were the mosquitoes. Though the
best minds in British medicine had not yet figured out the connection between certain illnesses and hordes of bloodsucking insects,
they were aware that something about the climate of the tropics promoted disease, particularly in those not born to the West African

coast. More pressing to Collier's immediate situation, the years 1823 and 1829 had shared a near-identical weather pattern.

Since the fatal symptoms had also been much the same, Boyle, as colonial surgeon, would be the first to directly compare the weather in the two outbreak years. In 1830, as he tried to make medical sense of the carnage of the previous year, he discovered the related and anomalous weather present in 1823 and 1829. Attempting to explain and differentiate all the fevers on the coast was a major undertaking, but clearly the situation could be one of life or death, and Boyle's resulting book-length analysis of the fevers of the West African coast revealed:

> These two records present a striking coincidence, with respect to the occurrence of rains as early as the month of March. Both in 1823 and 1829, during that month, the weather was unseasonable, and it afterwards became still more so. Frequent heavy showers of rain, alternated with a hot sun, and attended by thunder, lightning, or other unusual phenomena, occurred; and it is further remarkable, that these elementary commotions happened, as nearly as can be learned, on the same dates of the different years, and sometimes even at the precise hours of the respective dates. Indeed, so extraordinary is the similarity in the weather, that it renders the fatal consequences attendant upon the two periods [reconcilable], if not to be anticipated.

Clearly, the epidemics were related, both symptomatically and seasonally, and the March rains definitely had had something to do with the major outbreaks of what Boyle referred to as "epidemic fever." However, this was far from grasping the mode of transmission, as medical knowledge in the 1820s had yet to take many of the impressive leaps forward that would come later in the century. Boyle, for all his efforts, just couldn't see past the climate and ultimately attributed the fevers to unseasonable rain in March, finis.

It's hard to blame Boyle for getting it wrong in the end—almost no one had made the leap that, while tropical regions or unusual weather might readily coincide with bouts of epidemic, they did not directly transmit the disease. In this era, many doctors still propagated the idea of miasmas—bad air—as both the cause and method of transmission for any number of illnesses. This is key because Boyle's work was probably the best available analysis the Royal Navy had on fevers on the coast during this period, and it was published *after* the epidemic of 1829 had passed, with as much access to all available data that a world without modern communication could provide, and the full recognition that the events of 1823 and 1829 were related. If this was among the most advanced knowledge available in 1831, with all the benefits of hindsight, when Boyle could successfully compare and contrast two seasons of virulent fever, it's not surprising that, back in 1829, they hadn't stood a chance.

Unwitting of the dangers presented by the weird weather in the spring of 1829, the ships of the Squadron had continued about business as usual, and though both the *Eden* and, indirectly, the *Sybille* would be floated as the possible source, in retrospect it seems obvious that the mystery fever was developing simultaneously in multiple places, seemingly independent of one another. One site was, of course, the *Sybille*—for Collier's part, at the end of April, just over a month after retaking the *Hosse* and approximately six weeks after Boyle's suspicious rains, *Sybille* would uneventfully capture the *Panchita*, out of Havana and captained by Felipe Romez. Despite the fact that the slaver had just embarked over two hundred enslaved people from the Calabar River, had easily been won and easily been condemned, it's entirely possible that, if Collier could have taken back only a single decision in his entire time on the coast, it might have been the capture of this ship.

But that the commodore might have missed the warning signs was understandable. When the *Sybille* boarded its prize crew, sickly Africans were on board, but given the conditions on slavers, that was normal. It was also discovered that the *Panchita's* captain, first mate, and doctor had already succumbed to disease. This was, perhaps, a little more unusual, but given the sheer quantity of afflictions that could be contracted off the coast, not in itself alarming. So the *Sybille's* prize crew followed procedure. By May 18, the prize ship arrived in Freetown, where twenty of the diseased enslaved were immediately disembarked for care. The rest had to stay on board; the Liberated African Department was, it seems, already overcrowded with the sick and dying.

This was why Collier and some in Freetown ultimately blamed the *Eden*, which had arrived before *Panchita*, but was still in the harbor and topful of dead and dying sailors. Boyle boarded the *Eden* for the first time on May 17, a full day before the *Panchita* appeared in the harbor, meaning that whatever was decimating the crew of the former could not have come from the flagship's prize. Here, two diseases seemed to be operating at once: one presented somewhat like malaria but killed in two to three days; the other manifested as horrific ulcers and seemed to primarily affect the Africans, but was less fatal. The latter mystery was the easier one to solve, as Boyle discovered in conversation with the few sailors on the *Eden* still capable of communicating. They were certain that the enslaved had not had any such ulcerous malady when the ship on which they were found had been captured and were equally convinced that the five weeks the enslaved had spent in Fernando Pó waiting for transfer to Freetown was the source of what ailed the Africans, as the mystery affliction had already been spreading rapidly throughout the island settlement before the *Eden* had made its brief stop.

The malaria-like illness was what genuinely concerned Boyle. Malaria transmission may not have been understood, but the usual progression of symptoms was known, and though treatment did still occasionally include some form of bloodletting, many had converted to quinine bark, which was actually effective. Only in the most serious of cases was malaria still fatal, and in even those extreme circumstances, death rarely resulted before eight to ten days of symptoms; Boyle had neither heard of nor seen a case of someone dying from malaria before the fifth or sixth day, and even that was exceedingly rare. On the *Eden* the men had shown almost no symptoms before they collapsed, and only a scant twenty-five members of its original crew were now even on board—the rest had either died, usually within three days, or been invalided off the ship and continued to struggle with the disease, indicating that the illness continued to spread. A quick-killing disease that appeared to be highly contagious was nightmare enough, but when Boyle learned that no one with the second illness had presented any symptoms before the vessel's arrival in Freetown, whence the disease had come, at least in the most recent incarnation, seemed clear. Boyle could now be certain that whatever it was had rapidly been spreading through Freetown before either *Panchita*, *Sybille*, or *Eden* had sailed into port. Despite its grime, the *Eden* was less culprit and more victim—those on board had caught it from the town.

It's not shocking that ultimately, between the ships and Freetown itself, the latter had the earliest documented cases. There were all manner of fevers one might contract; one, probably malaria, was such a common affliction in Freetown that it was known as the "Sierra Leone Fever" and contracting it was expected for newcomers and those possessed of "weak constitutions." When the *Panchita* did arrive, with forty-three Africans already dead and members of the prize crew beginning to show signs of infection, the reason it had not been able to land the rest of the enslaved with the Liberated African Department was not just a matter of space—the judges and much of the staff of the Mixed Commission were already sick. Risk of illness had already made it difficult to recruit judges to serve on the Mixed Commission in Sierra Leone, as foreign judges were not generally eager to sacrifice their health on the altar of British policies that many of their countrymen barely tolerated. Appointed non-British commissioners regularly failed to show up in Freetown when expected, usually with a litany of excuses at the ready (conveyed by letter) for why. The events of 1829 didn't help matters. The suspected culprit among those in the colony—at least before both *Eden* and *Panchita* had arrived like so many scapegoats ready for sacrifice—was some other, as yet unidentified, slave ship whose officers or witnesses must have, in their interrogations, carried the malady right to the Mixed Commission's doorstep, weeks before the *Panchita* arrived. Though virulent and frequently deadly, the mystery ailment was not uniformly fatal—some, including one of the British commissioners and the new Brazilian commissioner, did survive it. Short-staffed and worse for the wear, the Mixed Commission was nonetheless able to once again confer by May 24, and it summarily condemned *Panchita* that very day. Given a disease that often killed in a couple of days, the time that passed between the prize's arrival and its condemnation could be ill afforded; sure enough, by the day the prize was condemned, it was already too late for the crew. Every *Sybille* sailor who'd helped usher the *Panchita* to Sierra Leone was dead but for one, and he didn't seem likely to make it. It hadn't even been four weeks since Boyle had seen the disease appear in Freetown, barely three since the *Eden* arrived, a scant week since the *Panchita* had put into port—and a full-blown epidemic was raging.

So what was it? Boyle, writing in 1830, detailed the varied symptoms, noting where they seemed to resemble nothing so much as superpowered malaria (what he refers to herein as "endemic fever"). Clearly a horrible way to die, even just the accounting is frightening:

> *With respect to the symptoms, it may be remarked that, as in the endemic fever [malaria], there will generally be pyrexia [fever], but rarely so marked or developed, and it will sometimes advance with so insidious a march as not to attract the particular attention of either the patient or medical attendant. In most cases the action of the pulse will be quickened, and the temperature of the*

*surface elevated; but it will frequently happen that the patient is first seen in a state of collapse, to which reaction [recovery] never succeeds. Some times pain in the head will be complained of as being very severe; but more frequently, however, it will be very slight, and not unfrequently [sic] altogether absent. Occasionally great giddiness will prevail. There will almost always be pains of the back, loins, or limbs, with pain in the chest, extending along the course of the oesophagus [sic], from its commencement [the throat] even to the stomach; and this pain will be said to be of a burning description. The state of the tongue varies greatly, it being at one time hard and dry, like a chip, and of a dark brown colour; the patient being unable to articulate for want of saliva. At other times the tongue will have a white centre, with edges of a bright red; and, still more commonly, in the worst cases, the tongue will be altogether without fur [papillae], and of a deep blood-red colour, and either very much enlarged and sponge-like, or elongated and contracted at the tip [glossitis]. There is generally thirst and a desire for cold liquids. The bowels are, for the most part, deranged; sometimes constipated, and sometimes, on the other hand, there is slight purging, attended with griping or tenesmus [cramping rectal pain]. The red appearance of the tongue, and the pains of chest, back, loins, or lower extremities, may be considered as the truest characteristics of the existence of the disorder.*

This seemingly exhaustive list didn't even cover the two other, extremely common symptoms of the epidemic that would provide the best hint to subsequent naval surgeons and modern readers alike as to precisely what affliction had struck and killed so many. In an early effort at contact tracing—there's even a map—Boyle's case studies of the 1829 epidemic tracked the progression of the disease across Freetown, and over and over, two phrases appear: "black vomit" and "yellowish cast of the skin."

The *Black Joke* returned to Freetown six weeks after it had left

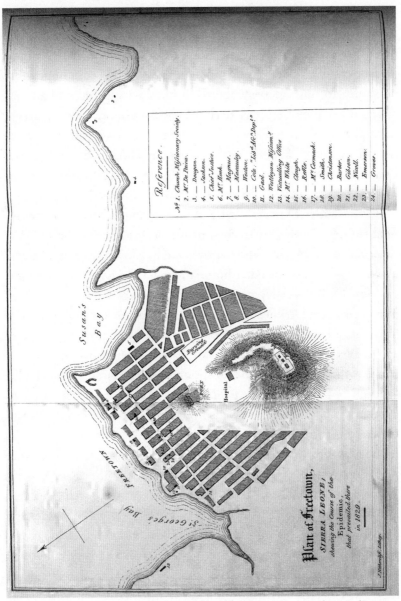

in mid-April. It unknowingly sailed directly into an epidemic's perfect storm and arrived just in time to be decimated by what turned out to be an especially awful incarnation of yellow fever. Though direct person-to-person transmission of yellow fever is impossible, mosquito-to-human-to-mosquito-to-human was more than feasible, and sailors often transferred between vessels. Downes might have gotten it in Freetown. He might also have gotten it when he met up with Captain Owen—currently aboard the *Medina*, but late of both the *Eden* and Fernando Pó—on May 27. Either way, the outcome was the same. Downes's logbook ends five days later.

Commander Downes—who upon arriving in Sierra Leone this final time had only just learned of his promotion for the *El Almirante* action of May 2—did survive, barely. However, he was so sick that he had to be invalided home to England just three days later, on May 30, 1829. After twenty-four years in the Royal Navy, Commander Henry Downes would never again serve on ship. His crew fared little better. In the few months it took for the epidemic to spend itself, just over half of its company—twenty-five of forty-five people—had died. With the exception of the *Primrose* (which hadn't touched in Freetown since February and wouldn't return until August) and *Clinker* (likewise cruising, and mostly far from the coast), Collier's flagship, *Sybille*, following in the wake of its prize *Panchita* to the now-deadly harbor, held out longer than just about any other Squadron vessel. Notoriously stringent about cleanliness and health, the commodore had made sure his lower decks were well ventilated and free of humidity, ensured his men stayed as dry as possible, sent only Kroomen (who were thought to be more immune) to accomplish *Sybille*'s "wooding and watering" onshore, fed every sailor who did go onshore "Peruvian bark" (quinine) and wine after breakfast regardless of ethnicity, and forbade any interaction with Freetown, Fernando Pó, or *Eden*, recently released from quarantine. It wasn't enough. On June 22, *Sybille* took on nine apparently healthy marines, eight of whom had previously served on the *Eden*. Four days later, a sailor came down with fever, presaging sixty-nine cases over the next two months, twenty-two of whom died. Out of the 792 sailors serving in the West Africa Squadron in 1829, 204 were felled by disease, almost all during that single terrible summer. Of those that died, 57 had come from the *Sybille* and its famous tender.

# Brazilian Brigantine "Carolina"

Register of Slaves, Natives of Africa Captured on board the said Vessel by the Brig "Black Joke" a Tender of His Majesty's

| No. | Names | Sex | Ag | Statue Ft. I. | Discription |
|---|---|---|---|---|---|
| 17,342 | Ogotoloo | Man | 28 | 5 7 | P. back of right shoulder & Cts. all over |
| | Ochoh | " | 27 | 5 0 | 2 on right breast & Ct. Filk on face with S.P |
| | Altahbay | " | 18 | 5 2 | Cuts all over |
| 17,345 | Ogosaday | " | 25 | 5 7 | Cuts on the body |
| | Lyonoday | " | 23 | 5 2 | A. A on left breast |
| | Babbah | " | 20 | 5 5 | P. on left Arm & Cut all over |
| | Olofoe | " | 29 | 5 7 | A.M. on right breast Do |
| | Chamokoo | " | 36 | 5 8 | N 3. Do Do |
| 17,350 | Madolah | " | 32 | 5 6 | W. above navel Do |
| | Aotang | " | 26 | 5 3 | B on right breast Do |
| | Ozahteay | " | 20 | 5 3 | V. Do |
| | Ammodoo | " | 24 | 5 5 | P. below left breast |
| | Olowoo | " | 29 | 5 7 | NR on right Do & Cut all over |
| 17,355 | Ahunahbee | " | 25 | 5 5½ | Cuts all over |
| | Sopahloo | " | 23 | 5 3 | B. back of left shoulder & Cts. all over |
| | Lahlo | " | 27 | 5 6 | R on left breast & Cts. all over |
| | Olahdaday | " | 29 | 5 1 | Do Do |
| | Oyahjomee | " | 36 | 5 6½ | Cuts all over |
| 17,360 | Mdhammah | " | 30 | 5 4 | Cuts on face |
| | Ozah | " | 32 | 5 6 | F.F. on right breast & Cuts all over |
| | Pokokong | " | 27 | 5 2 | A.M. Do Do |
| | Aoldim | " | 30 | 4 11 | P on left Do & Ct. on face |
| | Byakoo | " | 16 | 5 0 | Cuts on face & Talk. on breast |
| 17,365 | Dangannah | " | 29 | 5 2 | V on right breast & Cut all over |
| | Ahkabolah | " | 26 | 5 6 | C on right Arm & Cut on face |
| | Dajomoh | " | 31 | 5 6 | Cut all over |
| | Ogoi | " | 25 | 5 10 | Do |
| | Globe | " | 23 | 5 2 | 3 on right breast & Ct. on face |
| 17,370 | Edowoo | " | 26 | 5 1½ | SS. Do & Ct. all over |
| | Olofoe | " | 25 | 5 5 | P. below left Do & Ct. & Ct. on face with S.P |
| | Choge | " | 37 | 5 1 | K on left Arm & Cts all over |
| 17,373 | Arrow | " | 32 | 5 7 | A above navel Do |

Register, Carolina

Ship "Sybille": Francis Augustus Collier CB Commander, and Emancipated
by Decree of the British and Brazilian Court of Mixed Commission on the
Fourteenth day of April 1829. The said Brigantine having on the day
aforesaid been pronounced liable to Confiscation and accordingly condemned

| No | Names | Sex | Age | Stature ft in | Description |
|---|---|---|---|---|---|
| 7,374 | Ahwojobie | Man | | 5 9 | Cuts all over |
| | Lahlogo | " | 22 | 5 " | W on upper R. hand Cuts all over |
| | Songpay | " | 25 | 5 2 | MC on right Do . Do |
| | Ahot | " | 19 | 5 9 | Cuts all over |
| | Awoomee | " | 32 | 5 " | FN on left breast & Cuts all over |
| | Apsnah | " | 26 | 5 7 | V on right Do. Do |
| 7,380 | Osofeye | " | 33 | 5 11 | BC on Do Do |
| | Blowahlee | " | 27 | 5 2 | 4 Do Do |
| | Soteyee | " | 20 | 5 1 | Cuts all over |
| | Ochoh | " | 22 | 5 6 | R middle of breast & Cuts all over |
| | Sokilee | " | 29 | 5 7 | V on right Do Do |
| 7,385 | Ayenah | " | 21 | 5 7 | V Do & Cuts on face |
| | Kahjolah | " | 23 | 5 3 | W on left Do & Cuts all over |
| | Dasomee | " | 20 | 5 8 | ↓ below left Do & Cuts on face |
| | Damoleh | " | 18 | 5 6 | VB on left arm, Pitted on face with S. & Cuts all over |
| | Sobojo | " | 21 | 5 9 | MC on right breast and Cuts all over |
| 7,390 | Mahwodoo | " | 26 | 5 2 | R on left Do. Do. |
| | Ooho | " | 28 | 5 6 | MC on right Do Do. |
| | Yoadee | " | 22 | 5 3 | AM. Do. Do. |
| | Ooo | " | 36 | 5 4 | O on left Arm Do. |
| | Gjoggo | " | 25 | 5 3 | S on right breast Do. |
| 7,395 | Soahday | " | 38 | 5 5 | B. below the navel Do. |
| | Syolelay | " | 20 | 5 3 | CC on right breast Do |
| | Adoom | " | 18 | 5 " | 2. Do. Do |
| | Sodspay | " | 41 | 5 4 | Cuts all over |
| | Kolole | " | 38 | 5 6 | Do |
| 7,400 | Tahlesay | " | 19 | 5 2 | 2 on right breast & Cuts on face |
| | Awagay | " | 37 | 5 5 | O on the back & Cts all over |
| | Aysnah | " | 27 | 5 6 | 2 on right breast Do |
| | Bahhonee | " | 21 | 5 3 | S on back of right Shoulder, C on right breast & on face with S.S. |
| | Kahljole | " | 28 | 5 4 | No marks |
| 7,405 | Latee | " | 23 | 5 " | Cuts all over |

# CHAPTER SEVEN

*Cristina*

October 1829,

348 enslaved people

Considering the sheer quantity of sailors lost, especially since the *Sybille* was in no position to readily supply more, it's no surprise that the *Black Joke* was slow to recover, or that its next captain, Lieutenant Edward Iggulden Parrey, was a long time coming. The crew, what was left of them, weren't missing much. Rumors of the 1829 epidemic had, naturally, spread among seafaring vessels with business on the coast. Though most WAS ships were shorthanded and temporarily out of commission, the two that still cruised in the summer of 1829, *Primrose* and *Clinker*, saw few potential slavers and little action. Since the epidemic was thought to be seasonal—and it was, just not in the way the medical profession supposed—slavers were mostly content to wait it out. Toward the end of summer, action picked up as the epidemic showed signs of tapering off, and Collier became progressively more worried about the resumption of slaving traffic in West Africa, particularly in his preferred hunting grounds, the Bights. Even before the epidemic, the commodore had seen an alarming increase in Spanish slave traders in the area. Even the *Providencia*—the supposed privateer with whom the *Black Joke*, under Turner, had had its famously dubious run-in—had, by the beginning of the summer, been resold and was sighted sailing as the *Fama de Cadiz*, waiting to board the enslaved with several other ships near Ouidah.

The onset of the fever had, temporarily, altered the commodore's priorities. Collier felt compelled to sail south to St. Helena for the benefit of *Sybille*'s crew, regardless of his concerns regarding the quantities of slavers. As its familiar shores came into view—

> *the coast changed its hitherto monotonous and barren aspect, [. . .] relieved by a chain of small islands and rocks extending inshore, and bearing the most fantastic shapes. One [. . .] was a rock which appeared originally to have been of some height and extent, but the sea or some other cause had carried away the whole of its centre, excepting a surface of about twenty feet deep, which rested on the two extremities, leaving between them an immense archway or natural bridge, apparently capable of allowing a ship to sail under without lowering a mast. [. . .] The surrounding country is one continued sand, without a shrub as far as the eye can see. [. . .] A rock forms the north end of this bay, upon the top of which [. . .] a column and cross, which, in the adventurous and flourishing days of the Portuguese, was erected [. . . by Bartholomew Diaz, about the beginning of the fifteenth century].*

—Collier must've felt, in his gut, that it had been the right move. And it was; *Sybille* hadn't made a full recovery until it approached the healthful airs of St. Helena, but by August 28, the frigate reported no new cases of yellow fever. Though he'd left the understaffed *Black Joke* to keep a weather eye on Lagos and another ship to patrol near Ouidah, the precautions would prove unnecessary, at least for the month of July. By August, however, slave traders were willing to venture the risk, and slowly but inexorably, the traffic in Africans reemerged, soon picking up to the levels Collier had been so worried about a few months prior.

It wasn't only the slavers who bothered the commodore; in late spring, then throughout the summer and into the fall, interference from the Admiralty (and its affiliated boards), as well as the colonial administration in Sierra Leone, was beginning to give him fits. The various maladies at the onset of the epidemic had underscored that it didn't take a yellow fever epidemic to decimate the African population of a slaver, and what's more, that the lack of hygiene and medical care could, through illness, impact the safety and performance of the Squadron. (Though it wasn't as if no one had considered the question before, it might have been nice if there'd been more impetus to resolve this issue before 1829, if only for the sake of the enslaved.) The problem of filthy slavers and the myriad diseases they carried had persisted for decades before the West Africa Squadron had been impacted, and illnesses on slave traders had already killed far more people than the Squadron could ever fear to lose, even (or perhaps especially) in an epidemic. Nonetheless, the question of how to save lives was now at the forefront of everyone's mind, which should have been a good thing to a man as reputed for his cleanliness as Collier. What he took issue with, though, was not the concern, motivated by self-interest or not—it was the proposed solutions.

Nothing could be done about the conditions on slavers, short of capturing them. Debate also remained ongoing as to whether a slave ship or a prize ship had been at the root of the epidemic that had prompted the surge in interest in the prevention of disease (and with it, disease transmission). So those behind implementing the suppression effort turned their attention to something they could control—the conditions aboard prize ships. Boyle, the colonial surgeon, proposed what he thought was an easy fix: having ships of the Squadron supply their prize crews with medications to treat the enslaved. Collier, exasperated, pointed out that such a solution was ludicrous. The population on board a slave trader could be huge—four, five, even six hundred Africans—without question far larger than the population on any ship in the Squadron but for the *Sybille* itself, which, fully manned, would have carried about 240 men at most. Compare that to the population of one of the smallest ships, *Sybille*'s tender *Black Joke*, which not infrequently had a complement of under fifty. And what if a Squadron ship had to supply more than one prize crew before making it back to Freetown to resupply itself? Unless the stores at Sierra Leone were prepared to supply every ship of the WAS with, Collier estimated, ten times the number of medicines ordinarily provided to each craft, and the Admiralty was willing to approve changes to the regulations stipulating the amount of medical supplies a Royal Navy vessel could carry and pay for the higher costs, the idea made less than no sense, obvious though it may have seemed. Not one to naysay without at least contributing a counterproposal, Collier passed on a suggestion from the *Sybille's* own surgeon, Robert McKinnel, that was more feasible—warm clothing. The open sea at night could be frigid, so perhaps something as simple as being able to adequately warm the sick and feverish could make an immediate and appreciable difference in survival rates on prize ships. McKinnel's plan also had the advantage of being readily implementable across the Squadron. The advent of mass production had dramatically dropped the cost of cloth, while using these types of supplies circumvented much of the Admiralty's red tape. No one took Collier up on it.

The commodore was also in heated debate with the Victualling Board, the arm of the Royal Navy responsible for regulating and supplying food and drink. Captain Owen had gotten in its ear, and now the board was seriously considering moving the West Africa Squadron's store from Ascension, where it was now located, to Fernando Pó. Collier, unsurprisingly, disliked this idea about as much as he disliked Owen, which is to say *a whole lot*. Of course, their mutual antipathy wasn't part of Collier's rationale—his eventual reasoning for opposing the move didn't include something along the lines of "And also, I can't stand that guy"—but since the two hadn't seen eye to eye from the first moment they'd met, this context can't be ignored, especially given that Owen was the one goading the change. The story was that Captain Owen, in the years previous to 1827, had been seeking more productive relations with the native population of Fernando Pó. Noticing the prevalence of facial hair among the original locals as well as the respect they afforded bearded "Arabian" traders, he had grown a huge, perhaps verging on magnificent, beard and readily encouraged his men to do likewise, in direct contravention of the Royal Navy's rules governing the appearance of its officers. Collier, while a beloved captain who ran a well-contented ship, was widely known to be absolutely insistent about following regulations. The navy may have been in the process of extremely gradual modernization, but the commodore was a protégé of *Nelson's*, for goodness' sake; Collier wouldn't readily abandon the guidelines of the service, the way of life he'd known since childhood. Luxurious beards, no matter how practical, convenient, or useful, were out.

So when Collier arrived in Freetown, flush with the success of capturing the *Henriqueta*, only to have a lieutenant from Owen's *Eden* pay a call on the *Sybille* for the first time sporting not just any beard, but a full, lush, *well-established* beard, Collier was entirely uninterested in the rationale behind what he saw as a bushy spit in the navy's eye. He wanted that beard *gone*, yesterday if possible, and the commodore pulled rank and kicked the lieutenant off his frigate, telling him "not to presume again to disgrace the uniform of the Service and his Country by appearing so unlike a British officer." Rather than back Collier up, or at least accede to the reality that regulations were regulations, Owen wrote to Collier expressing surprise that a little facial hair "should have drawn from you such an extraordinary order." Nothing about following basic guidelines seemed extraordinary to Collier, so when it happened again when the commodore first visited Fernando Pó, the mutual dislike was a seed already planted. While there, Collier spied yet another lieutenant "in a state of tropical undress," and while surely a beard has never since been described in such a delightful manner, Collier was anything but amused. Since Owen was on the coast under ambit of the Colonial Office, Collier wasn't the lieutenant's direct superior, so he couldn't just order the man to shave, and the commodore did the next best thing and refused to meet with the lieutenant until he reappeared beardless (which he did).

Owen resented what he saw as Collier's interference in *his* squadron and overall inflexibility in the face of extenuating circumstances—i.e., a politic deference to local custom. Owen again wrote to Collier, this time pointing out that perhaps his lieutenant "may possibly in wearing his beard have been influenced by the example of his Captain who has worn his these six years." While Owen had stopped ever so short of saying that he had been actively encouraging his men to flout regulation, he might as well have. This was precisely the wrong tack to take with the rigid, at least in this respect, commodore. The relationship broke down almost as soon as it had commenced and would only get worse; soon the two senior officers were exchanging a flurry of increasingly testy letters concerning, of all things, beards. And while the beard issue might, in retrospect, seem awfully petty, note, first, that modern militaries still regulate facial hair, and, second, that it actually *was* emblematic of Owen's being, as a general rule, incredibly insubordinate. Regularly. About all manner of things, some of which were a lot more serious than shaving. Nuanced histories have chalked at least some of it up to the years Owen had spent in isolated, independent command, but the man unquestionably liked to cut corners and ignore orders, sometimes with genuinely deleterious impact. To wit, when Captain Owen decided to buy his own tenders and send them to cruise for slavers. Recall, this was the same man who'd complained of Collier's interference in the administration of Fernando Pó over *beards*, and now Owen was interfering in the operations of the whole West Africa Squadron by directly contravening orders to him from the Admiralty, which had, in no uncertain terms, told the captain that he was not to chase slavers.

And he was doing it badly. Foreign powers who weren't exactly enamored of their treaty obligations—ahem, Brazil (and Portugal and Spain)—would seize on any opportunity to help a slaver escape condemnation, and Owen's knowledge of, or perhaps respect for, the treaty obligations and restrictions surrounding British search and seizure of foreign vessels was shaky at best. The captain's willy-nilly pursuit of slavers—more than once, he detained and captured slave ships that weren't even subject to British jurisdiction—created headaches not just for Collier, but for the Mixed Commission, which was obliged to clean up the inevitable mess. Catching slavers made money, and while Owen was a committed abolitionist, he wasn't averse to using the cause to richly supplement his own income, which gave him a reputation to some for being a flagrant opportunist who had more commitment to his pocketbook than his duty. Then Owen, never one to miss a chance to make an enemy, wrote to the Admiralty and complained that he didn't have enough officers and men to appropriately staff the Fernando Pó settlement because they were all out on cruise looking for slavers, and could the Admiralty be obliged to send him more? The temerity of the request had to raise more than one eyebrow back in London. Owen's job was to try to launch Fernando Pó as a settlement, which he seemingly needed constant reminder of; the Royal Navy already had an entire squadron devoted to direct suppression in West Africa, namely, *Collier's* squadron. However, since it wasn't exactly clear who was Owen's boss, the Admiralty or the Colonial Office—and his ship had been issued treaty instructions that allowed it to legally cruise for slavers—there was only so much the Admiralty could do to reign him in. When it came to *Eden* (tenders inclusive), Collier was under orders not to interfere.

So while the commodore did not care one bit for Captain Owen, in fairness *a whole lot* of people agreed with Collier, and with cause. This new situation with the Victualling Board wasn't the first time a body operating out of Sierra Leone had strenuously resisted the idea of a move to Fernando Pó. Back in 1828, Owen had shown up in Freetown, with little warning, and declared that the island settlement had been made sufficiently ready for the Mixed Commission to move its operations there. Owen and the *Eden* would take them; he'd be glad to wait in the harbor until everyone was ready to go. If he'd asked before summarily showing up, Owen might have discovered that the British commissioners weren't ready to move to Fernando Pó and were never going to be ready, primarily because they had zero interest in being fourteen hundred miles farther from England, much less farther south. And if the Mixed Commission could barely get foreign commissioners to come to Freetown, which had been founded in 1792 and had decades' worth of infrastructure development, how on earth was it to convince anyone to move to Fernando Pó, a much more recently established settlement? In that instance, the Mixed Commission got out of the move by punting the matter upward, pointing out that while of course everyone knew that the general plan was to steadily move operations to Fernando Pó, "as no orders or arrangements of His Majesty's Government have yet been received [. . .] regarding their removal [. . .] it is quite impossible for the measure to be carried out."

Collier's problem in 1829 was twofold. He couldn't resort to the Mixed Commission's tactic from the previous year because if the Victualling Board told him to move the WAS supplies—which it might, if it kept listening to Owen—Collier would have to move them. Most important, he didn't want the Squadron's stores moved to Fernando Pó regardless of who was in command of the settlement. The commodore agreed with the Mixed Commission's assessment that the island was inconveniently located—true, it would have made many prize-crew journeys shorter if everything were at Fernando Pó, which would in turn save some lives among the enslaved, but it would make patrolling for slavers, particularly in the northern section of the WAS territory, that much harder. And clearly, everything—namely the Mixed Commission—was decidedly not at Fernando Pó. Additionally, Collier liked going to Ascension at least once a year, despite its distance, because he felt it was good for the men. In the commodore's opinion, its air was healthier than that of

Fernando Pó, still to his mind a possible source for the recent outbreak (or at least just as susceptible), and upon reading a description of Ascension, it's easy to understand why:

> The climate here is exceedingly grateful to our feelings, after the damp and [drizzly] atmosphere of the pestilent coast we have just left. From the very small quantity of rain that falls on the lower parts of this island, but little decomposition of its superficies has taken place in this situation; consequently there is here scarcely any vegetation, and the air is uncommonly pure and dry. The temperature at present is varying from seventy-two to eighty degrees during the day. The upper half of what is called the green mountain, which is about seven miles from the anchorage, is decomposing rapidly. The elevation of this spot is two thousand eight hundred and eighteen feet. It is almost constantly enveloped in mist, but is, notwithstanding, uncommonly healthy—the thermometer averaging ten or twelve degrees below its usual range at the garrison and anchorage. The soil at this spot is a loose black earth, very productive, and already extensively cultivated.—Fields of several acres of the common and sweet potato, turnips, and other esculent plants, adorn the sloping sides of the mountain; and the mountain house, besides its pleasure ground of English flowers and shrubs, has its kitchen garden, which produces almost every vegetable in great perfection and abundance.

Ascension additionally had plenty of water, cattle, and a climate the sailors could actually enjoy, and it was also more convenient to the Bights, where most of the WAS patrol occurred, than Sierra Leone. If not Ascension, Collier would have also willingly accepted St. Helena, whose medicinal and recreational benefits have previously been mentioned. Eventually, the Victualling Board dropped the idea.

The commodore's concern for his men didn't stop with those

who'd taken up service back in England. Kroomen were essential to the effective functioning of the West Africa Squadron, and Collier was appalled that the Kroomen who served on Squadron vessels were not being paid comparably to the mostly White sailors of the Royal Navy. These free African sailors were hired in Africa, usually in Freetown (which had an entire Kru section that, even with the transiency required of maritime life, could range from several hundred to over a thousand residents at any given time), to supplement inadequate complements of Royal Navy sailors. (So tight was the bond between English ships and the Kroomen that Liverpool *also* had a well-established Kru neighborhood and community.) Though Kroomen were salaried at a rate similar to the seamen of the WAS, as yet no Admiralty policy apportioned to them a portion of the prize money earned by Squadron ships. Historically, the average Royal Navy sailor was paid less than many of his merchant counterparts, which was likely no small part of why the Royal Navy was a relatively inexpensive investment for the British government. British politicians of the day would probably take issue with that characterization, but it's accurate—the thirty-odd years of war preceding 1815 had been expensive as all get-out, but the Royal Navy was a downright bargain, considering what the government was getting for the price. Setting aside the total cost, the real price of Britain's total defense expenditures at the time was getting roughly £1 per capita per *year*. This averages out to 2 to 3 percent of the annual national income; that's less than the United States spends on its military today (over 3 percent), and in the nineteenth century Britain was building what would become, by landmass, the largest empire ever recorded in the modern or ancient world.

So the Royal Navy saved the government's money by keeping salaries on the lower end, then made up the difference with the potential for prize money (which was also a major performance incentive). Though it wasn't quite as simple as throw a rock, hit a prize, during the wars this supplement had been spread across the whole of the service, and the sheer number of war zones plus the ability to attack enemy merchant shipping meant that prize ships were widely available nearly everywhere one served. Even if one had to harry the government to actually pay up on prize money—and one very much did, so much so that an entire profession grew up around the need (Collier's agent in Freetown, Macaulay, for instance)—and what pay there was, was diminished by numerous charges and reductions, it was money duly earned, and eventually (somewhat) duly paid. By the 1820s, however, the West Africa Squadron was one of the few places within the service that had ready and consistent access to prizes and their attendant bounties. It was one of the things that appeared to make a berth in the WAS worth risking the deadliest station in the service, even if the reality didn't exactly live up to the hype. Prize money from a single ship could double or triple a sailor's salary and was part of what made up for the difficult climate and risk of death from the frightening maladies British sailors often associated with the Bights and their environs. When a Squadron ship captured a prize, it was awarded a percentage of the money from the proceeds of the sale of the ship and the goods thereon, plus head money where applicable. This percentage was then apportioned among the ship's complement based on rank and rating, on a scale commensurate with the distribution of the sailors. While Commodore Collier was among the first (possibly the actual first) to try to do something about it, the source of the pay inequity was obvious. Kroomen were supplemental to the Royal Navy, not members of the Royal Navy; they were paid *like* seamen, not *as* seamen. They didn't have a rating. When it came to prize money, they got nothing.

Kroomen in the Squadron were members of West African tribes (the Kru, *Kroo* being an archaic anglicized spelling) who resided primarily, or at least originally, in coastal regions of modern-day Liberia and collectivized by language. The Kru were multitalented—they were also artisans, carpenters, coopers, cooks, interpreters, etc., plenty of whom worked in Freetown—but of most interest to the

Royal Navy was their experience with swimming, diving, and boating, which had its origins in a time long before Europeans arrived in Africa. (It's entirely likely, even probable, that the Kroomen might be the only people on a Squadron ship who *could* swim—since the Admiralty believed the ability to swim facilitated desertion, the Royal Navy had a long-standing policy of actively discouraging efforts to teach its sailors how to do it, counterintuitive though that may seem.) Since the 1780s, when legitimate (as opposed to slaving) trade to the West African coast began to sharply increase, Kroomen had been seen as valuable and useful hires on all sorts of marine craft.

As a larger cultural question, Europeans tended to afford the Kru a particular reputation for reliability and loyalty, distinct from any other African tribal group in the area. For the WAS, the Kru had another advantage over other tribes, uniquely useful to the Squadron, namely, a hierarchy the Royal Navy could easily understand and fit into its existing structure. Though anywhere from five to fifteen Kroomen might serve on a Squadron vessel, nearly all formal interactions were with a single man, the headman. The captain told the headman, the headman told his fellow Kru, and everything got done with a minimum of fuss. Orders to all of the Kroomen were distributed through the headman, likewise their pay—they were a crew within the crew and functioned just as cohesively and efficiently as any other unit of sailors or marines. The headman occupied a traditional place in Kru society, and the practice was often maintained even among Kru who ended up in England. The Kroomen appeared to have little concern that this man might take advantage of the situation—on land the headman could even serve as what Europeans might think of as a trusted bank, holding and distributing wages on his tribesmen's behalf and at their behest.

Collier understood better than most, it seemed, that the West Africa Squadron could not have accomplished even half as much as it did without the assistance of Kroomen. Not only was their indigenous knowledge of the geography of the area invaluable, neither

Collier nor any of his predecessors had ever been convinced that the Admiralty had assigned the Squadron enough ships or the personnel to fill them. The problem of ships had been somewhat addressed with the changes in the use of tenders; the problem of personnel had been mitigated by Kroomen, a development the recent epidemic had only sped up further. Since the Kru appeared to be at least partially resistant to some of the native illnesses found onshore, Collier was neither the first nor the last captain to near exclusively send Kroomen to do land work that was significantly more likely to kill a non-indigenous sailor. Kroomen did many of the "dirty" jobs of a ship and were also excellent sailors: they could interpret in some situations, they could swim or dive should the need arise, they could warn of potential hazards in the shallower waters near the shore, they knew the best ways to prepare the local foods that supplemented items the Victualling Board could not feasibly send from England, they often had other skills that were invaluable to shipboard life—in short, the WAS could not have functioned as well as it did, if at all, without the Kroomen who served aboard each ship. Collier knew it, and to his enduring credit, he did his best to make sure the distant Admiralty knew it, too. Via letter, the commodore had first asked that the Kru be given full food rations, as they then received only two-thirds of what a Royal Navy sailor was issued for both food and alcohol. (He left the rum ration untouched due to the Kru propensity to sell their share to their boozier British crewmates.) After the Admiralty relented, Collier then campaigned relentlessly for genuinely equitable pay for his Kru sailors. And he made a little headway here, too. The Admiralty relented and agreed to ask the Treasurer of the Navy for suggestions on how it might address the problem.

The commodore had other personnel issues to contend with. In the fall of 1829, with the Squadron still reeling from the echoes of the epidemic, there was a shortage of midshipmen—a real one, not like Owen's self-generated lieutenant problem—and Collier requested that the Admiralty be kind enough to send him more, as expeditiously as possible. The shortage was probably the result of the dynamic duo of death and promotion, but the practical result was that Collier was running low on prize masters, the sailors in charge of leading prize crews on their journey back to Freetown. Often the job was assigned to midshipmen, which worked out well for everyone—usually a ship could spare one, and since mids were on the commissioned-officer track, it provided them the opportunity to develop and demonstrate their command skills, and their captains an opportunity to evaluate them before recommending promotion. The use of tenders had already spread the officer corps on the coast thin, and the need for prize crews spread it still thinner, but on this issue the Admiralty was firm. Despite never having set foot or sail on the coast of Africa to see the problem for itself, the members of the Admiralty told Collier to make do—the West Africa Squadron's complement was sufficient, and on that the Admiralty could not be moved.

Rarely moved, at any rate. The Admiralty had no problem with sending smugglers who'd been caught and prosecuted to the Squadron to repay their debt to society and serve out their time doing something useful. Back in the eighteenth century, Parliament had approved naval acts that stipulated that magistrates could, as a sentencing option, ship anyone convicted of a crime (including vagrancy) to the navy. Since the Admiralty was not in the habit of letting criminals on its ships, most of these men were rejected out of hand. Two groups usually weren't: debtors owing less than £20, who could choose for themselves between debtor's prison and the Royal Navy; and smugglers. In the first instance, small-time debt was a pretty benign crime—these men hadn't exactly gone on a wild crime spree, they were just broke—so, especially during the war years when the need for sailors had been so great that the government resorted to legalized kidnapping off the street, petty debtors were in large part accepted into the navy as their skills and abilities warranted. Smugglers—who were criminals, sure, but their crime was not so much outright theft as buying a thing in one place and contriving to sell it in another without paying any applicable tax—weren't viewed as equally harmless, but tended to have the skill set the Admiralty was looking for. In England, its being an island and all, smuggling was a felony, yes, but also primarily accomplished by way of the sea, meaning that most smugglers knew their way around a boat. Collier had had several ex-smugglers on board the *Sybille*, and he, in turn, put at least two of them on the *Black Joke*, fifty-year-old William Fielder of Portsea and eighteen-year-old Thomas Atkinson of Liverpool. One wonders if the commodore had in mind their illicit experience with vessels smaller than a frigate, but whatever the reason, the ex-smugglers had been model sailors, giving him no reason to doubt them, and in his own words had "conducted themselves with the greatest gallantry." Due to their sentences, however, none of these men was allowed to return home without permission, and Collier, as their commanding officer, felt they merited reprieve. He went so far as to add that he would consider it a personal favor from the Admiralty if they'd be allowed to come home with the *Sybille* when it finished its tour—strong words in a system of patronage in which favors were currency. But Collier made the request at the beginning of the summer, before yellow fever claimed so many and drew the focus of all and sundry—neither Fielder nor Atkinson would ever see England again.

All in all, 1829 was a year of a multitude of frustrations for the commodore—even setting aside the horror of the epidemic and the resurgence of the slave trade in its aftermath—but only one of them seemed to send Collier into a genuine rage. That May, just as *Sybille* and *Black Joke* were arriving in Freetown's harbor to a pestilential welcome, Collier became aware of a letter from Judge Jackson of the British Mixed Commission to the Admiralty. In it, Jackson accused ships of the Squadron of plundering prizes before they reached the Mixed Commission and could have their total value officially tabulated for appropriate redistribution. By way of example, Jackson pointed the finger directly at Commander William Turner. Apparently even the memory of Turner—who'd been back in England for some six months by now—had stuck in someone's craw, and Judge Jackson had heard it from the Mixed Commission's registrar (record keeper), who heard it from "elsewhere," that Turner, while in command of *Black Joke*, had plundered an unnamed prize ship. Citing only this thirdhand rumor, Jackson passive-aggressively implicated the entire Squadron, claiming that he had "some reason to believe that the practice complained of [plundering prizes] is of too frequent occurrence." To remedy the issue, the judge suggested the Admiralty require that Squadron ships perform a complete survey and inventory of all prize ships at the instant of capture. And then, Jackson had promptly gotten sick—the sixth epidemic case in Freetown—and gone back to England on June 8.

To say Collier about lost it is putting it mildly—he was probably closer to apoplectic, and for several good reasons. Any such accusation implicated not just the Squadron, but its leadership; to accuse the WAS of malfeasance was to accuse its commodore of being either incompetent, ineffectual, or complicit. That it was a judge of the Mixed Commission passing nothing so much as malicious gossip up the chain of command was even more infuriating, because there certainly *were* prize ships being plundered, and unlike Judge Jackson's nebulous thirdhand rumor of Turner's alleged wrongdoing, the commodore had seen it happen in real time. He could name names.

Though the yellow fever epidemic of 1829 had wreaked as much havoc on the operations of the Mixed Commission as it had on the West Africa Squadron—three members had to be replaced due to death or sick leave, and a single Brazilian judge was the only non-British commissioner in Freetown—every prize ship that was brought in for judgment was nonetheless processed the same way in a routine that had been established since the first days of the Mixed Commission of Sierra Leone, which, alongside its opposite numbers in Brazil, Cuba, and Surinam, came into being in 1819. Once a prize sailed into the harbor, the responsibility for both the ship and any enslaved on board shifted from the prize crew—and by extension, the Squadron ship whence they came—to the marshal of the court, who was essentially the bailiff of the Mixed Commission. If present, the officer who'd captured the ship (up to this time either Turner or Downes, in the *Black Joke*'s case) then provided an affidavit to the registrar of the court, the secretary/record keeper to the Mixed Commission; otherwise, the officer leading the prize crew did it. Said officer then passed on all papers found on the prize as well as a declaration made at the time of the capture as to where the prize had been found, when it had been searched, the condition of the ship at that time, and the number of enslaved on board, plus a declaration of how many had been lost on the journey to Freetown. If present, "interested parties"—usually the captain or perhaps agents of the owner—were then called to present evidence of why the prize should not be condemned, after which the registrar, using a preset list of questions, would examine all relevant witnesses (usually the available crew of the alleged slaver, at the least). Once all of this material had been compiled, it was given to the proctors (attorneys) who would represent the two opposing claims in argument before two judges of the Mixed Commission.

The Mixed Commission operated from an assumption of guilt on the part of the accused slaver, but neither the lawyers nor the judges were required to have previous legal experience. Alongside each judge, a commissioner of arbitration was also appointed to represent each nation, creating a senior/junior partnership for each country represented on the Mixed Commission bench. If the judges couldn't agree on a ruling, they would flip a coin to determine which of their commissioners of arbitration should join the panel (thus creating a majority decision), meaning that the guilt or innocence of a prize could easily come down to a coin toss. (This outcome was most prevalent at commissions actually fielding a multinational slate of judges and arbitrators, as representatives from the same place tended to agree with each other.) Sentencing was meant to occur in twenty days, though only the Mixed Commission in Freetown (as opposed to those in Havana and Rio) regularly met this deadline, probably because judges in Sierra Leone tended to be uniformly British while those of the other two courts were genuinely "mixed," and at all the Mixed Commissions the majority of disputes between commissioners over the sentencing fell along the lines of nationality. British judges, inclined to agree with one another, could render decisions faster. If a prize was acquitted, the vessel and anything on it—including the enslaved—were immediately returned to the owner or his agent, who could make a claim for damages resulting from the cost of the suit and any losses sustained while the ship had been detained, whether from the initial capture or the subsequent journey to Freetown. The registrar and a third party, usually a "respectable merchant" or perhaps two, would then go on board to establish the liability of the Squadron ship, as 95 percent of all captured vessels tried by the Mixed Commissions were presented by the Royal Navy. This sum was to be paid back in a year or less by the captain who was legally responsible for the capture—only in the event of default by the captor did the cost of amends revert to the government (which Britain, at least, refused to pay if the ship had clearly been a slave trader, regardless of the adjudged illegality of the seizure).

Conversely, if a ship was condemned, its contents were disposed of systematically, and it was put up for public auction, where it could usually be purchased for a song by just about anybody. The monies from the auction, ranging from £100 to £5,000, were then split by the two governments being represented in the adjudication as a cover for the costs of maintaining the procedures of the Mixed Commission, including everything from the cost of the furniture in the courthouse to the auctioneer who'd sold the condemned vessel, and beyond. (In Britain's case, it was a percentage of these funds that made up the prize money for salvage.) Any enslaved person thereon would be "freed" to the Liberated African Department for registration, to be followed by a very limited set of options for future employment (some of which bore more than a passing resemblance to slavery).

From the moment a prize ship came into port to the instant it was either returned to its previous owner or presented to a new one, it remained in the custody of the marshal of the court. Collier, as the senior officer of the *Sybille*, had been called upon to give more than one affidavit, and as someone who had reason to be in Freetown often, he had seen this entire process play out many times. He knew, without a doubt, that plundering was being done, and that the fault lay entirely with the marshal of the court and his men, who, to escape detection, targeted only the condemned vessels, ships the Mixed Commission had ruled to be slave traders, and therefore not subject to an assessment of liability by the registrar. Collier had seen the marshal's men in the very act, with his own two eyes, on board one of the *Sybille*'s condemned prizes. In the present situation, it begged the question, who'd proffered Turner—one of the commodore's best officers, and conveniently not present to defend himself—as an alternative culprit?

For Collier's money, it had been some embittered Brazilian slave-ship captain, and Collier told the Admiralty, in no uncertain terms, what the word of such a man should be worth against the reputation of an officer so well regarded and promising, and on such little evidence. (Other possibilities might include the master himself, looking to deflect attention, or perhaps even Turner's old adversary Savage, who was the agent to a Brazilian slaver, and perhaps looking to return the favor of making trouble.) The commodore, though outraged on behalf of the honor of the entire Squadron, was protective of those who served under him and must have been concerned about how rank hearsay such as this—even unsubstantiated and, to Collier's mind, clearly fictitious—might impact Turner's future. Unlike, say, Lieutenant Butterfield, whose father was an admiral who would serve in the navy for sixty-one years, or Lieutenant Le Hardy, whose family had produced not one but three admirals and innumerable officers while enjoying centuries of prominence in Jersey, Commander Turner was the son of a merchant, and he had no familial naval connections to speak of, not even a brother in the service somewhere. Turner was extremely popular, maybe even popular enough that a court-martial against him would disgruntle many of those who'd served with him or knew him by reputation, but there was no guarantee that a good reputation alone, even one universally agreed upon, would be enough to protect him.

No charges were ever brought against Turner, so Collier's letter must've been convincing—perhaps too convincing, at least when it came to evidence that plundering was a real problem. The Admiralty, though officially finding no fault worth pursuing in either the Freetown Mixed Commission or the West Africa Squadron, did decide to nonetheless implement the former's suggestion requiring immediate inventory of prize ships, much to the commodore's chagrin. Collier tried to tell them, repeatedly, that such a policy wasn't feasible—the prize crew had a hard enough time creating an accurate count of the enslaved at the moment of capture, much less tallying every barrel of food and spare sail—but the Admiralty, as usual, wasn't all that interested in practical realities of service on the coast. Such a rule would make it difficult for anyone, in either the commission or the Squadron, to plunder, and that was good enough for the men who made Royal Navy policy. The year before, Collier had attempted to get an increase in the Squadron's allotment of weatherproofing hammock paint to account for the increased deterioration precipitated by the tropical climate, but the Navy Board hadn't thought dry bedding was worth worrying about, either. Again and again, the higher-ups in London had demonstrated how out of touch they were with the men who executed their will, who lived and died under their policies, and this new impracticality would be no exception. As Collier predicted, the rule requiring inventory was as hated, among the men of the WAS, as Commander Turner had been liked. While no doubt some sailors were skimming—not to cast aspersions, but by way of example, Lieutenant Harvey, while in command of Collier's other tenders, had at least two prizes that appeared to the Mixed Commission to have been looted in some fashion, and no one publicly accused him of anything—this change and other decisions like it made it evident that the distance the Admiralty had from the daily practicalities and privations of life in the WAS wasn't measured solely in miles.

Now, if those in administrative positions had *really* wanted to make sure no one sought any extracurricular cash, they probably shouldn't have again reduced the head money for liberated Africans from £10 per head to £5 the next year—not, perhaps, the most intuitive theft-prevention method. Yet the policy makers back in England continued their trend toward increasingly granular and unpopular rules that negatively impacted the lives and attitudes of men in the service. The expectations of bureaucracy existed, in many ways, in opposition to the realities of service in the WAS. But only so much could be done about it, particularly for the average sailor, so with much grumbling, life on the coast continued.

After spending all of summer and early fall of 1829 recovering from the devastating outbreak, the *Black Joke* was finally considered ready to recommence active cruising by October of 1829. Downes, who'd been near death, had been sent home with Collier's gratitude and yet another impressive gift, this time a beautiful oak-and-silver wine cooler engraved with "a tribute of admiration and respect from Commodore Collier to Lieut. Henry Downes, for his gallant conduct when in command of H.M. tender BLACK JOKE."

Since then, the tender had gotten a new captain, Lieutenant Edward Iggulden Parrey, the first of the *Black Joke*'s captains to come from a ship that wasn't *Sybille*. Parrey had been on the *Primrose* before his transfer to the tender and had acquitted himself well, but his performance in the WAS was likely just part of the reason he was promoted to the *Black Joke*. Though he wouldn't serve on the *Black Joke* for more than a few short months, just as the Squadron

Wine cooler made from the timbers of the slaver *El Almirante* [...]
wooden base made from the timber of the Spanish warship *Bahama*
captured at Trafalgar [...] inscribed: "A TRIBUTE OF Admiration
and respect FROM COMMODORE COLLIER C.B.
To Lieutenant Henry Downes for his gallant conduct in command
OF H.M. TENDER BLACK JOKE" (© NMM).

transitioned to a new decade, Parrey's connection to Collier went far
deeper than perhaps that of any other man the commodore selected
for the job. Parrey, alone among the tender's captains, had actually
served under then-captain Collier back in 1819 on the *Liverpool*, the
very ship on which Collier had spent so much time incapacitating
pirates in the Persian Gulf. Then an acting lieutenant, Parrey had
been severely wounded during that action and it was on that ship
that he had his officer's commission confirmed.

Parrey wouldn't have to wait long to prove himself again to his
old captain, though it wouldn't be a tricky game of flags or a particularly impressive bout of gunnery that would distinguish him. It was

a rescue mission. On October 10, the *Black Joke* happened upon the Spanish slaver *Cristina* stranded on the bank of the Scarcies River. The slave trader had hit the bank when navigating the tricky exit from the river and was clearly in distress. Though Parrey first attempted what seemed like the most expedient solution—getting the *Cristina* off the bank and back into the safety of deeper water—the slaver couldn't be made seaworthy, and what might have been a boarding party rapidly escalated into a desperate attempt to save the Africans still trapped in the slaver's hold before they drowned, a pressing matter made more urgent by Parrey's discovery that the *Cristina* had begun filling with water almost as soon as it had struck land. Though not the type of glamorous action that had made the *Black Joke*'s fame, the rescue of the *Cristina* might have been one of the tender's most impressive feats. *Black Joke*, coordinating with an English merchant, the *Sappho*, which was also in the river, pulled hundreds of people from the water and salvaged what supplies it could; miraculously, not a single life was lost. Realizing that the *Cristina* was a lost cause and couldn't be recovered, and knowing that the *Black Joke* could not even begin to adequately feed and care for over three hundred enslaved people if Parrey took them on board—the ship didn't have the space, besides—he had no choice but to land the enslaved and the crew of the *Cristina* onshore. Parrey sent an urgent message to Freetown, blessedly nearby, begging immediate assistance.

Though "immediate" was a relative concept in 1829, Collier's agent in Freetown, Dougan—Kenneth Macaulay having died in the yellow fever epidemic that year, after twenty years living in Sierra Leone—did everything in his power to render aid, and three days later a rescue ship, the *Frederick*, made it to the Scarcies to embark the population of the *Cristina* along with a prize crew from *Black Joke* (led by Slade) and ferry them to Freetown. The two-day trip from the Scarcies to Freetown was far shorter than the average prize journey, but the losses from the *Cristina*, almost all of which occurred in just forty-eight hours, were astronomical. Even if every lifesaving policy that had been debated throughout the year had been implemented, it would have been difficult for warm clothing or medicine to quickly make up for what ailed too many; smallpox would accomplish much of what the sea had not. It's unclear whether the Africans had been ill before the accident or had gotten sick during the three days they had been onshore, but it would have been difficult to not notice that the enslaved of the *Cristina* were on average particularly young. For every hour it took to get to Freetown, the prize crew watched on helplessly as adults and children—and there were so many children—died. So soon after the deaths of many of their crewmates from yellow fever, the Black Jokes must've been uncomfortably reminded of how helpless they, too, were in the face of unmerciful death. All told, 116 of the Africans embarked to the *Cristina* never saw the harbor that purported to hold their liberation. Sixteen more died after they arrived enslaved, and of the 216 still alive, 75 were children. When colonial surgeon Boyle went on board to examine the survivors the next day, he found most of them to be infected with smallpox, and those who weren't were suffering with either "craw-craw" (a skin disease) or ophthalmia. Rather than take the infected into Freetown, the *Frederick* was sent immediately to the colonial hospital at Kissy.

And almost as quickly as he'd come, Parrey was gone. Within a few short months, the lieutenant received word from the commodore that the savvy Captain Griffenhoofe, who'd so ably steered the *Primrose* to its place just behind the *Black Joke* on the list of the Squadron's most successful ships, had died at Ascension. Though the sudden loss of a captain as efficient and effective as Griffenhoofe was awful in its own right, the cold reality was that the Squadron's efforts on the coast couldn't afford to lose a ship as capable as *Primrose* to questionable leadership. So Collier turned to someone he knew, someone he trusted, someone he'd trained—Parrey, his once and current lieutenant. Parrey was already familiar with the *Primrose*, having just come from being second-in-command under

Griffenhoofe to captain the *Black Joke*, making him the most logical choice. His short time on the *Black Joke* had been marked by misery, though not of Parrey's making. His appointment to the *Primrose* was shrouded by grief, but Parrey could do nothing about that, either. He could only continue to serve where he was needed. Even after so much death, life in the Squadron went on.

Register of Slaves natives of Africa Captured on board the said vessel by the Brig "Black Joke" a Tender of His Majesty's ship Sybille. Francis Augustus

| No. | Names | Sex | Age | Stature ft. in. | Description |
|---|---|---|---|---|---|
| 19,836 | Alahmoque | Man | 25 | 5 4 | Cuts all over |
| | Ashem | " | 32 | 5 6 | Cuts on face |
| | Alackah | " | 28 | 5 4 | Cuts on Forehead in temples |
| | Ayelay | " | 31 | 5 4 | No marks |
| 19,840 | Annofelay | " | 22 | 5 7 | Cuts on temples |
| | Maggen | " | 24 | 5 6 | Cuts on Face |
| | Siedy | " | 21 | 5 3 | Cuts all over |
| | Mahjeah | " | 20 | 5 5 | Cuts on Face |
| | Dangannah | " | 19 | 5 8 | No marks |
| 19,845 | Abbah | " | 20 | 5 5 | Do. |
| | Mahjai | " | 24 | 5 1 | Cuts on temples |
| | Kakutah | " | 27 | 5 . | No marks |
| | Asai | " | 20 | 5 5 | Cuts on Face |
| | Asagee | " | 25 | 5 4 | Cuts all over |
| 19,850 | Opuannah | " | 21 | 5 4 | Pitted small pox face |
| | Allotoh | " | 23 | 5 2 | |
| | Opuannee | " | 19 | 5 3 | No marks |
| | Omammay | " | 21 | 5 6 | |
| | Ahguamay | " | 28 | 5 1 | Cuts on temples and Cheeks |
| 19,855 | Saidoo | " | 19 | 5 6 | No marks |
| | Moopay | " | 18 | 5 2 | Cuts on temples |
| | Lahcolay | " | 21 | 5 4 | Cuts on face and a scar on right arm |
| | Nrkoo | " | 26 | 5 1 | No marks |
| | Warkonobee | " | 22 | 5 7 | Cuts all over |
| 19,860 | Olobo | " | 17 | 5 . | Cuts on face |
| | Malartobah | " | 22 | 5 6 | No marks |
| | Mammah | " | 20 | 5 1 | Cuts all over |
| | Abbah | " | 23 | 5 8 | Cuts on face |
| | Warkooday | " | 21 | 5 5 | Cuts all over |
| 19,865 | Abelah | " | 31 | 5 3 | Scored forehead and Cuts on back |
| | Monjay | " | 24 | 5 5 | No marks |
| 19,867 | Azramee | " | 34 | 5 5 | Cuts on breast |

Register, Cristina

247.

Augustus Collier CB Commander and Emancipated by decree of the
British and Spanish Court of Mixed Commission Established in this
Colony of Sierra Leone on the 27th day of November 1829. the said Brigantine
having on the day aforesaid been pronounced liable to confiscation and

| No. | Names | Sex | Age | Stature F. I. | Description |
|-----|-------|-----|-----|------|-------------|
| 19,866 | Mammah | Man | 22 | 5 6 | No marks |
| | Onogoo | " | 24 | 5 6 | Cuts above navel |
| 19,870 | Abbay | " | 20 | 5 6 | Cuts on face |
| | Lahjay | " | 20 | 5 7 | Do |
| | Acheboe | " | 25 | 5 4 | Cuts all over |
| | Dimochay | " | 23 | 5 5 | Cuts on temples |
| | Anamonee | " | 35 | 5 5 | No marks |
| 19,875 | Amoconay | " | 22 | 5 5 | Cuts on forehead and temples |
| | Affoe | " | 28 | 5 10 | Cuts on temples |
| | Alasallagee | " | 34 | 5 6 | Do |
| | Namsay | " | 27 | 5 3 | No marks |
| | Ayamchay | " | 18 | 5 5 | Cuts on forehead and temples |
| 19,880 | Abbo | " | 19 | 5 4 | |
| | Abay | " | 32 | 5 1 | |
| | Dangannah | " | 17 | 5 . | No marks |
| | Aleboley | " | 18 | 5 4 | |
| | Ebarkoo | " | 32 | 5 6 | |
| 19,885 | Numaday | " | 20 | 5 5 | |
| | Asafoogee | " | 16 | 4 11 | Cuts on face |
| | Ahgalay | " | 22 | 5 3 | |
| | Allahsalakay | " | 24 | 5 8 | |
| | Ahdagah | " | 16 | 5 . | |
| 19,890 | Annabee | " | 25 | 5 3 | No marks |
| | Inchee | " | 26 | 5 4 | Cuts on face |
| | Appah | " | 35 | 5 3 | Cuts all over |
| | Arbagoo | " | 18 | 5 4 | No marks |
| | Ahgasee | " | 22 | 4 10 | Cuts all over |
| 19,895 | Jamonoo | " | 21 | 5 3 | Do |
| | Allebro | " | 20 | 5 . | Cuts on forehead and temples |
| | Rotamlay | " | 26 | 5 4 | Cuts all over |
| | Afoe | " | 22 | 5 4 | Do |
| 19,899 | Alakolamee | " | 38 | 5 8 | Scored forehead and cut down belly |

# CHAPTER EIGHT

*Manzanares*

April 1830,

354 enslaved people

P arrey had proved to be an excellent captain, but by March of
1830, when he officially left the *Black Joke* to assume command
of *Primrose*, the tender was in the midst of a serious dry spell. The little
brig with the outsize reputation had had no actual captures since that
of the *Carolina* the previous March. Parrey's timely aid to the *Cristina*
didn't count because, despite its being an impressive feat, the Admiralty saw it was more of a rescue operation than a prize capture, even
though the Spanish ship was eventually condemned as a slaver, for
which *Black Joke* was awarded prize money. This lack of action since
being hit by fever eleven months earlier wasn't the only bad news for
the *Black Joke*. Death, which had already claimed so many, continued
to plague the Squadron, and Collier was now, well and truly, short on
officers. Between the official ships of the WAS and his own tenders,
the commodore currently had no one available to officially replace
Parrey; in the name of expediency Collier temporarily promoted the
*Black Joke*'s senior mate, William Coyde, to acting lieutenant and gave
him command. It's unclear how much Collier expected of the acting
lieutenant, who'd previously served ably in the East in Britain's First
Burmese War—a particularly bloody and expensive two-year conflict
that decimated the Burmese Empire and solidified Britain's hold on
India—but Coyde didn't shrink from his new role.

On April Fools' Day 1830—it's a very long-standing holiday—

the *Black Joke* came across the Spanish brigantine *Manzanares* off Gallinas. Things started out well enough. The two ships were evenly matched in both complement and armament, but the captain of the brigantine, Manuel Alcontara, wasn't interested in a fight, opting instead to make a run for the quickest current to Havana. The *Black Joke* was beginning to show some of the wear of its two years of continual and vigorous service to the Royal Navy, but it was still more than a match for anything sailing; after a twelve-hour chase, Coyde had his prize. Or almost had it. Alcontara struck his colors and surrendered to boarding, and Coyde sent over a crew that included the *Black Joke's* resident medical officer, Lane, assistant surgeon to the *Sybille*, presumably in case any enslaved on board needed immediate care. Subsequent accounts attest to how extraordinarily crowded the *Manzanares* was, and prize-crew boardings could be rather chaotic—subduing the crew, releasing the enslaved from the hold, searching the ship, documenting everything, counting anything that wasn't nailed down; it was a lot. They could be particularly confusing for the enslaved, a sudden cacophony of English, and in this case Spanish, and perhaps snippets of whatever native African tongues any of the Black Jokes had picked up during their time in the service, all flying across the deck as the prize crew went about its standard procedures, sometimes with violence, depending on the disposition and sympathies of the sailors. But the Africans on the *Manzanares*, though unaware of who had boarded their disgusting prison—as it turned out, the *Manzanares* had been very busy, and besides being a slaver, was wanted by the US Navy for piratical activity committed on this very voyage, so it could have been just about anyone—were not in the least confused about their captivity or their chances of surviving the horrors of the Middle Passage and whatever hell waited on the other side. On the contrary, they had a plan. And at the moment of peak chaos, and with an unseen signal, they rose up and attempted to free themselves.

Shipboard slave revolts were not actually all that uncommon in the Atlantic slave trade; as the *Henriqueta*, the *Black Joke* itself had had one on its third voyage. They were infrequently successful and often bloody—in *Henriqueta's* case, upward of a fourth of the enslaved may have died in the uprising—but that does not mean that the Africans who'd been forcibly removed from the continent passively accepted their fate. Slavers took precautions against revolts, but regularly enough, some or all of the enslaved on a vessel tried anyway. That being said, revolts against WAS prize crews were rare. Because he was the assistant surgeon, Lane might well have been the British officer nearest to the enslaved—and the burgeoning revolt—but whatever the reason, he went down first. At the sight of their shipmate being overtaken, the other Black Jokes on board the *Manzanares* jumped into what was fast becoming an all-out melee. The prize crew, unlike the Africans, were armed with well-honed swords and well drilled with them; they'd been prepared to face resistance from the crew of the *Manzanares*, not the human cargo. The record is silent on what, precisely, happened next, but when the Spanish brigantine sailed into Freetown four days later, the result was obvious. The revolt had surely been quelled, and violently. Boyle, acting as surgeon to the court, reported the results of his examination of the prize:

> [That] amongst the slaves were a great many sabre wounds, and 3 amputated stumps, arising from the circumstance of their having mutinied; that there were about 40 cases of diarrhœa, and a few of purulent ophthalmia; and the "Manzanares," from her crowded state, was of necessity in an unclean and unhealthy condition.

Additionally, five of the Africans had died on the passage to Freetown, though whether from disease or wounds sustained in seeking their freedom on their own terms is unclear, and another died in Freetown before the *Manzanares* was condemned. Lane was the only person from the *Black Joke* seriously wounded, but he survived. Boyle recommended the soon-to-be-"liberated" Africans be landed as soon as possible, which they were, but after the slaver was condemned, there was some consternation about what to do with them. Normally, after having been registered at the Liberated African Department, the "free" Africans would be distributed at the discretion of the lieutenant governor of Sierra Leone. Perhaps fearing reprisals, the colonial administration in Freetown likely had no interest in maintaining a population of Africans that was able to organize and willing to be militant with it. By the thirteenth, with the help of Dougan, a plan had been reached to distribute the liberated Africans of the *Manzanares* in the "mountain villages" of Sierra Leone, the administration thereby washing its hands of the entire situation. That the vast majority of the Africans in question were, in all likelihood, not from this region was no impediment, as far as the colonial administration was concerned. It seems as if as long as the Africans were far enough away that the British could sleep soundly at night, that was good enough. So the *Black Joke* successfully secured its first prize of the new decade. Whether Collier, upon learning of the revolt, considered this a massive bungle or the natural result of having to make do in a bad situation is unknown. But Coyde would not retain the captaincy.

Collier might not have thought much of the situation at all; he was extremely preoccupied that April. At a reconnoiter with *Black Joke* back in January, a recent WAS addition, *Tyne*, passed by, and the commodore added an apparently healthy young sailor, a boy, from it to *Sybille's* crew. If this sounds familiar, it should, because by the end of the month, virulent yellow fever had broken out on the *Sybille* for the second time in less than a year. By February it had spread rapidly, resulting in the "most dreadful havoc among all classes on board," and the death of the beloved master, Tom Collins. Dealing with the fever again so soon after losing so many the previous summer was a huge blow to morale, which had always been high on the frigate, and many sailors became convinced that, no matter what anyone said, the malady had to be communicable from person to person. McKinnel, still the *Sybille's* surgeon, became exasperated with all of the talk of contagion, probably because fears that touching the sick made one sick would upend the commodore's commitment to cleanliness, which really would make everyone sick, and he asked his assistant, McKechnie, to collect a pint of the symptomatic black vomit from the next violently ill sailor. That in hand, and his curious assistant trailing behind, McKinnel took a stroll up to the half deck of the frigate, where the entire crew would have been at their dinner. As an incredulous McKechnie looked on:

*[McKinnel] called [Lieutenant Green] over, and filling a glassful of the black vomit, asked him if he would like to have some of it; being answered in the negative, he then said, "Very well, here is your health, Green," and drank it off. Dr. McKinnel immediately afterward went to the quarter-deck, and walked until two o'clock to prevent its being supposed that he had resorted to any means of counteracting its effects [. . .] It is almost unnecessary to add that it did not impair his appetite for dinner, nor did he suffer any inconvenience from it afterwards.*

To add to the visual, it was a wineglass.

After such a demonstration, it's hard to imagine the good surgeon had any more problems getting the decks clean. Subsequently, the commodore was effusive in his praise for McKinnel's medical care, stating, "The unremitting attention of Dr McKinnel to the sick surpassed anything I had ever experienced." It was a compliment surely earned.

Collier's men were still dying, though, and he tried what had worked the previous August and headed back to St. Helena; by the time he arrived in mid-March, eighty-seven men on the *Sybille* had come down with the fever and twenty-six were dead. But far from having a restorative effect, the disease seemed to gain traction, and another wave of yellow fever felled six more men from another twenty-two cases. Commodore Collier had had about enough—enough of dying, enough of sickness, enough of attempting to change the world while having to fight for scraps of support from his superiors. Just enough. Though at first the Admiralty had floated the idea of keeping the *Sybille* on the coast until 1831, the commodore had shot it down in no uncertain terms, as he feared the frigate would not hold out much longer. For once, the Admiralty reacted sympathetically and replied that Collier should use his best judgment as to when it was time to go. And it was time to go.

Even before leaving for St. Helena, Collier had more than an inkling that he might not be coming back to the coast. To that end,
he sent letters to the captain of the *Atholl*, Gordon, directing him to
meet the commodore in Ascension and, there, transfer command
of the WAS. Collier dispatched a schooner from St. Helena's small
fleet, also named *St. Helena*, but if anyone knew things on the coast
were rarely that simple, it was this commodore, who had spent three
years trying to make sense of incomprehensible orders while making
progress on an improbable mission. So he probably was resigned, but
not entirely surprised, when news came back that, before the schooner had ever reached Gordon and the *Atholl*, it had been set upon
by the aptly named pirate ship *Desperado*, whose crew, in typical pirate fashion, killed several, plundered the damaged ship for anything
worth stealing, and made off with Collier's letters. But he'd selected
Captain Gordon as his successor on the coast for a reason, no matter
how temporary the appointment. Gordon had also heard about the
schooner's unfortunate encounter with the *Desperado*, and suspecting

Shipping off Saint Helena (© NMM).

what might be afoot, the captain took the initiative. He was already in the company of *Primrose* and *Black Joke*, the latter now laboring and desperately in need of a refit, so much so that Gordon was afraid to let the tender cruise alone. Making an executive decision, the captain sent both ships together to find the *Desperado* and took the *Atholl* to Ascension, hoping to find Collier there, since surely if the commodore was truly headed back to England, he would first need to resupply.

The two men did find each other at Ascension. There, Commodore Collier at last laid down the burden of command, and Gordon shouldered it. An officer of long experience, it wouldn't be the first burden born of tragedy Alexander Gordon, the forty-nine-year-old son of a well-respected and extensive extended Scottish family, took on. Both of his brothers had already died well over a decade previous, one in action in Buenos Aires and the other of yellow fever while serving in Barbados. As for Francis Augustus Collier, the old commodore could claim responsibility for the liberation of several thousand enslaved Africans. Over his three years of leading the fight for suppression of the slave trade on the West African coast, he'd finished the reimagining of the West Africa Squadron initiated by Bullen. Collier was ready for a rest. And rest was the last thing on Gordon's mind. His appointment as acting commodore was only temporary—Collier chose his interim successor, and the post would be filled permanently by the Admiralty—but that didn't mean there wasn't plenty to do. With the acting title, Captain Gordon and the *Atholl* inherited the *Black Joke* as a tender, as the *Sybille*, which would be returning to England with Collier, would no longer need it. Though Gordon wasted no time in ordering a refit for the ship and would soon show himself to be an able interim commander, a fierce advocate for the sailors of the Squadron generally—and for the crew of the *Black Joke* specifically—had left the coast in the person of Commodore Collier. Whether his Admiralty-appointed permanent replacement would be as committed to his men was anyone's guess. No one could have known that Collier's departure would mark the beginning of the end of the era of the *Black Joke*.

## Spanish Brigantine "Manzanares":—

Register of Slaves, natives of Africa, Captured on board the said Vessel by His Majesty's Brig "Black Joke"; Tender of His Britannic Majesty's Ship

| No. | Names | Sex | Age | Stature ft. in. | | Description |
|-----|-------|-----|-----|----|----|-------------|
| 20,886 | Tom Caulker | Man | 25 | 5 | 3 | Cuts on Temples / a son of Chas. Caulker, sold by Isaac Gibson, a Sierraleone man, at Salinas.— |
| | Battay | „ | 30 | 5 | 5 | Tattoed on the body |
| | Yonee | „ | 24 | 5 | 9 | No marks |
| | Fenah | „ | 27 | 5 | 0 | D° |
| 20,890 | Doworro | „ | 30 | 5 | 4 | Pitted small pox face |
| | Yaccandoo | „ | 28 | 5 | 6 | No marks |
| | Prah | „ | 20 | 4 | 11 | D° |
| | Bannah | „ | 18 | 4 | 10 | Tattoed on the back |
| | Breah | „ | 22 | 5 | 7 | D° |
| 20,895 | Kong | „ | 28 | 5 | 4 | O. on back left shoulder |
| | Barrah | „ | 33 | 5 | 9 | D° right D° |
| | Barrah | „ | 26 | 5 | 8 | Tattoed all over body |
| | Sarrah | „ | 24 | 5 | 3 | D° on the belly |
| | Momodoo | „ | 22 | 5 | 6 | No marks |
| 20,900 | Fonee | „ | 26 | 5 | 7 | D° |
| | Doworro | „ | 20 | 5 | 6 | D° |
| | Barrah | „ | 19 | 5 | 3 | Tattoed on the back |
| | Roworro | „ | 25 | 5 | 5 | Scar on right arm |
| | Van | „ | 31 | 5 | 2 | No marks |
| 20,905 | Dowah | „ | 30 | 5 | 10 | Tattoed all over body |
| | Dammah | „ | 22 | 5 | 8 | O. on back right shoulder |
| | Sanbay | „ | 20 | 5 | 8 | No marks |
| | Fannah | „ | 34 | 5 | 7 | Pitted small pox face |
| | Doorey | „ | 29 | 5 | 2 | O. on back right shoulder |
| 20,910 | Kanday | „ | 24 | 5 | 2 | Tattoed all over body |
| | Barrah | „ | 24 | 5 | 8 | D° D° |
| | Wonee | „ | 20 | 5 | 4 | No marks |
| | Bangay | „ | 27 | 5 | 7 | O. on back left shoulder |
| | Bannah | „ | 18 | 5 | 0 | No marks |
| 20,915 | Doworro | „ | 28 | 4 | 11 | D° |
| | Bannah | „ | 25 | 5 | 5 | D° |
| 20,917 | Doorey | „ | 26 | 5 | 8 | Tattoed all over body |

Register, Manzanares

Esquire,

'Sybille' Francis Augustus Collier, CB. Commander, and Emancipates by
Decree of the British and Spanish Court of Mixed Commission, Established in
this Colony of Sierra Leone, on the 11th day of May 1830. The said Brigantine
having on the day aforesaid been pronounced liable to confiscation and accordingly
condemned.

| No. | Names | Sex | Age | Stature ft. in. | Description |
|---|---|---|---|---|---|
| 20,918 | Foo | Man | 29 | 5 4 | Pitted small pox face |
| | Wyaa | , | 32 | 5 5 | Tattoed all over body |
| 20,920 | Harray | , | 28 | 5 5 | Pitted small pox face |
| | Sammah | , | 26 | 5 3 | No marks |
| | Kammo | , | 24 | 5 3 | Do. |
| | Dowee | , | 27 | 5 2 | Tattoed all over the body |
| | Harday | , | 18 | 4 11 | O. on back right shoulder |
| 20,925 | Doray | , | 22 | 5 5 | Do.          Do. |
| | Katoo | , | 26 | 5 6 | Do.          Do. |
| | Torray | , | 19 | 5 1 | No marks |
| | Bombo | , | 27 | 5 4 | Do. |
| | Doguah | , | 17 | 5 . | D. on back right shoulder |
| 20,930 | Sarey | , | 21 | 5 5 | O. on back left Do. |
| | Fourree | , | 24 | 5 4 | D.   .   right Do. |
| | Tingua | , | 26 | 5 2 | ⎫ |
| | Dawrray | , | 20 | 5 5 | ⎪ |
| | Dambey | , | 21 | 5 4 | ⎬ No marks |
| 20,935 | Bokoh | , | 23 | 5 7 | ⎪ |
| | Nyaguay | , | 19 | 5 1 | ⎭ |
| | Norah | , | 25 | 5 2 | Tattoed all over the body |
| | Poguah | , | 26 | 5 6 | Do. on face & Do. |
| | Yanguah | , | 22 | 5 2 | Do. all over  Do. |
| 20,940 | Wyah | , | 20 | 5 3 | No marks |
| | Mommoh | , | 34 | 5 3 | Pitted small pox face |
| | Dorah | , | 31 | 5 8 | Tattoed all over |
| | Karay | , | 23 | 5 2 | No marks |
| | Poguah | , | 24 | 5 . | Tattoed all over body |
| 20,945 | Gooboo | , | 24 | 5 6 | Do.       Do. |
| | Kotoo | , | 24 | 5 6 | O. on back left shoulder |
| | Nyah | , | 29 | 5 4 | Tattoed all over body |
| | Vammah | , | 19 | 5 3 | No marks |
| 20,949 | Fangah | , | 30 | 5 3 | D. |

# CHAPTER NINE

*Dos Amigos*
November 1830,
563 enslaved people

The long-overdue refit of *Black Joke* began on June 14, 1830, when acting commodore Alexander Gordon arrived at Principe with the requisite materials from Fernando Pó. During Captain Owen's tenure as administrator of the Fernando Pó settlement, he'd built up a small but effective lumber industry, from which residents produced palm-oil casks for the coast and ships' masts for England and refit merchant ships besides. But the Fernando Pó settlement was also on its way out. Owen, for all his distractions and insubordinations, had been a capable steward of the settlement itself: he'd formed positive relationships with the Bubi, the resident tribe of Fernando Pó, from whom he purchased (rather than coerced or outright stole) the land for the site of the British base; cleared roads and built a town at Clarence Cove that included a hospital and a school for the children of the formerly enslaved; and, once a British style of infrastructure was established, promptly turned over the daily administration of the community to a council staffed by liberated Africans. Though his religious fervor did prompt him to compel everyone, Bubi included, to attend a church every Sunday at which Owen preached the sermons, it seems that Owen, while still incredibly paternalistic, was not quite as deeply wedded to the notion of African inferiority, inherent or otherwise, when compared to many others engaged in either the suppression effort or betimes the colonial government of

Sierra Leone (and for the rest of his life he remained confirmed in his absolute commitment to abolition).

However, for all the respect Owen had seemingly shown to the African residents of Fernando Pó—which, though perhaps exceptional for his era, was nonetheless limited and at the service of British colonialism, no matter how comparatively benevolently conceived—he could not muster much of the same for the English-men who commanded him. Owen was happy to give orders, but his disinclination toward taking them had made him enemies from Sierra Leone all the way back to London. The Admiralty had been the only division (both of the government generally and the suppression effort specifically) openly inclined in favor of moving the base of pre-ventive efforts to Fernando Pó, but Owen's disregard for its orders and input—namely, that perhaps he should do his actual job and leave the patrolling for slavers to the West Africa Squadron—had drained away much of that support. It probably didn't help that the British members of the Mixed Commission had escalated from sim-ply not wanting to move to Fernando Pó to running a smear cam-paign against its superintendent, one underwritten by the wealthier residents of Freetown. (At least some opposition from the colonial Sierra Leoneans was almost certainly due to Owen's habit at Fer-nando Pó of treating Africans as if they were capable of running not just their own lives, but maybe even a whole town.) Letters were sent back to England claiming that Owen was continuing to hold Afri-cans in bondage and asserting that the island was, far from Owen's glowing reports, a wasteland of disease where dead bodies were bur-ied at night to hide the truth of the situation.

Both accusations were patently false—and a sure irony coming from anyone at Freetown, given not just the town's own reputation for disease but the "apprenticeship" system utilized in the Liberated African Department, which was not half as liberatory as the name advertised. As one officer succinctly put it, the "Clarence Settlement [on Fernando Pó] is most unhealthy. The only question is, [w]hether it be more so than any other of our settlements on the western coast of Africa? It is, to say the least of it, equally as fatal as Sierra Leone, and that is saying a great deal." However, the charges did plant the seed of doubt in ground made fertile by Owen's own behavior. The Foreign Office was angry at him, too, given his penchant for attacking a slaver first and asking questions later, precipitating all sorts of diplomatic nightmares back in England; it also wasn't sold on the concept of Fernando Pó, since Spain had a viable claim to the island. Still, loath to turn its back on someone who was clearly having success as an administrator, regardless of what disgruntled Freetown residents might claim, the Colonial Office tried to offer Owen a permanent post if he would resign from the Royal Navy, thereby taking him off the Admiralty's hands and putting him out of the Foreign Office's mind, while utilizing the full extent of the captain's talents to keep the base viable in the face of ever-mounting opposition. Captain Owen was shocked. It may not have been his assignment, but his self-manufactured sideline uniquely satisfied both his opposition to slavery and his desire to enrich himself, and the captain hated to give up on his "honest and profitable command" in favor of a (far less remunerative) "petty superintendancy." In what one imagines may have been a fit of pique, Owen replied by asking to be relieved as administrator of Fernando Pó immediately. If he was surprised that he was at once taken up on the offer, he shouldn't have been. The captain was summarily replaced with Colonel Edward Nicholls, who'd been serving as the governor of Ascension.

And then the epidemic of 1829 happened. The primary argument in favor of gradually shifting the base of the suppression effort from Freetown to Fernando Pó had been the island's geographical advantages. As previously noted, it was well situated to a number of active slaving ports, and taking prize ships to Fernando Pó, rather than Sierra Leone (north in the West Africa Squadron's assigned territory), would have been easier for the enslaved and the prize crews alike. But up until 1829, it was also thought to be *healthier*. Sierra Leone had for years had a terrible reputation for illness. Captain Yeo had called it "the most unfit, and worst situation on the

whole coast" for both its remove from the main action of slave traders and its prevalence of disease, and nothing much had changed in
the intervening decade to alter that assessment in the minds of those
charged with administering the suppression effort. In a time when
the "climate" could be perceived as unhealthy, the second yellow fever
epidemic and the astronomical losses on Fernando Pó that followed
(the Bubi were nearly wiped out) were evidence that, at least in one
extremely key aspect—and unlike, say, St. Helena, where Collier
had run to escape the disease both times—Fernando Pó was no better than Freetown. (It wasn't just this instance, either; recall that at
the outset of the first outbreak, the *Eden* had had two different contagious diseases aboard, and the ulcerous one, the crew had insisted,
had been caught while anchored at the settlement.) This time, Nicholls was struck with the fever, and though he would survive, months
of resulting delirium left him incapable of performing his duties as
administrator of Fernando Pó, which promptly collapsed into disorder and disrepair in the wake of so much death and the resulting
near-complete lack of oversight.

Owen's tribulations with the epidemic and the *Eden* had meant
that he was away from the island for a large swath of 1829, and when
he finally returned to the town he'd built from the ground up, the
conditions appalled him so much that he got into an epic alterca-
tion with Nicholls over whose fault all of this was. That encounter—
in which Colonel Nicholls literally fled from a chasing Captain
Owen and barred himself inside his house and, when the captain
attempted to break in, tried to shoot him—didn't settle anything.
Owen was absolutely not going to allow himself to get blamed for
this turn of events when he'd already been attacked for things that
*hadn't* happened, so he held a show-trial-style court of inquiry that
found Nicholls to be "the cause of the almost total ruin of the settlement," then packed up any surviving laborers from Sierra Leone, all
the stores he could fit, and the entirety of the settlement's records,
and hied off to service on the South America Station.

So when acting commodore Gordon had shown up in Clarence

Cove to gather the supplies needed for *Black Joke* to become seaworthy again, it was not the thriving settlement with the complicated administrator of Gordon's predecessor's day. Collier's old nemesis Owen was gone, the town was a shadow of itself, and everyone was pretty much just waiting for official notice from England of what they already knew to be true—Fernando Pó was toast. The island still had plenty of lumber, though, and Gordon gathered some up for what was, at least for a little while, the *Atholl*'s new tender, and thus his responsibility. At Principe, Gordon met up with acting commander Parrey, still captaining *Primrose*, who'd had the tired brig hauled onshore in anticipation of Gordon's arrival, and after dropping off the materials, the acting commodore headed *Atholl* out to the Bights to patrol. Gordon was only doing what his old commodore had done, but as far as the governor of Sierra Leone was concerned, that was precisely the problem.

The colony at Sierra Leone had finally gotten a permanent lieutenant governor—the previous one, Lumley, had died shortly after the events of the *Esperanza* in 1828, and in a little over eighteen months, a series of four different acting lieutenant governors had rotated through the position. But Alexander Findlay was there now, and he had several opinions on how Collier had been doing his job, few of them favorable. Findlay, writing to the Colonial Office, felt that Collier's concentration of his limited WAS resources in the Bights had been a mistake, that for Gordon to continue the policy was a bigger mistake, and that all the Squadron wanted to do was get that head money and increase "the expense of the British Nation by bringing many thousands of slaves to this colony." Not only did that kind of math support Collier's choice to patrol in the Bights, it ignored the possibility that changes in the traffic were *due to* the WAS presence being effective south of Freetown; the trade up the coast near Sierra Leone was growing even as it began to shrink to the south as slavers went to greater and greater lengths to avoid the *Black Joke* specifically.

It may seem odd that Findlay was complaining about the Squadron doing its job—which was to capture slavers and then to bring the enslaved to be liberated in Sierra Leone, which had been founded as a colony specifically to resettle free Black people—but it makes more sense if one knows the new lieutenant governor was an unrepentant racist. Findlay would have liked to see a lot fewer Africans in his little slice of Africa, the entire population of which he described as "naturally lazy and indolent" and incapable of accomplishing anything "without a European to direct them." This attitude made the Sierra Leone colony a particularly bad posting for the new lieutenant governor, as the culture that had begun to take shape was formed, in large part, around groups of Black people: free and "liberated" Africans, the latter removed from the slave trade in Freetown, and the free Black communities that grew out of resettled Black residents from Nova Scotia and Jamaica.

Though a quick explanation does little justice to the topic, it will have to do. Back at the conclusion of the eighteenth century, the English abolitionist campaign did not focus solely on the abolition of the trade by the government, nor did it jump right into Parliament and demand an end to the trade. (Well, actually it did, it just wasn't very effective.) One facet of the groundswell was a recolonization effort for the relief of London's "Black poor" led by Granville Sharp. Many of these "Black poor" were formerly enslaved people left homeless by emancipation and destitute as the result of racism, and the idea was that the government might be willing to support killing several birds with a single stone by settling an entire community back in Africa, and laying claim to an excellent harbor besides. After the land was purchased (a few times, as the African chieftains with whom the English contracted regarded the relationship as more of a lease than a sale), a pamphlet was put out calling for volunteers to make the journey. Several hundred Black Londoners did sign up willingly, but the benefactors felt the ships weren't full enough and conscripted over a hundred White prostitutes and dozens of criminals to also make the trip to the coast of Africa. Since this was not perhaps the best population balance for a successful agricultural settlement and the benefactors behind the project knew nothing about running what was meant to become a full-fledged colony, unsurprisingly this first attempt failed fairly quickly. But those behind this "Province of Freedom" continued their efforts.

Over the same time, roughly, Black loyalists in Nova Scotia had begun to raise complaints over their treatment by the English. In return for their freedom and assurances of land, these Black people had sided with the English in the American Revolutionary War, but after the war, the British government tossed them into communities in Nova Scotia without guaranteeing that land, and the local White settlers took advantage of the situation. When the loyalists' advocate came to England to petition the Crown for redress, he met with Sharp and other Sierra Leonean advocates. The causes united, which eventually resulted in over a third of the Black loyalist population in Nova Scotia, approximately twelve hundred people, moving to Freetown. When land promises again weren't met, some of these new settlers revolted, leading the Sierra Leone Company, as Sharp's need for investors had prompted the previous organization to incorporate until the colony could become self-sustaining, to bring in over five hundred Jamaican Maroons to quell the unrest. And that was all by 1800. Though there was an increasing European presence, by the time of Findlay's appointment, these communities of independent, English-speaking Black people had solidified and commingled, and to them hundreds of Africans from across the continent were regularly added. In 1822, Freetown's demographics comprised:

*Europeans including the members of the government and of the civil, judicial, and religious establishments of the colony; the missionaries, merchants, mechanics, and adventurers of every description, (exclusive of the garrison) . . . . . . 128*

*The Maroons, who were sent from Jamaica, and their descendants, of whom many are now persons of consequence and property . . . . . . 601*

*The Nova-Scotians, being the original settlers, brought from America in 1791, and their descendants, several of whom are also persons of property and respectability . . . . . . 722*

*Exiles from Barbadoes [sic], in consequence of the insurrection of 1816, together with a few North-American Blacks who have settled in the colony . . . . . . 85*

*Natives of Africa, who have voluntarily taken up their abode in the colony. Of these a small part are natives of the peninsula of Sierra Leone; the remainder are natives of the surrounding and interior countries, who have, of their own accord, either settled permanently in the colony, or made it their temporary residence. Of this class the largest part are adults, and are either Mohammedans or Pagans, who adhere to the rites and customs of their own respective religions, and are quite indifferent to Christianity . . . . . . 3,526*

*Liberated Africans, comparatively few of whom, it must be recollected, have been long in the colony; and of whom there is imported, every year, a large additional number in the lowest state of ignorance and degradation . . . . . . 7,969*

*Discharged soldiers, principally liberated Africans, the rest having originally been purchased as slaves in the West Indies, and who were disbanded in 1820 and 1821 . . . . . . 1,103*

*Kroomen, a body of labourers who, though the total number is generally the same, are, individually, constantly changing. Strongly attached to their own country and its customs, though they will migrate freely for a time, no inducement can prevail with them to remain long absent from it, or to relinquish their native superstitions . . . . . . 947*

*[Total] 15,081*

As Macaulay makes clear, they didn't all stay, but Freetown had been founded as a Black settlement and became an ethnically and culturally diverse Black town in which only roughly 0.85 percent of the stable population was White, and despite the fact that this minuscule percentage of White Europeans held the majority of administrative power, the town's Blackness apparently irritated Findlay to no end. Nonetheless, his letter questioning the efficacy of the Squadron's deployment was passed on to the Admiralty.

Rather than looking to the WAS, Findlay might have better spent his time sweeping around his own front door. His racism meant he refused to hire qualified Black people for administrative posts in Freetown and had fired all of the Black people who had previously held those jobs, redistributing them to White European officers who were less qualified, in both experience and education (many of them being young enough to have just left school). And Findlay's race-baiting histrionics notwithstanding, the intelligence Captain Gordon had received regarding activity around the colony just a few weeks before Findlay sent his nasty note was less "predation by slavers running amok" and more "residents of Sierra Leone using a boat to run guns to French slavers on the Rio Pongas." Gordon sent the *Plumper*, back on patrol of the coast, to investigate. *Plumper* had left boats in the Pongas a couple of weeks prior while searching nearby rivers for quarry, and upon the ship's return, *Plumper's* boat crews had more bad news—the slave dealers were rumored to have arranged for four hundred locals to attack the Squadron vessel and its boats and kill everyone. This wasn't an idle threat; eight years earlier, a similar attack had been made against HMS *Thistle* in the same river, killing two and injuring several more. Anchoring under cover of night, *Plumper* soon waylaid a schooner attempting to sneak past it and discovered that, sure enough, the ship had sold guns to French slavers farther upriver and was owned by "Mr. Smith" of Freetown. After sending the schooner on for Lieutenant Governor Findlay to deal with, as that was a colonial matter, not a Squadron one, *Plumper* went even farther inland to investigate. They found a slaver to condemn, but though the assault had never been forthcoming, fever caught on the trip eventually killed twenty-seven members of the crew.

French slave traders had become a much bigger problem that year, and no one in the Squadron, at least, could do much about the reason. France had officially banned the slave trade back in 1818, but since then the government had done little to suppress the French traffic in the enslaved. In effect, all the 1818 measure had done was remove regulations on those traffickers who, much like the then

French government, were willing to simply ignore the law, and the trade continued. Administratively—especially given that France had already technically agreed to abolish the trade—its stance on suppression had shifted by 1826, when French abolitionists discovered and revealed undeniable evidence of France's ongoing participation in the slave trade, shaming the government into enacting further regulations and more stringently enforcing those already on the books. This had a marked chilling effect, cutting the number of trips by known French slavers in half (from seventy-two to thirty-six) in a single year. Then, in 1827, France passed an anti-slave-trade law with some force behind it—one that Charles X, king of France and noted conservative, was willing to sign—further dampening enthusiasm for the trade. Now, if caught, a French slave ship was subject to confiscation by the government, and all officers on French slavers would be charged a fine equivalent to the worth of both the ship and cargo and banished; noncommissioned crew would be jailed for three to five years, though whistleblowers who informed on their berth in a timely fashion upon arrival back in France would serve no time. Thus, by 1828, the number of French slave-trading voyages reached their nadir for the entire decade, with twenty-three voyages that year. Up until this point, French slavers still favored the Bights to embark enslaved Africans, and soon it became a not-uncommon sight for WAS ships arriving on their own cruise of the area to see the French Squadron, representative of their navy, detaining French slavers, since they were the only ones who legally could, as Britain and France still had no treaty entertaining a mutual right of search. Though surely a strange feeling after too many years of enmity, distrust, and warfare, that *someone* was finally doing something about French slavers had to have been heartening, particularly for those who believed more zealously in the abolitionist mission.

For years, slavers (whether actually French or not) had used the flag of France as a cover. (This was the white field of the Bourbon dynasty, not a variation on the revolutionary tricolor we know today, as the flag tended to change with the system of government, and to vastly oversimplify, France had gone through a lot of governments since the late 1780s.) Because no mutual right of search as yet existed between Britain and France, the Royal Navy's West Africa Squadron could do absolutely nothing, legally, about any ship that was of French extraction—or convincing enough in its game of colors and papers to seem French—and slavers of all nationalities knew it. There had been the bright spot of 1828, when control of France's navy was turned over to Hyde de Neuville, the first abolitionist to reach the heights of France's royal cabinet. Conservative though de Neuville undoubtedly was, his antislavery bona fides were solid, and he cautioned that the administration "must be vigilant that the French flag is not usurped to cover odious speculation; it must seek to know about the participation [. . .] of French subjects [. . .]; finally it must prevent our colonies from again becoming the theatre of criminal operations." That last one would prove the most difficult.

Both Lieutenant Governor Findlay's complaints of increased slaver traffic near the colony and free Africans being kidnapped off the edges of Sierra Leone and acting commodore Gordon's discovery of Sierra Leonean complicity with French slavers were facets of the same trend. British-colonized Sierra Leone was right down the coast from French-colonized Senegal, and by 1829, even de Neuville in Paris had heard the rumors that a robust traffic in the enslaved was departing from, among other places, Senegal to the Cape Verde islands. It was the same story across the French colonies—Guadeloupe, Martinique, Réunion (then called Bourbon) were taking on the slaver traffic too risk averse to depart from France directly, supplying the official papers that, though they could no longer be obtained in France, colonial governments seemed more than happy to issue. As reports of ongoing French slave trading continued to pour in from across the globe, de Neuville cajoled, remonstrated, even threatened to send special officers from France to accomplish what its territorial governments would not, to little avail. And things would get worse before they got better.

In 1829, the balance of power had once again shifted in the

French government, this time to an ultraconservative bloc—at the orchestration and behest of Charles X—and with that change, de Neuville was out at the ministry. Nearly all of the official political will behind meaningful suppression disappeared with him. The brief tenure of de Neuville had seen a sincere effort that, absent additional support (particularly from the colonies), had only yielded mixed results. As the months progressed into 1830 and a new decade, many in France's holdings continued to side with the slave traders. Slaving voyages from ports in France that dropped in 1827–28 had once again risen, while the brief surge in slaving ships leaving from French colonies returned to much the same levels as before the stricter measures were enacted—a trend that seemed bound to continue, especially after it became clear that the new national government's position on the reinvigorated slave trade was a shrug and a sigh and the telling public assertion that, really, it could do nothing else. In the French Squadron, even those who wanted to do their jobs felt stymied; the *commissaire général* of the *marine* at Nantes, France's largest slaving port, noted that more slave ships, once again, appeared to be departing, and "seem to regain here an activeness which I have no means at all to oppose, under existing legislation, which seems to me to leave still much to be desired."

Not only was there much to be desired, the government in Paris could still most definitely do something—it just *really* didn't want to. The reports from the WAS to British officials had also reflected an increasing frustration regarding the protections afforded slave traders by the French flag. Even before Collier returned home, he'd written the Admiralty to highlight the depth and extent of the problem, and rather succinctly, too: "The Slave-trade between the Gambia and Cape Palmas, is carried on solely almost under the French Flag." His opposite number commanding suppression efforts in the Caribbean, agreed, adding, "The chief evil under which all the pirates now cloke [*sic*] themselves, is the open manner in which the slave-trade is carried on between the French possessions in the West Indies and the Coast of Africa, under their flag," and with the full awareness, if not tacit approval, from colonial officials, who were at best apathetic and too often complicit. Even *Black Joke*, refit and raring to go under the new command of William Ramsay, Captain Gordon's first lieutenant on *Atholl*, couldn't help but sail into the enormity of the France problem.

Lieutenant William Ramsay was the son of privilege, and privilege somewhat unexpected, too—Ramsay had been born in Aberdeenshire to the Scottish nobility with the last name Burnett, the youngest surviving son of eight boys and three girls born to a father who inherited the Ramsay baronetcy from his uncle on his mother's side when young William was ten and changed the family's last name accordingly. There was no way Lieutenant Ramsay would inherit without an even more convoluted turn of events or substantial family tragedy, but he nonetheless grew up a son of the upper class with an idyllic childhood, at least if his older brother is to be believed. Dean Ramsay—aka the Reverend Dr. Edward Bannerman Ramsay, famous for his involvement with the Scottish Episcopal Church—wrote the book, proverbially and literally, on bucolic Scottish childhoods, *Reminiscences of Scottish Life and Character*. But his youngest brother, William, was destined for the navy, not the cloth, and after joining up in 1809 just after turning thirteen (slightly old for his upper-class cohort), the younger Ramsay had managed, unlike nearly every other officer in the Royal Navy, to stay fully employed ever since, spending the next twenty years moving from berth to berth with scarcely a gap in service.

The crew of the little brig must have been happy to be back on the water (if not to relieve the tedium, then at least for the opportunity for prize money), but the tender and its new captain spent an incredibly frustrating October chasing down five different French ships they now knew for a fact were carrying over sixteen hundred enslaved people, and had left ten more waiting to load them from the barracoons onshore to the slave ship off the Old Calabar River, yet still had nothing to show for it. Ramsay and the Black Jokes were not alone in their irritation; WAS officers and sailors complained of

French-flagged slavers who "literally laugh at us as we pass," and one lieutenant, Peter Leonard, arriving to the coast on *Dryad* in 1830, could clearly see that the *Black Joke's* fruitless month was emblematic of the problem that sapped effective suppression, bluntly writing:

> But when will the diabolical traffic in human beings, even on this part of the African continent, be annihilated [. . .] ? [. . .] Alas! the period seems as far distant as ever. France will do nothing towards it: under her flag there are ten vessels to one of any other nation engaged in the slave trade. During the month of October last, [. . .] his Majesty's brig Black Joke, boarded five French vessels, with [1,622] slaves on board, from the River Bonny alone; and in the month of November following, there were ten French vessels lying in the Old Calabar river, ready to take saves on board, the smallest of which would embark four hundred. She could not detain one of them: indeed had [Lieutenant Ramsay] strictly attended to the letter, or even the spirit of our feeble treaty with France, (than which nothing requires a more strict revision,) he must have known that he was not permitted even to board any vessel under French colours. So complete is the immunity of slave vessels sailing under this flag, owing to the disabilities under which our ships of war labour, and the perfect idleness and inactivity of the Gallic squadron, and so comparatively subversive are the laws enacted against the traffic to the northward of the equator by every other power under whose flag it has hitherto been carried on that, before long, there is not a doubt but the [French flag] [. . .] will, ere long, be the only flag employed to carry on the slave trade, and under this it will flourish, unless France is forced to grant the right of search—at least on the coast of Africa—and the right to capture all vessels under her flag fitted for the reception of slaves, or having slaves actually on board.

Allowing British ships the right of search—which the French government had fought since 1815 and was still fighting—was the thing it could do. It was also, by 1830, obviously the only solution that would make a real difference in the business practices of slavers; as long as there was a single flag to hide behind, the unscrupulous would exploit it. It's entirely possible that the ships the *Black Joke* had boarded weren't French at all—flying the flag and/or carrying the papers of whichever country suited one's purpose was incredibly common, and France's was the documentation of choice—but *Black Joke* was nonetheless stymied in its captures by ongoing political maneuvering over a thousand miles away. Negotiations between the British and the French empires had not been particularly fruitful in the previous years, but inexorably, the tide of public opinion had been turning against France's refusal to see what abolitionists would have called reason.

The international pressure had been building since 1815, but previously, French politicians had been able to hide their reluctance to accede to the right of search behind the will of the people. Back in 1815, the war had been fresh, the loss to Britain even fresher, and anti-English sentiment was fervent, even feverous. (And that's setting aside the hundreds of years of historical enmity and oppositional religious doctrines that had once and would again include vigorous anti-Protestant sentiment in France and still featured virulent—if slightly relenting—anti-Catholic sentiment in England.) In 1815, it is reasonably safe to generalize that if Britain wanted it, France almost certainly did not. And in 1815, Britain wanted abolition of the slave trade. There were abolitionists in France—most heavily represented in intellectual and radical circles—and the nation had already banned slavery once before (in 1794—Haiti began to throw off the yoke three years prior in 1791, and there'd been plenty of politicking in France to accompany the island's revolution). However, the rise of Napoléon had brought with it a return of French slavery, and with his fall, popular sentiment was against concessions to England, and military sentiment was against letting the Royal Navy search French naval vessels. Occasional talks would continue between the two European powers over the next several years, but against such a background, and with the conservative monarchy of Charles X, the political will to create real reform stagnated.

After fifteen years, things had changed. Abolitionist sentiment was more popular than it had ever been. Several newspapers in France now regularly ran articles lambasting the French government's complicity in slave trading. Even officers in the French Squadron, veterans of the Napoleonic Wars—who, now that the French Marine had begun genuine suppression efforts, were more familiar with the difficulties of policing the trade—were ready to accept that the mutual right of search was vital to suppression. The complaints from those charged with French prevention of the slave trade would have sounded incredibly familiar to their WAS counterparts: that their ships weren't fast enough to do the job, that ships could not be detained without the enslaved on board was intolerable, and that a flag—particularly the French flag—should not be the best protection a slaver could steal, bribe, borrow, or buy. The squadron of French ships assigned to the western coast of Africa was further hamstrung because French policy, as currently understood and practiced, meant that if the French Marine came upon a French slaver in British custody, it was obligated to liberate the slaver, not the enslaved. Sure, the French military on the coast could then take that slave trader into custody itself, but since it was also obliged to use force if need be to get the slaver from the British, every such encounter was an international incident (and potential pretext for war) waiting to happen. The French Squadron didn't have to like it—and it didn't, as shared duty on the coast tended to make these sailors sympathize with the West Africa Squadron's uphill battle these many years—but that's what the current state of affairs between the two nations dictated.

At the beginning of 1830, it must've seemed as if progress on slave trade reform in France had not just stalled but regressed. The "apparent laxity with which" the ultraconservative faction in power (that's not historical hindsight, they called themselves Ultras) approached France's "humane Intentions" provoked increasing consternation within Britain's Foreign Office. In 1827 British diplomats had been willing to take a wait-and-see approach to France's efforts to self-regulate the slave trade; by 1830, they'd seen enough. The French administration, for its part, wasn't particularly interested in what would happen to the slave trade (and some continued to profit from it), but was downright obsessed by the right of search and, more specifically, not granting it. The French Foreign Ministry reinvigorated suspicions that all this talk of British humanitarianism was a mere front for England's ongoing participation in the slave trade, that demands were made "to the profit of its maritime pretensions." The French government would be happy to rail "with force against all violations of the French flag," but Royal Navy actions such as, say, boarding French slavers when it had no hope to detain them, nor even a legal right to be there, had to stop. (*See* Lieutenant Ramsay, though he was by no means the only culprit.)

However, this wasn't the only kind of reform the Ultra government was stifling in 1830, and when Charles X and his handpicked politicians attempted to restrict the (already limited) franchise in that year's elections, the French had had enough. The people of France (notably the Parisians) had proven more than once that they were perfectly willing to overthrow an unsatisfactory government, yet even given this revolutionary tradition, the July Revolution of 1830 was shocking to many in both its appearance and speed. The Three Glorious Days went by exactly as quickly as it sounds, and whereas at the beginning ( July 27), Charles X was king of France, by the end ( July 29), his cousin Louis Philippe was king of the French, a not-at-all-small distinction that meant, among other things, sitting at the head of a constitutional, rather than absolutist, monarchy. Though France's involvement in the slave trade was not per se at issue—it doesn't even make an appearance in the incendiary rhetoric that precipitated the regime change—the July Revolution brought with it an onslaught of liberalism and a new, reform-minded monarch. Whatever antagonism the new king of the French had once felt toward British foreign policy had been tempered in no small part by several years spent in exile in England, and Louis Philippe's regime brought with it a slew of anti-slave-trade and outright abolitionist ministers. By 1831, France passed a far more stringent antitrafficking law than that of 1827, and the French Foreign Ministry acquiesced to opening talks regarding the conditions under which a slaver could be detained and captured and regarding a mutual right of search. A declaration of intent on the latter issue was signed—though meaningless in and of itself, the beginning of real negotiations (concluded successfully in 1833) marked a huge step forward in France's shift from defender of the slave trade to ally of suppression.

Back in late 1830, however, and despite the international upheaval that would revolutionize operations on the coast of Africa, the limitations of the treaties governing capture of slave vessels, and the extent to which the compromises in these agreements frustrated the twin causes of justice and liberty, were still on full display.

Not long after that frustrating October chasing down French-flagged slavers more bemused than concerned at the appearance of the Royal Navy, on November 13, the *Black Joke* was patiently waiting offshore near the Cameroons River. The tender had been sitting in the area for four days on the suspicion that a slaver would be emerging at any moment, having embarked enslaved people inland at King Bell's Town, and after so much frustration with the French, Ramsay was determined to make an actual capture. To that end, he'd sent the *Black Joke's* two boats, a gig and a cutter, under the commands, respectively, of R. K. Jenkins, mate, and William Coyde (back to being mate after his short and rather tumultuous tenure as acting captain of the *Black Joke*), into the mouth of the river to provide some warning of the ship's appearance to the crew back on the brig and hopefully forestall escape. Sure enough, early that morning a black-hulled Spanish brigantine full of African captives appeared in the river's mouth. However, at roughly 9:30 a.m.—having passed Jenkins, Coyde, and their boats, who'd signaled their fellows back on the tender—the slaver's captain saw *Black Joke* weighing anchor in preparation of pursuit and immediately turned his ship around and began lumbering back upriver, hoping to disembark his human cargo quickly enough to evade capture as a prize. Jenkins and Coyde took off to intercept the slaver, with Jenkins in the lead.

It was not just the contrary breeze that day that made the return trip slow going. This area, the Bay of Cameroons—an English bastardization of the Portuguese name of the river that fed it, the Rio dos Camarões (or, accurately translated, "River of Prawns")—was thick with treacherous reefs and lurking shoals, which made for hazardous sailing and compounded the difficulty by creating forceful currents that, even rowing at their utmost, the Black Jokes were only barely able to clear. It was nearly sundown before even the slaver made it the ten miles inland back to King Bell's Town and again anchored, with Jenkins and his men on oars only a scant half hour behind. From his leading position, two miles back and gaining, Jenkins watched as canoes streamed from the shore and the crew of the slaver hurriedly and unceremoniously removed every enslaved person on board; by the time the mate was only a pistol shot (roughly twenty yards) away, he could only watch helplessly as the canoes were being landed again and members of the Spanish crew, along with some residents of the town, dispersed those so recently confined within the slave ship's hold into the surrounding forest.

Not entirely helplessly—Jenkins did fire off two shots, but they had no effect on the frantic action in either the remaining few canoes or onshore. Coyde's boat arrived shortly thereafter, ten minutes to a half hour later, to much the same scene that the first boat had, with canoes recently landed and Black bodies being disappeared into the bush. Jenkins and his men boarded the slaver first, only to come across the smug captain of *Dos Amigos*, Juan Ramon de Muxica (the younger), waiting in all innocence, yet with the smell of slavery still clinging to his vessel. Jenkins and Coyde each searched the ship individually and found a slave deck, recently emptied and already covered in excrement—which the unfortunate Jenkins found out the hard way, namely by stepping in it—and old sail canvas lining the sides as makeshift and woefully inadequate "pillows," still wet with the sweat of the enslaved. On the same deck three tubs (one approximately seven gallons in capacity, the others ten to twelve) contained yet more excrement, which to the mates' estimation was far more than the crew of the slaver should have been able to produce in the time Ramon de Muxica claimed *Dos Amigos* had been upriver. (Jenkins, who searched after Coyde, had only seen one poop tub, but given that he only had a candle for light and could apparently barely take a few steps without stepping in human feces, it's likely he didn't explore nearly as much of the hold as the other mate and could see much less besides.) Seeing as it was by now completely dark, but satisfied that there was still more than enough evidence of wrongdoing to support their eyewitness accounts, they quit the slaver for fresher environs to finish the search when daylight returned.

When the next morning came, *Black Joke* could been seen approaching the town, having had much farther to go against the wind, and Jenkins and Coyde returned to the slaver to find many fewer supplies than had appeared to be there before. They nonetheless performed yet another search, which was interrupted not by their captain, but by the son of King Bell, who was less king and more famous Cameroonian middleman trader, locally known as kings, but not to be confused with contemporaneous leaders of African geographical areas and tribal groups. King Bell's son not-so-nonchalantly asked why *Black Joke* was there, and Jenkins, not mincing words, told him its purpose was likely to fire on the town if those enslaved people did not make a reappearance as sudden as their departure had been miraculous. (The "town" being little more than a slave-trading post surrounded by the requisite auxiliary buildings.) Jenkins knew his captain's mind well; Ramsay was driven and not exactly the type to simply take the loss and leave. By the time he caught up, bringing the full power and reputation of the *Black Joke* with him, Ramsay was confronted with an empty slaver, its likely still-smiling captain, and a seriously annoyed Jenkins and Coyde.

The two mates caught their lieutenant up and passed on the message King Bell's son had left with them, essentially, "Please ask your lieutenant not to do anything hasty." The two men also relayed that, sometime before dawn, a considerable portion of the slaver's stores of yams, rice, beans, and other foodstuffs seemed to have likewise disappeared, along with several other crucial items. These included the ship's "slave boilers," usually made of brass, copper, or iron and used for preparing the mass quantities of food such a voyage would require, as well as the quantities of food meant to go in them; though rations for those trapped in the hold would be minimal, given the hundreds of mouths to barely feed, the supplies did have to be plentiful in case the journey to the Americas took longer than expected. (In at least one documented case, a slaver's journey had lasted six weeks longer than expected, and concerned that his remaining stores wouldn't continue to stretch, the enterprising captain jettisoned a third of the enslaved on board into the ocean, alive, with the hope that insurance would cover the loss of life or, as he saw it, profit. It did not.) There was a stand for such a boiler, in this case thirty inches square and twenty inches deep, and fresh ashes underneath that stand, but the pot itself had vanished. Also missing were "a quantity of iron bars and rods, for running through leg-irons for slaves," and also used to connect the shackles of the enslaved to more bars bolted into the sides of the slave deck. The tubs of refuse had disappeared, not just emptied but nowhere in evidence. De Muxica—who was not just the captain, but also the owner of *Dos Amigos*—had done everything possible in the little time he'd had before *Black Joke* arrived to remove any evidence not just that any enslaved Africans had been held therein, but that he'd planned to embark any at all in the first place.

So, when Lieutenant Ramsay finally surveyed the deck of *Dos Amigos*, he was, to borrow the colloquial expression, *pissed*. King Bell's son had returned and inquired again as to the *Black Joke*'s reasons for being in the area, to which Ramsay reiterated very nearly the precise threat Jenkins had suspected he would, namely that his purpose was "to fire the town about your black wooly heads if you don't hand over the slaves of the *Dos Amigos*" (and the attendant provisions as well).

King Bell's son conveyed the threat to his father, who countered with an offer of twenty-five enslaved people, probably all that was left in the town's barracoons after reputedly loading over five hundred people into *Dos Amigos*, and an attitude of "Now please take them and go away." Ramsay declined King Bell's offer, and nothing else was forthcoming from Juan Ramon de Muxica, who'd likely produced his best "I have no idea what you're talking about" face throughout the entire affair. The slaver captain knew that Ramsay could do little about the situation—seeing as the *Black Joke* couldn't possibly feed and supply the transit of several hundred enslaved people back to Freetown from its own stores and Ramon had had his own provisions thrown overboard, thus preventing the crew from liberating those he'd purchased. Ramsay was enraged, but not deterred. One of the seamen from Jenkins's gig, Thomas Williams Osborne, had mentioned to his boat captain that he'd conversed with de Muxica during the night—probably in the town, more probably while drinking—and the slaver captain had mentioned not just embarking and then disembarking 563 slaves, but also that the copper boilers had been thrown overboard during the chase. Jenkins passed this information up the chain to Ramsay, who asked Osborne up to the brig's quarterdeck to question the sailor himself.

Ramsay was probably still furious, but it's possible that he was now the one smiling. The British treaty with Spain specifically allowed for condemnation of a ship if British witnesses could testify to the presence of the enslaved on board a vessel, even if, when the vessel was caught, none was present. An incredibly good-looking ship that appeared to be near the equal of the *Black Joke, Dos Amigos* had thirty-four crew armed with a cannon on a swivel, sixteen rifles, and fifteen pistols; it might have been a very different end to this story had the chase taken place on open water, rather than in slow motion on a day when the minimal breeze was headed in the wrong direction. So the lieutenant seized the "extremely fine" ship, for the prize money certainly, though it couldn't hurt that without it de Muxica would have a much tougher time embarking the captive Africans

HMS *Fair Rosamond* (ex-slaver *Dos Amigos*)
(© NMM).

he'd purchased, still hidden in the bush, while King Bell would have a much harder time finding a buyer if de Muxica decided to cut his losses—the trade in that area had slowed to a sliver of what it had once been, and even if King Bell kept de Muxica's money, he'd need to either feed and house (at his own expense) the enslaved still being hidden in the foliage or release them.

Even then, the Spanish slaver wasn't done being difficult. As expected, upon the prize crew's arrival in Freetown, de Muxica, along with *Dos Amigos's* cook, readily testified that they were shocked (shocked!) to find that anyone could believe their humble and entirely legitimate merchant vessel was engaged in something as nefarious and obviously illegal as the slave trade. He'd only fled because the *Black Joke* had hoisted Portuguese colors, and given its look, anyone could be forgiven for thinking it might be a pirate. As with the

Brazilian slaver *Carolina* before him, the slaver captain had papers attesting to the validity of this identity, surely nothing on his ship spoke of participation in the slave trade, and he was certain no one else had actually seen enslaved people on board, just a lot of over-stuffed canoes making for the shore. Fortunately for history, Coyde absolutely *had* seen what he believed to be many miserable Africans packed into the ship's hold—it had just been the morning, not evening, of the chase, when the Spanish brigantine had first been sighted attempting to leave the river. Juan Ramon de Muxica nonetheless fought the case for another two months, in what had to be one of the more dramatic trials the Mixed Commission ever witnessed. Both Jenkins and Coyde, along with de Muxica and his cook, stood for questioning multiple times, answering questions about what flag Ramsay had run up, what was and wasn't present on the deck, what was and wasn't still in the hold, who could see what, and how close they'd all been to one another during those crucial moments of fading sunset. George Duncan, a seaman who'd been a rower on Jenkins's gig and had witnessed the dumping of the excrement, had to attest to that unfortunate sight. Thomas Williams Osborne had to swear to what he'd told Jenkins and subsequently Ramsay, only to have his testimony stricken on the grounds of potential witness tampering from his own captain. Whatever Osborne said to the commission, it involved being threatened and prompted Ramsay to send a sworn affidavit to be read aloud in court that Osborne had said what he said, to both Jenkins and himself independently, had said he could swear to it, and further that the lieutenant "positively denied, ever having used any threatening or promising language whatever to [. . .] Osborne, relative to the evidence he might be required to give in this case." Jenkins corroborated Ramsay's version of events, but Osborne's statement was still removed from the record, just in case. These many issues having been argued, the Mixed Commission topped it off by undertaking its own inspection of the Spanish brigantine quiescent in the harbor.

The ship visit clinched it. The court, possibly annoyed at having had months of its time wasted and with the hope of forestalling any appeal, went off. The commissioners' incredulity drips from their opinion, of which this is only a small excerpt:

> The passport of the "Dos Amigos" certainly does state that she is bound for [Principe and São Tomé], for lawful commerce; but the passport of every Spanish vessel captured in carrying on the slave-trade, since Spain [. . .] totally abolished that traffick, has been of precisely the same [tenor]; and it remains with [de Muxica] to prove that he has been engaged in lawful commerce, and not the traffick in slaves. The Court is of opinion [sic], that he has totally failed in so doing. In endeavouring to account for several suspicious circumstances, he asserts, that the platform on board his vessel, was laid to stow away his outward-bound dry goods upon; that his returning up the river, when he saw the "Black Joke," was because he feared that vessel was a pirate; that he was going, first, he says, to [Principe],—secondly, to [São Tomé], to dispose of the remains of his outward-bound cargo; that the yams on board were for the use of his crew; but he says not one word about the immense quantity of the fresh water stowed in the hold.
>
> To ascertain the points connected with these assertions, the Court directed a Commission of Inspection of the "Dos Amigos" to issue. That Commission has been returned. The Commissioners therein state that the platform on board the "Dos Amigos" is placed immediately on the top of the water-casks, and that that platform extends the whole breadth, and, for and aft, the whole length of the vessel; that there were 87 to 90 bales of dry goods on board [. . .]; but those bales would take up but a small space of room, compared with the hold of the vessel; and the Court must, therefore, assume that the platform was for other purposes. His excuse for going out of the river in order to sell his remaining outward cargo, required the Court to learn what that remaining cargo consisted of; and there appears, by the Commissioners' report, to be onboard [a list follows], and some other trifling articles.

*The Cook swears that he was to have 60 dollars per month; no legitimate commercial voyage could pay such extravagant wages. Now, would any rational man believe, that a vessel, manned with from 35 to 40 men, therefore being navigated at an enormous expense, would go on a voyage for the purpose of disposing of so small a quantity of goods, as the "Dos Amigos" had on board. The Court does not believe it; nor does it believe the excuse that she was going to either of those islands to obtain a freight to the Havana. The Court will not aver that that is impossible; but it will say, it is extremely improbable. It would, if it were true, be the first case the Court ever heard of.*

*His returning upriver, armed and manned as his vessel was, because, according to his own account, the "Black Joke" had a Portuguese flag flying, and he took her for a pirate, is, in the opinion of the Court, very incredible; and here it is to be remarked that a national vessel has a right, and we know it is constantly [practiced], to hoist the flag of any nation when chasing a vessel, but certainly not to board under it. The probability is, seeing the British boats with the British flags flying, he made the best of his way back to disembark his cargo; and, in so doing, he would, of course, [endeavor] to obliterate every mark of a number of human beings having been on board. [. . .]*

*The Commissioners of Inspection have reported, that the "Dos Amigos" was, in every way, fitted for the slave trade [. . .]. If, therefore, the "Dos Amigos" came to this coast for lawful commerce, where was the necessity of such fitting? True it is that the subjects of Spain may fit up their vessels as they please, nor is such fitting-up of Spanish vessels grounds for condemnation by the Court; [. . .] such fitting-up is, and must, when other circumstances occur to support the Captor's allegation, be viewed as extremely suspicious, as it is well known that that fitting-up is only required for human cargo; and if the "Dos Amigos" were positively lawfully engaged, why is her log discontinued on the day she anchored off [Principe]? that is another circumstance that bears upon its face the stamp of fraud. The Court is, therefore, of opinion, that the evidence of [de Muxica] is insincere and fictitious.*

*Black Joke* was awarded the prize, and with it a particularly valuable salvage that some were already picturing as the West Africa Squadron's next tender, but what happened to the enslaved? It's most likely that, soon after *Dos Amigos's* capture, de Muxica or one of his officers either found another ship for transport or simply resold the Africans purchased for this journey; and it's doubtful that any enslaved people found freedom, or even "liberation," from this encounter, especially if the slaver captain felt pressured to recoup what losses he could. The Mixed Commission found a way to further sour the long-argued victory, charging Captain Gordon (ultimately responsible for *Black Joke's* prizes and failures as captain of *Atholl,* to which it was currently tender) £4.14s for inventory discrepancies regarding a slave ship known to have had most of its inventory tossed overboard in flight before lying in every capacity about what that inventory had been. Whatever happened next, with Lieutenant Governor Findlay, the French, or falsifying slavers, it was no longer Gordon's immediate problem. During the months that *Dos Amigos* waited in the harbor for the commission's disposition, the new year had arrived, and with it, John "Magnificent" Hayes, the new commodore of the West Africa Squadron, had sailed into Freetown on his flagship, HMS *Dryad.* Like his predecessor (and his predecessor before that), he was looking for a fast ship. But the *Black Joke* had disappeared.

# CHAPTER TEN

*Primero* (aka *Primeira*)
February 1831,
311 enslaved people

Aship might disappear into thin air for one of three primary reasons, and each was deadly—shipwreck, pirates, and storms. All three options carried with them the distinct possibility of a ship's never being heard from again: shipwrecks often sank, pirates frequently killed, and the crew of the *Sybille* twice saw a slaver they were pursuing batted around like a toy by a tornado at sea, and nothing was ever seen to fall out of the sky again. When Commodore John Hayes arrived in Freetown, in HMS *Dryad* and accompanied by his own tender, the *Seaflower*, no one knew which whirlwind, whether aquatic, bloodthirsty, or airborne, might have caught the *Black Joke* up, but all were feared.

After dispatching a prize crew to Freetown, the little brig had last been seen on the way to Ascension, the closest port to its location, for a much-needed resupply. The crew of the *Black Joke* had had no fresh provisions for two months before seizing *Dos Amigos*, and sending a prize crew (and with it, as a favor to the colonial governor, some fifty-odd Kroomen who'd previously been stranded in the area) on a ship that had had all of its food dumped meant extra rations gone, such that even the tender's by-now-tiresome dry goods, supplemented by a few fresh yams still remaining from *Dos Amigos's* stores, were looking scarily thin. The *Black Joke* left modern-day Cameroon for Ascension with just over three weeks of stores for the much smaller complement than it normally carried, as upward of seven to ten members of the crew had left the same place in the Spanish brigantine, bound for Freetown.

The prize crew had, for supplies, what de Muxica had left on board as food for his crew and what Ramsay believed the rest of the *Black Joke* crew could spare, but *Dos Amigos* now contained its captain and crew, the prize-crew Black Jokes, and the large group of Kroomen, and the journey to Sierra Leone could be treacherous and easily lengthened by adverse conditions. (To make sure everything lasted, the Black Jokes and Kroomen ate shortened rations, while they gave the slaver's crew the absolute minimum, which was sometimes nothing at all.) Obviously, the prize crew had made it and, given the length of the *Dos Amigos* trial, were in no hurry to leave, but as weeks passed, news of the *Black Joke* had yet to materialize. It had had enough supplies to make it to the island, and Ramsay had confiscated additional rope and hull-protecting paint the *Black Joke* desperately needed from the captured slaver. (These were part of the aforementioned inventory discrepancies, demonstrating how much sympathy for the exigencies of life at sea was available.) The *Black Joke* had, by all accounts, arrived at Ascension and departed again, but from there . . . nothing. At the end of 1830, the *Black Joke* was the first tender of the West Africa Squadron entered into the Royal Navy's *Navy List*, the official record of officers and their commands, but those on the ship still didn't know about the recognition that had finally been afforded the tender's service. Wherever it was, it was His Majesty's Brig *Black Joke* now, not just some auction-bought tender to the *Dryad*, meaning that its fate would ultimately be up to the Admiralty, rather than Commodore Hayes, to decide.

Hayes still had to find the little brig, though, and to that end sent *Plumper* out to search for the *Black Joke*. In the interim, the new commodore had a squadron to run—from administrative changes to ship deployment, Hayes was a man of ideas and planned to leave no aspect of the Squadron's functioning unexamined. This is not to say he didn't have the utmost respect for Collier—quite the opposite. The two men had almost certainly met during the interregnum between their respective services on the coast, after Collier had returned to England in 1830 and before Hayes left on September 30 of the same year. During that meeting, it's likely that Collier gave Hayes every piece of information he could to improve both the service and the Squadron, particularly considering that the first two issues the new commodore took up with the Admiralty upon his arrival were ones near and dear to Collier (thus beginning Hayes's own series of increasingly frustrated correspondence back to London). The first was the Kroomen, who were still not being paid prize money; Hayes was happy to add his voice to Collier's refrain, writing that these men had "done the deadly work of the Squadron" and "preserved many valuable European lives" and ought to be paid accordingly, in a manner equivalent to their Royal Navy counterparts. The second was the proliferation of French flags on the coast, still such a problem in 1831 that Hayes wrote that their number was "increasing daily" and that he was now seeing slavers skipping the formality of a flag and simply flying white tablecloths, as the effect from even a short distance was much the same as an actual French flag of the era. (Clearly the long-term effects of the July Revolution of the previous year—including a switch back to the tricolor—had yet to quite trickle down to the coast.) He'd also brought one more, rather memorable, element of Collier's tenure with him to the coast, a familiar face, perhaps to further ease the transition: Commander William Turner.

Cleared of any wrongdoing on the mysterious charges leveled against him of plundering prize ships, the first captain of the *Black Joke*, and still, perhaps, the best loved, Turner had returned to the coast in his new rank as the captain of the new flagship, *Dryad*. Though the fifth-rate frigate *Dryad* was, to be sure, Commodore Hayes's ship, a commander (or even a full-fledged post-captain— someone of appropriate rank to command a vessel) commonly saw to the day-to-day operations of the Squadron leader's vessel. This organizational structure allowed the leader of a squadron (in this case Hayes) to provide appropriate attention to the movements of the whole without getting bogged down by the full-time job of running his own ship.

Commodore Hayes had every intention of staying busy, because while he had certainly internalized Collier's advice, he was also determined to do at least a few things differently. Almost as soon as he arrived, Hayes began implementing changes to how the West Africa Squadron operated. True to his word, Hayes issued "most positive orders" on the use of "those valuable people," the Kroomen. Not only were the Kroomen to be protected from what Hayes referred to as unnecessary harassment (presumably resulting from racism, misplaced notions of cultural superiority, or both), the commodore demanded that the near-exclusive use of Kroomen for boat work in the interior cease. The commodore reasoned, correctly, that while the Kru might have more protections from some illnesses thought to be prevalent inland, as native inhabitants of the general vicinity (generously read), they were not immune to disease, and the Royal Navy was using the Kroomen as so much biological cannon fodder while failing to even pay them a truly equitable wage. (Given that the Kru were from in and near modern-day Liberia and, in accordance with the Squadron's official patrol, might work as far south as Benguela, roughly two thousand miles away from their native land as the crow flies, and as far north as Cape Verde, over eleven hundred miles away, they were indigenous only to a small area as one approached the center of the WAS's territory from the north, not to the West African coast entire.)

In fact, Commodore Hayes didn't want *anyone* risking exposure to "bad air" by going upriver anymore unless it was strictly necessary, and probably not even then—his exact words were "on no account whatever." (Hayes also didn't want small boats sent in chase if there was a chance that they might lose sight of their parent ship—one has to wonder if the ongoing deposition of *Dos Amigos* influenced his rationale, as that capture might not have happened had this rule been instituted weeks earlier.) Collier, well reputed for the cleanliness of his ships yet nonetheless more than once laid low by disease, had been shaken by the experience, and he no doubt warned Hayes that whatever extremity of measures he was contemplating, it was unlikely to be enough. This prompted the new commodore to think of additional measures he might take, beyond just disallowing trips to the "injurious climate" of the interior. Freetown was plenty coastal, yet had still clearly been a problem in this regard, so Hayes had the local agent of the Victualling Board convert the special launch allocated to the flagship in the town harbor reconfigured as a stores lighter, which would allow ships in the harbor to send small boats to do their resupply without a single sailor stepping foot on the dry land of Freetown proper. The new commodore instituted a lighter workday, ending at 4:00 p.m., for ships that were docked in Freetown, lest the sailors become overtaxed and thus more susceptible to illness, and at the Admiralty's behest committed to at least attempting to put a medical officer on every prize crew. It couldn't be done every time—there simply weren't enough medical personnel to go around—but the WAS, Hayes determined, would at the least make the effort.

This wasn't the only Admiralty policy Hayes publicly committed to, and the next was sure to be less popular than the sundry measures implemented to keep everyone healthy. No one was going to miss boat service upriver or balk at a shorter day when harbored in Freetown, but Hayes also reemphasized the Admiralty's position on improper use or removal of stores found in prizes and attached severe punishment to misconduct. Again, that the *Dos Amigos* Mixed Commission trial was happening during Hayes's first stay in Freetown—well, stay in the *Dryad* in the harbor of Freetown, because the commodore had no interest in tempting fate (or more aptly, mosquitoes) himself—seems relevant. The propriety of the *Black Joke*'s use of *Dos Amigos* supplies had wound its way to the top of the command chain well before Captain Gordon was charged for the discrepancies, in part *because* Hayes was already there. As the Mixed Commission itself wrote back to London, the "H.M.S. 'Dryad' lying in the [harbor] at the time, we deemed it necessary to desire the Registrar [. . .] to communicate with Commodore Hayes upon the subject of that deficiency, in order that an explanation thereof, might accompany our report of the case." Hayes was not an inflexible man, his seeming embrace of the Admiralty's much-loathed inventory policy notwithstanding, and in writing back to defend the *Black Joke*'s actions, it's obvious he sympathized with Ramsay:

> [Having] called upon the Commanding Officer of the "Black Joke" for his explanation of the case, which I have received, and examined with your attested inventory; and having duly considered the whole, and how likely it is for mistakes to arise, with respect to the contents of the different casks, and how exceedingly improbable that any improper transaction has taken place in this case, I can only add that I feel perfectly satisfied with the explanation given by Lieutenant Ramsay.

Because, yes, finally, the *Black Joke* was back. *Plumper* had returned from its aborted search mission none the wiser but not empty-handed, having run into the *Maria*, a Spanish schooner and slaver, during its search, and—in a rare turn of events for *Plumper*—on December 26, Boxing Day, they'd actually captured it. The *Black Joke*, unassisted, would limp into Freetown a fortnight later in January of 1831, over two months after it had last been sighted, and to this day no one knows where they were or what happened to so inordinately delay Ramsay and his crew. What Hayes did know was that, as commodore, the *Black Joke* was now his problem—Collier's bequest was that its service was tendered to the flagship—and it was desperately in need of yet another refit. Hayes liked the lines and the look of the little brig, even much abused by two months of mysterious hard sailing, and he certainly wasn't planning to abandon a beautiful ship, if more than a little worse for the wear, with such a reputation for speed and handling and the damnedest luck catching slavers.

Commodore Hayes *loved* ships. The tender he'd brought, the

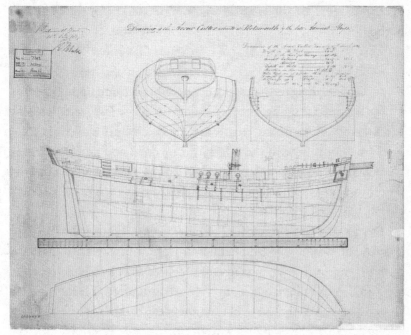

Plan [. . .] for *Arrow* (1823), a ten-gun single-masted cutter,
as designed and built by Captain Hayes (© NMM).

cutter *Seaflower*, was one of his own design. The Admiralty was, it
seems, tired of alternately relying on and cursing American shipwrights in the Chesapeake, and Hayes had already proven to have
the best designed craft in trials among various designers in 1826;
he'd given the design, which could be replicated in five different sizes,
to the Royal Navy in the hopes of persuading it to assume a complete standardization of shipbuilding, which Hayes believed would
both streamline the creation of ships and ensure the most efficacy in
their designs. (The *Seaflower*, constructed by the Royal Navy, was a
smaller version of the ship Hayes had run in the trials.)

But just because Hayes had brought his own tender didn't mean
he was averse to having more, and as the *Black Joke* spent the rest of
January undergoing its second refit in as many years, the commodore

eyed its prize, *Dos Amigos*, still waiting for a ruling in the Freetown harbor.

As soon as the brigantine was condemned and came up for auction, Hayes snapped it up as a "replacement" for *Black Joke*, rechristening it the *Fair Rosamond* and finally ending the former slaver's antagonistic relationship with the *Black Joke*, its crew, and nearly everyone employed by the Mixed Commission. The two former slavers would go on to have a significant and positive role in each other's future, almost like, well, two friends.

*Dryad* now had three ships assigned to it—*Black Joke, Fair Rosamond*, and *Seaflower*—and though it wouldn't be wise to discount the influence of advice passed from Collier as it had been received by him from Bullen, given how much attention Hayes paid to shipbuilding, it's unclear whether the new commodore had actually needed it. Hayes had a number of notable relations, but the most important for the purpose of understanding the man was his uncle Adam Hayes, Esq., the Master Shipwright of the Deptford Dockyard. Adam was childless and wanted to pass on his craft to someone in his family and help him rise as high as he had, or higher still, to Surveyor of the Navy. To that end the master shipwright had chosen one of young John's older cousins, but the boy just wasn't good enough for the old man, and when John showed exceptional promise at just seven years old, Adam abandoned the shipping education of his other nephew. Adam asked for and was granted custody of John, and for the next five years Adam was John's only family, his sole source of education, and essentially his boss, an arrangement that only ended with the old man's death from gout. Adam had been around the navy for a long time and knew all the tricks; seeking to give John a head start on seniority in the cutthroat competition in the officers' ranks, Adam entered the child onto a ship's books as soon as the boy arrived to stay with him at the dockyards. So John had been in the navy since he was seven but in truth spent his childhood under the wing of a master shipwright until, with his uncle's death, he finally went to sea, where he had the odd distinction of serving in both the first and last frigate battles in the wars with Napoléon. Hayes was something of a prodigy when it came to the operation of ships, and this, in conjunction with his previous training, ingenuity, and calm under pressure, earned him the appellation "Magnificent." (It was not a descriptor, although all agreed that such a superlative was apt, but the name of a ship he'd commanded that had been trapped in reefs and rocks during a terrible storm, and that would not have survived without a masterful display of seamanship that was still being used as a teachable moment decades later.) Even the death of his patron, usually an ominous portent for career prospects, couldn't keep Hayes down; after making post-captain at the young age of twenty-seven, he spent time as head of squadrons in Jamaica and elsewhere. One lieutenant serving under him described Hayes by saying his

*presence [. . .] was always a source of pleasure to those who served under him; he combined, with a high reputation as an officer, a scientific mind, and the kindest of tempers, a perfect knowledge of seamanship in its superior as well as subordinate branches. He could fit the rigging, rig the ship, govern and work her afterwards in so masterly a manner, that from the officer to the merest boy on board, he was sure of confidence and support in any enterprise in which he might engage; in short, he could build, rig, govern, and sail the ship with equal ease and credit.*

As commodore of the West Africa Squadron, Hayes would need every bit of flexibility and creativity he could muster, especially when dealing with Governor Findlay of Sierra Leone, who still had a strong penchant for complaining to anyone who would listen. Findlay still felt the WAS wasn't paying sufficient attention to (not entirely inaccurate) reports of increased slavery and predation near the colony, including incidents of "liberated" Africans being kidnapped and resold into slavery. As soon as Hayes arrived, he, too, was the recipient of an epistolary earful from the ever-noisome governor, complaining of both Collier's and Gordon's inattentiveness. Seeking to finally satisfy whatever Findlay was on about now and also perhaps ultimately solve the problem of protecting sailors from sickness in Freetown, Hayes sent Gordon to get a feel for the movements of the trade to better inform future deployment decisions, and stationed his two slowest ships in a novel manner—one would stay in the harbor to receive prize crews, meaning those men could spend even less time onshore, while the other would cruise the coast around Sierra Leone, and they would alternate every three weeks. Findlay still wasn't satisfied, especially when the commodore's new rules about going upriver stymied a capture the governor badly wanted, and Hayes would discover later that, staying on brand, Findlay had written a letter to the Admiralty complaining that Hayes had been utterly insensible to the governor's pleas for help and had provided none at all to the colony, a blatant falsehood. The colonial governor had gone so far as to request a ship of the Squadron be placed under his authority for the protection of the colony, but the Admiralty demurred, as such a posting—the placing of a Royal Navy vessel under the command of a colonial government—would be "contrary to custom." (In so many words, such a thing had never before happened, wasn't going to happen, and would never happen, at least not on its watch.)

Findlay wasn't the only person displeased with the new commodore. Gordon and Hayes didn't hit it off, which would culminate with Hayes, in a display of pettiness to rival Collier and Owen's battle of the beards, bringing Captain Gordon up on formal court-martial charges for, essentially, writing a nasty note about him. Collier was one of the judges for the trial, which occurred on board the *Victory* back in England in 1832, and Gordon was cleared of three charges and found guilty of two minor ones, for which he received what amounted to a slap on the wrist and a stern talking-to. Hayes got the stern talking-to as well—despite not being on trial, he was informally censured for bringing frivolous (if technically true in some aspects) charges. One of the allegations was that Hayes had transferred Ramsay without informing Gordon, and it's at least true that the *Atholl's* first lieutenant was doing a bit of ship hopping. Hayes had decided to replace the *Atholl's* first lieutenant, William Ramsay, with William Castle, first lieutenant from the *Dryad*, at the helm of *Black Joke*. (Castle would be the fourth William to serve as captain of *Black Joke*.) It's not that Castle didn't deserve the chance at promotion, given that he'd served as first lieutenant on multiple ships, including the flagship *Isis* in the West Indies Squadron, and more recently both *Sybille* and *Dryad*, and that after he'd commanded a schooner, *Speedwell*, in the fight against Cuban pirates in the early 1820s. Knowing, however, how difficult promotion was to achieve during this period, and how much the ability to make them happen could alter the perception of a captain as a patron worthy of following, the change irked Gordon at least a little, and Ramsay—still a lieutenant, though now the first lieutenant of the *Dryad*—possibly more. As far as Ramsay would have been concerned—and glad though he almost certainly was to take a break from the tiny tender on which he'd been effectively trapped for months for the roomier environs of the flagship—Castle couldn't earn promotion fast enough, as Hayes's actions strongly implied that Ramsay would get his tender back once Castle had had sufficiently meritorious success to reach commander. As for Gordon, one of the other court-martial charges against him had been complaining of Hayes's transfer of Ramsay in a letter using intemperate language, so Gordon's feelings can be surmised.

Castle, for his part, was happy to oblige; he'd convinced his superior to put him on the *Black Joke*, at least for one cruise, precisely because the tender was reputed to be lucky, and he only had to look to *Dryad's* own commander to see just how lucky the swift brig could be. *Black Joke* successfully completed its second refit in mid-February 1831, leaving Freetown to cruise for the first time since November of the previous year, and if Hayes hadn't been too sure how the ship that had barely made it into harbor a month ago could be considered fortuitous throughout the Squadron, he soon found out. Much like William Turner before him, scarcely a week had gone by since Castle's assumption of command when, on February 22, the *Black Joke* encountered the Spanish schooner *Primero*. All day—the *Primero* had been spotted at 8:00 a.m.—the crew of the *Black Joke* chased the slaver. As night settled over the water, the schooner's captain relaxed and eased up, assuming the *Black Joke* couldn't possibly chase him all night as well. He underestimated Lieutenant Castle, who'd likely done that and worse at night when chasing pirates across the Caribbean and back again, and using his night glass in conjunction with the cover of darkness, he not only caught up to the *Primero*, but cut off any viable means of its escape. The slave trader refused to accept defeat and again tried to run. Castle fired blank rounds at the schooner in warning, to no effect, as the captain remained primed to make a break for it if given even the tiniest gap.

Only then did someone see the tornado.

Castle's sense of urgency must have ratcheted up a hundredfold. He had to choose. The night had already been dark, and the storm that accompanied the approaching tornado wasn't helping. Rain had begun to fall, intensifying so much that Castle was convinced that if he didn't bring the slaver in, right here and now, it would escape into the storm. But if he took too long to capture the slaver, the *Black Joke* might not be successful in fleeing *a tornado*. The slaver's captain remained obdurate, certain that now the famous brig would have to relent and let him go. But the lieutenant had not waited so long to give up what could well be his last chance at promotion. He hadn't nigh on begged the commodore for this opportunity just to lose the *Primero* in the rain. The time for the niceties of the dance of flags and the guns aimed high had passed. Castle fired into the ship.

WAS captains tried to avoid firing into ships—as opposed to across their deck, or into their rigging, masts, and sails—for two primary reasons, and much like service in the Squadron itself, they were both mercenary and humanitarian. The more damaged a ship was, the less valuable it was as a prize, particularly if that damage was to the hull, rather than the more easily repaired or replaced rigging and masts, because a slave trader's salvage value was based on its price at auction, not its original value or an objective scale based on size as measured in "tons burthen." Also, the slave hold was belowdecks, meaning that any shot so aimed might kill or injure the captive people on board; the ostensible purpose of the WAS was to suppress the slave trade, and that included liberating or at least recapturing the enslaved, not killing them (though, realistically, they, too, were less valuable dead).

Castle's shot, which did halt the *Primero*, "with sails shaking and booms cracking," killed two enslaved children and wounded two more. The crew discovered this after a party from *Black Joke* boarded; beyond the losses among the enslaved, the slaver's crew had lost the cook to the blast, while its mate and four sailors were injured. It's hard to know how bad Castle felt about that first tally. Long service often engendered callousness in the men of the WAS, who, if not inured to the horrors of the slave trade, did become at least somewhat accustomed to the regular sight of its depravity in the visceral, living flesh. However, being directly responsible for the death of children would surely have weighed on all but the hardest (or most racist) of Squadron sailors. What they found in the hold probably eased Castle's mind a least a little, but not for any positive reasons.

The inhumanity with which slave ships were built and cruelty with which they were run were frequently one of the primary indictments of the trade used by abolitionists on the home front. The crew soon discovered that the confinements on the *Primero* were even more appalling than usual in a trade known for employing any degradation that might profit. At 130 tons burthen, the Spanish schooner was (very) slightly smaller than what could be considered a medium-size slaving vessel, but it was packed particularly tight, with 311 people trapped in the hold, made more squalid by the presence of animals, in this case, a number of exceedingly dirty monkeys. Of these 311, like an even more nightmarish version of Parrey's prize *Cristina*, 155 were young and 4 were babies, meaning over half the slaver's cargo had been imprisoned children. One of the babies was a newborn who had been born since the *Primero* had left Gallinas, just eight days before, and "whose mother, unhappy creature, sickly and emaciated, was [suckling] it on deck, with hardly a rag to cover either herself or her offspring." Those with pressing or infectious health problems—such as giving birth in utter filth in the former case and dysentery in the latter—remained on deck for limited medical care or to halt the spreading of contagion, but those considered "healthy" most likely spent at least sixteen hours a day, at minimum, on the brink of suffocation in the hold, impossibly confined to a slave deck that, on *Primero*, measured only twenty-six inches in height. (Thirty-six inches might have been closer to the standard usable height, and though still unbearable, the extra ten inches could be the difference between life spent, at least in part, as someone's chattel and excruciating death from slow suffocation, far from the sight of any shore.)

Slave hatches—latticed apertures, grates really, but made of either wood or iron—were placed between the deck and the slave deck to allow "a sufficiency of air" to reach below, but it was never enough. The hatches were sometimes accompanied by scuttles, small holes cut in the side of the ship, also for air, though if these existed, there were only two or three, and those were not always open. Some slavers held men and women in separate sections of the slave deck, some divided by age, and others didn't bother sorting through the misery. Crouched as best they could, the enslaved sat in the stink and wet of every discharge a body could produce, from the daily waste of urine and feces, to harbingers of illness such as pus and vomit, to the rotting flesh of those who had died in the hold and not yet had their lifeless bodies removed.

Peter Leonard, lieutenant to the *Dryad*, was serving on *Black Joke* and was on the *Primero* when the slaver's hatches were opened. It is his words that reveal the *Primero's* greatest horror:

> *The small space in which these unfortunate beings are huddled together is almost incredible [. . .] they can hardly even sit upright.*

*The [after] part of the deck is occupied by women and children, separated by a wooden partition from the other slaves. The horrors of this infernal apartment—the want of air—the suffocating heat—the filth—the stench—may be easily imagined; although it IS remarked that this ship is one of the cleanest that ever was brought to the colony.*

Of every act of deliberate and wanton cruelty aboard that schooner of horror, ultimately the worst thing about the *Primero* might have been that, as awful as it was, even the conditions described were barely a glimpse of the worst horrors the trade had to offer.

## Spanish Schooner

Register of Slaves, Natives of Africa captured on board the said Ship Dryad, John Hays, CB. Commander and emancipated by

| Nº | Names | Sex | Age | Stature ft | Stature in | Description |
|----|-------|-----|-----|----|----|-------------|
| 23,808 | Lamalle | Man | 24 | 5 | 3 | } No marks |
| | Mannoh | „ | 30 | 5 | 3 | |
| 23,810 | Bindee | „ | 18 | 5 | 4 | |
| | Bangar | „ | 18 | 5 | 5 | Tattooed on back |
| | Warbay | „ | 20 | 5 | 4½ | No marks |
| | Dove | „ | 22 | 5 | 6½ | Tattooed on Ribs |
| | Foimora | „ | 30 | 5 | 7 | dº arms |
| 23,815 | Jobangano | „ | 22 | 5 | 4½ | No marks |
| | Babo | „ | 16 | 5 | 2½ | dº |
| | Harbangau | „ | 21 | 5 | 1½ | Tattooed all over belly |
| | Miabob | „ | 26 | 5 | 3 | dº dº |
| | Jawalos | „ | 28 | 5 | 6 | No marks |
| 23,820 | Obbah | „ | 30 | 5 | 5 | Scars all over chin |
| | Jaye | „ | 21 | 5 | 1 | No mark |
| | Bannah | „ | 26 | 5 | 9 | Tattooed on back & belly |
| | Ompah | „ | 30 | 5 | 1½ | No marks |
| | Jor | „ | 18 | 5 | _ | dº |
| 23,825 | Beah | „ | 29 | 5 | 4½ | Tattooed back & belly |
| | Gampi | „ | 18 | 4 | _ | No marks |
| | Meme | „ | 30 | 5 | 5 | Tattooed on back |
| | Babbah | „ | 26 | 5 | 6 | No marks |
| | Ombah | „ | 20 | 5 | 3½ | dº |
| 23,830 | Kabaguoh | „ | 22 | 5 | 6 | Tattooed on belly & back |
| | Fang | „ | 30 | 5 | 2 | No mark |
| | Jendamay | „ | 24 | 5 | 5 | dº |
| | Bangay | „ | 28 | 5 | 9 | Tattooed on belly |
| | Feah | „ | 30 | 5 | 1 | dº all over |
| 23,835 | Paimoig | „ | 26 | 5 | 4½ | dº dº |
| | Hahoney | „ | 18 | 5 | ½ | |
| | Brlah | „ | 18 | 5 | 1 | No marks |
| | Sattoz | „ | 34 | 5 | 5½ | |
| | Miah | „ | 26 | 5 | 9½ | Tattooed on back |
| 23,840 | Bundos | „ | 36 | 5 | 4½ | dº dº & belly |
| | Jameah | „ | 40 | 5 | 9 | dº all over |
| | Jemoh | „ | 40 | 5 | 4½ | dº on belly |
| | Fain | „ | 20 | 5 | 3½ | dº on back |
| 23,844 | Dooa | „ | 20 | 5 | 1½ | dº dº |

Register, Primero

"Primera."

Captured by His Majesty's Brig "Black Joke," a Tender to His Majesty by decree of the British and Spanish Court of Mixed Commission established.

| № | Names | Sex | Age | Stature Feet | in. | Description |
|---|-------|-----|-----|------|-----|-------------|
| 23,845 | Darfuah | Man | 22 | 5 | 6 | No marks |
| | Shulay | " | 20 | 5 | 3 | d° |
| | Gragea | " | 19 | 5 | 5 | Tattoos on back & belly |
| | Famah | " | 30 | 5 | 3 | Left arm 3½ longer than the right |
| | Marfallah | " | 40 | 5 | 2½ | Tattoos on arms |
| 23,850 | Chelay | " | 16 | 5 | 3½ | No marks |
| | Forpah | " | 24 | 5 | 3 | Tattoos on belly |
| | Fah | " | 26 | 5 | 5 | d° back |
| | Besarka | " | 24 | 5 | 3½ | No marks |
| | Fah | " | 28 | 5 | 4 | d° |
| 23,855 | Barbannah | " | 26 | 5 | 6 | Tattoos on belly |
| | Bahsegaray | " | 22 | 4 | 10½ | d° back |
| | Wompay | " | 24 | 5 | 5 | d° d° |
| | Fah | " | 30 | 5 | 4 | d° d° |
| | Soso | " | 30 | 5 | 7½ | No marks |
| 13,860 | Fahbunde | " | 26 | 5 | 3 | Tattoos on arms |
| | Miah | " | 28 | 5 | 5½ | |
| | Bargue | " | 30 | 5 | 3½ | No marks |
| | Bannah | " | 30 | 5 | 11½ | |
| | Seboo | " | 30 | 5 | 6 | |
| 23,865 | Brnnay | " | 30 | 5 | 4½ | Tattoos on Back |
| | Formoroo | " | 28 | 5 | 2 | d° arms |
| | Boree | " | 28 | 5 | 3½ | |
| | Royeanda | " | 30 | 5 | 3½ | No marks |
| | Fuah | " | 20 | 5 | 4½ | |
| 23,870 | Karway | " | 19 | 5 | 3½ | Scar on right cheek |
| | Fah | " | 23 | 5 | 10½ | |
| | Yearkoo | " | 24 | 5 | 5 | |
| | Kahoota | " | 30 | 5 | 5 | No marks |
| | Quevoo | " | 16 | 5 | 3½ | |
| 23,875 | Fanguee | " | 32 | 5 | 6 | |
| | Suba | " | 20 | 5 | 1½ | |
| | Bah | " | 30 | 5 | 6 | Tattoos on back |
| | Solunangah | " | 30 | 5 | 5 | d° belly |
| | Karee | " | 30 | 5 | 5½ | d° back |
| 23,880 | Lemoh | " | 40 | 5 | 1½ | No marks |
| 23,881 | Kakai | " | 26 | 5 | 2½ | d° |

# CHAPTER ELEVEN

*Marinerito*
April 1831,
496 enslaved people

Commodore Hayes despised the slave trade as a business "of horrible crimes, worse than murder," and as prizes such as the *Primero* came into Freetown's harbor or escaped condemnation under the French flag, his disgust with the whole "nefarious traffic" undergirded each report he sent back to the Admiralty. These were official reports, and in most circumstances the standard language was a distanced, spare retelling of facts. The prize crew on the *Primero* lost only one more person on their journey back to Sierra Leone; only five (known) dead enslaved Africans since the time of embarkation—four of them killed as a result of the capture of the ship—was an astonishingly good result. Compare that description and result to this letter from Hayes to his superiors about two French slave ships the *Black Joke* had attempted to detain:

*The scalding perspiration was running down from one to the other, covered also with their own filth, and where it is no uncommon occurrence for women to be bringing forth children, and men dying by their side, with full in their view, living and dead bodies chained together, and the living, in addition to all their other torments, labouring under the most famishing thirst. [. . . Reflect] on what must be the sufferings of upwards of five hundred of these miserable people chained together, and crammed in between the decks of a vessel only half the tonnage of a Ten Gun Brig. Gracious God! Is this unparalleled cruelty to last for ever?*

It was going to last for a while longer, to be sure. Hayes's level of impassioned horror was not the norm, neither on the coast nor back in London, especially when British lives were lost in the pursuit and capture of a slave ship. Particularly back in England, abolitionist sentiment or no, the populace, in the commodore's estimation, had no notion of the grisly sights to be found on a slaver, nor the extent of the battle yet to be waged against the traffic. This work "where [English] blood is spilt," Hayes knew, was "viewed in England by many (who reflect not on, or take into their consideration, the sufferings, the unspeakable sufferings, of the poor unhappy Africans,) as most horrid affairs, but when their sufferings be considered, I think it will appear in another light."

Even still, the commodore's personal feelings could only make so much difference, even in his own command. Sailors in the West Africa Squadron were regularly exposed to the brutality of the slave trade, yet as far as Peter Leonard on the *Dryad* (and lately of the *Black Joke*) could tell, remained largely insensate to the greater aim of their collective efforts. Leonard seemingly had an attitude more typical to service on the coast than did his superior and was much more blasé about whether those effecting suppression actually cared about slavery. After witnessing the particularly violent action aboard one slaver, the lieutenant wrote, "It is gratifying to think that Jack"—Jack, or Jack Tar, was a common nickname for the average Royal Navy rating, those who weren't officers (commissioned, warrant, petty, or otherwise)— "is still the same—that he fights for the love of it just as he was wont to do—for it is not to be supposed that any notions concerning the inhumanity of slave-dealing, or the boon of emancipation which he is about to confer [. . .] enter into his thoughtless head." In using so broad a brush Leonard basically asserted that the lower decks were incapable of political thought and surely elided over at least some awareness among the sailors for the reasons and rationale for their service, particularly for any men who risked kidnapping and enslavement with every pirate and slaver encounter on account of their hue. However, Leonard wasn't entirely wrong about the general mindset in the WAS.

He was, though, mistaken in attributing the primacy of love of duty (and a good fight) to just the seamen. After his capture of the *Primero*, Castle continued to cruise for prey and, in February 1831, thought he had a line on a schooner near Cape Mesurado when he realized he wasn't alone in his pursuit. An unknown frigate was also firing on the schooner, which, out of options, decided it would rather risk the forty-four-gun frigate than the *Black Joke*. Surprising just about everyone, said frigate promptly hoisted an American flag and identified itself as the USS *Java*. Castle decided this definitely merited investigation, so as the schooner was being boarded by the frigate, he ordered his little brig to sidle up alongside to take a better look. All appeared to be in order, and even though the American captain, Kennedy, wouldn't allow a boarding party from the *Black Joke* (hey, the War of 1812 hadn't been *that* long ago), he did consent to receive Castle alone on the *Java* and was the picture of courtesy. The Americans were headed back to the United States, but Kennedy assured Castle that the *Black Joke* should give chase to any American-flagged slaver it might encounter, and the *Java* would do likewise should it happen upon a British slave trader, and, essentially, have a nice life. It wasn't much, considering that if British political will regarding policing the slave trade was low, American interest was lower still, and slavers didn't seem to have much bothered with American flags for years, but it was nice of him to say, and since the schooner had been boarded by the Americans and was thus out of the Royal Navy's purview, that would have been the end of it . . . if the *Black Joke* hadn't happened upon *Java* again two days later. This time, Kennedy assured Castle that should the US frigate happen upon a slaver, it would signal the tender and detain the quarry until the speedier ship could arrive. So of course it was this time that the *Black Joke* never saw or heard from the *Java* again.

The frigate had been stationed in the Mediterranean and had

only been in the area because Kennedy was looking in on the Colony of Liberia. Having conducted that business, USS *Java* left the
coast, continuing back to Norfolk, Virginia. Imperialist interests
notwithstanding, the US and the English home fronts didn't hold a
monopoly on disinterest in the disposition of the slave trade. The officer corps of the Royal Navy was as rife with apathy if not outright
antipathy toward the mission of the Squadron as it was abolitionist
fervor, and perhaps none typified this bent more than *Dryad* senior
lieutenant Henry Huntley, who was, in April 1831, presented with
a choice between three commands: the cutter from England, *Seaflower*; the proven, but tired, *Black Joke*; or its former prize and new
partner in arms, the freshly rechristened *Fair Rosamond*. However,
if Huntley picked *Black Joke*, which might "barely last six months"
before the ship had to be scuttled, the other assignments to the two
tenders would stand until a natural vacancy presented itself, and
Commodore Hayes couldn't guarantee Huntley would get another
opportunity to command.

Lieutenant Castle's time on the *Black Joke* was short-lived; soon
after his odd encounters with the *Java*, circumstances (read: death
and Commodore Hayes) conspired to transfer Castle to acting commander of another ship in the Squadron, the *Medina*, where that
October he would finally receive the promotion he sought. Hayes
had no intention of reneging on his understanding with Ramsay that
he'd get another chance at the helm, but Huntley had served with the
commodore longer, and that probably contributed to his having first
pick for a mission he felt was entirely pointless: not only could Africa
not be "civilized," but Huntley was certain that "to keep up a squadron
for the purpose of suppressing the Slave Trade is a monotonous and
idle absurdity." Huntley also believed in duty, however, and he took
the choice Hayes offered seriously, providing one of the only known
descriptions of how *Black Joke* and *Fair Rosamond* sailed respective
to the other. The lieutenant described the latter as "a fine schooner,
though not equal to the sailing of the *Black Joke* by the wind, but
she was certainly her superior when going well 'free.'" (These terms

describe the action of the ship on the water: in "by or on the wind" the sails were positioned such that a ship was propelled along its length, while "going free" or "sailing off the wind" was considered a more natural movement in which the ship was directly propelled forward by the wind.) Huntley apparently didn't put much stock in something so nebulous as "luck," and mindful of Hayes's warning, chose the newer, shinier *Fair Rosamond*, which had yet to even face a serious repair (seeing as, even when captured, the ship hadn't been fired upon), over the much-embattled and twice-refit *Black Joke*. His choice brought Lieutenant William Ramsay back to the famous tender that spring, only three months after his last command.

This bothered Ramsay, who apparently did put stock in the winds of fortune, not at all; had he been given the choice, he might well have ended up on the same ship he was assigned by default. It would have been the right choice. Commodore Hayes had intelligence on the possible whereabouts of heavily armed slave traders, and he wanted his lieutenants to act, sending the *Black Joke* for a cruise in its old stomping grounds, the Bight of Biafra, while he sent Huntley and the *Fair Rosamond* to the Bight of Benin. As for the rest of the Squadron, in the spring of 1831, it was more short of ships and men than it had arguably ever been—the *Atholl* remained and had been joined by *Favorite*; *Conflict* and *Plumper* held the rotating duty in Sierra Leone, and the *Dryad*, thought much too slow for duty on the coast, had lost most of its men to staffing the tenders. (The manpower problems went deeper than that as the complement of the *Plumper* consisted almost entirely of Kroomen, with only six White sailors aboard.) First, however, the *Black Joke* had to stop at Clarence Cove.

In a fit of irony—or perhaps just in the absence of Collier—the navy had finally elected to try Fernando Pó, which was still firmly in rapid (and ordered) decline under Colonel Nicholls, as the Victualling Depot for the West Africa Squadron. This made the island, however temporarily, the main rendezvous point for Squadron ships on patrol, much as Captain Owen had once dreamed and schemed of its being. Of more concern to Ramsay, awaiting him there were fresh sweeps (oars) sent from England. Given what the lieutenant had already been through on the *Black Joke*, it's no wonder he wanted them to hand before beginning the tender's cruise in earnest. While in harbor in Clarence Cove, the *Black Joke* chanced upon a friendly colonial vessel, a palm oiler, helmed by a Captain Mather. The two men swapped news, and Mather mentioned a heavily armed slave ship, with five guns and a well-disciplined crew, flying Spanish colors and nearing departure from nearby Duke's Town. It was, without question, the finest slave ship Mather had seen in the area for quite some time. The ship's captain was, Mather was certain, unworried by the prospect of capture.

Mather was so sure because, though no one was allowed on board this *Marinerito*, he'd had dinner onshore with its officers. This wasn't at all unusual, as the crews of licit and illicit traders who found themselves in the same settlements often interacted. There are numerous accounts of even men in the Squadron sharing meals with, and enjoying the hospitality of, slave traders. The mixed-nationality officers of this Spanish brig had boasted to the palm-oil captain that, if approached, they had every intention of fighting their way out, but on the whole, they weren't especially worried about the prospect. *Black Joke* was too weak to take them, seeing as it was small and out-gunned, they had assured Mather. As for the rest of the Squadron, well, that was even more laughable. Every other ship was too slow; they had nothing to fear from the British. It hadn't been surprising to Mather that *Black Joke* had come up in conversation—the brig's fame was global, and discussion of the bane of the trade was ubiquitous among slavers. But to then stumble on the notorious tender itself, and so nearby! That was something else, and Mather, ever helpful, could not only tell Ramsay where he'd left the cocky officers, but also provide a solid estimate of when they might disembark, fully laden with the enslaved.

The *Black Joke*, according to Mather's best guess, could get in position in time to intercept, but it was a tight window. Ramsay wasted no more time, scooping up the new equipment and his supplies at record pace, and immediately headed out to confront the confidence of the *Marinerito*. He anchored out to sea near the mouth of the Old Calabar River, but out of sight of the harbor, on the evening of April 23. The next morning, Ramsay moved the tender out to sea, in case a slaver came out of the river and spotted the little brig, then moved back to the river at night. Another morning broke, and the crew repeated the maneuver. It proved worth the trouble when, at 11:00 a.m. on the second day of their watch, April 25, 1831, someone on the *Black Joke* spotted the Spanish brig coming out of the Old Calabar River, headed in their direction from the northwest. If they'd remained in their nighttime spot, the tender would almost immediately have been spotted, which would not only have forced Ramsay to uncomfortably reminisce about how well chasing a ship upriver had worked out for him in pursuit of *Dos Amigos*, but also near certainly have warned every slaver in the vicinity and beyond of the *Black Joke*'s appearance in the Bights. Ships of all speeds and armaments had taken to avoiding the *Black Joke*'s patrol area entirely, if possible, and if the ship appeared while the slavers were in port, they stayed, sometimes for months, until they were sure the British brig had gone on its way.

Just in case, though, Ramsay ordered some of the sails struck to better disguise the distinctive ship. This worked well enough that the sublimely unconcerned *Marinerito* was in sight from the deck, not the rigging, of the *Black Joke* before recognizing the very subject of their amused dinner conversation with that friendly merchant captain of perhaps a week past. Once the Spanish brig recognized its foe, however, the joking stopped, and the *Marinerito* swiftly caught a southeasterly wind trying, unsuccessfully, to escape; Ramsay did have the only ship on the water they'd been worried about catching them. The two ships sailed all day, until suddenly, at nine o'clock at night, they both hit a dead calm, barely within gun range. The *Black Joke* asked for the Spanish brig's surrender with a warning shot aimed to cut the ship off in front; *Marinerito* answered as they said they would, with a three-gun broadside. The fight was on.

Stopping for replacement equipment had already been plenty fortuitous, since Mather's intel had been proven correct, and now Ramsay could be even more grateful he'd stopped—he was going to need those sweeps. In the bright moonlight on a totally calm sea, with the Cameroon mountains rising in the background, the *Black Joke*'s men rowed toward the slave ship under a barrage of grapeshot that only steadied as they approached. This was the scene that prompted Leonard to wax eloquent about the glory of the fighting spirit and the uncomplicated mind of Jack Tar, this strong beat of men eagerly rowing into a fight as deadly projectiles streamed overhead, with no thought to their place in a larger mission. For all the glory Leonard saw after the fact, the hour they spent—from 1:00 to 2:00 a.m., under the constant fire of grapeshot, round shot, and musketry—as the crew steadily rowed *toward* the barrage likely felt interminable to those manning the sweeps; they'd already had one man, Isaac Fail, wounded in the initial onslaught. Thankfully the wind finally came back and Ramsay was able to bring the tender alongside to taunting cries from the slaver, reputedly hearing a voice call out, "Come aboard, ye English blackguards, and fight us fairly!"

Ever since the sweeps had been ordered, Ramsay had been sitting on the port gunwale with eyes only for the *Marinerito*, sword point in the wood of the deck, and he laconically responded to the jeers from the other deck, "I'm coming, mon [sic], I'm coming as fast as I can." Bringing the brig alongside, Ramsay gave a signal to the grizzled, one-eyed boatswain's mate, Peter Kenney, who blew a loud whistle for all the crew to hear and called, "All hands to board! Give us a rope to lash the devil with!" As the ships met, he leaped across, followed by several men. Just then, at the crucial moment of boarding, the wind that Ramsay had been waiting for turned against him. With a sudden shift, *Black Joke* picked up speed so quickly that it practically ricocheted off the *Marinerito*. The movement was so swift that the sailors hadn't managed to lash the ships together for a proper boarding before *Black Joke* careened away, but as was the procedure, boarding had already commenced. Kenney, Ramsay, his mate C. J. Bosanquet, and nine others were the only ones to make it to the deck of the *Marinerito*, where they faced seventy-seven men long prepared for this moment. The Spanish brig had five eighteen-pounders to the *Black Joke*'s two, and as every gun on both ships fired, all hell well and truly broke loose.

It was a teenage midshipman who saved the day. Edwin Hinde, scarcely fifteen years old and tiny with it—and also quite possibly the highest-ranked individual still on the tender, what with so many officers having made the fateful leap to the *Marinerito*—had only been in the Royal Navy for two years, but he nonetheless rallied the crew of the *Black Joke* like the commander he hoped someday to become. Hinde ordered the men back to the starboard sweeps. A cry rose up from Isaac Fail, his young son looking on: "Hurrah, boys, hurrah! God bless King William!"—and with his final strength given to the call to rally, Fail died in assistant surgeon Douglas's arms. The crew managed to bring the ship alongside *Marinerito* once more, where the fighting was getting desperate, and Hinde successfully led a second boarding of nearly the entire crew to the slaver. The first boarding party, though heavily wounded, had held out until reinforcements arrived, and together they soon overcame the Spanish slaver.

Fail was the only man dead from the *Black Joke*, though Ramsay and Bosanquet were both severely injured, and five more were wounded. The *Marinerito*, by contrast, had thirteen men killed or drowned in the action, and another fifteen wounded. Now that the battle was won, the Black Jokes still standing noticed the slave hatches had been battened down and rushed to open them, only to discover a horrific scene: "The living were found sitting on the heads and bodies of the dead and dying below." The hatches had, it seemed, been closed since the chase began nearly twenty-four hours prior, and the enslaved Africans on board were simultaneously suffocating and dying of thirst, with the still-living crouched perilously on the bodies of the recently dead. The enslaved of the *Marinerito* had not been given water for days, since before the slaver had exited the river, and when they were released from belowdecks, a second, smaller pandemonium ensued as the Black Jokes began to hand out water. The enslaved crowded the tubs of fresh water, insensate from prolonged dehydration, lapping the deck for every spare drop, even attempting seawater when they could not access the tubs and jugs being hastily provided. Of the 496 enslaved people who had been embarked on the Spanish slaver, 26 were already dead of suffocation and/or dehydration, and 107 were so close to death that Ramsay believed that the only way to save their lives would be to land them at the nearest friendly harbor, Clarence Cove, rather than risk trying to get them to Freetown and the Mixed Commission for their formal liberation. Of those so landed, 60 still died. As for the *Marinerito*'s crew, "even the hardest heart" on *Black Joke* had been moved by the harrowing scene on the slave deck, and so close after a hard-fought victory, emotions were high.

Treaties dictated that a slaver's crew either be dropped at the nearest port—from thence to go forth and enslave again, presumably, but officially to be "tried and punished according to the laws of their country"—be placed on another ship, or be brought to Freetown as witnesses. Ramsay, taking the tenor of his men, went for a fourth option, much-discussed among naval officers but rarely carried out, particularly in the nineteenth century. The crew of the *Black Joke*, in rebuke of the abject misery they'd just witnessed, agreed to a man to first (and illegally) imprison the surviving crew of the *Marinerito* at Fernando Pó for a few weeks before conspiring with the crew of *Atholl*, Ramsay's previous berth, to set them "adrift," which in this case meant abandonment on an island, Anabona (modern-day Annobón), without any seacraft whatsoever. (*Black Joke* couldn't do it because Ramsay would be expected to testify against *Marinerito* before the Mixed Commission.) Describing the island, Leonard said:

*The Island of Anabona—in one degree twenty-two minutes south latitude, five degrees twenty-seven minutes forty-nine seconds east longitude—is about twenty-four miles in circumference, and its summit from two thousand to three thousand feet high. Its appearance, as we approach, is remarkably pleasing. Without either the romantic rocky outline of Prince's Island, or the deep forest shade of Fernando Po, its sunbright surface is surmounted by a few craggy and conical eminences, while its sloping sides consist of undulating hills, many of which are almost free from wood, and covered with waiving grass embrowned by the sun, forming bright yellow glades, which relieve the deep green of the spreading groves and clumps of trees covering the other hills in their vicinity. These hills are intersected with dells and ravines, shaded with numerous tall trees and leafy shrubs,—deep and wide gullies formed by the original convulsion of Nature, but now bearing in their bosom the placid brook, or affording a bed to the rushing mountain torrents during the periodical rains. In many places the island is steep and precipitous from the very beach. At others the ascent is more gradual; but, excepting a few acres in two or three places close to the sea shore, there is little or no level land, so far as I could observe, on the whole island.*

It doesn't sound like the worst place to be left, especially since Annobón was far from unpopulated. The poetic context is that Annobón was then administered by a native government extremely hostile to Spaniards, whom the whole of the island had successfully ousted as overlords, yet who still plagued the populace as kidnappers and sellers of flesh. In what could well be viewed as a rather cosmic justice, at least some of the slaver's crew—possibly those who were actually Spanish, as other nationalities likely received a comparatively warmer reception—attempted to canoe to São Tomé. Nine men in three canoes left Annobón. Two canoes were taken up in a tornado, while the third one barely survived. The storm took out nearly all of their stores, such that when the *Black Joke* happened upon that last canoe a month later, the two men left had been without food, drinking only what water fell from the sky, for ten days. The tender picked them up, but like so many from belowdecks on the *Marinerito*, these two from above were in dire straits, and unlikely to survive. Thus ever to slavers.

Once the *Black Joke* and the *Marinerito* prize crew arrived in Sierra Leone with the remaining African survivors, plus the few crew members of the slaver who'd traveled as witnesses, "liberation" began. Once a ship was spotted coming into Freetown, a signal gun was fired. Lookouts posted to the signal hill eyed the vessel and announced, by way of a colored ball lifted on a long stick or staff, its apparent make and origins—the *Marinerito* would have been announced as a brig from the south. Once arrived, an official boat would meet the prize and climb on board, and there witness a segregated group of enslaved Africans who were sick or dying; a deck "thronged with men, women and children, all entirely naked" and likely covered in all manner of filth; and the smell. This mass of people might be only a small portion of the prize's total human cargo, and if more enslaved were on board, they were still in the very slave deck on which they'd been embarked, if with slightly more space. Each individual would be subject to an inspection, which reads less like a liberation and more like the precursor to an auction:

> [The enslaved were] drawn up through the small hatchway from their hot, dark confinement. A black boatswain seized them one by one, dragging them before [the inspectors] for a moment, when the proper officer at a glance decided the age, where above 14; and they were instantly swung again by the arm into their [loathsome] cell, where another negro boatswain sat, with a whip or stick, and forced them to resume the bent and painful attitude necessary for the stowage of so large a number.

There the enslaved remained until the prize was condemned, unless their health merited landing or transfer. (Suddenly, *Dos Amigos* being taken without 560-odd enslaved Africans on board has a rather peculiar silver lining.) Presuming it was condemned—*Marinerito* certainly was—the enslaved were rowed to the King's Yard in Free-town to receive their much-ballyhooed liberation. It was not freedom. The newly liberated Africans became British, whether they wanted to or not, and the adults were given three options—they could become "free apprentices in the West Indies," join a segregated regiment of troops, or settle on one of the estates bordering Freetown. There was an unofficial fourth option, as those who attempted to liberate them-selves on the *Manzanares* could tell anyone, which was to cause or seem like enough trouble that the colonial government shipped the lot of you off to the hinterlands and ceased to interfere. And a fifth possibility, as as many as 15 percent of the newly arrived Africans succumbed to illnesses contracted on board slave ships or in Free-town itself and died within four months of their arrival.

One could easily be forgiven for forgetting that this process was ostensibly meant to be liberatory. Apprenticeship was rather slavery adjacent, in that the people who "chose" it would be shipped, usu-ally (but not always) against their will, to one of the British colonies in the Americas, where they were required to perform labor, with minimal or no compensation, for a term "not exceeding" fourteen years. (After the British abolished slavery in all its colonial hold-ings, guess what 80 percent of relocated "liberated" Africans did as "apprenticeship"? Harvested sugarcane in Jamaica, British Guiana, and Trinidad.) When joining a regiment, the British registrar might change someone's name because it was hard for the registrar to say or just for a lark—one such secretary changed *every* African's name, just so his records would be preemptively alphabetized. And settling on an estate might also sound disturbingly familiar—this option came with an allotment of land, one the "liberated" were to work for a supervisor (each responsible for upward of a thousand similarly situated Africans), and provided a cook pot, a shovel, and a spoon, plus one and a quarter yards of fabric for some clothes, since noth-ing, sometimes not even slavery, seemed to offend British sensibili-ties like nudity.

This hadn't always been the policy. The nature and goals of the

Liberated African Department had, for a stretch, appeared to be entirely at the whim of the colonial government of Sierra Leone. Kenneth Macaulay, who'd himself served as acting governor for six months in 1826, summed up this history in 1827:

> The colony [of Sierra Leone] has been grievously injured by the want of any systematic plan or rule of conduct having been laid down for its government, by which its prosperity might have been promoted. [. . .] Every Governor has been left to follow his own plans, however crude and undigested; and no two succeeding Governors have ever pursued the same course. This remark applies more particularly to the management of the liberated Africans. Mr. [Thomas] Ludlam [1806–08, his third tenure] pursued the system of apprenticing them. Mr. [Thomas Perronet] Thompson [1808–10] set that aside, and turned them loose in the colony, without any other superintendance than its general police. Captain [Edward H.] Columbine [1810–11] employed them on the public works, or apprenticed them. Colonel [Charles William] Maxwell [1811–15], after delivering over [. . .] all the men fit for his Majesty's service, apprenticed a part of the remainder, and then commenced forming villages with those who could not be so disposed of. Sir Charles MacCarthy [1815–20; 1821–24] gave up apprenticing, except in particular cases, and adopted the plan of forming them into villages, under such civil superintendance and religious instruction as he could command, keeping the youths and children in schools, or making mechanics of them; neglecting perhaps too much, in his successful attempt to make them orderly and quiet citizens, the equally desirable object of making them industrious agriculturalists and growers of exportable produce. [Major] General [Sir Charles] Turner [1824–26] dissolved, in great measure, the schools, and the institutions for mechanics, and threw the people more on their own resources; but did not afford, indeed he did not possess, the means of duly superintending their settlement and progress, or directing their energies.

In essence, some governors had allowed the apprentice system to be used as a proxy slavery, where the contract could be bought, sold, and extended for transgressions. Others placed more emphasis on conscription, and for a few years nearly 80 percent of recaptive African men were sent to the Royal Army. Some governors thought the colony, especially Freetown and its immediate environs, was too full and focused on shipping recaptives back out to places such as the West Indies for "apprenticeships," again proxy slavery, usually harvesting sugar; others felt there wasn't enough farming and focused on increasing the population of the colony for the benefit of the agricultural economy. The common bond throughout was colonization; the jobs being assigned to recaptive Africans were unquestionably in service of British empire. From an account of the *Primero*:

> [The children] were singing on board the schooner, in anticipation of the boat's return, and continued their song all the way on shore, laughing and clapping their hands. But the men and women, after they reached the yard, when the momentary gratification of setting foot on land once more had passed away, looked sullen and dissatisfied, but not dejected. It struck me that on landing they expected to be allowed to go wherever they pleased, and were consequently disappointed and angry when they found themselves still under control.

Recognizing that emancipation without freedom was nothing much to speak of, some Africans pretended to docilely accept their new name or their new job, then melted away, either to escape the rigidity of British conceptions of liberty in Freetown, avoid being shipped out again, or simply to finally return to their homeland.

# Spanish Brigantine "Marinerito"

## Register of Slaves Natives of Africa captured on board the said

| No. | Names. | Sex. | Age | Stature. Feet In. | Description. |
|---|---|---|---|---|---|
| 24,118 | Fimbah. | Man | 30 | 5 8 | Cuts on temples. |
| | Mouchee. | " | 28 | 5 9 | No marks. |
| 24,120 | Gam. | " | 33 | 5 4 | d⁰ |
| | Ayale. | " | 35 | 5 10½ | Cuts on right breast. |
| | Lottoe. | " | 38 | 5 4 | d⁰ " breasts |
| | Fonjay. | " | 25 | 5 1½ | Cuts on right breast |
| | Cachay. | " | 28 | 5 3½ | No marks. |
| 24,125 | Wang. | " | 30 | 5 8½ | Tattooed breast, belly and back. |
| | Dong. | " | 33 | 5 4 | Scars on breast |
| | Faffea. | " | 22 | 5 5 | No marks. |
| | Cab | " | 30 | 5 4 | Scar on breast. |
| | Besong. | " | 27 | 5 6 | Cuts on belly |
| 24,130 | Defon. | " | 36 | 5 2 | " " temples. |
| | Oryaw. | " | 30 | 5 0½ | Tattooed breast |
| | Famsee. | " | 26 | 5 8 | d⁰ d⁰ belly & back. |
| | Farcong. | " | 28 | 5 8 | d⁰ d⁰ d⁰ |
| | Fambang. | " | 25 | 5 8½ | No marks. |
| 24,135 | Gai | " | 19 | 5 5½ | Scars on left arm. |
| | Longo. | " | 20 | 5 4 | Tattooed breast, belly and back. |
| | Geb | " | 32 | 5 0 | No marks. |
| | Larharta. | " | 35 | 5 8½ | Tattooed on back. |
| | Cong. | " | 22 | 5 2½ | No marks. |
| 24,140 | Cuhm. | " | 24 | 5 3 | Tattooed on back. |
| | Montem. | " | 33 | 5 8½ | Cuts on breast |
| | Yamsa. | " | 28 | 5 2 | No marks. |
| | Fymashe. | " | 30 | 5 6 | Tattooed right breast. |
| | Engar. | " | 32 | 5 11½ | d⁰ belly. |
| 24,145 | Fat | " | 33 | 5 3½ | No marks |
| | Younge. | " | 36 | 5 6 | Tattooed belly |
| | Subot | " | 38 | 5 4½ | Scar on right arm. |
| | Fung. | " | 25 | 5 4 | Cuts on belly and right arm. |
| | Whm | " | 26 | 5 4 | d⁰ d⁰ and temples. |
| 24,150 | Cummatier | " | 29 | 5 3½ | Tattooed breast and belly. |
| | Fong | " | 22 | 5 3 | No marks |
| | Mosong | " | 27 | 5 3 | Tattooed temples and belly. |
| | Chub | " | 30 | 5 5 | d⁰ breast and arms |
| 24,154 | Dong. | " | 24 | 5 3 | No marks. |

Register, Marinerito

said Vessel by His Majesty's Brig "Black Joke"; a Tender to His
and emancipated by decree of the British and Spanish Court
on the 3rd day of June, 1831 –   He said Brigantine having on the

| No. | Name. | Sex | Age | Stature Feet In. | Description. |
|---|---|---|---|---|---|
| 24,155 | Byong. | Man | 32 | 5 6½ | Tattooed breast, belly & back |
|  | Megam. | " | 19 | 5 4 | do. belly. |
|  | Farlay. | " | 28 | 5 7½ | do. right arm. |
|  | Allegedah. | " | 28 | 5 7½ | No marks. |
|  | Renmoh. | " | 15 | 5 2½ | do. |
| 24,160 | Mepah | " | 26 | 5 2 | Tattooed all over. |
|  | Monday. 1st | " | 28 | 5 2 | No marks. |
|  | Do. 2nd | " | 30 | 5 2 | do. |
|  | Enjowah. | " | 15 | 4 11 | Tattooed on belly. |
|  | Fobance. | " | 23 | 5 7 | No marks |
| 24,165 | Nong. | " | 28 | 5 5½ | Tattooed on temples. |
|  | Demboy. | " | 26 | 5 0 | No marks. |
|  | Embangah. | " | 26 | 5 3½ | do. |
|  | Emboo. | " | 22 | 5 8½ | do. |
|  | Emoko. | " | 10 | 4 11 | do. |
| 24,170 | Ahyo. | " | 23 | 5 5½ | Tattooed face. |
|  | Etango. | " | 25 | 5 5 | do. |
|  | Offo. | " | 25 | 5 3 | No marks. |
|  | Samms. | " | 22 | 5 7 | do. |
|  | Nancy. | " | 26 | 5 9½ | Tattooed on temples. |
| 24,175 | Fahds. | " | 26 | 5 5½ | |
|  | Defum. | " | 23 | 5 0 | |
|  | Ewatoo. | " | 22 | 5 7 | |
|  | Engasop. | " | 23 | 5 4 | |
|  | Wanckey. | " | 25 | 5 6 | |
| 24,180 | Whorah. | " | 26 | 5 3 | |
|  | Ogombah. | " | 20 | 5 2 | No marks |
|  | Vobah. | " | 22 | 5 3 | |
|  | Enso. | " | 26 | 5 4 | |
|  | Ennan. | " | 23 | 5 2½ | |
| 24,185 | Moosah. | " | 22 | 5 3 | |
|  | Fahfungah. | " | 20 | 5 1 | |
|  | Eghds. | " | 27 | 5 5 | |
|  | Cabe. | " | 26 | 5 8½ | Tattooed all over. |
|  | Shaw. | " | 26 | 5 6 | Do. |
| 24,190 | Bangah. | " | 25 | 5 8 | No marks. |
| 24,191 | Enjong. | " | 22 | 5 3 | Do |

# CHAPTER TWELVE

*Regulo*
September 1831,
460 enslaved people

*Rapido*
September 1831,
450 enslaved people

The courageous action against the *Marinerito* would prompt another spate of promotions across the *Black Joke*—nobody mentioned the direct contravention of obligations under the treaty vis-à-vis the slaver's crew—but the ship had suffered considerable damage and was once again in need of repair. Even before the latest damage, Hayes had begun to worry about the state of the *Black Joke*. He only had five regular navy ships—*Atholl, Conflict, Dryad, Favorite*, and the oft-maligned *Plumper*, still holding on—while the bulk of the work of the Squadron was being done by *Dryad's* tenders, *Seaflower, Fair Rosamond*, and the eldest, *Black Joke*. Hayes had received eight sets of official Instructions (with blanks where a tender's name might appear) in January 1831, but major changes in government in Britain were a portent of likewise seismic changes in the Admiralty, the sort of shifting and political maneuvering that could well have rendered those signatures worthless for the commodore's purposes.

There really isn't a short version, but again risking massive over-simplification, the attempt must be made. Events could have been said to commence near the end of June 1830, when "George IV put an end to his unpopularity by dying" and made William IV king of England. William was a third son who was never expected to rise to the throne and was thus raised in the service, which was only part of the reason he had the appellation the "Sailor King." William was also pretty much obsessed with all things Royal Navy; he'd even served as the first Lord High Admiral in over a century in 1827 (an appointment that, coincidentally, occurred the same year his older brother Frederick died, making William the heir presumptive) before being forced to resign after only a year. This had been during the previous administration, an administration embodied in the Duke of Wellington, victor over Napoléon at Waterloo, but more recently known as the only man who could be trusted to successfully wrangle the previous monarch, George IV, who had been . . . excessive. (His taste was superb, his spending was outrageous, his love life was an entire buffet of scandal, and though he may or may not have been addicted to laudanum, he undoubtedly was a drinker.)

This was the *previous* administration because escalating reform movements and news of France's July Revolution, also in 1830, prompted many in England (those with the franchise, anyway) to back the Whigs, rather than the conservative Tories. The big Whig win, also in 1830, was nevertheless an upset. Whigs were in favor of the suppression of the slave trade, and of working with France to finally effect real change. Conversely, William IV was not particularly liberal, he did not care to be entangled in foreign matters, and he did not like countries whose navies could approach his own, France very much included, and inevitably insulted their diplomats at state dinners. William IV very much wanted a say in who served on the Admiralty Board, and he was king. Commodore John Hayes had Ship's Instructions signed by Lord Melville and Sir George Cockburn. Lord Melville resigned when the 1830 elections fundamentally altered the balance of political power. Sir George Cockburn was a precipitating factor of William IV's forced resignation from the position of Lord High Admiral (back when he was Duke of Clarence) and then took the job for himself. Neither of them would be on the next Admiralty Board, clearly.

Though the commodore couldn't yet tell which way the wind was blowing, the horizon didn't look promising. Though it would never dissipate entirely, popular support for the Squadron's mission in England was ebbing. Perhaps if Hayes was expecting a board heavily influenced by the liberal Whigs in Parliament, rather than a conservative king, he might have had more optimism, but he wasn't foolish. First Bullen, then Collier, had lauded the benefits of the tender system as practiced within the West Africa Squadron. Though the government was liberalizing, the Admiralty had already been conservative and would in some ways only become more so with the regime change, and the conservative view was dim on tenders in the WAS, in part because some, including the new sovereign, were dubious on the project of the Squadron as a whole. (While still the Duke of Clarence, William had advocated against abolishing the slave trade in the first place.) That tenders were more effective had been amply demonstrated, and that they were cheaper was plain to see; with half the money it took to send a single newly designed ship from England, Hayes could buy enough tenders to patrol the coast for three *years*. The commodore had the papers for all the tenders he could hope to buy and didn't even know if he had the requisite permissions to purchase more. So even as he fought to preserve the tender system in the WAS, Hayes prepared for its demise. He told the Admiralty that he'd acquired the *Black Joke*'s wily quarry *Dos Amigos* in February of 1831 as a replacement for the *Black Joke*, but then had the *Black Joke*'s hull caulked and the entire ship repaired when it came back from its fierce contest against the *Marinerito*, assuring anyone who asked that he was just doing a mild refit to prepare the tender to cruise in the immediate vicinity of Freetown. The commodore had staved off the end for as long as he could, but he must have been deeply disappointed when his worst fears were realized, and the news he didn't want (but definitely expected) arrived. It was official—the Admiralty had decreed that, effective immediately, no more tenders would be purchased for the West Africa Squadron.

But none of this meant the commodore couldn't use the ones he had. The first of the new-style tenders and the last, the *Black Joke* and her former prize *Fair Rosamond*, would become frequent companions that year. Hayes was still leery of the *Black Joke*'s seaworthiness, given the sheer quantity of repairs alone, not to mention the disappearing act, and tended to station the ships somewhat near each other, usually in the Bights. In September of 1831, Huntley, aboard the *Fair Rosamond*, was again stationed in the Bight of Benin, while Ramsay, on the *Black Joke*, waiting for news of his near-certain promotion for his action against the *Marinerito*, was back in the Bight of Biafra, but this time it was Huntley who ran into an informative skipper in Clarence Cove. The skipper had heard tell of two heavily armed slavers that had decided to sail together for better protection from the West Africa Squadron and told Huntley they were headed through the *Black Joke*'s patrol area. Now it was Huntley's turn to move with all possible speed. The *Fair Rosamond* quickly finished resupplying at Fernando Pó's (recently arrived) full Victualling Depot and hurried over to the Bonny River, hoping to find Ramsay and the *Black Joke* nearby. Huntley's timing was excellent, as a lookout on the *Fair Rosamond* sighted the *Black Joke* that afternoon near the mouth of the Bonny.

What happened next might have been awkward in most other circumstances, but Ramsay and Huntley were close friends. (This is despite what appears to be differing views on the merits of the Squadron's mission: Huntley thought it pointless; Ramsay would fire up no less than Charles Darwin to even greater heights of abolitionist fervor with stories of the horrors of the *Marinerito* and slavers like it.) When the two tender captains met on board *Fair Rosamond*, Huntley shared his news, and far from its catching the other lieutenant off guard, Ramsay proffered that he'd recently boarded a French slaver who'd told him about the same two ships and said they'd be more than a match for even "the dread *Black Joke*." Now Huntley was still angling for a promotion, and probably kicking himself for discounting whatever magic the *Black Joke* clearly had, while Ramsay knew, positively *knew*, he'd be promoted any day now, so as the longtime friends resolved to battle together, Ramsay offered Huntley the leading position in the hope that he might soon join Ramsay at the rank of commander. Uniting forces would turn out to be an excellent idea, and the two moved farther out to sea, out of view of the river.

When the two slave ships, the *Regulo* and the *Rapido*, ambled out of the Bonny, sailed past the hazards near the shore, and finally noticed what was on their horizon, they hadn't been expecting anyone; however, if they *had* been expecting anyone, it was certainly the *Black Joke* alone. The two fastest ships of the West Africa Squadron were not a problem the slavers wanted to tackle. Then again, who'd ever seen two such vessels stationed together? Maybe it wasn't the British at all, and if they were pirates, well, the *Regulo* and the *Rapido* were definitely prepared for that. The two slavers stopped and conferred, eventually opting to wait for the unidentified ships to come closer and see what they decided to do.

As the *Black Joke* and *Fair Rosamond* rapidly approached, the slavers recognized them and, realizing that it was much too late to change course, weighed anchor and made ready to stand and fight, using a light wind that had sprung up to ideally position themselves relative to the British brig and brigantine. For the next half hour, the four ships moved ever closer, until just, almost, the *Black Joke* and *Fair Rosamond* were in gun range. The captain of the *Rapido* broke, lost his nerve, and made to run back upriver with the hopes of landing the enslaved on board his vessel. The *Regulo*, now unequivocally outnumbered, was forced to do likewise, but for either ship to make it, they would have to navigate the treacherous outer banks back to the mouth of the Bonny.

The slave traders each had pilots on deck, but Huntley—by now leading Ramsay due to the better condition of his ship and the graciousness of his fellow lieutenant—had only recent survey maps to guide the tenders in their pursuit. As each ship carefully threaded its way forward, balancing risk of disaster with speed, the more ably crewed *Fair Rosamond* and the *Black Joke* steadily gained on the two slavers during their last-ditch efforts to elude capture. The route took them past the anchorage of several palm-oil ships working the area, all of which were British manned, and some few of which likely had former Royal Navy sailors of their own. When the WAS tenders passed, a resounding cheer rose up, one that followed the two tenders up the river and only faded as the last merchant vessel disappeared from sight. There, as the Squadron ships maneuvered deeper into the Bonny's tributary waters and then farther upriver, the slavers could only still be seen from high up in the rigging, trees and dense bush blocking visibility on the winding river. Suddenly, a lookout sounded pained alarm; both ships appeared to be tossing people overboard. As *Fair Rosamond* and the *Black Joke* cleared the last bend, the situation became clearer, and uglier—the *Regulo* had become wedged in the mud of the river and was a panic of bodies and canoes as the crew ungently tried to disembark as many slaves as possible into the waiting boats below, literally pushing the enslaved off the decks with no regard to their landing and little for their survival.

Huntley, still in the lead, had seen more than enough and fired a warning shot across the *Regulo*'s bow, declaring that if a single person on the slaver was off-loaded into a single canoe, he'd open fire on everyone. Clearly, Huntley and Ramsay were friends for a reason—even if their political differences meant that Huntley didn't care one whit about the suppression of the slave trade, while Ramsay had gone out of his way to maroon the larger part of a slaver crew in direct contravention of international law on account of its being incredibly inhumane in a business built on inhumanity. Beyond threats to fire on whatever was most inconveniencing them at the moment, the two shared a pettiness that could be potentially fatal to the recipient. Huntley had once chased a slaver and caught it, only to find no enslaved on board. When he asked the captain of the ship why he'd run if he had no illegal cargo, and the captain replied that he just wanted to see how his vessel might fare against a Royal Navy cruiser, Huntley, displeased but realizing he couldn't just destroy a ship for wasting his time, instead set his men to unbend every sail, dismantle every inch of rigging, throw anything movable overboard, including the guns, and drop the anchors on the slave ship as far as they would go, then abandoned the captain to the disarray. And this time both lieutenants were irritated. Everyone on the *Regulo* stopped moving.

Ramsay, mindful of his secure promotion and of his word to let Huntley take whatever action presented itself, kept the *Black Joke* back to stay and deal with the mess of the subdued *Regulo*, allowing the *Fair Rosamond* to continue up the river, around Bonny Island, and catch *Rapido*. The geography of the area allowed for some wiggle room around Hayes's order to avoid going upriver, but Huntley did not risk a leisurely pace; across the still-wide water he could see that something monstrous was happening. Where the *Regulo* had had canoes sort of waiting and was attempting some kind of landing— dangerous and haphazard though it had been—the crew of the *Rapido* was simply throwing the enslaved overboard, still shackled in twos, to drown or be eaten by crocodiles and sharks. (Sharks were known to sometimes follow slave ships, waiting for the inevitable bodies from above.) The crew of the *Fair Rosamond* saved one pair of men by catching them by their shackles with a hook as the ship passed the place they'd gone in, but these were the only known survivors of the enslaved on the *Rapido*. The ship didn't end up faring much better than the *Regulo*—by the time both ships had been taken, the tide had run out and everyone was grounded.

During the week it took to free the ships, the *Black Joke*'s medical staff, namely Douglas, discovered a number of cases of smallpox among the 220 enslaved people who had not been drowned or successfully landed by the *Regulo*'s crew. Ramsay refused to risk it and ordered the sick landed as well, lest the crew of the *Black Joke* take ill. These people had already been through a lot that day; they weren't from this area of Africa and had likely been brought to the coast by caravan—none of them spoke the local language. They were comprehensible enough to be heard begging, pleading, to be taken back on board for much of the night. Then in the morning, when Ramsay looked to see how they'd fared, they'd completely disappeared—no one remaining. Neither the crews of *Black Joke* and *Fair Rosamond*, the crews of the slavers, the 164 other survivors of the *Regulo*, nor the two survivors of the *Rapido*, ever saw them again.

The easy cruelty with which these two ships sought to evade capture—and that the *Rapido* might actually have avoided condemnation via the expedient of murdering its unwilling cargo had those two men not been pulled from the river—reverberated across the ocean, particularly for Huntley. He had a model of the *Rapido* made and exhibited in London and, upon his return, regaled crowds by turns horrified and fascinated with his tales of evil slavers and their appalling degradations, playing on abolitionist sympathies he didn't share. (One has only to look to his memoir, *Seven Years' Service on the Slave Coast of Western Africa*, for the evidence of that.) Nonetheless, Huntley's cash grab was (inadvertently) helpful to the cause, as the publicity his exhibition and others like it—Butterfield once commented offhandedly about just bringing back an actual slave ship and had several serious offers—generated kept the horrific acts of the *Rapido*s of the slaving world in the news and on the minds of those back in England, the same citizens that Hayes had been so intent on making understand the true nature of the fight against slavery and why it was worth the cost.

It was the scandal Britain needed to push harder for equipment clauses, amendments to treaties that would allow ships equipped for slaving to be detained with or without bodies on board, which would have prevented the incident. These efforts were assisted by the rise of King Louis Philippe in France, whose pro-abolition regime would, in a few years, accomplish what Collier and Hayes had spent years saying was the only thing that could make this entire project work—denying slavers the protection of the French flag, and thereby ridding the slave coast of nearly all French slavers. Diplomatic developments happening in this moment, all around the world, would once again fundamentally alter the laws of the sea with reverberations for decades to come. The world the *Black Joke* would soon leave behind had been difficult to imagine four years prior.

# Spanish Brig

Register of Slaves Natives of Africa captured on board the said Britannic Majesty's Ship "Dryad" Commodore John Hayes, CB. Commander Commissions established in this Colony of Sierra Leone, on the 22nd day of

| No. | Names | Sex | Age | Stature Feet In. | | Description |
|---|---|---|---|---|---|---|
| 24,677 | Damardoo | Man | 30 | 5 | 6 | Cuts on breast T on right shoulder. |
| | Ardoogah | — | 22 | 5 | 2 | Cuts all over ⊃ do. do. |
| | Awoarhoo. | — | 21 | 5 | 7 | do. do. T do. do. |
| 24,680 | Okonkowoo | — | 20 | 5 | 5 | Cuts on temples breast & down right arm T on right shoulder |
| | Boonoo. | — | 21 | 5 | — | Cuts on breast T on right arm. |
| | Oha. | — | 19 | 5 | 6 | Cuts on temples & down the belly. |
| | Chukoomapa. | — | 18 | 5 | 5 | do. do. |
| | Ayahoo. | — | 32 | 5 | 5 | Scored on forehead T on right shoulder |
| 24,685 | Chamah. | — | 18 | 5 | 5 | Cuts on face & belly. |
| | Goolahdee. | — | 17 | 5 | 5 | Cuts on forehead breast & right shoulder. |
| | Ojeeboo. | — | 22 | 5 | 5 | Cuts on breast & belly. |
| | Inguzrah. | — | 23 | 5 | 3 | Cuts on temples & forehead |
| | Allubelley. | — | 37 | 5 | 6 | Cuts all over |
| 24,690 | Mellog. | — | 20 | 5 | 7 | do. do. |
| | Appah. | — | 36 | 5 | 4 | Cuts down right & left & arm & T on right shoulder |
| | Ogoolazelaunah. | — | 17 | 5 | 5 | T on right arm. |
| | Oroo. | — | 17 | 5 | 2 | Cuts on temples. |
| | Eguay. | — | 19 | 5 | 2 | do. do. |
| 24,695 | Akdkay. | — | 18 | 5 | 3 | do. do. & forehead. S on left shoulder. |
| | Nozrom. | — | 28 | 5 | 3 | T on right shoulder. |
| | Maddoo. | — | 25 | 5 | 6 | do. do. & cuts on face. |
| | Imbautah. | — | 18 | 5 | 4 | do. do. & Cuts on temples. |
| | Woogoo. | — | 22 | 5 | 5 | do. do. Y from breast to navel. |
| 24,700 | Mayboocha. | — | 26 | 5 | 5 | do. do. & Scored on forehead. |
| | Woogoo. | — | 27 | 5 | 2 | do. do. Cuts on temples & breast. |
| | Annogah. | — | 33 | 5 | 2 | do. do. Cuts on face |
| | Chengah. | — | 19 | 5 | 4 | do. do. do. do. & temples. |
| | Crroom. | — | 30 | 5 | 5 | do. do. do. do. do. |
| 24,705 | Azsekah. | — | 16 | 5 | 3 | do. do. |
| | Innaboo. | — | 23 | 5 | 8 | do. do. Cuts on temples. |
| | Nooscesee. | — | 20 | 5 | 1 | do. do. Scored on forehead. |
| | Fargoo. | — | 18 | 5 | 4 | do. do. |
| | Wankoo. | — | 19 | 5 | 6 | do. do. & pitted with small pox |
| 24,710 | Ocho. | — | 17 | 5 | 2 | Cuts all over. |
| | Ineaguarrah. | — | 33 | 5 | 5 | T on right shoulder. Scored on forehead & down back |
| 24,712 | Okarakay. | — | 22 | 5 | 3 | do. do. do. do. |

"Regulo"

Vessel, by His Britannic Majesty's Brig "Black Joke", a tender to His
and emancipated by decree of the British and Spanish Court of Mixed
October, 1831. The said Brig having on the day aforesaid been pronounced
liable

| No. | Names | Sex | Age | Stature Feet In. | | Description |
|---|---|---|---|---|---|---|
| 24,713 | Achatubelly | Man. | 16 | 5 | 3 | T on right shoulder. |
| | Kookoo | | 16 | 5 | 1 | do. do. |
| 24,715 | Amallahoo | — | 17 | 5 | 0 | Scored on forehead & cut all over belly. |
| | Obillakay | — | 37 | 5 | 2 | Cuts on temples, face & belly. |
| | Oyeamau | — | 21 | 5 | 5 | T on right shoulder Cuts on temples & belly. |
| | Artammahshah | — | 16 | 5 | 1 | do. do. cuts on temples, forehead, breast & belly. |
| | Ayearbassa | — | 20 | 5 | 2 | do. do. |
| 24,720 | Woogoo | — | 21 | 5 | 5 | do. do. Cuts on face. |
| | Orkah | — | 22 | 5 | 7 | do. do. scored on forehead ✳ on each side & belly. |
| | Onnoocubba | — | 32 | 5 | 1 | do. do. cuts of face & belly. |
| | Oboo | — | 15 | 5 | 5 | Cuts on temples. |
| | Annoosam | — | 28 | 4 | 11 | T on right shoulder cuts on face. |
| 24,725 | Boonaquarrah | — | 27 | 5 | 4 | Cuts on face and belly. |
| | Arbarja | — | 30 | 5 | 2 | T on right shoulder. Cuts on face. |
| | Evain | — | 15 | 5 | 1 | do. left do. |
| | Ennah | — | 18 | 5 | 5 | do. right do. |
| | Edowodoo | — | 22 | 5 | 5 | do. do. |
| 24,730 | Cponnotuck | — | 16 | 4 | 11 | do. do. |
| | Mooden | — | 18 | 5 | 6 | do. do. |
| | Apparbeyea | — | 36 | 5 | 7 | do. do. Cuts on face & belly. |
| | Workoo | — | 17 | 5 | 3 | do. do. Cuts on forehead & temples. |
| | Orkoo | — | 30 | 5 | 4 | do. do. Cuts on belly. |
| 24,735 | Ocorree | — | 17 | 5 | — | do. do. |
| | Cssacott | — | 36 | 5 | 3 | do. do. Cuts on breast. |
| | Maryuguah | — | 25 | 5 | 5 | Cuts on temples. |
| | Webroo | — | 26 | 5 | 6 | O on left shoulder. |
| | Dooseyea | — | 30 | 5 | 7 | T on right shoulder. Cuts on temples. |
| 24,740 | Messobee | — | 19 | 5 | 6 | do. do. |
| | Narwoochee | — | 20 | 5 | 6 | do. do. pitted with small pox face. |
| | Ekajahoo | — | 32 | 5 | 1 | do. do. |
| | Arguaradah | — | 19 | 5 | 1 | do. do. Cuts on temples, forehead & belly. |
| | Aryasegea | — | 29 | 5 | 7 | Cuts on temples & down the back. |
| 24,745 | Bemmallah | — | 17 | 5 | 1 | T on right shoulder. Cuts on temples. |
| | Boboo | — | 17 | 5 | 2 | do. do. do. do. |
| | Pargoo | — | 15 | 5 | — | do. do. |
| 24,748 | Ennaboo | — | 16 | 4 | 11 | Cuts on face and breast. |

## Spanish Brig "Rapido."

Register of Slaves Natives of Africa captured on board the said Vessel, by His Britannic Majesty's Brigantine "Fair Rosamond," a tender to His Britannic Majesty's Ship "Dryad," Commodore John Hayes, CB. Commander, and emancipated by decree of the British and Spanish Court of Mixed Commissions established in this Colony of Sierra Leone, on the Seventh day of November, 1831. The said Brig having on the day aforesaid been pronounced liable to confiscation; and accordingly condemned by the said Commission for having been at the time of capture and seizure thereof engaged in the illicit traffic in Slaves.—

| No. | Names. | Sex. | Age. | Stature Feet. | In. | Description. |
|---|---|---|---|---|---|---|
| 24,841 | Okoorie | Man | 26 | 5 | 1 | Tattooed on forehead, temples & down the back. |
| 24,842 | Olubaroo | — | 28 | 5 | 1 | Cuts on cheeks, neck and back. |

## Abstract.

| | Number Registered | Number died before Registration but Emancipated | Number Emancipated | |
|---|---|---|---|---|
| Potosi. | 183 | " | 183 | |
| Regulo. | 164 | " | 164 | |
| Rapido. | 2 | " | 2 | |
| | 349 | " | 349 | |

Mem:

Number registered up to the 5th July, 1831 } 24,493.

Number registered from 5th July 1831 to 5th January, 1832 } 349

Total. 24,842

5th January, 1832.

# CHAPTER THIRTEEN

*Frasquita*
February 1832,
290 enslaved people

Though Ramsay's choice to land and functionally abandon the sick of the *Regulo* was ruled by the Foreign Office to be "unprecedented and improper," he'd been right about a forthcoming promotion. So when the *Black Joke* underwent yet another secretive refurbishment to hide its condition from the Admiralty, as being stuck in the mud of the Bonny had had a rather deleterious effect, command of the ship shifted from Ramsay, promoted to commander, to Huntley, who'd recanted on his previous decision about which tender he wanted to captain. Even though Huntley was already at the helm of the *Fair Rosamond*, he'd finally realized that there was something that wouldn't be denied about the *Black Joke*, and he was ready to steer the lucky ship toward his own promotion. This wasn't the only change afoot. Higher up the ranks, the Admiralty was making major moves as well.

The appellation "Sailor King" should have been more comfort to Commodore Hayes—it certainly was to much of the rest of the navy, and stunts such as Huntley's exhibition might not have been half so popular were everything navy-related not all the rage. In Hayes's case, however, there may have been few worse places to be stationed than the West Africa Squadron when one's king is less than enthusiastic about abolition, the West Africa Squadron when one's king doesn't enjoy foreign entanglements, or, look at that, the West Africa

Squadron when one's king likes to avoid the reminder that other places have decent navies, too, because it might require him to treat with their governments as if their sea power could possibly come to rival his own. Since the spark of the July Revolution in France, reformist zeal—at least from the populace, if not the monarchs— had raged across Europe and throughout England (and hadn't yet flagged enough to ignore), and the Admiralty knew that dismantling the West Africa Squadron outright was out of the question. That being said, the budget, deployment, manpower, and refusal to enact a tender policy that would make the Squadron function efficiently and as intended all told the same story—though the First Lord of the Admiralty since the 1830 political shake-up, Sir James Graham, was, for now, a Whig (the party representing liberal reform ideals; he switched to the conservatives a few years later in 1834 over reform of the Church in Ireland), the new predominately Tory Admiralty Board was just as disinterested in the WAS as its old Tory forebears, and perhaps even more so.

Both Hayes and Collier had written, argued, begged, and sworn that suppression was a job that could be done, and done right, if anyone was willing to fund it or had the political pull to firmly back it. So it probably particularly stung for Hayes that, just as the flag of France—of which he'd complained mightily as the last obstacle to making real progress with suppression—was no longer of real use to slavers, the West Africa Squadron was being collapsed into the Royal Navy's Cape of Good Hope Station. Graham, in his position atop the Admiralty, was genuinely interested in reform of naval policy and practice and made many key changes throughout the service (despite leaving impressment as a problem for someone else, at another, later, date); this, unfortunately, was not one of his better ideas. Such a huge shift in how the oceans surrounding Africa would be managed and policed necessarily came with major changes, not the least of which was Hayes's job. The commodore's position at the top of the WAS was folded into the responsibilities of the commander in chief of the Cape Station, currently Commodore Schomberg. Rather than choose one over the other—and given how things turned out, something both Hayes and Schomberg would likely have preferred, no matter who ended up employed—the Admiralty wanted someone in charge who was a little more in its image, a bit more aligned with its policies, goals, and direction. So neither commodore would keep his job as currently constituted; the Admiralty chose to replace them both with Rear Admiral Warren, a move that would not be without conflict or drama.

Descended from famous doctors on both sides of the family—his father, Richard, was a personal physician of George III's, his maternal grandfather, the same to Georges II and III—Frederick Warren was fifty-six years old in 1831 and had just made rear admiral the previous year. His naval career had already taken him to Halifax, China, the West Indies, the Baltic, Lisbon, and the Mediterranean, but he had no experience, absolutely none, on the coast of Africa, where he was now charged with the administration of two once-independent stations tasked with a heinously difficult mission several thousand miles apart. Sailing on the *Isis*, Warren brought with him two redesigned coffin brigs, *Charybdis* and *Brisk*, both commanded by star lieutenants who'd made names in service on the coast, the latter by Lieutenant Edward Harris Butterfield, once a master's mate on *Black Joke* under Turner, when the brig had been new to the mission and taken its first prize, *Gertrudis*. Warren was also accompanied by some of the latest naval technology going, the *Pluto*, a paddle steamer that could be powered by wood or coal, in order to document the ship's capabilities and fuel performance. As he cruised along the coast of Gambia toward Freetown, Warren didn't get off to a popular start. One of his first moves as commander of both stations had been to recommend to the Admiralty that any wine purchases made for the public service must be from the Cape, where it was cheaper than in the Wine Islands (Madeira, Tenerife, etc.), entirely ignoring the thousands of miles anyone stationed more northerly who needed (or wanted) to purchase wine for his ship would have to go to get this supposedly "cheaper" wine. The Admiralty took the recommendation. The policy was not well received, nor were Warren's other recommendations, likely on behalf of the lieutenant governor of Gambia, that the Mixed Commission should be moved to the settlement at Bathurst (now the capital, Banjul) and recaptive Africans placed around the nearby river. (On the other hand, he, like every head of the Squadron before him, had little good to say about Fernando Pó.)

These suggestions weren't as readily embraced as changing wine suppliers, but Warren was obviously there, at least in part, to cut costs and to make the suppression effort less expensive. The Admiralty could not have been pleased to hear, then, that even Warren, arriving at the coast in the wake of major international developments that prompted a relative ebb in the trade, could not see a way to operate on the Western coast with fewer than six ships—though he seemed to be the first head of the Squadron to fail to insist that, to do an effective job, they'd ideally have quite a few more. His recommendations weren't based on hard-won experience, or terrible images burned into the mind; even now, Warren had yet to see a slaver, much less experience the difficulties to be had in chasing or boarding one. Though possessed of an impressive record during the Napoleonic Wars (two court-martials notwithstanding), the rear admiral was now, in essence, a bureaucrat, one who cared more for the Admiralty's ledgers than for the comforts of the men in his command or the ultimate duty to which they'd been assigned. So, lacking, it seemed, both finesse and geographical knowledge of the area, the rear admiral then sent word to Hayes to meet him in Freetown upon his arrival. (This being accomplished by using swifter boats for post than Warren's flagship.) Hayes happened to be near the area and received the message in time, and managed to arrive in Sierra Leone in late January 1832, only a day after Warren himself.

Whatever reception Hayes was expecting, it certainly wasn't the one he got. Without fanfare or even pleasantries—much less refreshments—the rear admiral reiterated his purpose on the coast before brusquely insisting that Hayes could either bring down his broad pennant, which indicated the presence of a commodore on a ship, and remain in the West Africa Squadron as post-captain under Warren's command, or Hayes could leave for England with pennant still flying. This might have been wholly unnecessary. *Commodore* was used to describe someone in command of multiple ships, and seeing as Warren, a rear admiral, was now in charge of two stations over thirty-six hundred miles apart, maintaining some degree of localized control by retaining commodores for each squadron seems like it could have been a workable administrative compromise. (It's unclear whether the immediate-ultimatum part was the Admiralty's idea or Warren's.) Hayes was taken completely by surprise by the demand—he'd had no idea he was being replaced and less idea any such action was being contemplated, so much so that he'd preemptively off-loaded the precise sorts of provisions his crew would have needed for a long journey to England to improve the ventilation on *Dryad* for continued service on the coast. He'd need to make those stops again, now, to resupply, and after receiving what must have felt like curt permission to do so, Hayes had no problems with immediately foisting one of his most pressing problems—as the *former* WAS commodore—directly into Warren's lap.

The reasons people might already not like Warren, if piling up, were simple and seem not to have been all that personal, but do speak to the sort of leader he was. After Collier and Hayes, the difference for the men must have been dishearteningly stark. And the Admiralty wasn't done with unpopular decisions. As Hayes relayed to Warren, the Admiralty had ordered the *Black Joke* destroyed the previous fall—a choice that was its to make once *Black Joke* entered the *Navy List*—but when Hayes prepared to dismantle the vessel, the *Dryad*'s carpenter, Mr. Roberts, had discovered the ship was savable and had repaired it "at trifling expense." Whether Hayes prevaricated on *how much* work had had to be done to make the *Black Joke* seaworthy is an open historical question, but the ship had literally sailed, and now, as of February 1832 and contrary to Hayes's warning to Huntley, HM Brig *Black Joke* was "now as strong as when first built," both crewed and condemned; Warren would have to decide what to do. The rear admiral was not the sort to let his lack of experience get in the way of his decision making, but records suggest that he did initially make at least some effort on behalf of the *Black Joke*. He tried transferring its service to the colonial government in Sierra Leone, where Governor Findlay had finally received permission (from the Colonial Office, the Admiralty still refused) to buy a harbor guard and short-haul messenger ship, a task for which the *Black Joke* would have been well suited, even in mild disrepair. Warren suggested that Findlay take the tender, rather than purchase another ship entirely, and Findlay agreed, but the Admiralty shot this solution down for what could have been a few, possibly intersecting, reasons: the Admiralty wouldn't give *Black Joke* to Findlay because it had already refused to give Findlay a ship of the Royal Navy that was under his authority and not the Admiralty and hadn't changed its mind; Findlay couldn't buy the *Black Joke* due to policy surrounding the sale of tenders; or it wanted the tender system destroyed utterly, and why not start with the most famous one to prove the point. Regardless of the rationale—and that Findlay was always a problem—it's not uncharitable to wonder at the decision making.

It couldn't have been a question of seaworthiness. After Huntley got Hayes to give him another chance at the helm, the *Black Joke* was cruising alone, several hundred miles from Freetown's safe harbor, and in February 1832 made the most of its temporary reprieve from the Admiralty's order of the previous year. Though no slaver had been captured by *any* ship in the West Africa Squadron since the *Regulo* and *Rapido* the previous September, only two weeks after Warren's arrival in Freetown, the little brig, now officially declared "unfit," would end that over-four-month drought. The *Black Joke* detained the Spanish schooner *Frasquita* with ease fifty miles south of the Bonny, and the slaver came quietly, though sixty-two of the re-captive Africans were still lost on the voyage back to the Mixed Commission. It did not go down without a legal fight, however, when its master refused to appear in court, claiming to have some sort of pox. After weeks of back-and-forth, a house visit from a representative of the Mixed Commission and colonial surgeon Boyle amply demonstrated that the master was not remotely sick, and since malingering is not contagious, he was brought forth to appear, and *Frasquita* was summarily condemned.

A week later, that same February, Warren requested that Huntley put the *Black Joke* through its paces against *Brisk* and *Charybdis*, the two new additions to the WAS that had been specially remodeled and refitted for service against slavers, representing the Royal Navy's latest efforts to build, rather than source, an effective fleet. As the rear admiral had brought them down himself, one imagines he felt rather certain of the outcome, the capture of the *Frasquita* notwithstanding, sure enough, at least, to pull Huntley and his crew for the sailing trial from where they were awaiting a trafficker embarking the enslaved upriver. (The slaver was Downes's old quarry and subject of *Black Joke*'s most famous action, *El Almirante*, repurchased by slavers and renamed *Cherouka*.) The *Black Joke*, presumably worn-out, nonetheless sailed circles around the two other ships in the trials—something Warren was loath to report, as these were his "pet" ships. So he didn't. After the *Black Joke*'s triumph, Warren ordered yet another onboard inspection of the tender, to be conducted personally. After this survey, on his word alone and the brig's having just beat the pants off his ships, Warren declared the *Black Joke* unfit for service, again, despite heaps of evidence to the contrary. Only this second report made it back to his superiors in London, meaning he sat on the results of the trial, and just . . . didn't reveal them to the Admiralty. The ambivalence, if not outright animosity, that many in naval command felt toward the *Black Joke* could have been a function of what this last, meaningless victory represented. As much as the tender typified the best of the West Africa Squadron to its sailors and the people of the "Slave Coast," perhaps when the Admiralty looked at it, all it saw was the embodiment of the Royal Navy's failures—the failure of British shipyards to come up with a better-designed ship, the failure of the Mixed Commission to prevent slave ships from reentering the market and eventually the water, the failure of the Admiralty to use the tender system to supplement the WAS's preventive efforts, and the failure of the Squadron (and policy) to halt transatlantic slavery. What is certain is that the Admiralty did not have the best information regarding *Black Joke* in this, arguably the most crucial moment in the ship's storied history.

Whatever the rationale, without all of the relevant details, the *Black Joke*'s fate was sealed. It's impossible to know if anything would have changed had Warren reported the actual results of the *Black Joke*'s sailing trial, but the ship remained consigned to unceremonious decommission. In a move some historians believe must have been born out of spite or animosity, though no one has yet found the source, Warren decided that Hayes, who'd done his duty by the navy but also tried quite hard to save the *Black Joke*, should preside over the tender's demise on the *Dryad*'s way home to London. Furthermore, rather than simply taking the ship apart, as had been the plan—a customary practice used to note the construction and design of ships for future use or replication—the legendary *Black Joke* was so worthless it was just to be burned. One wonders if this was a deliberately cruel yet entirely practical move to protect Warren's lie of commission regarding the fitness of the ship, or his lie of omission in failing to report the results of the trial. The move was deeply unpopular on *Dryad* and, as the news spread, throughout the Squadron—the tender had been the men's mascot and their brightest star over four difficult years. It was equally unpopular among the nonslaving population of the African coast—indeed, the free Africans of Freetown presented a petition to save the *Black Joke*, saying they would raise money for its purchase and assume responsibility for its care. While Hayes was picking up supplies in Fernando Pó for the return to England, the freed Africans there presented him with yet another petition, and when he was leaving the island for Freetown and the irretrievable moment, a crowd gathered to entreat the previous commodore, one last time, to not go through with it, reaching out to the already reluctant Hayes, who had always loved beautiful ships, wrapping their arms around him, pleading with him not to destroy something so clearly worth saving.

It was of no use. Fifty-two months after the *Black Joke* had been rechristened into service of the Royal Navy, the terror of the illicit seas was soon to be so much ash. The little brig was stripped of the hogsheads, barrels, casks, and kegs that had sustained its ever-shifting population of volunteers and conscripts, former smugglers and formerly enslaved, free Africans and British subjects alike. The canvas hammocks, normally lashed on board with nets in case of tempests man- or nature-made, in which the sailors slept and were often buried, were swept away, the rigging and sails removed. As emotional onlookers watched—some, residents of Sierra Leone released from the holds of slave ships due to the extraordinary success of this very vessel; others, sailors who'd crewed it, made livelihoods from it, been inspired by it—the soon-to-be ex-commodore did as he'd been directed. On orders from Rear Admiral Frederick Warren, John "Magnificent" Hayes, in his penultimate act at sea after a lifetime of service, deliberately set the *Black Joke* ablaze.

Huntley would be left to dispose of its carcass—its salvaged masts, sails, and stores. Hayes took the *Dryad*'s remaining tenders with him, lest they face the same fate. And slave traders celebrated. The ship's destruction would be "hailed as the happiest piece of intelligence that has been received [in Havana], and wherever else the slave trade is carried on, for many years," wrote Peter Leonard. Whether with the opening of dark, wax-sealed bottles of fine rum and whiskey or the finest European wine, whether with smiles in spite or victory or relief, *Black Joke*'s demise was toasted in places as far-flung as Jamaica and Nantes, Bahia and Ouidah. The ship had "done more towards

Wooden snuff box [...] made from the timbers of the brig
*Black Joke*. [...] The lid of the snuff box shows a view of the ship
fully rigged. The back and sides are carved in deep relief with
representations of African life; the front is similarly carved
with a scene copied from the medal commemorating
the abolition of the slave trade in 1807 (© NMM).

putting an end to the vile traffic in slaves than all the ships of the station put together," and arguably more than any other single ship ever
would, but all that was left was a snuffbox made from its timbers and
the samples of the wood sent back to London to condemn it, the latter long since crumbled into dust in the naval archives.

The year 1832 saw big changes in the Royal Navy—soon there
would be no more tenders on the coast at all. The Navy Board was
collapsed into a larger, more streamlined command structure, Fernando Pó would be abandoned as a depot before the settlement finally failed two years later, and the pace of modernization increased,
both technologically and as an organization. These next few years
saw other significant shifts, beyond the navy's scope. In 1833, Britain
finally abolished slavery, not just the trade, employing a gradualist

approach in most (but not all) of its colonies, and France followed suit and abolished slavery for a second time in 1848. Back in England, 1837 saw the death of William IV, the coronation of Victoria, and the passage of the Slave Compensation Act, to redress the economic losses slaveholders sustained with broader abolition. But the quasi-enslaved in the "apprentice" system would continue to be a point of contention in British politics for years to come. And it would be decades before anyone would call the battle for suppression won.

Spanish Schooner "Frasquita" (alias) "Centella".

Register of Slaves, Natives of Africa, captured onboard the said vessel by His Britannic Majesty's Brig "Black Joke" a Tender to His Britannic Majesty's Ship "Dryad", Commodore John Hayes C.B. Commander and emancipated by Decree of the British and Spanish Court of Mixed Commissions Established at Sierra Leone, on the Twentieth day of March 1832 – The said Schooner having on the day aforesaid been pronounced liable to Confiscation and accordingly condemned by the said Commission for having been at the time of Capture and Seizure thereof engaged in the illicit traffic in Slaves. –

| Nº | Names. | Sx | Age | Stature Ft | In | Description. |
|----|--------|-----|-----|------|-----|--------------|
| 24, 843 | Marmah | Man | 23 | 5 | 7 | Cuts all over |
| | Ahgogah | " | 24 | 5 | 4 | Cuts on face & Tattooed on breast & Belly |
| 24, 845 | Jonnesew | " | 25 | 5 | 4 | Cuts on face and Tattooed on back & neck |
| | Onobah | " | 22 | 5 | 6 | Cuts on face & Tattooed on breast & Body |
| | Hoobahjoe | " | 26 | 5 | 3 | Cuts on Face |
| | Altam | " | 27 | 5 | 9 | Cuts on the Temples |
| | Leggadoo | " | 20 | 5 | 4 | Cuts on Face |
| 24, 850 | Morloud | " | 21 | 5 | 4 | No marks |
| | Abdigbah | " | 24 | 5 | 10 | Cuts on Face |
| | Leggadoo | " | 19 | 5 | 4 | do |
| | Alkarrakah | " | 38 | 5 | 10 | Cuts on forehead and Temples |
| | Bannanor | " | 20 | 5 | 6 | do do |
| 24, 855 | Acparpan | " | 27 | 5 | 5 | Cuts on Temples |
| | Awrakong | " | 39 | 5 | 11 | do |
| | Acpan | " | 36 | 4 | 9 | Cuts on forehead and Temples |
| | Harakah | " | 28 | 5 | 5 | Cuts on Temples |
| | Bean | " | 36 | 5 | 5 | Cuts on Face |
| 24, 860 | Olgoeo | " | 29 | 5 | 5 | Tattooed on Face, breast & belly |
| | Leesanee | " | 32 | 5 | 7 | Cuts on Face |
| | Achydee | " | 20 | 5 | 4 | do and around navel |
| | Acpan | " | 27 | 5 | 5 | Cuts on Temples & Tattooed down breast & Belly |
| | do | " | 26 | 5 | 4 | No marks |
| 24, 865 | do | " | 20 | 5 | 3 | Cuts on the Temples |
| | Acpannador | " | 39 | 5 | 4 | Tattooed all over |
| | Ahwarpan | " | 25 | 5 | 5 | Cuts on the Temples |
| | Alferver | " | 19 | 5 | 3 | Tattooed all over |
| | Akopan | " | 38 | 5 | 4 | Cuts on Face breast and Belly |
| 24, 870 | Ako | " | 29 | 5 | 4 | Cuts on forehead and Temples |
| | Fooloy | " | 19 | 5 | 0 | Cuts on Temples |
| 24, 872 | Arahpan | " | 25 | 5 | 3 | Cuts on forehead and Temples |

Register, Frasquita

Spanish Schooner "Frasquita" (alias) "Centella."

Register of Slaves Continued.—

| Nº | Names | Sex | Age | Stature Ft | In | Description |
|---|---|---|---|---|---|---|
| 24,873 | Ctean | Man | 47 | 5 | 3 | Cuts on forehead and Temples |
| 24,874 | Apahlee | " | 39 | 5 | 6 | Do   Do |
| 24,875 | Appau | " | 27 | 5 | 6 | Tattooed on Face, Breast and Belly |
| 24,876 | Mann | " | 24 | 5 | 8 | No marks |
| | Indolah | " | 25 | 5 | 4 | do |
| | Oloh | " | 19 | 5 | 1 | do |
| | Pamahnee | " | 21 | 5 | 3 | Cuts on Temples |
| 24,880 | Lohgoure | " | 31 | 5 | 4 | Tattooed on Face and Breast |
| | Clayfour | " | 28 | 5 | 7 | Cuts on face and Tattooed on belly |
| | Orah | " | 30 | 5 | 5 | Cuts on forehead and Temples |
| | Appau | " | 26 | 5 | 1 | do   do |
| | Oloh | " | 24 | 5 | 5 | Cuts on Temples |
| 24,885 | Dowdow | " | 32 | 5 | 3 | do |
| | Otawa | " | 20 | 5 | 3 | No marks |
| | Bowres | " | 27 | 5 | 5 | Cuts on the Temples |
| | Clyppos | " | 28 | 5 | 2 | Tattooed on Face |
| | Manna | " | 24 | 5 | 2 | No marks |
| 24,890 | Kayanjah | " | 28 | 5 | 4 | Tattooed on forehead and Temples |
| | Okollo | " | 30 | 5 | 6 | Tattooed all over |
| | Intong | " | 27 | 5 | 8 | Cuts on forehead and Temples |
| | Okomah | " | 40 | 5 | 3 | Cuts and Tattooed all over |
| | Arahkam | " | 32 | 5 | 8 | No marks |
| 24,895 | Okoue | " | 23 | 5 | 4 | Scalded forehead |
| | Woomah | " | 37 | 5 | 7 | Tattooed all over |
| | Okoosandah | " | 26 | 5 | 1 | Tattooed on forehead and Temples |
| | Amargah | " | 21 | 5 | 3 | Tattooed on Temples, breast & belly |
| | Cheffemah | " | 26 | 5 | 5 | Tattooed on Face and belly |
| 24,900 | Akolay | " | 18 | 5 | 4 | Cuts on the Temples |
| | Alaykan | " | 29 | 5 | 5 | Tattooed on Temples and right arm |
| | Mahdadbehee | " | 30 | 5 | 7 | Cuts on Temples |
| | Kolongpan | " | 27 | 5 | 5 | Tattooed on Temples |
| | Eba | " | 29 | 5 | 6 | Tattooed on forehead and Temples |
| 24,905 | Chahee | " | 42 | 5 | 3 | Cuts on Face |
| | Chaykay | " | 28 | 5 | 4 | Tattooed all over |
| | Akakay | " | 30 | 5 | 3 | No marks |
| | Okaytoo | " | 25 | 5 | 0 | do |
| 24,909 | Egaytoo | " | 27 | 5 | 8 | Tatt. down middle of Face, breast & belly |

# VALEDICTION

1832–2015,

too many

Francis Augustus Collier died of apoplexy in the Royal Navy's service in Hong Kong in 1849.

William Turner's final appointment was to the *Dryad*—he could only get work in the Coast Guard after his time in the West Africa Squadron and never commanded again. Due to time served, he nonetheless died a rear admiral in his home in Portsmouth in 1866.

Henry Downes won a navy medal for inventing an annular scupper for ships' decks, helped found a museum dedicated to military service, and partially funded as well as led a naval mission trip to Japan. He never entirely recovered from his illness on the coast and died a bachelor in 1852.

Edward Iggulden Parrey died sometime between 1863 and 1877; he was survived by his wife of at least thirty years.

William Coyde may have made lieutenant, and either died of lingering illness in a naval hospital, survived by his young wife, or unmarried and at sea, where his personal effects would have been auctioned off to those who could still use them. If the latter, the Royal Navy gave his mother the receipt.

William Ramsay commanded steamships until the mid-1850s and, when he retired, moved in with his older brother Dean. He died a bachelor, and a rear admiral, in 1871.

William Langford Castle also never fully recovered from an illness he contracted on the coast and became a widower in 1837. He remarried and the date of his death is unknown to this author.

Henry Vere Huntley served as the lieutenant governor of Gambia for a single year (because of course he did), before becoming the eleventh governor of Prince Edward Island. He died in 1864.

John "Magnificent" Hayes had published several pamphlets on naval architecture, and the Admiralty continued to use and modify his designs until the advent of steam made wooden ships fully obsolete. His actions aboard the *Magnificent* continued to be the stuff of legends, and classrooms.

Today, one can purchase a model of the *Fair Rosamond*, one of the only extant examples to be found anywhere in the world of how a slaver was built. The *Black Joke*, by comparison, is a symbol without a legacy. There was never the drive to make it more than that because its story, and by extension the story of slavery, does not come down to the impossibility of the mission, nor the attitudes of the age. It comes down to the political will to do the right, hard thing. The *Black Joke* existed, it triumphed, and it burned. Nothing remains but a snuffbox, an envelope, a logbook, and some sketches, old newspaper notices, and faded memories—not the optimism or the system that briefly enabled it, not the people who championed it, not the design that made it the most effective ship on the water. By way of contrast, the Slave Compensation Act—which, despite its name, did not compensate those who suffered and sometimes died in the holds of ships too small to contain their grief, nor those who suffered and sometimes died in the service of ending one of the most loathsome episodes in human history, but instead those who fought to perpetuate their indolence and wealth atop whip-marked backs and dead bodies and ships lost at sea—endured until 2015, when it was finally paid off. Political will had something to do with that, too.

# ACKNOWLEDGMENTS

This was not the book I'd set out to write what feels like a lifetime ago, but was really only a couple of years back. In 2019, I thought I'd be spending the majority of my time mining muster rolls and difficult-to-read letters for personal tidbits about the sailors aboard *Black Joke* and exploring the city and archives of Freetown, and I was ridiculously excited to see all the things and do all the history. Not knowing any better—baby's first rodeo, as it were—I decided to break my research trips into two, London that fall, to be followed by Sierra Leone and England again in the spring of 2020. Since I was coming back, I spent most of my time during this first trip at the Caird Library and Archive at the National Maritime Museum in Greenwich, the home of, among many other fascinating things, Downes's logbook, and there the staff was patient, helpful, and kind, and made the whole experience rather lovely, which I appreciate.

I came back to the States ready to work and eager to get back into the archives in a few months, but as we all experienced, a world-changing pandemic intervened. Travel was impossible (and irresponsible), archives were closed, and I needed a new plan. It seemed I would not get a chance to read Hayes's and Collier's correspondence with the Admiralty firsthand, or to try to discover where Ramsay and *Black Joke* disappeared for two months, and there was still a book to write. Taking a step back and turning toward the ship's context, rather than its contents, would not have been possible without the scores of scholars who've made it their life's work to study subjects I may have referenced repeatedly or only touched on for a line or few; every contribution to the historical discourse was immensely helpful to me, and while obviously all works cited are listed in the sources, I want to take this time to actually thank the people who created them. (All mistakes are assuredly my own.) Of particular note—and setting aside primary sources—I think it would have been next to impossible for me to complete this project without the work of Peter Grindal, Basil Lubbock, Sîan Rees, Mary Wills, Christopher Lloyd, W. E. F. Ward, David Eltis, Leslie M. Bethell, Paul Michael Kielstra, N. A. M. Rodger, Michael Lewis, William Law Mathieson, Marcus Rediker, Sowande Mustakeem, Daniel Domingues da Silva, Christopher Fyfe, and W. E. B. Du Bois.

This is definitely not to say no other archives and repositories were directly engaged in this project. The folks of the New York Public Library Archives, especially Tal Nadan, could not have been more accommodating when it came to figuring out how to get me access to *Dryad*'s logbook under these circumstances, a feat that would not have been possible without the additional help of Sara Rodberg, who went above and beyond the call of friendship. HathiTrust's pandemic guidelines were crucial for access to books I could not physically access. Though mentioned in the author's note at the outset of the book, I'd be remiss if I did not again laud the work of Henry Lovejoy and the Liberated Africans project (https://liberatedafri cans.org), the National Archives, Kew (Digital Microfilm Project), and the Sierra Leone Public Archives for preserving these records and getting them into the public eye.

Of course, on a meta level, what you're holding would not have been possible without my wonderful agent, Jess Regel of Helm Literary; my editors, Sally Howe, who is surely one of the most understanding souls on the planet, and Daniel Loedel, for believing in the book in the first place; as well as the whole production team at Scribner, who not only entertained ideas like "what if we included all the pages from the Liberated African registers" but actually found ways to make them reality—they all have been everything an author could ask for. And last, though certainly not least, if there was one person who was there for the highs and lows and the late nights, every step of the way, reading (and correcting) every draft of every iteration from the proposal to the final product, it was my mother, Elizabeth Rooks. Her critiques were valuable, her support was invaluable, and though obviously I'm biased, I'll go out on a limb here and say there is no better mom in the history of moms. Thank you.

# NOTES

## Chapter One: *Henriqueta*

7 Henriqueta: Also can sometimes be found under *Henriquetta* (multiple sources) or *Henri Quatre*, James Holman, *A Voyage round the World* (London: Smith, Elder, & Co.,1834), 107–8.

7 *American built*: Peter Grindal, *Opposing the Slavers* (London, I.B. Tauris, 2016), chap. 8.

7 *João Cardozo dos Santos*: Hugh Thomas, *The Slave Trade: The Story of the Atlantic Slave Trade* (New York: Simon & Schuster, 1997), chap. 30, Kindle, indicates that Cardozo dos Santos was the owner, but Dinizulu Gene Tinnie, in "The Slaving Brig *Henriqueta* and Her Evil Sisters," *Journal of African American History* 93 (2008): 509–31, begs to differ—given other evidence (including *Umbelina* capture record) that would suggest that Cardozo dos Santos was the captain. This text relies on Tinnie's research regarding the *Henriqueta*'s ownership and stewardship.

7 *but did little to stop the trade*: Correspondence with British Coms. at Sierra Leone, Havana, Rio de Janeiro, and Surinam on Slave Trade (Class A) 1827; Correspondence with Foreign Powers on Slave Trade (Class B) 1827, 254.

8 *must have thought a fool's bargain*: For a general overview of Anglo-Brazilian relations regarding slavery during this period as part of the larger Brazilian narrative, see E. Viotti da Costa, *The Brazilian Empire*, rev. ed. (Chapel Hill: University of North Carolina Press, 2000), chap. 6; for a more specific focus on this relationship generally over a longer period of time, see L. Bethell, *Brazil: Essays on History and Politics* (London: University of London Press, 2018), chap. 2, and L. Bethell, "The Independence of Brazil and the Abolition of the Brazilian Slave Trade," *Journal of Latin American Studies* 1, no. 2 (1969): 115–47.

8 *Cardozo dos Santos sat on deck unbothered*: For more about life on board a slave ship, see M. Rediker, *The Slave Ship: A Human History* (New York: Penguin, 2007).

8 *Brazil . . . market for the slave trade . . . unsurpassed*: D. Eltis, D. Richardson, D. Davis, and D. Blight, *Atlas of the Transatlantic Slave Trade* (New Haven: Yale University Press, 2010).

8 *approximately 44 percent of enslaved people shipped . . . from Africa*: Trans-Atlantic Slave Trade Database, Slave Voyages, 2019, https://www.slavevoyages.org/voyage/database.

8 *working on . . . plantations or in . . . mines across Brazil's*: Daniel Domingues da Silva, "The Atlantic Slave Trade from Angola," *International Journal of African Historical Studies* 46, no. 1 (2013): 116.

8 *expedient to . . . work . . . to death and buy more*: Viotti da Costa, *The Brazilian Empire*; P. A. Aufderheide, "Order and Violence: Social Deviance and Social Control in Brazil, 1780–1840," PhD diss., University of Minnesota, 1976.

8 *onerous labor . . . thought to be inappropriate . . . for most women*: Which is not to say

# NOTES

women never performed it—Richard Follett, "'Lives of Living Death': The Reproductive Lives of Slave Women in the Cane World of Louisiana," *Slavery & Abolition* 26, no. 2 (2005): 289–304, provides a more northerly example from Louisiana, particularly noting the additional impact the arduous nature of the work and other contextual factors may have had on fecundity beyond gender ratios.

8  *ratios of the enslaved population*: Viotti da Costa, *The Brazilian Empire*, 135.

8  *sustaining Brazil's booming agricultural economy*: Bethell, "The Independence of Brazil," 117–18.

9  *ownership stake . . . in the future*: Daniel Domingues da Silva, *The Atlantic Slave Trade from West Central Africa, 1780–1867* (New York: Cambridge University Press, 2017), 46–48.

9  *originally named the Griffin*: Geoffrey Marsh Footner, *Tidewater Triumph* (Centreville, MD: Tidewater Publishers, 1998), 155.

9  *the Bight of Benin*: Specifically in Molembo, Tinnie, "The Slaving Brig *Henriqueta*," 513; a "bight" is a geographical term that simply means a curve, bend, or recess on a coastline or of a river, or a bay that's created by such a feature.

9  *profiting . . . approximately £80,000*: Siân Rees, *Sweet Water and Bitter* (Durham: University of New Hampshire Press, 2009), 123; Tinnie, "The Slaving Brig *Henriqueta*," citing Howard I. Chapelle, *The History of American Sailing Ships* (New York: W. W. Norton; New York: Bonanza Books, 1935), lists the figure as $400,000, which, when similarly adjusted for inflation, is fairly close to the same.

9  *over forty thousand . . . Africans were trafficked each year to that country*: David Eltis, *Economic Growth and the Ending of the Transatlantic Slave Trade* (Oxford, UK: Oxford University Press, 1987), 244.

9  *de Cerqueira Lima was . . . a city councilman that year*: J. J. Reis, *Death Is a Festival: Funeral Rites and Rebellion in Nineteenth-Century Brazil* (Chapel Hill: University of North Carolina Press, 2003), 263.

9  *a fleet of at least a dozen slavers*: Tinnie, "The Slaving Brig *Henriqueta*," 517.

9  *handsome, if blood-soaked, profits*: Eltis, *Economic Growth*, 150.

9  *insuring them against capture by the Royal Navy*: P. Verger, *Flux et reflux de la traite des nègres entre le Golfe de Bénin et Bahia de Todos os Santos: du XVIIe au XIXe siècle* (Paris: Mouton, 1968), 404; P. Hudson, "Slavery, the Slave Trade and Economic Growth: A Contribution to the Debate," in *Emancipation and the Remaking of the British Imperial World*, edited by C. Hall, N. Draper, and K. McClelland (Manchester, UK: Manchester University Press, 2014), 36–59, for British involvement in maritime insurance for the transatlantic slave trade.

9  *Henriqueta . . . insured by an outfit in Rio*: Great Britain, British and Foreign State Papers, 1826–1827, London H.M.S.O., 357.

9  *treaties forced on them by a foreign empire*: Bethell, "The Independence of Brazil"; Leslie Bethell, "Britain, Portugal and the Suppression of the Brazilian Slave Trade," *English Historical Review* 80, no. 317 (1965): 761–84; Bethell, *Brazil: Essays on History and Politics*.

10  *reported by the nearby American schooner Lafayette*: Tinnie, "The Slaving Brig *Henriqueta*," 513.

10  *abetted . . . yet . . . found by . . . HMS Maidstone*: A third, more middle-ground possibility is that the *Lafayette* was actually either owned or chartered by de Cerqueira Lima alongside *Henriqueta*, and thus was detained by the *Maidstone* and pressured to reveal information about the location of *Henriqueta*. According to William Pennell, Consul to Brazil, in a letter to Canning about the incident, apparently there was a

common practice at this particular historical moment of simply sending two ships for the same journey—profits were such that it was worth it to preemptively send a backup that would be able to make the trip, in this case the *Lafayette*, if the first ship, here the *Henriqueta*, was apprehended by the British (British Parliamentary Papers, 11/26-0727, 88). Whatever might be the case in this instance, the end result was nonetheless the escape of *Henriqueta* and an uneventful arrival back in Brazil for the *Lafayette*. Great Britain, British and Foreign State Papers, 356–57.

10  *coffles of the enslaved stood packed in barracoons*: See Robin Law, *Ouidah: The Social History of a West African Slaving Port, 1727–1892* (Oxford, UK: Boydell & Brewer, 2005), for more on the origins of barracoons (137–38) and more generally for a study of a major slaving port crucial to this history before, during, and after the era of *Black Joke*.

10  *it could be weeks, even months*: Robert Burroughs, "Eyes on the Prize," *Slavery and Abolition* 31, no. 1 (2010): 101.

10  *arrived in Salvador, only slightly delayed*: Based on Tinnie's chart of *Henriqueta's* voyages, 111 days from initial departure to eventual arrival this eventful trip wasn't even the slaving brig's longest journey, so any delay as a result really was quite minimal. Tinnie, "The Slaving Brig *Henriqueta*," 513.

11  *one of the most prolific slavers on the coast*: Grindal, *Opposing the Slavers*.

11  *more liable to show its age and wear*: Ibid., chap. 8. The French *Hébé*-class was equivalent to the British fifth rate. (The rating system is based on classifications of ship, not its quality.)

11  *dozens more guns*: *Sybille* carried (or at least was pierced for) thirty-eight guns (eighteen pounders); Rif Winfield, *British Warships in the Age of Sail, 1793–1817* (Yorkshire, UK: Seaforth Publishing, 2008), 483.

11  *combat a "piratical scourge" in the Persian Gulf*: *Memoir of Admiral Sir Francis Augustus Collier* (London: G. Myers, 1850), 8–10; Grindal, *Opposing the Slavers*, chap. 8.

11  *resistance to British economic colonialism*: Muhammad Al-Qasimi, *The Myth of Arab Piracy in the Gulf* (London: Routledge, 1986).

12  *prompted some raids of British vessels*: James Onley, *The Arabian Frontier of the British Raj* (Oxford, UK: Oxford University Press, 2007), 44.

12  *provoke just this sort of military response*: Al-Qasimi, *The Myth of Arab Piracy*.

12  *a resounding success*: Ibid., in chapter 5, explores the action in which Collier participated from a more modern perspective; a somewhat contemporary—and very British—viewpoint on Collier's activities can be found in *Memoir*, 8–10. The historiography of the results of the engagement (namely, informal British control of the area for the next 150 years) is explored in James Onley, "Britain's Informal Empire in the Gulf, 1820–1971," *Journal of Social Affairs* 22, no. 87 (2005): 29–45.

12  *on service in the West Indies*: J. K. Laughton and Andrew Lambert, "Collier, Sir Francis Augustus (1785–1849), Naval Officer." *Oxford Dictionary of National Biography*, September 23, 2004.

12  *eliminating . . . piracy from an entire . . . area*: *Memoir*, 10.

12  *without which the campaign might have failed*: Ibid., 8–9.

12  *disallowed Collier's wearing of it*: Ibid., 10, doesn't indicate who that sovereign was, but based on the year, Denis Wright, *The English amongst the Persians: During the Qajar period, 1787–1921* (London: Heinemann, 1977), 187, indicates it would have been Fath-'Ali Šâh (Shah) Qâjâr, who reigned from 1798 to 1834.

13  *recognition from his own government*: *Memoir*, 10.

13  *not . . . uniformly beloved by his superiors*: Ibid., 5.

13  *this was a job*: Though this assessment of Collier's aptitude was drawn from Grindal,

*Opposing the Slavers*, chap. 8, the characterization of his attitude toward abolition as more workmanlike than not is derived from Mary Wills, *Envoys of Abolition* (Liverpool, UK: Liverpool University Press, 2019), 193–94.

13 *corporal punishment*: Basil Lubbock, *Cruisers, Corsairs & Slavers* (Glasgow: Brown, Son & Ferguson, 1993), 159.

13 *a child's eagerness to adventure*: Memoir, 3–4; Collier was a midshipman, and though most ratings did not yet have a standardized uniform, midshipmen did, as they were officers-in-training, Nicholas A. M. Rodger, *The Wooden World: Anatomy of the Georgian Navy* (Glasgow: William Collins Sons & Co., 1986), 65; that being said, there was a trend toward uniformity that would continue during the era of *Black Joke* before ultimately resolving into official uniforms in the 1850s, Michael Lewis, *The Navy in Transition, 1814–1864* (London: Hodder and Stoughton, 1965), 254–56.

13 *great success harassing the American colonists*: *Naval Chronicle for 1814: Containing a General and Biographical History of the Royal Navy of the United Kingdom; with a Variety of Original Papers on Nautical Subjects*, vol. 32 (from July to December) (London: Joyce Gold, 1814), 266, refers to the senior Collier's father as "a private gentleman."

14 *made him enemies . . . in the navy*: Louis L. Tucker, "'To My Inexpressible Astonishment': Admiral Sir George Collier's Observations on the Battle of Long Island," *New-York Historical Society Quarterly* 48, no. 4 (1964): 297; Julian Gwyn, "Collier, Sir George," in *Dictionary of Canadian Biography*, Volume 4, University of Toronto/ Université Laval (revised 1979); J. K. Laughton, "Collier, Sir George (1738–1795)," *Dictionary of National Biography*, vol. 11, *Clater–Condell*, 339–41 (London: Smith, Elder, & Co, 1887), 340.

14 *product of Sir George's second marriage*: J. K. Laughton and Nicholas Tracy, "Collier, Sir George (1738–1795), Naval Officer," *Oxford Dictionary of National Biography*, September 23, 2004, citing *Naval Chronicle, for 1814*, 265.

14 *could only be granted for adultery*: Sybil Wolfram, "Divorce in England 1700–1857," *Oxford Journal of Legal Studies* 5, no. 2 (1985): 157.

14 *only about 325 occurred*: Douglas James, "Parliamentary Divorce, 1700–1857," *Parliamentary History* 31 (2012): 169–89; Wolfram, "Divorce in England," 155–56.

14 *the problems that existed in his first marriage*: Though George Collier's divorce Act seems to have either been printed privately or not at all, as Wolfram, "Divorce in England," notes was customary, the proceedings and some details regarding the circumstances can be found in *Journal of the House of Lords*, vol. 33, *1770–1773* (London: His Majesty's Stationery Office, 1767–1830), February through April, but particularly March 21–31.

14 *a wealthy merchant's daughter from Exeter*: Presumption of wealth rests on the terms of her father's will—dated the same year as Elizabeth's now husband's death. Will of William Fryer, Merchant of Exeter, Devon, July 7, 1795 (PROB 11/1263/122), National Archives, Kew, Richmond, Surrey, UK.

14 *forced to resign the active command*: Laughton, "Collier, Sir George (1738–1795)," 340.

14 *dead by April*: Laughton and Tracy, "Collier, Sir George."

14 *entered his first ship's books*: Francis Collier was assigned to the *Magnanime*, under Captain Isaac Schomberg, who had in turn previously served as a first lieutenant under George Collier. Memoir, 3, and William Richard O'Byrne, *A Naval Biographical Dictionary* (London: John Murray, Albemarle Street, 1849), 215.

14 *rarely served . . . distant harbors*: Rodger, *Wooden World*, 113–15, and Lewis, *The Navy in Transition*, 99–112.

16 *"complexion fair"; his hair light*: Laughton and Tracy, "Collier, Sir George," citing *Naval Chronicle, for 1814,* 265.

16 *sought permission to call on Francis's mother*: Memoir, 3–4.

16 *leaving for sea almost as soon as the captain did*: Rodger, *Wooden World,* 276, and Edmund Lodge, *Portraits of Illustrious Personages of Great Britain,* vol. 11 (London: Harding and Lepard, 1835), "Alexander Hood," 1–2.

17 *came with some strings attached*: Memoir, 3–4; some of the correspondence between Nelson and Collier's mother survives and is held in the archives of the National Maritime Museum in Greenwich.

17 *war resumed in May*: Ibid., 4–5.

18 *depended on . . . enslavement . . . products the practice produced*: Just how much of the economy remains a site of historical debate, but a recent and compelling exploration of this relationship can be found in Sven Beckert, *Empire of Cotton: A Global History* (New York: Vintage Books, 2015).

18 *immeasurably enriched by human bondage*: Christopher Lloyd, *The Navy and the Slave Trade* (New York, Routledge, 2012), chap. 1; Bernard Edwards, *Royal Navy Versus the Slave Traders* (Barnsley, UK: Pen & Sword Books, 2008), chap. 3; under the 1799 Slave Trade Act, the slave trade in England was specifically restricted to these three ports, National Archives, "Britain and the Slave Trade," http://www.nationalarchives.gov.uk/slavery/pdf/britain-and-the-trade.pdf.

18 *a leading manufacturer of cloth*: Thomas, *The Slave Trade,* chap. 9, and Beckert, *Empire of Cotton.*

18 *insatiable craving for sugar*: Edwards, *Royal Navy Versus the Slave Traders,* chap. 2; David Eltis, *The Rise of African Slavery in the Americas* (New York: Cambridge University Press, 2000); and Sidney Wilfred Mintz, *Sweetness and Power: The Place of Sugar in Modern History* (London: Penguin Books, 1985).

18 *England's participation in . . . the triangular trade*: Mintz, *Sweetness and Power,* 43.

19 *eighty thousand newly enslaved . . . of British extraction*: Anthony Sullivan, *Britain's War Against the Slave Trade* (Barnsley, UK: Pen & Sword Books, 2020), 6.

19 *upward of 75 percent of total regional exports*: Ibid., 17.

19 *without creating perceptible change regarding slavery*: Philip Hans Franses and Wilco van den Heuvel, "Aggregate Statistics on Trafficker-Destination Relations in the Atlantic Slave Trade," *International Journal of Maritime History* 31, no. 3 (August 2019): 625, adapted from Stanley L. Engerman, Seymour Drescher, and Robert L. Paquette, *Slavery* (Oxford, UK: Oxford University Press, 2001).

19 *merit the Admiralty's involvement*: Sullivan, *Britain's War Against the Slave Trade,* 16.

19 *a comprehensive fact-finding mission*: Thomas, *The Slave Trade,* chap. 25.

19 *consideration of the movement's ultimate goals*: Sullivan, *Britain's War Against the Slave Trade,* 11.

20 *one of several licit ways to make a living at sea*: A loose comparison of wages and other considerations that might impact a sailor's choice of workplace—provided they'd had one—in the eighteenth and nineteenth centuries can be made using Rodger, *Wooden World,* 124–37, Thomas, *The Slave Trade,* chap. 15, and Lewis, *The Navy in Transition,* 209–42.

20 *risking pay in weaker West Indian currency*: Sullivan, *Britain's War Against the Slave Trade,* 7; Isaac Land, *War, Nationalism, and the British Sailor, 1750–1850* (New York: Palgrave Macmillan, 2009), 110.

20 *switched between seafaring industries*: Rodger, *Wooden World,* 113.

20  *130,000 British sailors may have worked in the trade*: Edwards, *Royal Navy Versus the Slave Traders*, chap. 3.

20  *piqued the Privy Council's*: The Privy Council is a group that advises the British monarchy.

20  *partway through the trip*: Sullivan, *Britain's War Against the Slave Trade*, 8, lists figures from the year 1786 by way of example. Out of 5,000 British sailors who worked on slavers, "1,130 men died and a further 1,550 were discharged or deserted ship in the West Indies or Africa."

20  *tasked with making the new law reality*: Thomas, *The Slave Trade*, chaps. 26, 27.

20  *to avoid detection*: Sullivan, *Britain's War Against the Slave Trade*, 15.

21  *early captures in the West Indies*: Grindal, *Opposing the Slavers*, chap. 4.

21  *unassigned to an official squadron or station*: Lloyd, *The Navy and the Slave Trade*, chap. 5.

21  *West Africa Squadron to come into being*: William Ernest Frank Ward, *The Royal Navy and the Slavers* (London: Pantheon Books, 1969), 43; however, Sullivan, *Britain's War Against the Slave Trade*, 347–49, provides a differing timeline for when the squadron became official.

21  *Sybille would not fundamentally change*: Lloyd, *The Navy and the Slave Trade*, Appendix C.

21  *the market Britain had (mostly) left*: Mostly, but not at all entirely. Eltis, *Economic Growth*, 47–61.

21  *it was a populace divided*: Ward, *The Royal Navy and the Slavers*, 126–27; Paul Michael Kielstra, *The Politics of Slave Trade Suppression in Britain and France, 1814–48* (London: Palgrave Macmillan UK, 2000), 108–13, for the diplomatic and political perspective, particularly as it relates to France, in the five years preceding *Henriqueta's* capture; Wills, *Envoys of Abolition*, for division of opinion regarding the mission within the squadron itself over the course of its existence; Burroughs, "Eyes on the Prize," and Robert Burroughs, "Slave-Trade Suppression and the Culture of Anti-Slavery in Nineteenth-Century Britain," in *The Suppression of the Atlantic Slave Trade: British Policies, Practices and Representations of Naval Coercion*, eds. Robert M. Burroughs and Richard Huzzey (Manchester, UK: Manchester University Press, 2016), 125–45, on the interaction between published squadron narratives and public opinion, particularly as the century progressed to its midway point.

22  *the unparalleled speed of his slaver*: Lubbock, *Cruisers*, 140–41.

22  *forced to surrender to boarding from armed British sailors*: Grindal, *Opposing the Slavers*, chap. 8; Lubbock, *Cruisers*, 140–41.

22  *alter his course forever*: Lubbock, *Cruisers*, 140.

23  *a prize crew of perhaps a dozen men*: This numerical supposition is based on Burroughs, "Eyes on the Prize," 103, citing Pascoe Grenfell Hill, *Fifty Days on Board a Slave-Vessel in the Mozambique Channel* (London: Charles Gilpin, 1848; Baltimore, MD: Black Classics Press, 1993), in regards to the composition of a squadron prize crew a little over ten years after *Black Joke* sailed, or forty after Collier came aboard *Osprey*.

23  *the adjudication of slaving ships*: Leslie Bethell, "The Mixed Commissions for the Suppression of the Transatlantic Slave Trade in the Nineteenth Century," *Journal of African History* 7, no. 1 (1966): 79–93.

23  *make problem sailors someone else's problem*: Burroughs, "Eyes on the Prize," 101–2, mentions that someone noted this practice in the context of American antislavery ships, not British vessels, but given the transient nature of berths for ratings in the

navy that persisted during the Georgian era, it seemed like an expedient the Royal Navy might have utilized as well. Rodger, *Wooden World*, 113, characterizes the transience of sailors thusly: "A man entered for wages on the books of a King's ship had joined the King's service until he was discharged or the ship paid off, but in constitutional theory and in everyday practice, he was primarily a member of a ship's company and not of the Navy as a whole. Men joined a King's ship or a merchant's as opportunity or preference suggested, and they moved easily from one to another."

24 *complement of forty-five sailors*: Memoir, 5.

24 *succumbed to disease, insurrections . . . rebellion*: Burroughs, "Eyes on the Prize," 101–2.

24 *Osprey . . . become its first lieutenant*: Memoir, 5.

24 *Admiralty mate named Frederick Mather*: Sullivan, *Britain's War Against the Slave Trade*, 137.

24 *close to the coast for safety reasons*: Ward, *The Royal Navy and the Slavers*, 45–47, provides details about why coastal service was necessary at all and some of the issues it presented; David Northrup, "African Mortality in the Suppression of the Slave Trade," *Journal of Interdisciplinary History* 9, no. 1 (1978): 51–52, focuses on the impact on the enslaved.

24 *a voyage of several months*: Burroughs, "Eyes on the Prize," 101.

25 *rebellion from their slaver prisoners*: "For example, the Brazilian *Volcano do Sud*, whose crew, when captured by an English cruiser, HMS *Pheasant*, in 1819, murdered the boarding party and delivered their cargo of 270 slaves at Bahia as if nothing had happened." Thomas, *The Slave Trade*, chap. 29.

25 *"had died from that complaint"*: Lloyd, *The Navy and the Slave Trade*, chap. 3, citing Parliamentary Papers 1828, vol. 26, 89.

26 *no one noticed until morning*: Holman, *A Voyage round the World*, 108.

26 *make the slave trade more "humane"*: Tinnie, "The Slaving Brig *Henriqueta*," 520.

26 *while maximizing profits*: Ibid., 516, 522–23.

26 *all manner of insects and pests*: Ibid., citing Rev. Robert Walsh, *Notices of Brazil in 1828 and 1829*, vol. 2 (London: Frederick Westley and A. H. Davis, 1830), as to why this was likely and what sorts of pests, including but not limited to roaches, centipedes, and rats.

26 *"dense mass of human beings was suffocating"*: Holman, *A Voyage round the World*, 108.

26 *Henriqueta . . . ready to be tried in court*: Captured September 6, 1827, sentenced October 29, 1827. Correspondence (Class A) 1828, 34.

26 *maritime crimes, prize cases, and the occasional commercial conflict*: Bethell, "The Mixed Commissions"; Jenny S. Martinez, *The Slave Trade and the Origins of International Human Rights Law* (Oxford, UK: Oxford University Press, 2011), 67–97.

27 *the ability to police the seas*: Paul M. Kennedy, *The Rise and Fall of British Naval Mastery* (New York: Penguin, 2017).

27 *£900 of his own money*: There's a bit of a historical dispute here as Tinnie, "The Slaving Brig *Henriqueta*," 513, says it was £330, rather than the Grindal, *Opposing the Slavers*, figure in the text; £900 in 1827 is worth approximately £98,000 (~$135,000) today, while £330 is roughly £35,000 (~$48,000). I freely admit I have no idea who's correct and went with the higher number because it demonstrates that, even at their most expensive, auctioned slavers were way more cost effective.

27 *house provincial presidents and Bahia's governors*: Tinnie, "The Slaving Brig *Henriqueta*," 522.

27 *shipping of enslaved people worldwide*: Ibid.; Eltis, *Economic Growth*, 145–63, for a more in-depth examination of the slave-trade "firm" during the illegal slave-trade era.

28  *made reality far less satisfying*: Bethell, "The Independence of Brazil," and Eltis, *Economic Growth*, 43–46.

28  *American shipbuilding worthy of royalty*: Footner, *Tidewater Triumph*, 155.

28  *rechristened and repurposed, the now Black Joke*: Lubbock, *Cruisers*, 140–41.


**Chapter Two: *Gertrudis***

33  *the titular object of a bawdy jig*: Basil Lubbock, *Cruisers, Corsairs & Slavers*: (Glasgow: Brown, Son & Ferguson, 1993), 141–42; J. G. Muddiman, "H. M. S. the Black Joke," *Notes and Queries* 172, no. 12 (March 1937): 200, citing Pierce Egan and Francis Grose, *Grose's Classical Dictionary of the Vulgar Tongue: Revised and Corrected with the Addition of Numerous Slang Phrases Collected from Tried Authorities* (London: Pierce Egan, 1823), "Black Joke" entry, which states "a popular tune to a song, having for the burden, 'Her black joke and belly so white'; figuratively, the black joke signifies the monosyllable. See Monosyllable." The same work defines "Monosyllable" as "a woman's commodity." In short (though not monosyllabic), a vulva.

33  *"with a black joke, and belly so white"*: History and lyrical variations can be found in the Traditional Tune Archive, "Annotation: Black Joke (1) (The)." Accessed July 21, 2021, https://tunearch.org/wiki/Annotation:Black_Joke_(1)_(The).

33  *two Black Jokes had been on the water*: Lubbock, *Cruisers*, 141.

33  *Burla Negra, or "Black Joke"*: Natalie Jane McManus, "The Pirate Pathway: The Trajectory of the Pirate Figure in Peninsular Spanish Literature from the Nineteenth to the Twenty-First Century," PhD diss., University of Virginia, 2012, 249–310.

34  *a veritable ocean full of pirates and "pirates"*: William Ernest Frank Ward, *The Royal Navy and the Slavers* (London: Pantheon Books, 1969), 73; Hugh Thomas, *The Slave Trade* (New York: Simon & Schuster, 1997), chap. 29. Obviously British law only applied to British citizens, and likewise when the United States had implemented similar legislation back in 1820. Peter Grindal, *Opposing the Slavers* (London: I.B. Tauris, 2016), chap. 6, explains that Britain did try to convince other European powers to agree that "the slave trade should be denounced as piracy under the Law of Nations" in 1822, but had no takers. Though Britain would use subsequent treaties to add piracy clauses saying as much, that sort of loose consensus wouldn't be reached until the mid-1800s, as slave trading approached the end of the journey from legitimate enterprise to "crime against humanity," and not without contention. Jenny S. Martinez, *The Slave Trade and the Origins of International Human Rights Law* (Oxford, UK: Oxford University Press, 2011), 114–39.

34  *for further maltreatment and eventual sale*: Lubbock, *Cruisers*, 155.

34  *existence of ex-slaver tenders . . . a point of contention*: Grindal, *Opposing the Slavers*, chap. 8.

34  *as much use of former slaver tenders as the Admiralty . . . would permit*: Ibid.

35  *liberated approximately ten thousand enslaved people*: William Richard O'Byrne, *A Naval Biographical Dictionary* (London: John Murray, 1849), 141–42; Anthony Sullivan, *Britain's War Against the Slave Trade* (Barnsley, UK: Pen & Sword Books, 2020), 135; J. K. Laughton and Roger Morriss, "Bullen, Sir Charles (1769–1853), Naval Officer," *Oxford Dictionary of National Biography*, September 23, 2004.

35  *this point of maritime law*: Grindal, *Opposing the Slavers*, chap. 8; *State Papers Presented by Command of His Majesty Relating to the Slave Population in the West Indies, on the Continent of South America, and at the Cape of Good Hope: Also, Correspondence with*

the British Commissioners at Sierra Leone, the Havannah, Rio de Janeiro, Surinam, and Foreign Powers, Relating to the Slave Trade, Volume XXVI, Volume 2 (Session 21 November 1826–2 July 1827), Pre–1833 Command Paper, 1827, 36–37.

36  the Hope, a former slaver: Ward, The Royal Navy and the Slavers, 128.

36  an outwardly minor technical point: Grindal, Opposing the Slavers, chap. 8, and State Papers (1827), 36–37.

36  to whatever end might best suit: HMS Sybille itself was evidence of that—Paul M. Kennedy, The Rise and Fall of British Naval Mastery (New York: Penguin, 2017), 124, details just a sampling of British ship seizures in the most recent conflict with France alone.

37  nations in their own right: Leslie Bethell, "The Independence of Brazil and the Abolition of the Brazilian Slave Trade," Journal of Latin American Studies 1, no. 2 (1969): 115–47.

37  Canning, a vocal proponent of abolition: Paul Michael Kielstra, The Politics of Slave Trade Suppression in Britain and France, 1814–48 (London: Palgrave Macmillan, 2000), 111–13.

37  "the Treaties for the repression of the Slave-trade": State Papers (1827), 37.

38  ship that supervised it had done the deed: Grindal, Opposing the Slavers, chap. 8. Indeed, the High Court of the Admiralty had actually issued letters of marque to two privateers to catch slavers after abolition of the slave trade went into effect. Grindal, Opposing the Slavers, chap. 4.

38  supportive of the WAS efforts: Canning would, within months of sending this letter, move on up the political ladder to the position of prime minister. Within a year and a half he'd be dead. Derek Beales, "Canning, George (1770–1827), prime minister and parodist," in Oxford Dictionary of National Biography (Oxford, UK: Oxford University Press, 2004; online ed., 2011), article published September 23, 2004; last modified September 25, 2014.

38  expensive and time-consuming: Lubbock, Cruisers, 169–99, for discussion of British shipping design efforts and costs during this era.

38  press gangs . . . had ceased by 1815: Michael Lewis, The Navy in Transition, 1814–1864 (London: Hodder and Stoughton, 1965), 32–33, 171–72, marks the end of the practice of press gangs to this year, but takes especial pains to note that impressment as a concept—as a right retained by the government in war—was not particularly disputed, did not cease then, and laws sanctioning it have never been repealed.

38  the pesky British tendency to impress American nationals: Gerald S. Graham, Empire of the North Atlantic (Toronto: University of Toronto Press, 1950), 237–42.

38  employed only 20,000 just five years later: Nicholas A. M. Rodger, The Admiralty (Suffolk, UK: Terence Dalton, 1979), 93–94.

39  concerned . . . sailors . . . would also be put out of work: Reginald Coupland, The British Anti-Slavery Movement, 2nd ed. (London: Frank Cass & Co, 1964), 37.

39  the Industrial Revolution: When defined as 1760–1840.

39  fifty-four near copies finished or under construction: William Q. Force, Army and Navy Chronicle, and Scientific Repository: Being a Continuation of Homans' "Army and Navy Chronicle," vols. 1–3 (Washington, DC: Wm. Q. Force, 1843), 629.

40  Successful innovations . . . not yet forthcoming: Grindal, Opposing the Slavers, chap. 9, though the author does highlight that the frigates, at least, were not without some advantages on the coast, not the least of which was that their larger crews could sustain the losses that staffing tenders required. Howard I. Chapelle, The History of American Sailing Ships (New York: W. W. Norton; New York: Bonanza Books, 1935), 156, and

Lubbock, *Cruisers*, 169–99, detail the progression of the improvements in British naval ship design when they did arrive in the 1830s.

40 *crafting progressively faster ships*: Chapelle, *History of American Sailing Ships*, 130–31, 133, 150–52.

40 *putting out arguably the best ships on the water*: Ibid., 144, referencing William James, *The Naval History of Great Britain* (6 vols.) (London: Richard Bently, 1837).

40 *double the speed of the frigates*: Chapelle, *The History of American Sailing Ships*, 149.

40 *privateers became a model for slavers*: Ibid., 158.

40 *"race-horse beauty"*: Coupland, *The British Anti-Slavery Movement*, 161.

40 *northeastern United States . . . Chesapeake (Baltimore) region . . . integral to the . . . trade*: Howard I. Chapelle, *The Baltimore Clipper: Its Origin and Development* (New York: Bonanza Books, 1930), 8–14, on what that author believes to be the most probable history of the origins of the Baltimore clipper; Id. at 107–8, and Chapelle, *The History of American Sailing Ships*, 154, on the relationship between Baltimore clippers, the War of 1812, and the slave trade; Sherry H. Olson, *Baltimore: The Building of an American City* (Baltimore: Johns Hopkins University Press, 1997), 26–27, 83–85, for Baltimore's involvement with international trade; Christy Clark-Pujara, *Dark Work: The Business of Slavery in Rhode Island* (New York: New York University Press, 2016), 44, 49–50; and Christopher Phillips, *Freedom's Port: The African American Community of Baltimore, 1790–1860* (Urbana: University of Illinois Press, 1997), 17, 68, 78–80, on the interaction of slavery and shipyards in Rhode Island and Baltimore, respectively.

41 *strongly influencing their design*: Chapelle, *The History of American Sailing Ships*, 154–155, 158–61; Chapelle, *The Baltimore Clipper*, 107–11; Joseph Goldenberg, "Shipbuilding," in *The Historical Encyclopedia of World Slavery*, vol. 2, *L–Z*, ed. Junius P. Rodriguez (Santa Barbara: ABC-CLIO, 1997), 583–84.

41 *two ports simply wasn't worth the risk*: Chapelle, *The History of American Sailing Ships*, 158.

41 *several ways to be murdered on a slave ship*: Marcus Rediker, *The Slave Ship* (New York: Penguin, 2007); Sowande M. Mustakeem, *Slavery at Sea* (Urbana: University of Illinois Press, 2016); David Northrup, "African Mortality in the Suppression of the Slave Trade," *Journal of Interdisciplinary History* 9, no. 1 (1978): 47–64.

41 *loss of life . . . acceptable . . . to maximize profits*: Chapelle, *The History of American Sailing Ships*, 158; Dinizulu Gene Tinnie, "The Slaving Brig Henriqueta and Her Evil Sisters," *Journal of African American History* 93 (2008): 520–22.

41 *the slave deck*: Tinnie, "The Slaving Brig Henriqueta," 513, 515; Chapelle, *The Baltimore Clipper*, 110; Goldenberg, "Shipbuilding," 584; Rediker, *The Slave Ship*, chap. 10; Larry Gragg, "Middle Passage," in *The Historical Encyclopedia of World Slavery*, vol. 2, *L–Z*, ed. Junius P. Rodriguez (Santa Barbara: ABC-CLIO, 1997), 434; and Daniel P. Mannix, *Black Cargoes: A History of the Atlantic Slave Trade, 1518–1865* (New York: Viking Press, 1962), 106–7.

42 *temperature . . . surpassed ninety degrees*: Mustakeem, *Slavery at Sea*, 106–7; Tinnie, "The Slaving Brig Henriqueta," 515, citing Rev. Robert Walsh, *Notices of Brazil in 1828 and 1829*, vol. 2 (London: Frederick Westley and A. H. Davis, 1830), 481–82; and Rediker, *The Slave Ship*, chap. 2.

43 *a place to retreat in the event of an uprising*: Rediker, *The Slave Ship*, chap. 2, and Mustakeem, *Slavery at Sea*, 143–49.

43 *cheaper to put into use than . . . England's best*: The rationale behind the Admiralty's resistance remains a mystery. Grindal, *Opposing the Slavers*, chap. 9.

# NOTES

43 *a tenth, even a twentieth, of the cost*: For instance, using figures from Lubbock, *Cruisers*, 199, one can compare the size and cost of the American-built, Sierra Leone–auctioned *Henriqueta*, £330/£900 (roughly £35,000/$47,000 or £98,000/$135,000 today) for a ship about 260 tons burthen with a single pivot gun, to that of the English-built HMS *Bonetta* (1836), 319 tons burthen with three guns, but at a price of £6,510 (or approximately £692,500/$939,500 today). And *Bonetta* was one of the cheaper ships the yard put out during the 1830s.

43 *the elements of their construction documented*: Lubbock, *Cruisers*, 142, and Grindal, *Opposing the Slavers*, chap. 11, and fn. x.

44 *quality, gently used shipping at an extremely low price*: Leslie Bethell, "The Mixed Commissions for the Suppression of the Transatlantic Slave Trade in the Nineteenth Century," *Journal of African History* 7, no. 1 (1966): 79–93; and Padriac Xavier Scanlan, "The Rewards of Their Exertions," *Past & Present* 225 (2014): 113–42.

44 *any benefits weren't worth the risk of scandal*: Grindal, *Opposing the Slavers*, chaps. 8 and 9.

45 *near-complete control of internal policy*: A list of members of the Admiralty and Navy Boards during this (and indeed, most any) era can be found in Rodger, *The Admiralty*, 91–92.

45 *his expedient . . . had worked*: Grindal, *Opposing the Slavers*, chap. 8.

45 *allowing the ship to fall back into a slaver's hands*: Ibid., chap. 9.

46 *only the buying, selling, and shipping of the enslaved was forbidden*: David Eltis, *Economic Growth and the Ending of the Transatlantic Slave Trade* (Oxford, UK: Oxford University Press, 1987).

46 *necessitated positive public opinion*: Seymour Drescher, *Abolition: A History of Slavery and Antislavery* (New York: Cambridge University Press, 2009), 248, asserts that the influence of British public opinion on the slave trade was at its zenith during the 1820s; Bernard Semmel, *Liberalism and Naval Strategy* (Boston: Allen & Unwin, 1986), 123, on the power and influence of liberal public opinion in regards to naval strategy; Isaac Land, *War, Nationalism, and the British Sailor, 1750–1850* (New York: Palgrave Macmillan, 2009), 110, regarding how less than glowing accounts and descriptions of service in the navy were disincentivized.

46 *not brook . . . Britain doing anything that might facilitate the trade*: See, e.g., abolitionist reaction to the results of the Congress of Vienna in Kielstra, *The Politics of Slave Trade Suppression in Britain and France*, 25–33.

46 *righteously snuffed out*: Richard Huzzey, "The Politics of Slave-Trade Suppression," in *The Suppression of the Atlantic Slave Trade*, eds. Robert M. Burroughs and Richard Huzzey (Manchester, UK: Manchester University Press, 2016), 17–22; Ward, *The Royal Navy and the Slavers*, 165; and Thomas, *The Slave Trade*, chap. 29.

46 *the power to judge those so captured*: James Bandinel, *Some Account of the Trade in Slaves from Africa as Connected with Europe and America from the Introduction of the Trade into Modern Europe, Down to the Present Time* (London: Frank Cass & Co., 1842), 126–32, 150–63; Leslie Bethell, "Britain, Portugal and the Suppression of the Brazilian Slave Trade," *English Historical Review* 80, no. 317 (1965): 761–66; Foreign and Commonwealth Office Historians, "Slavery in Diplomacy: The Foreign Office and the Suppression of the Transatlantic Slave Trade," *History Notes* 17, Britain: The Foreign, Commonwealth, and Development Office, 2013, https://issuu.com/fcohistorians/docs/history_notes_cover_hphn_17; and J. P. van Niekerk, "British, Portuguese, and American Judges in Adderley Street . . . (Part 1)," *Comparative and International Law Journal of Southern Africa* 37, no. 1 (2004): 1–39.

46  *an ongoing process of spectacular collapse*: Kennedy, *The Rise and Fall of British Naval Mastery*, 159–60.

47  *previously stipulated obligations of its former rulers*: Bethell, "The Independence of Brazil," 120–21.

47  *honor Portugal's previous agreements with Britain*: Leslie Bethell, *Brazil: Essays on History and Politics* (London: University of London Press, 2018), 57–66.

48  *subject to legitimate capture by the British*: Bethell, "The Independence of Brazil," 115–47.

48  *reasons to deceive . . . and plenty of practice*: A sampling of examples: Bernard Edwards, *Royal Navy Versus the Slave Traders* (Barnsley, UK: Pen & Sword Books, 2008), chap. 5; Christopher Lloyd, *The Navy and the Slave Trade* (New York: Routledge, 2012), chap. 12; and Grindal, *Opposing the Slavers*, chaps. 4 and 6.

49  *"a picture of the most agreeable character"*: Peter Leonard, *Records of a Voyage to the Western Coast of Africa* (Edinburgh: William Tait, 1833), 38.

49  *what was then known as interest*: Lewis, *The Navy in Transition*, 27–28, and Rodger, *Wooden World*, 273–302.

49  *a man and an officer*: Rodger, *Wooden World*, 119–24.

49  *Black Joke would be led by a lieutenant*: The practice of the second-in-command on a larger ship being a commander was completing the process of becoming standard practice by 1827 (Lewis, *The Navy in Transition*, 86), so despite the fact that Turner already did this job on *Sybille*, he was still a first lieutenant at this juncture.

49  *even the occasional petty officer*: Specifically master's mates. Nicholas A. M. Rodger, *Naval Records for Genealogists* (London: Her Majesty's Stationary Office, 1988), 18.

50  *the rank was distinct from the duty*: Ibid., 15, and Lewis, *The Navy in Transition*, 84.

50  *more officers than berths to contain them*: Lewis, *The Navy in Transition*, 78–84.

50  *it took all three . . . to advance . . . to post-captain*: Rodger, *Wooden World*, 263, 273–302.

50  *comparative relaxing of class distinctions*: Ibid., 252–72.

51  *an officer who could not help their career*: Ibid., 275–77.

51  *could . . . completely destroy the career*: Ibid., 280.

51  *Nelson . . . notorious personal life*: Michael Ryan, "Lord Nelson: Hero and . . . Cad!," *Smithsonian Magazine*, February 2004, https://www.smithsonianmag.com/history/lord-nelson-hero-andcad–105811218/.

51  *demand . . . outstripped the supply of available commissions*: Lewis, *The Navy in Transition*, 72–88.

52  *the backroom coin of the Royal Navy*: Rodger, *Wooden World*, 282–83.

52  *William Turner . . . second berth on Sybille*: O'Byrne, *A Naval Biographical Dictionary*, 1215.

52  *the new brig's captain*: Lubbock, *Cruisers*, 140.

53  *until he was thirteen or fourteen*: Edward Cave, *The Gentleman's Magazine and Historical Review*, vol. 220 (January–June 1866) (London: Bradbury, Evans, & Co., 1866), 297. He would have been born in 1802 or 1803 and entered the Navy in 1816.

53  *the gentlemen's class with whom he had to compete*: Rodger, *Wooden World*, 254.

53  *a village near Portsmouth*: Bedhampton Historical Collection, "The Time Travellers Guide to Bedhampton Village," January 2019, https://secure.toolkitfiles.co.uk/clients/21710/sitedata/files/Time-Travellers-Guide-to-Bedhampton-Village-2019-02–18–121424.pdf, 3-4.

53  *the complications involved in procuring French wines*: Gavin Daly, "Napoleon and the 'City of Smugglers,' 1810–1814," *Historical Journal* 50, no. 2 (2007): 333–52, especially 337.

53  *a centuries-long reputation for heavy drinking*: R. C. Riley and Philip Eley, *Public Houses*

*and Beerhouses in Nineteenth Century Portsmouth* (Portsmouth, UK: Libraries, Museums and Arts Historical Publications Sub-Committee of the Portsmouth, 1983), 3–4.

53 *constant improvements to the family's country estate*: Bedhampton Historical Collection, "The Waterloo Room at The Elms: 'The Gem of Bedhampton,'" https://secure.tool kitfiles.co.uk/clients/21710/sitedata/files/The%20Waterloo%20Room%20at%20 The%20Elms.pdf, 1–2.

53 *the grip of an economic downturn*: Bedhampton Historical Collection, "The Time Travellers Guide," 1.

53 *then the largest known industrial complex*: Niall Ferguson, *Empire: The Rise and Demise of the British World Order and the Lessons for Global Power* (New York: Basic Books, 2004), 27.

54 *attractive option . . . to progress their families socially*: Rodger, *Wooden World*, 266–67.

54 *return to the Sybille's quarterdeck*: O'Byrne, *A Naval Biographical Dictionary*, 1215.

54 *jaunt back to Freetown*: Lubbock, *Cruisers*, 141.

54 *a war of words*: David Lambert, "Sierra Leone and Other Sites in the War of Representation over Slavery," *History Workshop Journal* 64 (2007): 103–32.

55 *schools and churches aplenty*: Kenneth Macaulay, *The Colony of Sierra Leone Vindicated from the Misrepresentations of Mr. Macqueen of Glasgow* (London: J. Hatchard and Son, 1827).

55 *public dinners, and all-night dancing*: James W. St. G. Walker, *The Black Loyalists: The Search for a Promised Land in Nova Scotia and Sierra Leone* (Toronto; Buffalo; London: University of Toronto Press, 1992), 308–9.

55 *better suited to the climate*: Macaulay, *The Colony of Sierra Leone Vindicated*.

55 *disorganized and ill-fated arrival of the first settler colonizers*: Accounted historically in Christopher Fyfe, *A History of Sierra Leone*, 3rd ed. (London: Oxford University Press, 1968), 13–52, and contemporaneously, at least between 1791 and 1793 and from a British perspective, by Anna Maria Falconbridge, *Two Voyages to Sierra Leone, During the Years 1791–2–3, in a Series of Letters* (London: Anna Maria Falconbridge, 1794). Fyfe, *A History of Sierra Leone*, 1–12, provides a brief overview of the history of Sierra Leone from European contact in the fifteenth century; and P. E. H. Hair, "Aspects of the Prehistory of Freetown and Creoledom," *History in Africa* 25 (1998): 111–18, explores the Portuguese influence on Freetown's evolution.

55 *the brig was a mere extension of the frigate*: Grindal, *Opposing the Slavers*, chap. 9.

55 *cut a distinct profile*: Chapelle, *The History of American Sailing Ships*, 156, 158. "Rake" simply refers to the angle of something, in this instance, "the inclination of the stem and sternpost beyond the ends of the keel; also, the inclination of the masts from the perpendicular," J. Richard Steffy, "Illustrated Glossary of Ship and Boat Terms," in *The Oxford Handbook of Maritime Archaeology*, eds. Ben Ford, Donny L. Hamilton, and Alexis Catsambis (New York: Oxford University Press, 2012), a not uncommon adjustment in clippers engineered to perfect a ship's buoyancy, balance, and/or motion through the water, John W. Griffiths, *The Progressive Shipbuilder*, vol. 2 (New York: John W. Griffiths, 1876).

55 *"a most symmetrical specimen of naval architecture"*: Chapelle, *The History of American Sailing Ships*, 156, 158; Lubbock, *Cruisers*, 141; and Leonard, *Records of a Voyage*, 131.

56 *barely room to breathe, much less move*: Tinnie, "The Slaving Brig Henriqueta," 512.

56 *two days in Sierra Leone in early January*: Henry Downes, Logbook of HMS SYBILLE and HMS BLACK JOKE 1827–1829 (LOG/N/41). National Maritime Museum, Greenwich, London.

56 *purchasing the* Henriqueta *at auction:* Tinnie, "The Slaving Brig *Henriqueta,*" 513.

56 *the area had traded in people, and only people:* Thomas, *The Slave Trade,* chap. 32.

56 *capturing its first slaver:* Grindal, *Opposing the Slavers,* chap. 9.

56 *John Ouseley Kearney:* Thomas, *The Slave Trade,* chap. 32.

58 *sailing alongside the Sybille and HMS* Esk: Sullivan, *Britain's War Against the Slave Trade,* 141.

58 *his ship taken with little fuss:* "Portsmouth, Saturday March 29, 1828," *Hampshire Telegraph* (March 31, 1828); Correspondence (Class A) 1829, 20.

59 *condemned . . . processed into Freetown:* Trans-Atlantic Slave Trade Database; Correspondence (Class A) 1829, 20.


## Chapter Three: *Providencia*

63 *over a thousand slave voyages:* Trans-Atlantic Slave Trade Database.

63 *no combatant . . . better shape than England:* Paul M. Kennedy, *The Rise and Fall of British Naval Mastery* (New York: Penguin, 2017), 150.

64 *"formal" control of territorial possessions:* Ibid., 152.

64 *England's overseas interests actually increased:* Ex: James Onley, "Britain's Informal Empire in the Gulf, 1820–1971," *Journal of Social Affairs* 22, no. 87 (2005); Britten Dean, "British Informal Empire: The Case of China," *Journal of Commonwealth & Comparative Politics* 14, no. 1 (January 1976): 64–81; Martin Lynn, "British Policy, Trade, and Informal Empire in the Mid-Nineteenth Century," in *The Oxford History of the British Empire,* vol. 3, *The Nineteenth Century,* by Porter, Andrew, and Wm Roger Louis, ed. Andrew Porter (Oxford, UK: Oxford University Press, 1999, Oxford Scholarship Online, 2011).

64 *a base capable of comparatively rapid response:* Kennedy, *The Rise and Fall of British Naval Mastery,* 154; Kennedy also cites Graham, *Empire of the North Atlantic* (Toronto: University of Toronto Press, 1950), 264, who has an even more detailed list accompanied by additional information regarding the strategic value of some of these particular holdings for British sea power.

65 *Royal Navy was a primary mechanism:* Kennedy, *The Rise and Fall of British Naval Mastery,* 157.

65 *the golden age of piracy ended:* Marcus Rediker, *Villains of All Nations: Atlantic Pirates in the Golden Age* (Boston: Beacon Press, 2004), 8, defines piracy's golden age as between "roughly 1650 to 1730."

65 *the waters were nonetheless rife with predation:* Kennedy, *The Rise and Fall of British Naval Mastery,* 164–65.

65 *precipitated a particular rise in nefarious activity:* J. L. Anderson, "Piracy and World History: An Economic Perspective on Maritime Predation," *Journal of World History* 6, no. 2 (1995): 194.

65 *protected them from interference:* Howard Chapelle, *The History of American Sailing Ships* (New York: W. W. Norton; New York: Bonanza Books, 1935), 130.

65 *pirates were the bane of nearly all:* Anderson, "Piracy and World History," 194.

66 *the cost of protective measures:* Ibid., 179.

66 *served British trade interests rather well:* Oded Lowenheim, "'Do Ourselves Credit and Render a Lasting Service to Mankind': British Moral Prestige, Humanitarian Intervention, and the Barbary Pirates," *International Studies Quarterly* 47 (2003): 23–48 (35–43).

66  *universal cessation of slave trading*: Reginald Coupland, *The British Anti-Slavery Movement* (London: Frank Cass & Co, 1964), 154–55.

66  *pervaded many of the intellectual and diplomatic circles*: Brian E. Vick, *The Congress of Vienna* (Cambridge: Harvard University Press, 2014), 194, 201, 203.

66  *not yet reached their future popularity*: Ibid., 208–10.

66  *national self-interest, not altruism*: Ibid., 223–24.

67  *a relatively simple matter . . . before the Congress began*: Ibid., 202.

67  *newfound antislavery political attitude*: Lowenheim, "'Do Ourselves Credit,'" 39–44.

67  *regularly ransomed, rather than sold, back to Europe*: Vick, *The Congress of Vienna*, 214–15.

67  *eradicate the Barbary pirate problem in 1816*: Lowenheim, "'Do Ourselves Credit,'" 30–35.

67  *role of the Royal Navy in the coming age*: Kennedy, *The Rise and Fall of British Naval Mastery*, 164–65, notes that the eradication of Barbary piracy in the area wasn't accomplished until 1830.

68  *the signatories'*: England, Austria, France, Portugal, Prussia, Russia, Spain, and Sweden. James Bandinel, *Some Account of the Trade in Slaves from Africa as Connected with Europe and America from the Introduction of the Trade into Modern Europe, Down to the Present Time* (London: Frank Cass & Co., 1842).

68  *"no proper means for accelerating that period are to be neglected"*: Ibid., 148–49.

68  *the Netherlands and Denmark . . . moved to abolish*: Johannes Postma, *The Dutch in the Atlantic Slave Trade, 1600–1815* (Cambridge, UK: Cambridge University Press, 1990), 284–89; Denmark had gone the gradual abolition of the trade route, so it should be noted that its gradual decrease was preceded by several years of aggressively stockpiling an enslaved population in its Caribbean holdings, Seymour Drescher, *Abolition: A History of Slavery and Antislavery* (New York: Cambridge University Press, 2009), 97, 169.

68  *a robust domestic slave trade*: Drescher, *Abolition*, 118–19, 127, 296, 311.

68  *British abolition left a market vacuum . . . to fill*: David Eltis, *Economic Growth and the Ending of the Transatlantic Slave Trade* (Oxford, UK: Oxford University Press, 1987), 52–53.

68  *met with their opposite numbers from Portugal and Spain*: Vick, *The Congress of Vienna*, 202–4.

69  *any reason to simply acquiesce to British demands*: Bandinel, *Some Account of the Trade*, 126–30, and Christopher Lloyd, *The Navy and the Slave Trade* (New York: Routledge, 2012), chap. 4.

69  *Portugal . . . was to be paid . . . with additional payments to come*: This was less than a third of what England ultimately ended up paying to Portugal alone by 1853, Lloyd, *The Navy and the Slave Trade*, chap. 4.

70  *Mixed Commission . . . established in Sierra Leone*: Leslie Bethell, "Britain, Portugal and the Suppression of the Brazilian Slave Trade," *English Historical Review* 80, no. 317 (1965): 763–64.

70  *Mixed Commission to be established in Cuba*: Bandinel, *Some Account of the Trade*, 160.

70  *slave trading south of the equator*: Lloyd, *The Navy and the Slave Trade*, chap. 4.

70  *less interested . . . right to search French ships*: Vick, *The Congress of Vienna*, 197–98, and Paul Michael Kielstra, *The Politics of Slave Trade Suppression in Britain and France, 1814–48* (London: Palgrave Macmillan UK, 2000), 63–67.

70  *make any other move to prevent human trafficking*: Kielstra, *The Politics of Slave Trade*

*Suppression in Britain and France*, 76, and Peter Grindal, *Opposing the Slavers* (London: I.B. Tauris, 2016), chap. 6.

70 *"right of search"*: Kielstra, *The Politics of Slave Trade Suppression in Britain and France*, 63.

71 *a nonnegotiable feature of British foreign relations*: Edward Keene, "A Case Study of the Construction of International Hierarchy: British Treaty-Making against the Slave Trade in the Early Nineteenth Century," *International Organization* 61, no. 2 (April 1, 2007): 311–39.

71 *an international naval force*: Vick, *The Congress of Vienna*, 216–17.

71 *and again the next year*: Kielstra, *The Politics of Slave Trade Suppression in Britain and France*, 64–65.

71 *fought a war . . . over this very issue*: It would continue to be a contentious issue with the United States for decades to come. William Beach Lawrence, *Visitation and Search: or, An Historical Sketch of the British Claim to Exercise a Maritime Police over the Vessels of All Nations, in Peace as Well as in War* (Boston: Little, Brown and Company, 1858).

71 *"any of His Majesty's Ship or Vessels of War"*: Act for the Abolition of the Slave Trade, 1807, 47 Geo. III, c. 36; the language in the subsequent Felonies Act (1811) is almost exactly the same. *British and Foreign State Papers, 1817–1818* (London: James Ridgway and Sons, 1837), 575.

71 *weren't ships available to create a dedicated patrol*: William Ernest Frank Ward, *The Royal Navy and the Slavers* (London: Pantheon Books, 1969), 43.

72 *what was supposed to happen next*: Padraic Xavier Scanlan, *Freedom's Debtors* (New Haven: Yale University Press, 2017), 67.

72 *Derwent . . . Solebay*: Ward, *The Royal Navy and the Slavers*, 43.

72 *a misdemeanor . . . to a felony*: *British and Foreign State Papers*, 571–76.

72 *a relatively simple endeavor*: Coupland, *The British Anti-Slavery Movement*, 81.

72 *astronomical returns on investment still brought enslavers*: Grindal, *Opposing the Slavers*, chap. 4.

73 *Yeo . . . Columbine . . . Irby . . . Browne*: Ibid., Appendix D.

73 *"no less than eighty" like-missioned vessels*: Siân Rees, *Sweet Water and Bitter* (Durham, University of New Hampshire Press, 2009), 28.

74 *"stipulations contained therein"*: Ward, *The Royal Navy and the Slavers*, 43–44.

74 *the Squadron was tiny*: Grindal, *Opposing the Slavers*, chap. 6.

74 *little help would be forthcoming*: Ibid. The colonial schooner *Princess Charlotte* didn't stay serviceable for long and was replaced by a captured brig then renamed *Prince Regent*, and *Queen Charlotte*, also a captured vessel, joined the colonial side of the efforts. *Inconstant* didn't stay serviceable for long, either, and its crew was later transferred to HMS *Semiramis*. Despite these changes, however, and the fact that captured ships were already doing some work as tenders, the official number of Royal Navy ships available for deployment during Yeo's tenure maxed out at two.

74 *were as yet uninterested*: Eltis, *Economic Growth*, 94–96.

74 *Domestically the situation was little better*: Ibid., 90–94.

74 *send those ships . . . to guard Napoléon instead*: Basil Lubbock, *Cruisers, Corsairs & Slavers* (Glasgow: Brown, Son & Ferguson, 1993), 100.

74 *natural harbors . . . confined to the major slaving rivers*: Ward, *The Royal Navy and the Slavers*, 45–47; Rees, *Sweet Water and Bitter*, 35–36.

75 *practically give the information away*: Kennedy, *The Rise and Fall of British Naval Mastery*, 164–65; Captain William Fitzwilliam Owen, who will join the narrative later, was one such surveyor before his subsequent time on the coast as the administrator

of Fernando Pó, charting the coasts of Africa both east and west, the latter from the Congo to Gambia Rivers, and it was then that he'd managed to earn the ire of Commodore Bullen. Grindal, *Opposing the Slavers*, chap. 8.

75 *instructions would have to be more honored in the breach*: Hamlet (act 1, scene 4). I had to look it up myself, so hopefully this saves you some trouble if you're likewise inclined.

75 *lengthen a two-week cruise along the coast to over five*: Ward, *The Royal Navy and the Slavers*, 45–47; by way of extreme example, Robert Burroughs, "Eyes on the Prize," *Slavery and Abolition* 31, no. 1 (2010): 101, recounts a prize-ship trip that should have been three weeks and instead took nearly five months.

75 *Yeo . . . would die from illness*: J. K. Laughton and Michael Duffy, "Yeo, Sir James Lucas (1782–1818), Naval Officer," *Oxford Dictionary of National Biography*, September 23, 2004.

75 *the size of the Squadron would again stall*: Lloyd, *The Navy and the Slave Trade*, Appendix C.

75 *quantity of enslaved . . . exported . . . would precipitously rise*: These figures are from Eltis, *Economic Growth*, 250; however, more recent data from the Trans-Atlantic Slave Trade Database suggests the numbers are distinctly higher, closer to almost 62,000 in 1815 to over 112,000 in 1829.

76 *number of ships . . . near stagnant . . . through 1832*: Lloyd, *The Navy and the Slave Trade*, Appendix C.

76 *Opponents . . . declared the goal . . . impossible*: Grindal, *Opposing the Slavers*, Prologue.

76 *outnumbered by slave traders by almost thirty to one*: 228 slave voyages embarked enslaved people from Africa in 1827 (Trans-Atlantic Slave Trade Database), divided by 6 WAS ships, excluding tenders (Lloyd, *The Navy and the Slave Trade*, Appendix C), is 38.

76 *Royal Navy . . . notably low-cost*: Kennedy, *The Rise and Fall of British Naval Mastery*, 150.

76 *£60 million to £100 million per year*: Eltis, *Economic Growth*, 92.

77 *Royal Navy usually held the advantage*: Daniel K. Benjamin and Anca Tifrea, "Learning by Dying: Combat Performance in the Age of Sail," *Journal of Economic History* 67, no. 4 (2007): 968–1000; Thomas Malcomson, *Order and Disorder in the British Navy, 1793–1815* (Woodbridge, Suffolk, UK; Rochester, NY: Boydell & Brewer, 2016), 74–80.

77 *promotion and . . . prize money*: Michael Lewis, *The Navy in Transition, 1814–1864* (London: Hodder and Stoughton, 1985), 231–42; Padriac Xavier Scanlan, "The Rewards of Their Exertions," *Past & Present* 225 (2014): 113–42; Daniel K. Benjamin and Christopher F. Thornberg, "Comment: Rules, Monitoring, and Incentives in the Age of Sail," *Explorations in Economic History* 40 (2003): 195–211; Daniel K. Benjamin and Christopher Thornberg, "Organization and Incentives in the Age of Sail," *Explorations in Economic History* 44 (2007): 317–41.

77 *promotion ladder was congested and opportunities few*: Lewis, *The Navy in Transition*, 58–59, 61–63.

77 *only 3 percent of . . . personnel . . . West Africa in the late 1820s*: Eltis, *Economic Growth*, 92.

77 *one in ten officers were fully employed*: Lewis, *The Navy in Transition*, 68–70.

77 *territory . . . divided at first into four sections*: Ward, *The Royal Navy and the Slavers*, 45.

77 *Senegal . . . the equatorial line*: Lloyd, *The Navy and the Slave Trade*, chap. 5.

78 *resupply in Fernando Pó*: Robert T. Brown, "Fernando Po and the Anti-Sierra Leonean

Campaign," *International Journal of African Historical Studies* 6, no. 2 (1973): 252, and Ibrahim K. Sundiata, *From Slaving to Neoslavery: The Bight of Biafra and Fernando Po in the Era of Abolition, 1827–1930* (Madison: University of Wisconsin Press, 1996), 22–24.

78 *rest and refresh in Ascension*: Grindal, *Opposing the Slavers*, chaps. 3 and 6.

78 *prizes . . . near the Bonny and Calabar Rivers*: Lloyd, *The Navy and the Slave Trade*, chap. 5.

79 *trolled for information*: Grindal, *Opposing the Slavers*, chap. 5.

79 *Black Joke had forty-three men on board*: John Marshall, *Royal Naval Biography*, Part 3 (London: Longman, Rees, Orme, Brown, and Green, 1829), 297–98.

79 *finally "the watch was set" at eight*: Brian Lavery, *Life in Nelson's Navy* (Stroud, UK: The History Press, 2007), chap. 4.

79 *likely leaving his boatswain, Harvey*: William Richard O'Byrne, *A Naval Biographical Dictionary* (London: John Murray, Albemarle Street, 1849), 1215.

80 *may . . . sleep on deck*: Lavery, *Life in Nelson's Navy*, chap. 4.

80 *in position to pounce*: Lloyd, *The Navy and the Slave Trade*, chap. 5.

80 *receive an £8 bonus*: Ibid.

80 *Coates, who acted as chief medic for the tender*: Joseph Allen, *The New Navy List and General Record* (London: Parker, Furnivall, and Parker, 1850), 175, lists Coates in this position for a subsequent action under Turner, so I have inferred his presence here.

80 *and nothing to sneeze at for them, either*: Lewis, *The Navy in Transition*, 212–13.

80 *those particular characteristics . . . that might mark a slaver*: Chapelle, *The History of American Sailing Ships*, 159.

80 *usually a short-lived mystery*: Lloyd, *The Navy and the Slave Trade*, chap. 5.

80 *agricultural exploitation rather than human trafficking*: Eltis, *Economic Growth*, 164.

81 *Black Joke first sighted the* Providencia: Anthony Sullivan, *Britain's War Against the Slave Trade* (Barnsley, UK: Pen & Sword Books, 2020), 141–42.

81 *10 percent . . . under French or US flags*: Trans-Atlantic Slave Trade Database; 1,069 ships are listed leaving the area from 1825 to 1830, 135 of them flew the flag of France or the United States. It was not an even distribution, as almost all these ships were French.

82 *the resources to acquire fake flags*: Jenny S. Martinez, *The Slave Trade and the Origins of International Human Rights Law* (Oxford, UK: Oxford University Press, 2011), 4–5.

82 *solid-white flag of France's Bourbon restoration*: France's flag changed with its system of government, so, though it had been the tricolor we've come to expect and would be again, during this historical moment, yes, it was an entirely white flag.

82 *Dutch vessels were scarce on the water*: Trans-Atlantic Slave Trade Database.

82 *apprehended . . . less than a fortnight previous*: *La Fanny*, flying a French flag. Grindal, *Opposing the Slavers*, chap. 9.

82 *not above lying their entire faces off*: David Joseph Blair, "All the Ships That Never Sailed," PhD diss., Georgetown University, 2014, 245–311.

82 *lie of the vessel's actual affiliation*: The question of how to consistently determine a ship's nationality for the purposes of adjudication would be an issue of unagreed upon international maritime law between Britain, Portugal, and Brazil for some years yet. Grindal, *Opposing the Slavers*, chap. 16.

82 *carry multiple commissions*: See, e.g., the aforementioned *La Fanny*.

83 *depending on . . . position relative to the equator*: Lubbock, *Cruisers*, 115.

83 *pretend not to speak English at all*: Lloyd, *The Navy and the Slave Trade*, chap. 5.

83 *personally liable for . . . his mistake*: Leslie Bethell, "The Mixed Commissions for the

Suppression of the Transatlantic Slave Trade in the Nineteenth Century," *Journal of African History* 7, no. 1 (1966): 88.

83 *indemnify . . . against reasonable error*: Benjamin and Thornberg, "Organization and Incentives," 198.

83 *redress for slave ships illegally captured*: Grindal, *Opposing the Slavers*, chap. 6.

84 *already an exceptional occurrence*: Lewis, *The Navy in Transition*, 19–32.

84 *sizable increases in income*: Ibid., 209–48.

84 *mechanisms of social mobility*: Nicholas A. M. Rodger, *The Wooden World* (Glasgow: William Collins Sons & Co., 1986), 263–72, discusses what the promotion system previously looked like for officers in the long eighteenth century, compare to Lewis, *The Navy in Transition*, 101–2, for the nineteenth-century shifts.

84 *hoisted the Red Ensign*: John Marshall, *Royal Naval*, Vol. 3, Part 1 (London: Longman, Rees, Orme, Brown, and Green, 1831), 297.

84 *used to indicate a British merchant or passenger ship*: Robert Carse, *The Twilight of Sailing Ships* (New York: Galahad Books, 1965), 60. For the visually inclined, it has a solid red field and a Union Jack in the upper left corner.

84 *now identifying itself as Spanish*: Anthony Sullivan, *Britain's War Against the Slave Trade*, 142.

84 *Turner and his speaking trumpet*: Lloyd, *The Navy and the Slave Trade*, chap. 5, notes the regular use of speaking trumpets in service on the coast, as otherwise it would be very difficult to be heard on another vessel in many circumstances.

85 *"no boat that could swim"*: Marshall, *Royal Naval Biography*, Vol. 3, Part 1, 297.

85 *demanded to see the Black Joke's identification papers*: Lubbock, *Cruisers*, 143.

85 *the diversity of faces that graced its navy*: I draw this conclusion by way of the example provided in Ray Costello, *Black Salt: Seafarers of African Descent on British Ships* (Liverpool, UK: Liverpool University Press, 2012), 60–61, of HMS *Victory* at Trafalgar, on which the author notes there were, in addition to likely populations of British-born Black seamen and possible pockets of Canadian and US-born ones who are difficult to distinguish from their White crewmates on account of Anglicized naming conventions, "small numbers of seamen of other nationalities including Swedish, Dutch, Maltese, Italians, Portuguese, Danes, Russians, Indians and even Frenchmen—22 Americans, nine West Indians and one African." And despite the complaints of the United States, odds are that many volunteered, rather than being impressed. J. Ross Dancy, *The Myth of the Press Gang* (Suffolk, UK: Boydell & Brewer, 2015), 149–50.

86 *the ubiquitous Kroomen*: John Rankin, "Nineteenth-Century Royal Navy Sailors," *African Diaspora* 6, no. 2 (2014): 179–95; John Rankin, "British and African Health in the Anti-slave-trade Squadron," in *The Suppression of the Atlantic Slave Trade*, eds. Robert M. Burroughs and Richard Huzzey (Manchester, UK: Manchester University Press, 2016), 95–121.

86 *sometimes flamboyant*: Lewis, *The Navy in Transition*, 254–58, and Lavery, *Life in Nelson's Navy*, chap. 4.

86 *jib . . . used . . . to identify the nationality of a ship*: Nicholas A. M. Rodger, *The Command of the Ocean: A Naval History of Britain, 1649–1815* (New York: W. W. Norton, 2005), 757, for a more technical definition of a jib; *The Naval Chronicle, for 1805: Containing a General and Biographical History of the Royal Navy of the United Kingdom; with a Variety of Original Papers on Nautical Subjects*, vol. 14 (*from July to December*), (London: Joyce Gold, 1805), 97, for evidence of the genesis of the idiom, even though the word "jib" is not actually used.

86 *the two empires fought to retain their colonial holdings*: D. A. G. Waddell, "British Neu-

trality and Spanish-American Independence: The Problem of Foreign Enlistment," *Journal of Latin American Studies* 19, no. 1 (1987): 1–18; Leslie Bethell, *Brazil: Essays on History and Politics* (London: University of London Press, 2018), 62–64.

86  *joined the naval effort for South American liberation*: Waddell, "British Neutrality."

86  *Thomas Cochrane, the Sea Wolf*: Ibid.; Bethell, *Brazil: Essays on History and Politics*, 63, citing: Thomas Cochrane, *Narrative of Services in the Liberation of Chile, Peru and Brazil, from Spanish and Portuguese Domination* (2 vols.) (London: James Ridgway, 1858–59); Brian Vale, *Independence or Death! British Sailors and Brazilian Independence, 1822–25* (London: I.B. Tauris, 1996); and Brian Vale, *The Audacious Admiral Cochrane* (London: Conway Maritime Press, 2004).

89  *better at aiming than their average opponent*: Rodger, *Wooden World*, 56–59; Geoffrey J. Marcus, *Heart of Oak: A Survey of British Sea Power in the Georgian Era* (London: Oxford University Press, 1975), 39–40; Jeremy Black and Cheryl Fury, "The Development of Sea Power, 1649–1815," in *The Social History of English Seamen, 1650–1815*, ed. Cheryl A. Fury (Suffolk, UK: Boydell & Brewer, 2017), 5–32 (24).

90  *"intrepidity and judgment on the occasion"*: Account of the *Black Joke's* encounter with the *Providencia* is compiled from the following sources: Marshall, *Royal Naval Biography*, Vol. 3, Part 1, 297–98; Lubbock, *Cruisers*, 143–44; Grindal, *Opposing the Slavers*, chap. 9; Sullivan, *Britain's War Against the Slave Trade*, 142; O'Byrne, *A Naval Biographical Dictionary*, 1215; and Rees, *Sweet Water and Bitter*, 123–24.

90  *a sword worth £220*: In O'Byrne, *A Naval Biographical Dictionary*, 1215, the actual figure given is 200 guineas. A guinea was worth £1 s.1, or one pound one shilling. There was a massive recoinage in 1816 that eliminated the guinea and replaced it fully with the pound, but apparently guineas had a more "aristocratic" association and continued to be used as reference for luxury goods, like, say, superfancy engraved swords.

90  *over a year and a half of a lieutenant's sea-pay*: Lewis, *The Navy in Transition*, 212. Monthly pay for a senior lieutenant was £11 s.14 at the time the *Black Joke* sailed, there are 20 shillings in a pound, so 220/11.7=18.8 months.

90  *"gallantry while Lieutenant-commanding the Black Joke tender"*: O'Byrne, *A Naval Biographical Dictionary*, 1215.

90  *Harvey . . . was also promoted*: Ibid., and *The Navy List, Corrected to the 25th of September, 1828* (London: John Murray, 1828), 28.

## Chapter Four: *Vengador, Presidente & Zepherina*

93  *the Black Joke would find its next chance*: Account of *Black Joke's* encounter with the *Vengador* is compiled from the following sources: Basil Lubbock, *Cruisers, Corsairs & Slavers* (Glasgow: Brown, Son & Ferguson, 1993), 144; Peter Grindal, *Opposing the Slavers* (London: I.B. Tauris, 2016), chap. 9; Anthony Sullivan, *Britain's War Against the Slave Trade* (Barnsley, UK: Pen & Sword Books, 2020), 143; Siân Rees, *Sweet Water and Bitter* (Durham: University of New Hampshire Press, 2009), 124; Rif Winfield, *British Warships in the Age of Sail, 1817–1863* (Yorkshire, UK: Seaforth Publishing, 2014), 1076–77; Trans-Atlantic Slave Trade Database; "Naval Intelligence," *Observer*, September 15, 1828; Correspondence (Class B) 1828, 4; and Correspondence (Class A), 1828, 76.

94  *only to have it . . . hie off*: Christopher Lloyd, *The Navy and the Slave Trade* (New York: Routledge, 2012), chap. 5.

94  *this wasn't unusual*: Kevin Dawson, "Enslaved Watermen in the Atlantic World,

1444–1888," PhD diss., University of South Carolina, 2005; Emma Christopher, "Slave Ship Sailors: A Roundtable Response," *International Journal of Maritime History* 19, no. 1 (June 2007): 333–41; and Stephen D. Behrendt, "Human Capital in the British Slave Trade," in *Liverpool and Transatlantic Slavery*, eds. David Richardson, Suzanne Schwarz, and Anthony Tibbles (Liverpool, UK: Liverpool University Press, 2007), 78.

94 *perhaps Netto didn't like his odds*: If Netto's paperwork was in order, this might not matter as, at least in some treaties, Britain had acquiesced to the right of vessels to carry (and thus retain in the case of condemnation) enslaved "bona fide household servants," provided their identities were stipulated in the ship's passport, which would have been issued from the voyage's origin point. J. P. van Niekerk, "British, Portuguese, and American Judges in Adderley Street . . . (Part 1)," *Comparative and International Law Journal of Southern Africa* 37, no. 11 (2004): 32, fn. 131.

95 *owned by . . . Jose de Cerqueira Lima*: Correspondence (Class) A 1828, 76; Dinizulu Gene Tinnie, "The Slaving Brig *Henriqueta* and Her Evil Sisters," *Journal of African American History* 93 (2008): 517.

95 *an unfortunately accurate assessment*: Tinnie, "The Slaving Brig *Henriqueta*."

95 *despite the rising costs*: William Ernest Frank Ward, *The Royal Navy and the Slavers* (London: Pantheon Books, 1969), 133–34; David Joseph Blair, "All the Ships That Never Sailed," PhD diss., Georgetown University, 2014, 323–24, citing William Law Mathieson, *Great Britain and the Slave Trade, 1839–1865* (London: Longmans, Green and Co., 1929), 17, 135, and David Eltis, *Economic Growth and the Ending of the Transatlantic Slave Trade* (Oxford, UK: Oxford University Press, 1987), 138.

96 *penalties for slave traders*: Grindal, *Opposing the Slavers*, chap. 6.

96 *these punishments were . . . never applied*: Correspondence (Class B) 1829, 35.

96 *Vengador . . . once known as the* Principe de Guine: "From the London Gazette, Tuesday, Dec. 12: Admiralty Office," *London Times*, December 13, 1826; Correspondence (Class A) 1827; and Correspondence (Class B) 1827, 46.

96 *sold that ship . . . at auction once again*: Ward, *The Royal Navy and the Slavers*, 128, and Grindal, *Opposing the Slavers*, chap. 9.

96 *Jose de Cerqueira Lima's slave-trading outfit*: Sullivan, *Britain's War Against the Slave Trade*, 143.

97 *had to have a certain number of British sailors*: This was a requirement imposed by the Navigation Acts, which weren't entirely repealed until 1849. J. H. Clapham, "The Last Years of the Navigation Acts," *English Historical Review* 25, no. 99 (1910): 482, and Isaac Land, *War, Nationalism, and the British Sailor* (New York: Palgrave Macmillan, 2009), 19.

97 *"a most notorious Vessel" under its new name*: Correspondence (Class B) 1829, 29.

98 *"purchased by Agents here and sent to the Brazils"*: Ibid., 28.

98 *Esperanza was formerly known as . . . the* Hope: Ward, *The Royal Navy and the Slavers*, 128.

98 *already been condemned as a slaver captain*: On the *Trajano*, which was also part of the controversies being discussed in this exchange of letters. Correspondence (Class B) 1829, 30.

98 *Hoop—it was originally of Dutch extraction*: Ward, *The Royal Navy and the Slavers*, 128.

99 *Turner . . . refused to let the schooner leave*: Except where otherwise noted, the details of the *Esperanza/Hope* incident are drawn from Correspondence (Class B) 1829, 24–29.

100 *became ridiculously rich on a percentage of the profit*: Padriac Xavier Scanlan, "The Rewards of Their Exertions," *Past & Present* 225 (2014): 114.

100 *Kenneth Macaulay . . . prominent . . . public citizens*: James W. St. G. Walker, *The Black Loyalists: The Search for a Promised Land in Nova Scotia and Sierra Leone* (Toronto; Buffalo; London: University of Toronto Press, 1992), 308, and Scanlan, "The Rewards of Their Exertions," 123–24, 127.

101 *"neither did he take the Bill of Sale, and the other Documents away"*: Correspondence (Class B) 1829, 24–29.

102 *Ajuda*: Just another name for Ouidah.

102 *Australia on the first available boat*: Grindal, *Opposing the Slavers*, chap. 4. Fourteen years of exile was just one of the possible punishments listed in the Slave Trade Felonies Act of 1811, but given how few people were actually prosecuted and how many ways there were to profit from the trade, the law's overall value as a deterrent remains arguable. Emily Haslam, "Redemption, Colonialism and International Criminal Law: The Nineteenth Century Slave-Trading Trials of Samo and Peters," in *Past Law, Present Histories*, edited by Diane Kirkby (Canberra, Australia: ANU Press, 2012), 10.

103 *disposition of those ships once an officer left*: Ward, *The Royal Navy and the Slavers*, 128–29.

103 *captains even had to pay for the expenditures . . . of a prize*: Grindal, *Opposing the Slavers*, chap. 8; and if one purchased it for use in the service, one had to pay for upkeep as well. Lubbock, *Cruisers*, 41.

103 *called prizes long before suppression*: Daniel K. Benjamin, "Golden Harvest: The British Naval Prize System, 1793–1815" (unpublished, 2009), 2.

103 *disciplinary system . . . no stranger to the whip*: Michael Lewis, *The Navy in Transition, 1814–1864* (London: Hodder and Stoughton, 1965), 168–69, asserts that the rates of flogging and punishment after 1815 were consistent with those before, at least until much later in the nineteenth century. Thomas Malcomson, *Order and Disorder in the British Navy, 1793–1815* (Woodbridge, Suffolk, UK; Rochester, NY: Boydell & Brewer, 2016), 189–220, provides an idea of what those rates were.

103 *accounts of prize crews resorting to such means*: Robert Burroughs, "Eyes on the Prize," *Slavery and Abolition* 31, no. 1 (2010): 102.

104 *resorting to violence if the crews felt it warranted*: Lloyd, *The Navy and the Slave Trade*, chap. 5, quoting F. Harrison Rankin, *The White Man's Grave*, vol. 2 (London: Richard Bentley, 1836).

104 *denying prize crews their daily allotment of alcohol*: Burroughs, "Eyes on the Prize," 102; Mary Wills, *Envoys of Abolition* (Liverpool, UK: Liverpool University Press, 2019), 111–12.

104 *can't absolve its sailors of any crimes against humanity*: Wills, *Envoys*, 103–12.

104 *Prize duty created a lot of work*: Ibid., 97–103, and Lloyd, *The Navy and the Slave Trade*, chap. 6.

104 *prize crews . . . never be discovered*: By way of example: Lloyd, *The Navy and the Slave Trade*, chap. 5, and Grindal, *Opposing the Slavers*, chap. 8.

104 *supplement his income*: Wills, *Envoys*, 78–81.

105 *an ideal prize, no matter the risk*: Lewis, *The Navy in Transition*, 231–38.

105 *the money to which their work entitled them*: Scanlan, "The Rewards of Their Exertions," 125–26.

106 *ship purchases . . . through official channels*: Ward, *The Royal Navy and the Slavers*, 129, and Grindal, *Opposing the Slavers*, chaps. 5, 8, and 13.

106 *purchase slave-trading vessels from Lloyd's*: Lubbock, *Cruisers*, 144; Stephen D. Beh-

rendt and Peter M. Solar, "Sail on, Albion: The Usefulness of Lloyd's Registers for Maritime History, 1760–1840," *International Journal of Maritime History* 26, no. 3 (2014): 568–86, detail the type and utility of historical information about ships, slave and non, that can be found in Lloyd's sundry Registries and Lists.

106 *ties to the slave-trading industry*: P. Hudson, "Slavery, the Slave Trade and Economic Growth," in *Emancipation and the Remaking of the British Imperial World*, eds. by C. Hall, N. Draper, and K. McClelland (Manchester, UK: Manchester University Press, 2014), 36–59; Lubbock, *Cruisers*, 144; and Mark Landler, "Britain Grapples with Its Racist Past, from the Town Square to the Boardroom," *New York Times*, June 18, 2020, https://www.nytimes.com/2020/06/18/world/europe/uk-slavery -trade-lloyds-greene-king.html.

106 *move that depot to Fernando Pó*: Robert T. Brown, "Fernando Po and the Anti-Sierra Leonean Campaign," *International Journal of African Historical Studies* 6, no. 2 (1973): 249–64; Ibrahim K. Sundiata, *From Slaving to Neoslavery* (Madison: University of Wisconsin Press, 2006), 21–37; and Grindal, *Opposing the Slavers*, chap. 8.

106 *one hell of an administrative error*: Grindal, *Opposing the Slavers*, chap. 9.

107 *stuck in Freetown*: Ibid.

107 *effectively trapped in Sierra Leone*: Ibid.

107 *no one in Freetown wanted the change, the commodore . . . included*: Brown, "Fernando Po"; Sundiata, *From Slaving to Neoslavery*, 21–37; and Grindal, *Opposing the Slavers*, chap. 8.

107 *Captain Owen had his own tenders*: Grindal, *Opposing the Slavers*, chap. 8.

108 *brig and two schooners near "Whydah Roads"*: Account of *Black Joke*'s encounter with the *Presidente* is compiled from the following sources: Lubbock, *Cruisers*, 145–46; Grindal, *Opposing the Slavers*, chap. 9; Sullivan, *Britain's War Against the Slave Trade*, 145–46; Rees, *Sweet Water and Bitter*, 124–27; Trans-Atlantic Slave Trade Database; J. G. Muddiman, "H. M. S. the Black Joke," *Notes and Queries* 172, no. 12 (March 1937): 200–201; "The Forty Pirates," *London Times*, February 9, 1829; "Miscellaneous," *Devizes and Wiltshire Gazette*, February 12, 1829; and Correspondence (Class B) 1929, 72.

108 *upsurge in dangerous maritime activity*: Blair, "All the Ships That Never Sailed," and Howard I. Chapelle, *The History of American Sailing Ships* (New York: W. W. Norton; New York: Bonanza Books, 1935).

108 *erase the legal distinction between slave trading and piracy*: John B. Hattendorf, "Maritime Conflict," in *The Laws of War: Constraints on Warfare in the Western World*, eds. Michael Howard, George J. Andreopoulos, and Mark R. Shulman (New Haven: Yale University Press, 1994), 108.

108 *most pirates didn't discriminate*: It should be noted that some very much *did* mind, as multiple eighteenth-century examples can attest. Peter Linebaugh and Marcus Rediker, *The Many-Headed Hydra: Sailors, Slaves, Commoners, and the Hidden History of the Revolutionary Atlantic* (Boston: Beacon Press, 2000), 165–73.

109 *supply the barracoons he kept . . . up and down the coast*: For more on de Souza, see Silke Strickrodt, *Afro-European Trade in the Atlantic World: The Western Slave Coast, c.1550–c.1885* (Woodbridge, Suffolk, UK; Rochester, NY: Boydell & Brewer, 2015), 199–200; Robin Law and Kristin Mann, "West Africa in the Atlantic Community: The Case of the Slave Coast," *William and Mary Quarterly* 56, no. 2 (1999): 323–29; Robin Law, *Ouidah: The Social History of a West African Slaving Port* (Oxford, UK: Boydell & Brewer, 2005), 155–88; Ana Lucia Araujo, "Forgetting and Remembering the Atlantic Slave Trade," in *Crossing Memories: Slavery and African Diaspora*, eds.

Ana Lucia Araujo, Mariana P. Candido, and Paul E. Lovejoy (Trenton, NJ: Africa World Press, 2011), 79–103; and Sundiata, *From Slaving to Neoslavery.*

111 *"and I must have her"*: Emphasis added.

112 *sailing at over seven knots*: Lubbock, *Cruisers*, 155, says over seven, while Grindal, *Opposing the Slavers*, says six knots.

113 *the Surrey County Sessions House on Horsemonger Lane*: On a modern map, this would now be the Inner London Crown Court on Harper Road.

114 *Zepherina . . . case . . . to the High Court of the Admiralty*: Account of *Black Joke's* encounter with the *Zepherina* and the distribution of its prize money is compiled from the following sources: Grindal, *Opposing the Slavers*, chap. 9; Sullivan, *Britain's War Against the Slave Trade*, 147; Winfield, *British Warships, 1817–1863*, 1076–77; Trans-Atlantic Slave Trade Database; Correspondence (Class A) 1829, 6, 35–36; and John Haggard, *Reports of Cases Argued and Determined in the High Court of Admiralty, During the Time of the Right Hon. Lord Stowell*, vol. 2, *1825–1832*, ed. by George Minot (Boston: Little, Brown and Company, 1853), 318–22.

115 *"in the same manner as if the seizure was made by the said ship or vessel"*: Haggard, *Reports of Cases.*

116 *new captain, Lieutenant Henry Downes*: Grindal, *Opposing the Slavers*, chap. 9.


### Chapter Five: *El Almirante*

123 *acting under the authority of Buenos Aires*: "The Forty Pirates," London Times, February 9, 1829, and Anthony Sullivan, *Britain's War Against the Slave Trade* (Barnsley, UK: Pen & Sword Books, 2020), 148.

124 *crew . . . couldn't even be tried*: "Money Market and City Intelligence," London Times, November 8, 1828; "London, Saturday; February 14, 1829," London Times, February 14, 1829; "An Extensive Failure, Caused by Speculations in Indigo, Took Place on Saturday at Liverpool," London Times, June 22, 1829; and Adrian Desmond and James Moore, *Darwin's Sacred Cause* (New York: Houghton Mifflin Harcourt, 2009), 85.

124 *merchants . . . intimately tied to . . . slave trade*: David Eltis, "The British Contribution to the Nineteenth Century Trans-Atlantic Slave Trade," *Economic History Review* 32, no. 2 (1979): 211–27; David Eltis, *Economic Growth and the Ending of the Transatlantic Slave Trade* (Oxford, UK: Oxford University Press, 1987), 81–84; and Daniel Domingues da Silva, "The Atlantic Slave Trade from Angola: A Port-by-Port Estimate of Slaves Embarked, 1701–1867," *International Journal of African Historical Studies* 46, no. 1 (2013): 105–22, 27–28, citing Eltis, "The British Contribution," 211.

124 *the impossibility of ending the slave trade*: David Lambert, "Sierra Leone and Other Sites in the War of Representation over Slavery," *History Workshop Journal* 64 (2007).

124 *detail the other nineteen*: Siân Rees, *Sweet Water and Bitter* (Durham: University of New Hampshire Press, 2009), 37.

125 *beliefs . . . inherent inferiority of Africans*: On the navy, specifically, Mary Wills, *Envoys of Abolition* (Liverpool, UK: Liverpool University Press, 2019), 85, and Ray Costello, *Black Salt* (Liverpool: Liverpool University Press, 2012), 95–106. Attitudes among policy makers and administrators, generally, Emma Christopher, "'Tis Enough That We Give Them Liberty?' Liberated Africans at Sierra Leone in the Early Era of Slave-Trade Suppression," in *The Suppression of the Atlantic Slave Trade: British Policies, Practices and Representations of Naval Coercion*, eds. Robert M. Burroughs and Richard Huzzey (Manchester, UK: Manchester University Press, 2016), 56–57;

Brian Vick, *The Congress of Vienna* (Cambridge: Harvard University Press, 2014), 208–9, 214; Leslie Bethell, "Britain, Portugal and the Suppression of the Brazilian Slave Trade," *English Historical Review* 80, no. 317 (1965): 63; Bernard Semmel, *Liberalism and Naval Strategy* (Boston: Allen & Unwin, 1986); and Reginald Coupland, *The British Anti-Slavery Movement*, 2nd ed. (London: Frank Cass & Co., 1964), this last has examples of this type of thinking but also *is* an example of same.

125 *globally dominant . . . position . . . strengthened . . . by suppression efforts*: Paul M. Kennedy, *The Rise and Fall of British Naval Mastery* (New York: Penguin, 2017), 165–66.

125 *Religion . . . source to justify slavery*: Seymour Drescher, *Abolition* (New York: Cambridge University Press, 2009), 83–85.

126 *Black men . . . on Victory at . . . Trafalgar*: Costello, *Black Salt*, 34, 58–59.

126 *empire's planter-colonists in the Americas*: Lambert, "Sierra Leone and Other Sites."

126 *Britain's holdings . . . expanded after . . . 1815*: Kennedy, *The Rise and Fall of British Naval Mastery*, 157.

126 *Jamaica's planters . . . against ending . . . slave trade*: Coupland, *The British Anti-Slavery Movement*, 102–3, and William Law Mathieson, *British Slavery and Its Abolition, 1823–1838* (London: Longmans, Green and Co., 1926), 11–20.

127 *winning the war to preserve slavery*: Mathieson, *British Slavery*.

127 *cheap way to maintain their business model*: Eltis, *Economic Growth*, 17–27.

127 *realities of crop cultivation in the Americas*: Laird W. Bergad, *The Comparative Histories of Slavery in Brazil, Cuba, and the United States* (Cambridge, UK: Cambridge University Press, 2007), 96–98; Sidney Wilfred Mintz, *Sweetness and Power* (London: Penguin Books,1985), 25, who notes that while historically sugar had been grown as far north as Spain, that was in spite of the challenges of the climate.

127 *slavery . . . banned yet . . . freely profited from*: Eltis, *Economic Growth*, 185–86, and Sven Beckert, *Empire of Cotton: A Global History* (New York: Vintage Books, 2015).

127 *sugar . . . production process . . . fatal*: Bergad, *The Comparative Histories of Slavery*, 102; Mintz, *Sweetness and Power*, 46–50; for the nuts and bolts of the operations on a British sugar plantation post-slave-trade abolition, Mathieson, *British Slavery*, 60–71. It should be noted that I am using "United States" broadly, and statements about systems of slavery as they relate to crop choice, reproductivity, mortality, and import are more about cultivation and geography more than national borders, as Louisiana's distinctive practices and slaughterhouse reputation can attest. Richard Follett, *The Sugar Masters* (Baton Rouge: Louisiana State University Press, 2005).

128 *rapidly diverging systems of enslavement*: Bergad, *The Comparative Histories of Slavery*, 23–24, 52–54.

128 *harvesting sugarcane . . . men's work*: Ibid., 102–3, and Richard Follett, "Lives of Living Death," *Slavery & Abolition* 26, no. 2 (2005): 290, for an example of exceptions to the trend.

128 *enslavement . . . contravention of English precedent*: Edmund S. Morgan, *American Slavery, American Freedom* (New York: W. W. Norton, 1975), 333, and Thomas D. Morris, *Southern Slavery and the Law, 1619–1860* (Chapel Hill: University of North Carolina Press, 1996), 43–49.

128 *cheaper source of equivalent labor*: Enslaved women were apparently more expensive to acquire in Africa (Eltis, *Economic Growth*, 69), but usually comparatively cheaper to purchase in the Americas, or at least in the United States (Daina Ramey Berry, *The Price for Their Pound of Flesh* [Boston: Beacon Press, 2017]).

128 *United States . . . trade . . . domestic*: Joshua D. Rothman, *The Ledger and the Chain* (New York: Basic Books, 2021).

128 *sugar reigned, and sugar killed:* Bergad, *The Comparative Histories of Slavery*, 102.

129 *claimed by disease:* Leslie Bethell, "The Independence of Brazil and the Abolition of the Brazilian Slave Trade," *Journal of Latin American Studies* 1, no. 2 (1969): 117–18.

129 *dying from the injury:* Follett, *The Sugar Masters*.

129 *life expectancy . . . seven years:* Sharon Landers, "Sugar Cultivation and Trade," in *The Historical Encyclopedia of World Slavery*, vol. 2, *L–Z*, ed. Junius P. Rodriguez (Santa Barbara: ABC-CLIO, 1997), 1619.

129 *get as much work . . . before they passed on:* Joseph Martin Mulhern, "After 1833: British Entanglement with Brazilian Slavery," PhD diss., Durham University, 2018, 70, citing BFASS, *Proceedings of the General Anti-Slavery Convention, called by the Committee of the British and Foreign Anti-Slavery Society, and Held in London, from Friday, June 12th, to Tuesday, June 23rd, 1840* (London: 1841), 516, provides a contemporary abolitionist perspective: " . . . in Cuba, 'because no slave-holder can keep up a sufficient number of labourers by natural increase, he must be an annual purchaser in the slave market, and consequently every slave-holder is a slave-dealer.'" Howard M. Prince, "Slave Rebellion in Bahia, 1807–1835," PhD diss., Columbia University, 1972, 54, quotes a nineteenth-century British consul in Brazil, "the annual mortality on many slave plantations is so great, that unless their numbers were augmented from abroad the whole slave population would become extinct in the course of about twenty years; the proprietors act on the calculation that it is cheaper to buy male slaves than to rear Negro children."

129 *an expected business expense:* Prince, "Slave Rebellion in Bahia," 54; Viotti da Costa, *The Brazilian Empire*, rev. ed. (Chapel Hill: University of North Carolina Press, 2000); Eltis, *Economic Growth*, 192, 321; and Follett, "Lives of Living Death," 290.

130 *slaveholders . . . acted accordingly:* There is plentiful scholastic debate as to (a) why the British really did it, morals, economics, or a combination thereof, and as a corollary (b) were British slave colonies even still collectively profitable in regard to sugar cultivation and export. Eltis, *Economic Growth*, gets into it, but I'm not going to.

130 *slave trading spiked:* Eltis, *Economic Growth*.

130 *demand for the products of those industries:* Ibid., 46.

130 *in Brazil, the year of reckoning was 1830:* Bethell, "The Independence of Brazil," 146.

131 *Kearney . . . a particularly infamous example:* Hugh Thomas, *The Slave Trade: The Story of the Atlantic Slave Trade* (New York: Simon & Schuster, 1997), chap. 32, citing William Ernest Frank Ward, *The Royal Navy and the Slavers* (London: Pantheon Books, 1969), 73–75.

131 *resell the enslaved on board:* Wills, *Envoys*, 85.

131 *first Commodore Collier, George . . . cause for ending his life:* Ibid., 74–85.

131 *allegations of both incompetence and cowardice . . . published:* Ibid., 78, referencing the original publication of William James, *The Naval History of Great Britain* (6 vols.) (London: Richard Bently, 1837).

131 *ennobling and sanctifying language for . . . their mission:* Robert T. Brown, "Fernando Po and the Anti-Sierra Leonean Campaign," *International Journal of African Historical Studies* 6, no 2 (1973): 234.

132 *selfless conception of their service:* Wills, *Envoys*, 70–85.

132 *risk of being . . . a "prize Negro" . . . lowered:* Costello, *Black Salt*, 73, and Charles R. Foy, "Eighteenth Century 'Prize Negroes,'" *Slavery and Abolition* 31, no. 3 (2010): 379–93.

132 *definition of "British" was explicitly expanded:* Costello, *Black Salt*, 35.

132 *every vessel . . . one to four Black seamen:* John Rankin, "Nineteenth-Century Royal

Navy Sailors," *African Diaspora* 6, no. 2 (2014): 179–95, and John Rankin, "British and African Health in the Anti-slave-trade Squadron," in *The Suppression of the Slave Trade*, eds. Robert M. Burroughs and Richard Huzzey (Manchester, UK: Manchester University Press, 2016), 95–121.

133 *some diversity . . . could be found on board*: Rankin, "Nineteenth-Century Royal Navy Sailors."

133 *separate and/or sub-Anglo races unto themselves*: Seymour Drescher, "The Ending of the Slave Trade and the Evolution of European Scientific Racism," *Social Science History* 14, no. 3 (1990): 415–50; Nell Irvin Painter, *The History of White People* (New York: W. W. Norton, 2010), and Ex. Thomas Winterbottom, "Account of the Native Africans in the Neighbourhood of Sierra Leone (September 1825)," in *The African Repository and Colonial Journal*, vol. 1, edited by the American Colonization Society (Washington City: 1826; New York: Kraus Reprint Corporation, 1967), 193–204.

134 *demoted, with . . . regrets, for this reason*: Costello, *Black Salt*, 95–99.

134 *English translations . . . the "Accou" language*: Wills, *Envoys of Abolition*, 104.

134 *"aguardiente [sic]"*: Henry Downes, Logbook of HMS SYBILLE and HMS BLACK JOKE 1827–1829 (LOG/N/41). National Maritime Museum, Greenwich, London.

135 *"no supplies of fresh stock except at long intervals"*: Coupland, *The British Anti-Slavery Movement*, 161.

135 *"cruising, cruising, cruising, and very unprofitably too"*: Rees, *Sweet Water and Bitter*, 168.

135 *sketched while at sea*: A few of his sketches still survive at the National Maritime Museum.

135 *anything to relieve the tedium*: Brian Lavery, *Life in Nelson's Navy* (Stroud, UK: The History Press, 2007), chap. 4.

135 *where sailors' advances . . . welcomed*: Peter Grindal, *Opposing the Slavers* (London: I.B. Tauris, 2016), chap. 9, and Peter Leonard, *The Western Coast of Africa: Journal of an Officer Under Captain Owen. Records of a Voyage in the Ship Dryad in 1830, 1831, and 1832* (Philadelphia: E. C. Mielke, 1833), 34–35.

135 *the 29th Article of War*: "If any person in the fleet shall commit the unnatural and detestable sin of buggery and sodomy with man or beast, he shall be punished with death by the sentence of a court martial." Barry Richard Burg, *Boys at Sea: Sodomy, Indecency, and Courts Martial in Nelson's Navy* (New York: Palgrave Macmillan, 2007), 1.

136 *buggery . . . carried a death sentence*: Indecency was a bit harder to pin down, in part because enumerating every possible sexual impropriety a sailor might conceive would have been prohibitive in more ways than one. Ibid., 67.

136 *HMS Africaine*: Barry Richard Burg, "The HMS *African* Revisited: The Royal Navy and the Homosexual Community," *Journal of Homosexuality* 56 (2009): 173–94, and Burg, *Boys at Sea*.

136 *Downes . . . service on the Africaine . . . tour to Asia*: William Richard O'Byrne, *A Naval Biographical Dictionary* (London: John Murray, Albemarle Street, 1849), 302.

136 *perceived sexual transgressions . . . on its decks*: Burg, "The HMS *African* Revisited," 178.

136 *a ship only 154 feet in length*: Burg, *Boys at Sea*, 129, and Burg, "The HMS *African* Revisited," 182.

137 *the sex would have been extremely difficult to miss*: Burg, "The HMS *African* Revisited," 183–86.

137 *pious in the manner of his day*: Which is to say after his service he cofounded a naval mission to send a series of ships to proselytize in Japan, and that just seems like it's above and beyond the average expression of faith, even in the aggressively evangeli-

cal context of the early to mid-nineteenth century. Robert S. G. Fletcher, "'Returning Kindness Received?' Missionaries, Empire and the Royal Navy in Okinawa, 1846–57," *English Historical Review* 125, no. 514 (2010): 612–20.

137 *clearing their captain of wrongdoing*: Burg, "The HMS *African* Revisited," 191.

137 *acted surreptitiously enough . . . ignore them*: Burg, *Boys at Sea*, 66; there is potentially one known incident of Downes reporting homosexual activity on *Africaine*, depending on the level of coincidence required for both a Lieutenant Downe and a Lieutenant Downes to be serving as two of the four lieutenants on the same ship. If it's the same man, a witness approached him complaining of two men "committing unclean acts in the forechains." (The chains were "the place where the leadsman stood to cast the lead for the purpose of taking soundings; forward near the bows and outside the bulwarks, directly over the water" [Ward, *The Royal Navy and the Slavers*, 233]). He duly reported it to the captain, but since there was no evidence, it came to naught. If that seems too close to informing for comfort, compare his behavior to that of his coworker, the lieutenant who heard word in the wee hours of the morning that a different pair of men clad in only their shirts were "lying together" on the deck. That guy immediately grabbed two mids who were close by, rounded up the quartermaster and master of arms as well, and ordered this newly formed posse to interrupt the coitus and catch the offenders in the act. For what it's worth, they were also too late, and nothing came of that, either, but clearly Downes did rather less than he could have, even when the opportunity presented itself, to zealously guard against the supposed scourge of homosexual sex (Burg, *Boys at Sea*, 131).

137 *the notorious slaver El Almirante*: The account of *Black Joke*'s encounter with *El Almirante* is compiled from the following sources: Basil Lubbock, *Cruisers, Corsairs & Slavers* (Glasgow: Brown, Son & Ferguson, 1993), 146–48; Grindal, *Opposing the Slavers*, chap. 9; Christopher Lloyd, *The Navy and the Slave Trade* (New York: Routledge, 2012), chap. 5; Sullivan, *Britain's War Against the Slave Trade*, 152–53, 156; O'Byrne, *A Naval Biographical Dictionary*, 302; Joseph Allen, *The New Navy List and General Record* (London: Parker, Furnivall, and Parker, 1850), 94, 175; Rif Winfield, *British Warships, 1817–1863* (Yorkshire, UK: Seaforth Publishing, 2014), 1076–77; Trans-Atlantic Slave Trade Database; Geoffrey Marsh Footner, *Tidewater Triumph* (Centerville, MD: Tidewater Publishers, 1998); Downes, Logbook; Correspondence (Class A) 1829, 6, 22–23; Correspondence (Class A) 1830, 76, 105–12; and J. G. Muddiman, "H. M. S. the Black Joke," *Notes and Queries* 172, no. 12 (March 1937): 200–201

143 *letters . . . warned . . . escaping capture*: Grindal, *Opposing the Slavers*, chap. 9.

### Chapter Six: *Carolina*

147 *promotions rained down on the crew*: As did songs—Henry Downes, Logbook of HMS SYBILLE and HMS BLACK JOKE 1827–1829 (LOG/N/41). National Maritime Museum, Greenwich, London, contains two composed in honor of the action, questionable bits of transcription enclosed in brackets:

> *Come all you gallant sailors bold/ and listen to my song.*
> *The truth to you I'll tell/ although not very long.*
> *It is of a Noble Brig my Boys/ The Black Joke is her name*
> *Commanded by bold Downes/ a man of well known fame.*

*It was on the first of February/as you must understand*
*Along the Coast of Africa/Not very far from land.*
*We cruised about the Leagues/and their[sic] we did espy*
*a Brig with Spanish Colours/Which proved our Enemy.*
*And now the time arived[sic]/To show ourselves like men*
*For sweeping of our [repell]/It was our full Design.*
*And as we came up to her/We gave to her a gun*
*Old Neptune sat upon the waves/a laughing at the fun.*
*Be Cool and steady my brave boys/Our Captain he did say*
*Before this day is Ended/We will show them British Play*
*Although their force is greater/We ne'er shall yield to [them]*
*For ere the setting of the sun/Their Colours we'll pull down.*
*Our men as bold as lions/Unto their Quarter flew*
*With Courage bold Undaunted/We hoisted Colours Blue.*
*Like hearts of Oak we boarded her/She tried to get away*
*[Four thirty] of her bravest men/Upon her Decks did Lay.*
*And as the battle Raged/In Dismal and [Surprise]*
*The Spanyards [sic] fled from their [quarters]/and aloud for mercy cried.*
*Give us our lives and liberty/From you we ask no more*
*The Brig and all her slaves/and also [sic] of [great store].*
*Their's [sic] Downes for ever my brave Boys/And all his Valiant Crew*
*Who bravely beat the Spanyards[sic]/And brought their Courage low.*
*Likewise our gallant Commodore/and all the Sybille's men*
*and all the force that they can bring/shall ne'er Conquer them.*

by "Thomas [Larou], one of the Black Jokes
Crew on 1 Feb 1829"

*But that little brig the Black Joke*
*That brig of high reknown*
*She did engage the Almirante*
*And hauled her colours down*
*Here's a health to all the Black Joke's crew*
*And may that health go [round]*
*I hope they'll see many happy days*
*When they are homeward bound*

author unknown

147 *slated for a promotion . . . join them as a lieutenant*: Peter Grindal, *Opposing the Slavers* (London: I.B. Tauris, 2016), chap. 9.

147 *the Brazilian brigantine Carolina*: The account of *Black Joke*'s encounter with *Carolina* and the subsequent adjudication is compiled from the following sources: Grindal, *Opposing the Slavers*, chap. 9; Anthony Sullivan, *Britain's War Against the Slave Trade* (Barnsley, UK: Pen & Sward Books, 2020), 156; Rif Winfield, *British Warships in the Age of Sail, 1817–1863* (Yorkshire, UK: Seaforth Publishing, 2008), 1076–77; Trans-Atlantic Slave Trade Database; Correspondence (Class A) 1829, 55–56, 71; and *Colonies and Slaves*, vol. 19, 1831.

149 *tacit . . . coordination . . . entirely expected*: Correspondence (Class A) 1829, 31–34, 57, 62–63; Leslie Bethell, "The Mixed Commissions for the Suppression of the Transatlantic Slave Trade," *Journal of African History* 7, no. 1 (1966): 87; and William

Ernest Frank Ward, *The Royal Navy and the Slavers* (London: Pantheon Books, 1969), 120–21.

150 *legitimate or no, if it didn't have to*: Edward Keene, "A Case Study of the Construction of International Hierarchy," *International Organization* 61, no. 2 (April 1, 2007): 311–39.

150 *commercial passport . . . issued . . . since at least the seventeenth century*: John B. Hattendorf, "Maritime Conflict," 105, in *The Laws of War*, ed. Michael Howard, George J. Andreopoulos, and Mark R. Shulman (New Haven: Yale University Press, 1994), 98–115.

150 *catch someone red-handed and full-berthed*: A demonstration of how the establishment of an equatorial boundary impacted the suppression effort can be found in Ward, *The Royal Navy and the Slavers*, 122–23.

150 *ignorant of slave traders' lies . . . complicit in them*: Alexandre Vieira Ribeiro, "The Transatlantic Slave Trade to Bahia, 1582–1851," in *Extending the Frontiers: Essays on the New Transatlantic Slave Trade Database*, eds. David Eltis and David Richardson (New Haven: Yale University Press, 2008), 139–40.

150 *enslaved people physically present*: J. P. van Niekerk, "British, Portuguese, and American Judges in Adderley Street . . . (Part 1)," *Comparative and International Law Journal of Southern Africa* 37, no. 1 (2004): 18–19, and Bethell, "The Mixed Commissions," 86–87.

151 *even if the hold was just as empty*: For instance, Grindal, *Opposing the Slavers*, chap. 9.

151 *"beyond what it may otherwise receive from such Evidence"*: Correspondence (Class A) 1829, 56.

151 *every conceivable incentive to lie*: David Eltis, *Economic Growth and the Ending of the Transatlantic Slave Trade* (Oxford, UK: Oxford University Press, 1987), 138–39, 161.

152 *picking up the* Hosse *. . . again*: The account of the dispositions of *Hosse* and *El Almirante* is compiled from the following sources: Grindal, *Opposing the Slavers*, chap. 9; as the *"Josse"* in Sullivan, *Britain's War Against the Slave Trade*, 157, 187; Correspondence (Class A) 1828, 3, 69–70; Correspondence (Class A) 1829, 71–72; Correspondence (Class B) 1829, 29–30; and Correspondence (Class A) 1830, 10, 76, 105–12.

153 *inescapably noxious and unbearably nauseating*: By way of example: "noxious smell" in Sowande M. Mustakeem, *Slavery at Sea* (Urbana: University of Illinois Press, 2016), 108; "filth so foul and stench so offensive as not to be imagined," in Ward, *The Royal Navy and the Slavers*, 87–88; "the stench from the holds being almost insupportable," in Grindal, *Opposing the Slavers*, chap. 13; "the smell of slaves was as strong as if they had still been on board," in Grindal, *Opposing the Slavers*, chap. 16; "stench at times was almost beyond endurance," in Marcus Rediker, *The Slave Ship: A Human History* (New York: Penguin, 2007), chap. 2; "it was said in Charleston, South Carolina, that when the wind blew a certain way people could *smell* a slave ship before they could *see* it" (emphasis original), in Marcus Rediker, *Villains of All Nations* (Boston: Beacon Press, 2004), 202; and "a ship that stank of excrement, so that, as with any slaver, 'You could smell it five miles down wind,'" in Daniel P. Mannix, *Black Cargoes: A History of the Atlantic Slave Trade, 1518–1865* (New York: Viking Press, 1962), 113.

153 *smell the presence of the enslaved on board*: Grindal, *Opposing the Slavers*, chap. 9, and Basil Lubbock, *Cruisers, Corsairs & Slavers* (Glasgow: Brown, Son & Ferguson, 1993), 164.

153 *the Mixed Commission had, too*: Bethell, "The Mixed Commissions," 86.

153 *incidence of both diseases dropped precipitously*: James Watt, "Some Forgotten Contributions of Naval Surgeons," *Journal of the Royal Society of Medicine* 78 (1985): 759.

# NOTES

153 *"pissing from his hammock upon the deck"*: Barry Richard Burg, *Boys at Sea* (New York: Palgrave Macmillan, 2007), 67.

154 *fundamental element of daily shipboard life in the Royal Navy*: Thomas Malcomson, *Order and Disorder in the British Navy: 1793–1815* (Woodbridge, Suffolk, UK; Rochester, NY: Boydell & Brewer, 2016), 84–86.

154 *less rigorous . . . cleaning . . . punishment . . . excelled*: Rediker, *The Slave Ship*, chap. 7.

154 *cleaned whenever the captain happened to decide*: Mustakeem, *Slavery at Sea*, 108.

154 *There was usually a surgeon*: Apparently Brazilian ships were generally known to not carry doctors. David Northrup, "African Mortality in the Suppression of the Slave Trade," *Journal of Interdisciplinary History* 9, no. 1 (1978): 57.

154 *a corpse left to rot beneath the living*: Grindal, *Opposing the Slavers*, chap. 6, and Ward, *The Royal Navy and the Slavers*, 60, detail the same incident.

154 *bodies dead of suffocation in the hold*: Mustakeem, *Slavery at Sea*, 106–7, and Peter Leonard, *Records of a Voyage to the Western Coast of Africa* (Edinburgh: William Tait, 1833), 134.

154 *flesh rubbed off from the motion of the ship*: Grindal, *Opposing the Slavers*, chap. 2.

154 *Bight of Biafra . . . worst . . . mortality rates . . . region*: Northrup, "African Mortality"; Herbert S. Klein, Stanley L. Engerman, Robin Haines, and Ralph Shlomowitz, "Transoceanic Mortality: The Slave Trade in Comparative Perspective," *William and Mary Quarterly* 58, no. 1 (2001): 101–2.

154 *did not have access to the same supplies and . . . knowledge*: Manuel Barcia, *The Yellow Demon of Fever* (New Haven: Yale University Press, 2020), 86, and again, the presence and qualifications of medical personnel on slave ships could be a hit or miss affair. Rediker, *The Slave Ship*; Northrup, "African Mortality," 57; and Barcia, *The Yellow Demon of Fever*, 69–70.

155 *"with few exceptions, either are, or have been ill"*: Leonard, *Records of a Voyage*, 229; however, how much of Fernando Pó's eventual reputation was the result of the upcoming epidemic and how much was manufactured by the pro–Sierra Leone faction is a bit of an open question, Robert T. Brown, "Fernando Po and the Anti-Sierra Leonean Campaign," *International Journal of African Historical Studies* 6, no. 2 (1973): 249–64.

156 *"cuts the slight thread of his existence"*: Peter Leonard, *The Western Coast of Africa: Journal of an Officer Under Captain Owen. Records of a Voyage in the Ship Dryad in 1830, 1831, and 1832* (Philadelphia: E. C. Mielke, 1833), 66–67.

156 *leprosy, elephantiasis, and guinea worm*: Grindal, *Opposing the Slavers*, chap. 3.

156 *climate, as well as water quality*: James Boyle, *A Practical Medico-Historical Account of the Western Coast of Africa Embracing a Topographical Description of its Shores, Rivers, and Settlements . . .* (London: S. Highly, 1831), 334–41, 360–62; potential misdiagnosis of hepatitis in areas with yellow fever, Sheldon Watts, *Epidemics and History* (New Haven: Yale University Press, 1997), 218.

156 *disappear, never to be heard from again*: Barcia, *The Yellow Demon of Fever*, 62–64; Grindal, *Opposing the Slavers*, chap. 2; Rediker, *The Slave Ship*, chap. 9; and Lubbock, *Cruisers*, 108–11, for a particularly harrowing example of ophthalmia on board a slaver.

156 *suicide on slave ships was not uncommon*: Mustakeem, *Slavery at Sea*, 172–74, 176–79, and Robert L. Stevenson, "Jumping Overboard: Examining Suicide, Resistance, and West African Cosmologies During the Middle Passage," PhD diss., Michigan State University, 2018.

157 *Once was in 1823*: Boyle, *A Practical Medico-Historical Account*, 269–83.

157 *the other was in 1829*: Ibid., 201.

157 *over 25 percent ... succumb to a terrifying malady*: Grindal, *Opposing the Slavers*, chap. 9.

157 *Black Joke ... departed ... April 13*: Correspondence (Class A) 1829, 56.

157 *first case ... colonial secretary's office*: Boyle, *A Practical Medico-Historical Account*, 223 (Case I: Loughnan).

157 *Eden arrived May 1*: Grindal, *Opposing the Slavers*, chap. 9.

157 *boat trip to the Scarcies River on May 4*: Boyle, *A Practical Medico-Historical Account*, 229 (Case II: Gibson).

157 *Bannister, who'd barely been in the colony a year*: Elizabeth Elbourne, "The Bannisters and Their Colonial World: Family Networks and Colonialism in the Early Nineteenth Century," in *Within and Without the Nation: Canadian History as Transnational History*, eds. Karen Dubunsky, Adele Perry, and Henry Yu (Toronto; Buffalo; London: University of Toronto Press, 2015), 62–63.

157 *succumbing to a relapse a few months later*: Boyle, *A Practical Medico-Historical Account*, 214–15 (Case V: Banister [sic]).

157 *apprentice of ... Savage was fifth*: Ibid., 216–17 (Case V: Williams).

157 *sixth case ... Judge Jackson's house*: Ibid., 214 (Case VI: Jackson).

157 *Sybille's prize crew was dead*: Grindal, *Opposing the Slavers*, chap. 9.

158 *Eden ... arriving in Sierra Leone in early May*: Boyle, *A Practical Medico-Historical Account*, 237–42.

158 *reasons that many distrusted ... Owen*: Brown, "Fernando Po," 258–59, and Grindal, *Opposing the Slavers*, chap. 9.

158 *what the commodore might do about it*: Boyle, *A Practical Medico-Historical Account*, 237–42.

158 *during one such episode*: Grindal, *Opposing the Slavers*, chap. 9.

158 *commodore ... kept a clean and well-run ship*: Ibid.

158 *connection between ... illnesses and ... insects*: Watts, *Epidemics and History*, 213–68, on the evolution and impact of knowledge of yellow fever and malaria.

158 *in those not born to the West African coast*: Barcia, *The Yellow Demon of Fever*, 36–39.

159 *1823 and 1829 ... near-identical weather pattern*: Boyle, *A Practical Medico-Historical Account*, 204–10.

159 *"[reconcilable], if not to be anticipated"*: Ibid., 210.

160 *bad air ... method of transmission ... illnesses*: Barcia, *The Yellow Demon of Fever*, 36–39.

160 *the most advanced knowledge available in 1831*: And it was, actually. Ibid., 22.

160 *Sybille would uneventfully capture the* Panchita: Grindal, *Opposing the Slavers*, chap. 9; Boyle, *A Practical Medico-Historical Account*, 241, 244–47; Trans-Atlantic Slave Trade Database; Correspondence (Class A & B) 1830, 23; and Correspondence (Class A) 1829, 26–28.

161 *overcrowded with the sick and dying*: Grindal *Opposing the Slavers*, chap. 9.

162 *Eden ... caught it from the town*: Boyle, *A Practical Medico-Historical Account*, 201–68, for a full accounting of the believed origins and progress of the 1829 epidemic, as well as conclusions drawn contemporaneous to the epidemic's conclusion and aftermath.

162 *all manner of fevers one might contract*: Barcia, *The Yellow Demon of Fever*, 13–14, 29.

162 *newcomers and those possessed of "weak constitutions"*: Boyle, *A Practical Medico-Historical Account*, 120–51. It should be noted that Boyle regards malaria as another affliction entirely and also mentions some extreme symptoms of what he refers to as "endemic" or "local bilious remittent fever" or "Sierra Leone fever" that are more

analogous to yellow fever. However, Barcia, *The Yellow Demon of Fever*, 13, notes that "remittent fever" in primary sources of this period usually refers to what we now know as malaria, which seems, at least to this untrained eye, about right for the illness Boyle describes.

162 *staff of the Mixed Commission were already sick*: Boyle, *A Practical Medico-Historical Account*, 211–30.

163 *excuses at the ready . . . for why*: Brown, "Fernando Po," 251, and Bethell, "The Mixed Commissions," 87–88.

163 *1829 didn't help matters*: Barcia, *The Yellow Demon of Fever*, 102.

163 *British . . . Brazilian commissioner, did survive it*: Boyle, *A Practical Medico-Historical Account*, 212 (Case XXVIII: De Paiva, though his wife succumbed), 214 (Case VI: Jackson).

163 *a full-blown epidemic was raging*: Grindal, *Opposing the Slavers*, chap. 9; Siân Rees, *Sweet Water and Bitter: The Ships That Stopped the Slave Trade* (Durham: University of New Hampshire Press, 2009), 142–43.

164 *"truest characteristics of the existence of the disorder"*: Boyle, *A Practical Medico-Historical Account*, 203.

164 *there's even a map*: Ibid., 256–57.

166 *Downes . . . met up with Captain Owen . . . May 27*: Henry Downes, Logbook of HMS SYBILLE and HMS BLACK JOKE 1827–1829 (LOG/N/41). National Maritime Museum, Greenwich, London.

166 *invalided home . . . May 30, 1829*: Grindal, *Opposing the Slavers*, chap. 9, and Lubbock, *Cruisers*, 148.

166 *Downes would never again serve on a ship*: William Richard O'Byrne, *A Naval Biographical Dictionary* (London: John Murray, Albemarle Street, 1849), 302.

166 *With the exception of the Primrose . . . and Clinker*: Grindal, *Opposing the Slavers*, chap. 9.

166 *Kroomen . . . thought to be more immune*: John Rankin, "British and African Health in the Anti-slave-trade Squadron," in *The Suppression of the Atlantic Slave Trade*, ed. Robert M. Burroughs and Richard Huzzey (Manchester, UK: Manchester University Press, 2016), 111–13.

167 *57 . . . from the Sybille and its famous tender*: Grindal, *Opposing the Slavers*, chap. 9.

### Chapter Seven: *Cristina*

171 Providencia . . . *sailing as the* Fama de Cadiz *. . . near Ouidah*: Peter Grindal, *Opposing the Slavers* (London: I.B. Tauris, 2016), chap. 9.

172 *concerns regarding the quantities of slavers*: Ibid.

172 *"Bartholomew Diaz, about the beginning of the fifteenth century"*: Peter Leonard, *The Western Coast of Africa: Journal of an Officer Under Captain Owen. Records of a Voyage in the Ship Dryad in 1830, 1831, and 1832* (Philadelphia: E. C. Mielke, 1833), 9.

172 *levels Collier . . . worried about a few months prior*: Grindal, *Opposing the Slavers*, chap. 9.

173 *even (or perhaps especially) in an epidemic*: Herbert S. Klein, Stanley L. Engerman, Robin Haines, and Ralph Shlomowitz, "Transoceanic Mortality," *William and Mary Quarterly* 58, no. 1 (2001): 93–118; David Northrup, "African Mortality in the Suppression of the Slave Trade," *Journal of Interdisciplinary History* 9, no. 1 (1978): 47–64; Manuel Barcia, *The Yellow Demon of Fever* (New Haven: Yale University Press, 2020)

and Sowanade M. Mustakeem, *Slavery at Sea* (Urbana: University of Illinois Press, 2016).

173 *Nothing could be done . . . short of capturing them*: In fact, critics of the squadron asserted that the suppression effort made the practices of the slave trade more inhumane, which wasn't an inaccurate critique, Robert Burroughs, "Eyes on the Prize," *Slavery and Abolition* 1, no. 1 (2010): 99–115.

174 *No one took Collier up on it*: Grindal, *Opposing the Slavers*, chap. 9.

174 *Collier, unsurprisingly, disliked this idea*: Ibid.

175 *rules governing the appearance of its officers*: J. Holman, *A Voyage round the World* (London: Smith, Elder, and Co., 1834), 383–85, and Grindal, *Opposing the Slavers*, chap. 8.

175 *the commodore was a protégé of Nelson's, for goodness' sake*: Basil Lubbock, *Cruisers, Corsairs & Slavers* (Glasgow: Brown, Son & Ferguson, 1993), 159–60.

176 *increasingly testy letters concerning . . . beards*: Siân Rees, *Sweet Water and Bitter* (Durham: University of New Hampshire Press, 2009), 137–38; Grindal, *Opposing the Slavers*, chap. 8; and Anthony Sullivan, *Britain's War Against the Slave Trade* (Barnsley, UK: Pen & Sword Books, 2020), 140.

176 *sometimes with genuinely deleterious impact*: Grindal, *Opposing the Slavers*, chap. 8.

176 *told the captain that he was not to chase slavers*: Ibid., chap. 9.

177 *under orders not to interfere*: Ibid., chaps. 8, 9, and Robert T. Brown, "Fernando Po and the Anti-Sierra Leonean Campaign: 1826–1834," *International Journal of African Historical Studies* 6, no. 2 (1973): 253, 258–59.

178 *"quite impossible for the measure to be carried out"*: Brown, "Fernando Po," 252, and Grindal, *Opposing the Slavers*, chap. 9.

178 *he felt it was good for the men*: Grindal, *Opposing the Slavers*, chap. 9.

179 *"every vegetable in great perfection and abundance"*: Peter Leonard, *Records of a Voyage to the Western Coast of Africa* (Edinburgh: William Tait, 1833), 216–17.

179 *the Victualling Board dropped the idea*: Grindal, *Opposing the Slavers*, chap. 9.

180 *Kroomen . . . not being paid comparably*: Ibid.

180 *a thousand residents at any given time*: Padriac Xavier Scanlan, *Freedom's Debtors* (New Haven: Yale University Press, 2017), 65, and David A. Chappell, "Kru and Kanaka: Participation by African and Pacific Island Sailors in Euroamerican Maritime Frontiers," *International Journal of Maritime History* 6, no. 2 (1994): 93.

180 *well-established Kru neighborhood and community*: Diane Frost, "Diasporan West African Communities: The Kru in Freetown & Liverpool," *Review of African Political Economy* 29, no. 92 (2002): 285–300.

180 *prize money earned by Squadron ships*: Grindal, *Opposing the Slavers*, chap. 9.

180 *paid less than many of his merchant counterparts*: Brian Lavery, *Life in Nelson's Navy* (Stroud, UK: The History Press, 2007), chaps. 1 and 4.

180 *2 to 3 percent of the annual national income*: Paul M. Kennedy, *The Rise and Fall of British Naval Mastery* (New York: Penguin, 2017), 150.

180 *United States spends on its military today (over 3 percent)*: Based on US gross national income (2019) $21.69 trillion, military spending (2019) $732 billion, for 3.37 percent. SIPRI, "Trends in World Military Expenditure, 2019," https://www.sipri.org/sites/default/files/2020-04/fs_2020_04_milex_0.pdf.

180 *largest empire ever recorded in the . . . world*: The empire didn't actually reach this size until the early twentieth century, Niall Ferguson, *Empire* (New York: Basic Books, 2004), 43, but the point remains.

181 *prize ships were widely available nearly everywhere one served*: Michael Lewis, *The Navy in Transition, 1814–1864* (London: Hodder and Stoughton, 1965), 231.

181  *eventually (somewhat) duly paid*: Padriac Xavier Scanlan, "The Rewards of Their Exertions," *Past & Present* 225 (2014): 113–42.

181  *consistent access to prizes*: Lewis, *The Navy in Transition*, 231, 234–38.

181  *the reality didn't exactly live up to the hype*: Grindal, *Opposing the Slavers*, chap. 4; Christopher Lloyd, *The Navy and the Slave Trade* (New York: Routledge, 2012), Introduction; and John Rankin, "British and African Health in the Anti-slave-trade Squadron," in *The Suppression of the Atlantic Slave Trade*, ed. Robert M. Burroughs and Richard Huzzey (Manchester, UK: Manchester University Press, 2016), 95–121 (99).

181  *apportioned among the ship's complement based on rank and rating*: Lewis, *The Navy in Transition*, 232–33, 235; and Lloyd, *The Navy and the Slave Trade*, chap. 6, for how prize apportionment continued to evolve.

181  *they were paid like seamen, not as seamen*: The headman was paid more, akin to a petty officer.

181  *They didn't have a rating*: Rankin, "British and African Health in the Anti-slave-trade Squadron," 97.

181  *Liberia and collectivized by language*: Jane Martin, "Krumen 'Down the Coast': Liberian Migrants on the West African Coast in the 19th and Early 20th Centuries," *International Journal of African Historical Studies* 18, no. 3 (1985): 401–2, 405–6; L. B. Breitborde, "City, Countryside and Kru Ethnicity," *Africa: Journal of the International African Institute* 61, no. 2 (1991): 187, 189–91; and Chappell, "Kru and Kanaka," 91–92.

182  *swimming, diving, and boating . . . before Europeans arrived in Africa*: G. E. Brooks, *The Kru Mariner in the Nineteenth Century* (Newark, DE: Liberian Studies Association in America, 1972).

182  *discouraging efforts to teach its sailors how to do it*: Kevin Dawson, "Enslaved Swimmers and Divers in the Atlantic World," *Journal of American History* 92, no. 4 (2006): 1327–55 (1327, 1331); Kevin Dawson, "Swimming, Surfing and Underwater Diving in Early Modern Atlantic Africa and the African Diaspora," in *Navigating African Maritime History*, ed. Carina E. Ray and Jeremy Rich (Liverpool, UK: Liverpool University Press, 2009), 86, 95, 97; Chappell, "Kru and Kanaka," 85–86; and Thomas Malcomson, *Order and Disorder in the British Navy: 1793–1815* (Woodbridge, Suffolk, UK; Rochester, NY: Boydell & Brewer, 2016), 129; this policy would begin to change in the 1830s (Brian Lavery, *Royal Tars: The Lower Deck of the Royal Navy* [London: Conway Publishing; Annapolis, MD: Naval Institute Press, 2010], 336).

182  *useful hires on all sorts of marine craft*: Chappell, "Kru and Kanaka," 97, 98; Grindal, *Opposing the Slavers*, chap. 3; and Brooks, *The Kru Mariner*.

182  *distinct from any other African tribal group in the area*: For example, W. R. Greg, *Past and Present Efforts for the Extinction of the African Slave Trade* (London: Ridgway, 1840), 83–84; T. R. Griffith, "On the Races Inhabiting Sierra Leone," *Journal of the Anthropological Institute of Great Britain and Ireland* 16 (1887): 303–4; E. J. Burton, "Observations on the Climate, Topography, and Diseases of the British Colonies in Africa," *Provincial Medical & Surgical Journal (1840–1842)* 3, no. 13 (1841): 250.

182  *functioned . . . efficiently as any other unit of sailors or marines*: Rankin, "British and African Health in the Anti-slave-trade Squadron," 97.

182  *on his tribesmen's behalf and at their behest*: Ray Costello, *Black Salt: Seafarers of African Descent on British Ships* (Liverpool, UK: Liverpool University Press, 2012), 104.

182  *indigenous knowledge . . . invaluable*: Brooks, *The Kru Mariner*.

183  *WAS could not have functioned . . . without the Kroomen*: Rankin, "British and African Health," 97; Brooks, *The Kru Mariner*; and Chappell, "Kru and Kanaka."

183 *sell their share to their boozier British crewmates*: Grindal, *Opposing the Slavers*, chap. 9.

183 *suggestions on how it might address the problem*: Ibid.

184 *complement was sufficient . . . could not be moved*: Ibid.

184 *between debtor's prison and the Royal Navy*: Nicholas A. M. Rodger, *The Wooden World: Anatomy of the Georgian Navy* (Glasgow: William Collins Sons & Co., 1986), 158–59; Denver Brunsman, *The Evil Necessity: British Naval Impressment in the Eighteenth-Century Atlantic World* (Charlottesville: University of Virginia Press, 2013), 60–61; and Stephen Taylor, *Sons of the Waves: The Common Seaman in the Heroic Age of Sail* (New Haven: Yale University Press, 2020), 224.

185 *smugglers knew their way around a boat*: Rodger, *Wooden World*, 170–71; Brunsman, *The Evil Necessity*, 60–61; and Taylor, *Sons of the Waves*, 224.

185 *Thomas Atkinson of Liverpool*: Taylor, *Sons of the Waves*, 480.

185 *a system of patronage in which favors were currency*: Grindal, *Opposing the Slavers*, chap. 9.

185 *neither Fielder nor Atkinson would ever see England again*: Taylor, *Sons of the Waves*, 483.

186 *complete survey . . . at the instant of capture*: Grindal, *Opposing the Slavers*, chap. 9.

186 *gone back to England on June 8*: James Boyle, *A Practical Medico-Historical Account of the Western Coast of Africa Embracing a Topographical Description of Its Shores, Rivers, and Settlements* (London: S. Highly, 1831), 214.

186 *the only non-British commissioner in Freetown*: Sullivan, *Britain's War Against the Slave Trade*, 159.

186 *opposite numbers . . . came into being in 1819*: Leslie Bethell, "The Mixed Commissions for the Suppression of the Transatlantic Slave Trade," *Journal of African History* 7, no. 1 (1966): 79–81.

189 *a very limited set of options for future employment*: Leslie Bethell, "Britain, Portugal and the Suppression of the Brazilian Slave Trade," *English Historical Review* 80, no. 317 (1965): 84–89.

189 *on board one of the Sybille's condemned prizes*: Grindal, *Opposing the Slavers*, chap. 9.

189 *and on such little evidence*: Ibid.

189 *commodore . . . protective of those who served under him*: For example, ibid., and Lubbock, *Cruisers*, 159–60.

189 *Butterfield . . . serve in the navy for sixty-one years*: William Richard O'Byrne, *A Naval Biographical Dictionary* (London: John Murray, Albemarle Street, 1849), 156.

190 *Le Hardy . . . centuries of prominence in Jersey*: Ibid., 646.

190 *Turner was extremely popular*: Lubbock, *Cruisers*, 140.

190 *practical realities of service on the coast*: Grindal, *Opposing the Slavers*, chap. 9.

190 *dry bedding was worth worrying about*: Ibid.

190 *as hated . . . Turner had been liked*: Grindal, *Opposing the Slavers*, chap. 9.

191 *Harvey . . . no one publicly accused him of anything*: Correspondence (Class A & B) 1831, 59–60, and Correspondence (Class A & B) 1830, 54–57.

191 *£10 per head to £5 the next year*: Lewis, *The Navy in Transition*, 236.

191 *"in command of H.M. tender BLACK JOKE"*: Grindal, *Opposing the Slavers*, chap. 9.

191 *Parrey . . . performance in the WAS . . . promoted*: Lubbock, *Cruisers*, 148–49; Grindal, *Opposing the Slavers*, chap. 9; and O'Byrne, *A Naval Biographical Dictionary*, 863–64.

192 *had his officer's commission confirmed*: O'Byrne, *A Naval Biographical Dictionary*, 863–64.

193 *a rescue mission*: Account of *Black Joke's* rescue of *Cristina* is compiled from the following sources: Grindal, *Opposing the Slavers*, chap. 9; Lubbock, *Cruisers*, 207; Sullivan,

*Britain's War Against the Slave Trade*, 163; Trans-Atlantic Slave Trade Database; Foreign Slave Trade (1837), 50; and Correspondence (Class A & B) 1830, 21–22, 23.

193 *after twenty years living in Sierra Leone*: Boyle, *A Practical Medico-Historical Account*, 219.

194 *so many children—died*: Benjamin N. Lawrance, *Amistad's Orphans: An Atlantic Story of Children, Slavery, and Smuggling* (New Haven: Yale University Press, 2014), 27–36, provides more context on transatlantic child enslavement during this period.

194 *Parrey, his once and current lieutenant*: Grindal, *Opposing the Slavers*, chap. 9.

195 *continue to serve where he was needed*: Parrey would receive his promotion to commander a few months later in February 1830 (Lubbock, *Cruisers*, 207).

## Chapter Eight: *Manzanares*

199 *for which Black Joke was awarded prize money*: Correspondence (Class A & B) 1830, 22.

199 *William Coyde . . . gave him command*: Peter Grindal, *Opposing the Slavers* (London: I.B. Tauris, 2016), chap. 9, and Basil Lubbock, *Cruisers, Corsairs & Slavers* (Glasgow: Brown, Son & Ferguson, 1993), 207.

199 *served . . . in Britain's First Burmese War*: John Marshall, *Royal Naval Biography*, Vol. 3, Part 1 (London: Longman, Rees, Orme, Brown, and Green, 1831), 40–50, 62–63, 66, 81, 108–10; William Laird Clowes, *The Royal Navy: A History from the Earliest Times to the Present*, vol. 6 (London: Sampson Low, Marston and Company, 1901), 243–44, 249.

200 *the Spanish brigantine Manzanares*: Account of *Black Joke's* encounter with *Manzanares* is compiled from the following sources: Grindal, *Opposing the Slavers*, chap. 9; Anthony Sullivan, *Britain's War Against the Slave Trade* (Barnsley, UK: Pen & Sword Books, 2020), 167; Lubbock, *Cruisers*, 207; Trans-Atlantic Slave Trade Database; Correspondence (Class B) 1829, 159; Correspondence (Class A & B) 1830, 25–26, 28–29, 98; Correspondence (Class A & B) 1831, 10, 88–89; and Letter (1832), 10–11.

200 *Shipboard slave revolts were not . . . uncommon*: Eric Robert Taylor, *If We Must Die* (Baton Rouge: Louisiana State University Press, 2006), 63–66.

200 *Henriqueta . . . had one on its third voyage*: Great Britain, British and Foreign State Papers, 1826–1827, London H.M.S.O., 366.

201 *a fourth of the enslaved may have died in the uprising*: The then captain, likely Cardozo dos Santos, claimed only 18 enslaved people died due to the revolt; however, Pennell, British Consul to Brazil, reveals that other reports placed the number much higher, noting that though *Henriqueta* was authorized to bring 600 enslaved people on the voyage, only 441 actually made it into port. Great Britain, British and Foreign State Papers, 366.

201 *"was of necessity in an unclean and unhealthy condition"*: Correspondence (Class A & B) 1830, 29.

202 *Coyde would not retain the captaincy*: He would, however, achieve his promotion to lieutenant the following year, in October 1831. *Navy List, Corrected to the 20th of June, 1834* (London: John Murray, 1834), 33.

203 *McKinnel took a stroll*: Grindal, *Opposing the Slavers*, chap. 9; Lubbock, *Cruisers*, 159–61; and Christopher Lloyd, *The Navy and the Slave Trade* (New York: Routledge, 2012), chap. 9.

203 *"nor did he suffer any inconvenience from it afterwards"*: Grindal, *Opposing the Slavers*, chap. 9.

203 *"surpassed anything I had ever experienced"*: Ibid.

203 *best judgment as to when it was time to go*: Ibid.

205 *and Gordon shouldered it*: Ibid.

205 *An officer of long experience*: John Marshall, *Royal Naval Biography*, Part 3 (London: Longman, Rees, Orme, Brown, and Green, 1829), 224–27; Constance Oliver Skelton and John Malcolm Bulloch, *Gordons Under Arms* (Aberdeen, Scotland: University Press, 1912), 28–30.

205 *Both of his brothers had already died*: Skelton and Bulloch, *Gordons Under Arms*, 213–14, 264.

205 *the liberation of several thousand enslaved Africans*: Grindal, *Opposing the Slavers*, chaps. 8 and 9.

205 *left the coast in the person of Commodore Collier*: Lubbock, *Cruisers*, 161–62, details Collier's send-off from St. Helena.

## Chapter Nine: *Dos Amigos*

209 *requisite materials from Fernando Pó*: Peter Grindal, *Opposing the Slavers* (London: I.B. Tauris, 2016), chap. 9.

209 *when compared to . . . betimes the colonial government of Sierra Leone*: Robert T. Brown, "Fernando Po and the Anti-Sierra Leonean Campaign," *International Journal of African Historical Studies* 6, no. 2 (1973): 255–57, 260.

210 *drained away much of that support*: Ibid., 262.

210 *to hide the truth of the situation*: Ibid., 259, and Grindal, *Opposing the Slavers*, chap. 9.

211 *"as fatal as Sierra Leone, and that is saying a great deal"*: Peter Leonard, *Records of a Voyage to the Western Coast of Africa* (Edinburgh: William Tait, 1833), 152.

211 *Spain had a viable claim to the island*: Ibrahim K. Sundiata, *From Slaving to Neoslavery: The Bight of Biafra and Fernando Po in the Era of Abolition, 1827–1930* (Madison: University of Wisconsin Press, 1996).

211 *Nicholls, who'd been serving as the governor of Ascension*: Brown, "Fernando Po," 259–60, and Grindal, *Opposing the Slavers*, chap. 9.

212 *those charged with administering the suppression effort*: Brown, "Fernando Po," 249–52, 260, and Manuel Barcia, *The Yellow Demon of Fever* (New Haven: Yale University Press, 2020), 45.

212 *the Bubi were nearly wiped out*: Brown, "Fernando Po," 261.

212 *the resulting near-complete lack of oversight*: Ibid., 260–61; Siân Rees, *Sweet Water and Bitter: The Ships That Stopped the Slave Trade* (Durham: University of New Hampshire Press, 2009), 128–44, provides a comprehensive overview of Owen's time on the coast during this period.

212 *hied off to service on the South America Station*: Brown, "Fernando Po," 261, and Paul G. Cornell, "Owen, William Fitzwilliam," in *Dictionary of Canadian Biography*, vol. 4 (University of Toronto/Université Laval, revised 1979), http://www.biographi.ca/en/bio/owen_william_fitz_william_8E.html.

213 *Fernando Pó was toast*: Brown, "Fernando Po," 261, and Sundiata, *From Slaving to Neoslavery*.

213 *Lumley, had died . . . in 1828*: Grindal, *Opposing the Slavers*, chap. 9.

213 *four different acting lieutenant governors had rotated through the position*: A drama-filled

series of incidents in its own right, the quick rundown is that Lumley had been in office for only two months after succeeding a guy (Denham) who'd had the gig for only one month. Lumley was followed by Samuel Smart for three months, who passed it off to Henry John Ricketts, who had a bit of a booze-assisted breakdown after the 1829 epidemic, at which point there was functionally a soft coup attempt among the European residents, creating factional divides until the arrival of a senior military officer, Augustine Fitzgerald Evans of the 2nd West India Regiment, and Ricketts promptly decamped to England. Evans was declared acting governor for "a few weeks," until the arrival of an even more senior officer, Alexander Maclean Fraser of the Royal African Colonial Corps, who then declared himself acting governor and interfered in the functioning of the Mixed Commission for a month or three by refusing to swear in one of the original instigators of the whole affair as a judge. That was pretty much the state of things when the officially promoted Alexander Findlay arrived in April 1830 to take over and put an end to the shenanigans, which didn't immediately work, as Fraser spent the next year contesting Findlay's appointment. Christopher Fyfe, *A History of Sierra Leone*, 3rd ed. (London: Oxford University Press, 1968), 171–78.

213 *"by bringing many thousands of slaves to this colony"*: Grindal, *Opposing the Slavers*, chap. 9.

213 *greater lengths to avoid the Black Joke specifically*: Blair, "All the Ships That Never Sailed," PhD diss., Georgetown University, 2014, 81, fn. 8, citing Rees, *Sweet Water and Bitter*.

214 *"without a European to direct them"*: Janes W. St. G. Walker, *The Black Loyalists: The Search for a Promised Land in Nova Scotia and Sierra Leone* (Toronto; Buffalo; London: University of Toronto Press, 1992), 337.

214 *resettled Black residents from Nova Scotia and Jamaica*: Padriac Xavier Scanlan, *Freedom's Debtors* (New Haven: Yale University Press, 2017), 28, 30–31.

214 *this first attempt failed fairly quickly*: Fyfe, *A History of Sierra Leone*, and Scanlan, *Freedom's Debtors*.

215 *over five hundred Jamaican Maroons to quell the unrest*: Walker, *The Black Loyalists*.

216 *"[Total] 15,081"*: Kenneth Macaulay, *The Colony of Sierra Leone Vindicated from the Misrepresentations of Mr. Macqueen of Glasgow* (London: J. Hatchard and Son, 1827), 16–17.

217 *young enough to have just left school*: Walker, *The Black Loyalists*, 337.

217 *arranged for four hundred locals to . . . kill everyone*: Grindal, *Opposing the Slavers*, chap. 9.

217 *HMS Thistle . . . killing two and injuring several more*: Ibid., chap. 14.

217 *fever . . . killed twenty-seven members of the crew*: Ibid., chap. 9.

217 *French slave traders . . . bigger problem that year*: Ibid.

218 *willing to simply ignore the law, and the trade continued*: Paul Michael Kielstra, *The Politics of Slave Trade Suppression in Britain and France, 1814–48* (London: Palgrave Macmillan UK, 2000), 18.

218 *more stringently enforcing those already on the books*: Ibid., 108.

218 *whistleblowers who informed . . . would serve no time*: Ibid., 134–35.

218 *the French Squadron . . . detaining French slavers*: Ibid., 146.

219 *That last one would prove the most difficult*: Ibid., 141.

219 *things would get worse before they got better*: Ibid., 141–43.

220 *really, it could do nothing else*: Ibid., 143, 146–47.

220 *"seems to me to leave still much to be desired"*: Ibid., 143.

220 *His opposite number*: Vice Admiral C. E. Fleeming.

221 *colonial officials . . . apathetic and too often complicit*: Kielstra, *The Politics of Slave Trade Suppression in Britain and France*, 142, 144.

221 *changed the family's last name accordingly*: William Anderson, *The Scottish Nation; or, the Surnames, Families, Literature, Honours, and Biographical History of the People of Scotland*, vol. 3 (*Mac–Zet*) and Supplement (Edinburgh: A. Fullarton & Co., 1877), 322, and William Richard O'Byrne, *A Naval Biographical Dictionary* (London: John Murray, Albemarle Street, 1849), 952.

221 *berth to berth with scarcely a gap in service*: O'Byrne, *A Naval Biographical Dictionary*, 952.

221 *yet still had nothing to show for it*: Grindal, *Opposing the Slavers*, chap. 9, and Basil Lubbock, *Cruisers, Corsairs & Slavers* (Glasgow: Brown, Son & Ferguson, 1993), 207.

222 *"literally laugh at us as we pass"*: Kielstra, *The Politics of Slave Trade Suppression in Britain and France*, 127; Leonard, *Records of a Voyage*, 153; and Anthony Sullivan, *Britain's War Against the Slave Trade* (Barnsley, UK: Pen & Sword Books, 2020), 171.

222 *"or having slaves actually on board"*: Leonard, *Records of a Voyage*, 149–51.

223 *France's was the documentation of choice*: Kielstra, *The Politics of Slave Trade Suppression in Britain and France*, 126.

223 *if Britain wanted it, France almost certainly did not*: William Ernest Frank Ward, *The Royal Navy and the Slavers* (London: Pantheon Books, 1969), 79–81.

223 *Napoléon had brought . . . return of French slavery*: Kielstra, *The Politics of Slave Trade Suppression in Britain and France*, 17.

224 *French government's complicity in slave trading*: Ibid., 139.

224 *an international incident . . . waiting to happen*: Ibid., 145.

225 *boarding French slavers . . . had to stop*: Ibid., 146–147.

226 *a slew of anti-slave-trade and outright abolitionist ministers*: Ibid., 148, and William Law Mathieson, *England in Transition, 1789–1832* (London: Longmans, Green and Co., 1920), 263.

226 *France's shift . . . to ally of suppression*: Kielstra, *The Politics of Slave Trade Suppression in Britain and France*, 138.

226 *Black Joke was patiently waiting offshore near the Cameroons River*: Account of *Black Joke*'s encounter with and subsequent disposition of *Dos Amigos* is compiled from the following sources: Grindal, *Opposing the Slavers*, chap. 9; Sullivan, *Britain's War Against the Slave Trade*, 171–72; Lubbock, *Cruisers*, 207–9; Dinizulu Gene Tinnie, "The Slaving Brig *Henriqueta* and Her Evil Sisters," *Journal of African American History* 93 (2008): 509–31; Trans-Atlantic Slave Trade Database; and Correspondence (Class A & B) 1831, 15–24, 34.

228 *poop tub*: The giant defecation tubs were a standard slave ship feature, and somehow even more disgustingly inhumane than their function and location implies. Sowande M. Mustakeem, *Slavery at Sea* (Urbana: University of Illinois Press, 2016), and Marcus Rediker, *The Slave Ship: A Human History* (New York: Penguin, 2007).

228 *leaders of African geographical areas and tribal groups*: Ralph A. Austen, "The Metamorphoses of Middlemen: The Duala, Europeans, and the Cameroon Hinterland, ca. 1800–ca. 1960," *International Journal of African Historical Studies* 16, no. 1 (1983): 5–6.

229 *the quantities of food meant to go in them*: Rediker, *The Slave Ship*.

229 *insurance would cover the loss of life . . . It did not*: Ibid., chap. 8, and Christopher Lloyd, *The Navy and the Slave Trade* (New York: Routledge, 2012), chap. 1.

231 *trade . . . a sliver of what it had once been*: Grindal, *Opposing the Slavers*.

235 *"the evidence of [de Muxica] is insincere and fictitious"*: Correspondence (Class A & B) 1831, 16–21.

235 *John "Magnificent" Hayes . . . his flagship, HMS Dryad*: Lubbock, *Cruisers*.

## Chapter Ten: *Primero*

237 *nothing was ever seen to fall out of the sky again*: A tender of *Sybille*, *Paul Pry*, had a service-ending experience with a tornado as well when, during a chase, the weather prompted a munitions explosion on deck. The tender was limped into harbor and sold. Peter Grindal, *Opposing the Slavers* (London: I.B. Tauris, 2016), chap. 9, and Basil Lubbock, *Cruisers, Corsairs & Slavers* (Glasgow: Brown, Son & Ferguson, 1993), 150–51 (*Paul Pry*), 153 (additional example, HMS *Redwing*).

238 *sympathy for the exigencies of life at sea was available*: Correspondence (Class A & B) 1831, 21–24.

238 *entered into the Royal Navy's* Navy List: Grindal, *Opposing the Slavers*, chap. 9.

238 *sent Plumper out to search for the Black Joke*: Ibid., chap. 9, and Anthony Sullivan, *Britain's War Against the Slave Trade* (Barnsley, UK: Pen & Sword Books, 2020), 174.

239 *much the same as an actual French flag of the era*: Grindal, *Opposing the Slavers*, chap. 9.

239 *the captain of the new flagship, Dryad*: Ibid., chap. 9.

239 *the fifth-rate frigate Dryad*: Phoebe class, originally had thirty-six guns and subsequently had six more added. Rif Winfield, *British Warships in the Age of Sail, 1793–1817* (Yorkshire, UK: Seaforth Publishing, 2008), 445–46, and Rif Winfield, *British Warships in the Age of Sail, 1817–1863* (Yorkshire, UK: Seaforth Publishing, 2014), 532–35.

240 *bogged down by the full-time job of running his own ship*: Michael Lewis, *The Navy in Transition, 1814–1864* (London: Hodder and Stoughton, 1965).

240 *Kroomen for boat work in the interior cease*: Grindal, *Opposing the Slavers*, chap. 9.

240 *so much biological cannon fodder*: John Rankin, "British and African Health in the Anti-slave-trade Squadron" in *The Suppression of the Atlantic Slave Trade*, ed. Robert M. Burroughs and Richard Huzzey (Manchester, UK: Manchester University Press, 2016), 95–121; Manuel Barcia, *The Yellow Demon of Fever* (New Haven: Yale University Press, 2020), 39, 105–6; and Stephen Taylor, *Sons of the Waves: The Common Seaman in the Heroic Age of Sail* (New Haven: Yale University Press, 2020), 481

241 *attempting to put a medical officer on every prize crew*: Grindal, *Opposing the Slavers*, chap. 9.

241 *attached severe punishment to misconduct*: Ibid.

242 *"an explanation thereof, might accompany our report of the case"*: Correspondence (Class A & B) 1831, 15–16.

242 *"satisfied with the explanation given by Lieutenant Ramsay"*: Ibid., 23.

242 *it was desperately in need of yet another refit*: Grindal, *Opposing the Slavers*, chap. 9.

243 *constructed by the Royal Navy . . . ship Hayes had run in the trials*: Lubbock, *Cruisers*, 202.

244 *rechristening it the* Fair Rosamond: Grindal, *Opposing the Slavers*, chap. 11.

245 *head of squadrons in Jamaica and elsewhere*: J. K. Laughton and Roger Morriss, "Hayes, John (1775–1838), Naval Officer," *Oxford Dictionary of National Biography*; Lubbock, *Cruisers*, 200–202; Grindal, *Opposing the Slavers*, chap. 9; and John Marshall, *Royal Naval Biography*, Vol. 2, Part 2 (London: Longman, Rees, Orme, Brown, and Green, 1825), 673–83.

245 *"he could build, rig, govern, and sail the ship with equal ease and credit"*: Henry Huntley, *Seven Years' Service on the Slave Coast of Western Africa*, vol. 1 (London: Thomas Cautley Newby, 1850), 143–44.

245 *"liberated" Africans . . . resold into slavery*: Lubbock, *Cruisers*, 206, and Grindal, *Opposing the Slavers*, chap. 9.

246 *"contrary to custom"*: Grindal, *Opposing the Slavers*, chap. 9. Hayes minced fewer words, calling it "a question too absurd for Their Lordships to entertain for a moment."

246 *frivolous (if technically true in some aspects) charges*: *The Nautical Magazine* (London) 1 (1832): 494–95.

247 *Speedwell . . . Cuban pirates in the early 1820s*: Lubbock, *Cruisers*, 74, 209; Grindal, *Opposing the Slavers*, chap. 9; William Richard O'Byrne, *A Naval Biographical Dictionary* (London: John Murray, Albemarle Street, 1849), 178–79.

248 *the Spanish schooner* Primero: Account of *Black Joke*'s encounter with *Primero* is compiled from the following sources: Lubbock, *Cruisers*, 209; Grindal, *Opposing the Slavers*, chap. 9; O'Byrne, *A Naval Biographical Dictionary*, 179; Sullivan, *Britain's War Against the Slave Trade*, 175; Peter Leonard, *Records of a Voyage to the Western Coast of Africa* (Edinburgh: William Tait, 1833), 104–7; Trans-Atlantic Slave Trade Database; and Correspondence (Class A & B) 1831, 24–25.

249 *"with sails shaking and booms cracking"*: Lubbock, *Cruisers*, 209.

249 *primary indictments . . . on the home front*: Reginald Coupland, *The British Anti-Slavery Movement*, 2nd ed. (London: Frank Cass & Co., 1964).

249 *slightly smaller than . . . a medium-size slaving vessel*: Marcus Rediker, *The Slave Ship: A Human History* (New York: Penguin, 2007), chap. 2, indicates 140 TB average.

249 *a number of exceedingly dirty monkeys*: Ibid. notes that animals on slave ships were not uncommon; Lubbock, *Cruisers*, highlights the regular appearance of dogs on slave ships, and *Dos Amigos* had goats, Correspondence (Class A & B) 1831, 21.

250 *a slave deck that . . . measured only twenty-six inches*: Leonard, *Records of a Voyage*.

250 *only two or three, and those were not always open*: Rediker, *The Slave Ship*.

250 *the daily waste of urine and feces . . . pus and vomit*: Sowande M. Mustakeem, *Slavery at Sea* (Urbana: University of Illinois Press, 2016).

251 *"one of the cleanest that ever was brought to the colony"*: Leonard, *Records of a Voyage*.


### Chapter Eleven: *Marinerito*

255 *a distanced, spare retelling of facts*: Mary Wills, *Envoys of Abolition* (Liverpool, UK: Liverpool University Press, 2019).

255 *Primero . . . journey back to Sierra Leone*: Peter Grindal, *Opposing the Slavers* (London: I.B. Tauris, 2016), chap. 9.

255 *an astonishingly good result*: Manuel Barcia, *The Yellow Demon of Fever* (New Haven: Yale University Press, 2020), and David Northrup, "African Mortality in the Suppression of the Slave Trade," *Journal of Interdisciplinary History* 9, no. 1 (1978): 47–64.

256 *"Is this unparalleled cruelty to last for ever?"*: Wills, *Envoys of Abolition*, emphasis original to Hayes.

256 *"I think it will appear in another light"*: Grindal, *Opposing the Slavers*, chap. 9, and Wills, *Envoys of Abolition*.

256 *"enter into his thoughtless head"*: Peter Leonard, *Records of a Voyage to the Western Coast of Africa* (Edinburgh: William Tait, 1833).

256 *awareness among the sailors . . . rationale for their service*: Isaac Land, *War, Nationalism,*

*and the British Sailor, 1750–1850* (New York: Palgrave Macmillan 2009), 105–30, on sailor-authors' awareness of and reaction to systemic issues in the broader context of the late eighteenth and early to mid-nineteenth centuries; see Wills, *Envoys of Abolition*, for an exploration specific to the WAS.

257 *kidnapping . . . on account of their hue*: Ray Costello, *Black Salt: Seafarers of African Descent of British Ships* (Liverpool, UK: Liverpool University Press, 2012), 18–22, 83.

257 *the general mindset in the WAS*: Wills, *Envoys of Abolition*.

257 *USS* Java: Account of *Black Joke*'s encounter with USS *Java* is compiled from the following sources: Grindal, *Opposing the Slavers*, chap. 11; Anthony Sullivan, *Britain's War Against the Slave Trade* (Barnsley, UK: Pen & Sword Books, 2020), 175; Judd Scott Harmon, "Suppress and Protect: The United States Navy, the African Slave Trade, and Maritime Commerce, 1794–1862," PhD diss., College of William and Mary, 1977; and American Colonization Society, *The African Repository and Colonial Journal*, vol. 7 (Washington: American Colonization Society, 1832; New York: Kraus Reprint Corporation, 1967).

257 *American interest was lower still*: W. E. B. Dubois, *The Suppression of the African Slave-Trade to the United States of America, 1638–1870* (Williamstown, MA: Corner House Publishers, 1970); Harmon, "Suppress and Protect"; and William Ernest Frank Ward, *The Royal Navy and the Slavers* (London: Pantheon Books, 1969).

258 *continuing back to Norfolk, Virginia*: American Colonization Society, *The African Repository*, vol. 7, 153–57.

258 *presented with a choice between three commands*: Christopher Lloyd, *The Navy and the Slave Trade* (New York: Routledge, 2012); Grindal, *Opposing the Slavers*, chap. 9; Henry Huntley, *Seven Years' Service on the Slave Coast of Western Africa*, vol. 1 (London: Thomas Cautley Newby, 1850), 143–46.

258 *get another opportunity to command*: Huntley, *Seven Years' Service*, 144–45.

258 *that October he would finally receive the promotion he sought*: Grindal, *Opposing the Slavers*, chap. 9.

258 *"a monotonous and idle absurdity"*: Huntley, *Seven Years' Service*, 301.

258 *"she was certainly her superior when going well 'free'"*: Ibid., 145.

259 Fair Rosamond *to the Bight of Benin*: Grindal, *Opposing the Slavers*, chap. 9.

259 *staffing the tenders*: Ibid., chap. 11.

259 *dreamed and schemed of its being*: Robert T. Brown, "Fernando Po and the Anti-Sierra Leonean Campaign," *International Journal of African Historical Studies* 6, no. 2 (1973): 249–64.

260 *no one was allowed on board this* Marinerito: Account of *Black Joke*'s encounter with *Marinerito* is compiled from the following sources: Grindal, *Opposing the Slavers*, chap. 11; Siân Rees, *Sweet Water and Bitter* (Durham: University of New Hampshire Press, 2009), 174–76; Sullivan, *Britain's War Against the Slave Trade*, 177–81; Basil Lubbock, *Cruisers, Corsairs & Slavers* (Glasgow: Brown, Son & Ferguson, 1993), 213–16; Trans-Atlantic Slave Trade Database; *Journal* (1833), 87–88; and Correspondence (Class A & B) 1831.

261 *avoiding the* Black Joke*'s patrol area entirely, if possible*: David Joseph Blair, "All the Ships That Never Sailed," PhD diss., Georgetown University, 2014, 81 fn. 8, referencing Rees, *Sweet Water and Bitter*.

263 *his mate C. J. Bosanquet*: William Richard O'Byrne, *A Naval Biographical Dictionary* (London: John Murray, Albemarle Street, 1849), 98–99.

263 *Hinde . . . had only been in the Royal Navy for two years*: Ibid., 518.

266 *announced as a brig from the south*: Lloyd, *The Navy and the Slave Trade*, chap. 5, and

Christopher Fyfe, *A History of Sierra Leone*, 3rd ed. (London: Oxford University Press, 1968).

266 *still in the . . . slave deck . . . if with slightly more space*: Lloyd, *The Navy and the Slave Trade*, chap. 5.

266 *"painful attitude necessary for the stowage of so large a number"*: Leonard, *Records of a Voyage*.

267 *rowed to . . . receive their much-ballyhooed liberation*: Lloyd, *The Navy and the Slave Trade*, chap. 5.

267 *died within four months of their arrival*: Barcia, *The Yellow Demon of Fever*, 156.

267 *process was ostensibly meant to be liberatory*: As a captain on the coast in later years put it, ". . . if [recaptive Africans] are not slaves their condition is so near it that I was unable to perceive the difference." Costello, *Black Salt*, 37.

269 *jobs . . . in service of British empire*: Richard Anderson, "The Diaspora of Sierra Leone's Liberated Africans," *African Economic History* 41 (2013): 101–38. For a non–Sierra Leonean example of these policies carried out, see Andrew Pearson, *Distant Freedom: St Helena and the Abolition of the Slave Trade, 1840–1872* (Liverpool, UK: Liverpool University Press, 2016), 201–41.

269 *"angry when they found themselves still under control"*: Leonard, *Records of a Voyage*.

## Chapter Twelve: *Regulo & Rapido*

273 Seaflower, Fair Rosamond, *and the eldest*, Black Joke: Peter Grindal, *Opposing the Slavers* (London: I.B. Tauris, 2016), chap. 11.

273 *worthless for the commodore's purposes*: Ibid.

274 *"George IV put an end to his unpopularity by dying"*: William Law Mathieson, *England in Transition, 1789–1832* (London: Longmans, Green and Co., 1920), 263.

274 *forced to resign after only a year*: Nicholas A. M. Rodger, *The Admiralty* (London: T. Dalton, 1979).

274 *he undoubtedly was a drinker*: Steven Parissian, "George IV: The Royal Joke?," *BBC History*, https://www.bbc.co.uk/history/british/empire_seapower/george_fourth_01 .shtml.

274 *rather than the conservative Tories*: Mathieson, *England in Transition*, 263–64, and Edith F. Hurwitz, *Politics and the Public Conscience* (London: George Allen & Unwin, 1973), 48–76.

274 *working with France to finally effect real change*: Paul Michael Kielstra, *The Politics of Slave Trade Suppression in Britain and France, 1814–48* (London: Palgrave Macmillan, 2000), 149–53.

274 *insulted their diplomats at state dinners*: Andrew Lambert, "Introducing William IV: A 'Sailor King'?," *Georgian Papers Programme Blog*, https://georgianpapers .com/2018/02/20/introducing-william-iv-sailor-king/.

275 *Neither of them would be on the next Admiralty board*: Rodger, *The Admiralty*.

275 *popular support . . . in England was ebbing*: William Ernest Frank Ward, *The Royal Navy and the Slavers* (London: Pantheon Books, 1969), 126–27.

275 *dubious on the project of the Squadron as a whole*: Hurwitz, *Politics and the Public Conscience*, 48–76.

275 *enough tenders to patrol the coast for three years*: Grindal, *Opposing the Slavers*, chap. 11.

275 *cruise in the immediate vicinity of Freetown*: Ibid.

276 *no more tenders . . . purchased for the West Africa Squadron*: Ibid.

276  *near each other, usually in the Bights*: Ibid.

276  *two heavily armed slavers*: Account of *Black Joke's* encounter with *Regulo* and *Rapido* is compiled from the following sources: Ibid.; Siân Rees, *Sweet Water and Bitter* (Durham: University of New Hampshire Press, 2009), 176–77; Anthony Sullivan, *Britain's War Against the Slave Trade* (Barnsley, UK: Pen & Sword Books, 2020), 181–82; Basil Lubbock, *Cruisers, Corsairs & Slavers* (Glasgow: Brown, Son & Ferguson, 1993), 219–24; Trans-Atlantic Slave Trade Database; *Journal* (1833), 154–57; Correspondence (Class A & B) 1832; and Daniel P. Mannix, *Black Cargoes: A History of the Atlantic Slave Trade: 1518–1865* (New York: Viking Press, 1962), 210–11.

276  *stories of the horrors of the Marinerito and slavers like it*: Adrian Desmond and James Moore, *Darwin's Sacred Cause* (New York: Houghton Mifflin Harcourt, 2009), 73, 86.

279  *abandoned the captain to the disarray*: Lubbock, *Cruisers*, 218–19, and Christopher Lloyd, *The Navy and the Slave Trade* (New York: Routledge, 2012), chap. 5.

279  *Sharks . . . waiting for the inevitable bodies from above*: Marcus Rediker, *The Slave Ship: A Human History* (New York: Penguin, 2007), chap. 1.

280  *reverberated across the ocean*: Grindal, *Opposing the Slavers*, chap. 11.

280  *abolitionist sympathies he didn't share*: Mary Wills, *Envoys of Abolition* (Liverpool, UK: Liverpool University Press, 2019), 187–88.

280  *had several serious offers*: Ibid., 189.

280  *equipment clauses . . . would have prevented the incident*: Kielstra, *The Politics of Slave Trade Suppression*, 149–53.

281  *ridding the slave coast of nearly all French slavers*: Grindal, *Opposing the Slavers*, chap. 11.

## Chapter Thirteen: *Frasquita*

285  *"unprecedented and improper"*: Peter Grindal, *Opposing the Slavers* (London: I.B. Tauris, 2016), chap. 11.

285  *right about a forthcoming promotion*: Ibid.

285  *being stuck . . . had a rather deleterious effect*: Ibid.

285  *were everything navy-related not all the rage*: Andrew Lambert, "Introducing William IV: A 'Sailor King'?" *Georgian Papers Programme Blog*.

286  *reformist zeal . . . hadn't yet flagged enough to ignore*: Reginald Coupland, *The British Anti-Slavery Movement*, 2nd ed. (London: Frank Cass & Co., 1964).

286  *reform of the Church in Ireland*: Nicholas A. M. Rodger, *The Admiralty* (London: T. Dalton, 1979), and William Law Mathieson, *England in Transition: 1789–1832* (London: Longmans, Green and Co., 1920).

286  *just as disinterested . . . perhaps even more so*: Edith F. Hurwitz, *Politics and the Public Conscience* (London: George Allen & Unwin, 1973), 48–76.

286  *this . . . was not one of his better ideas*: Basil Lubbock, *Cruisers, Corsairs & Slavers* (Glasgow: Brown, Son & Ferguson, 1993), 226.

287  *currently Commodore Schomberg*: Grindal, *Opposing the Slavers*, chap. 11.

287  *replace them both with Real Admiral Warren*: Ibid.

287  *the same to Georges II and III*: William Richard O'Byrne, *Naval Biographical Dictionary* (London: John Murray, Albemarle Street, 1849), 1251.

287  *difficult mission several thousand miles apart*: J. K. Laughton and Andrew Lambert, "Warren, Frederick (1775–1848), Naval Officer," *Oxford Dictionary of National Biography*, September 23, 2004; accessed June 21, 2021; and Lubbock, *Cruisers*, 226.

287 Brisk . . . commanded by . . . Edward Harris Butterfield: Grindal, Opposing the Slavers, chap. 11.

287 document the ship's capabilities and fuel performance: Lubbock, Cruisers, 226.

288 The policy was not well received: Grindal, Opposing the Slavers, chap. 11.

288 recaptive Africans placed around the nearby river: Ibid.

288 little good to say about Fernando Pó: Ibid.

288 prompted a relative ebb in the trade: Paul Michael Kielstra, The Politics of Slave Trade Suppression in Britain and France, 1814–48 (London: Palgrave Macmillan UK, 2000).

288 they'd ideally have quite a few more: Grindal, Opposing the Slavers, chap. 11.

288 an impressive record during the Napoleonic Wars: Laughton and Lambert, "Warren, Frederick."

288 two court-martials notwithstanding: Marshall, Royal Naval Biography, vol. 2 (London: Longman, Rees, Orme, Brown, and Green, 1824), 414–16.

288 Hayes happened to be near: Grindal, Opposing the Slavers, chap. 11.

288 only a day after Warren himself: Ibid.

290 both crewed and condemned: Ibid.

290 the Admiralty shot this solution down: Ibid.

290 policy surrounding the sale of tenders: Ibid.

291 Frasquita was summarily condemned: Account of Black Joke's encounter with Frasquita is compiled from the following sources: Ibid.; Anthony Sullivan, Britain's War Against the Slave Trade (Barnsley, UK: Pen & Sword Books, 2020), 187; Lubbock, Cruisers, 225–26; Trans-Atlantic Slave Trade Database; Journal (1833), 171–74; and Correspondence (Class A & B) 1832.

291 build, rather than source, an effective fleet: Lubbock, Cruisers, 169–99, for how the navy's shipbuilding and design efforts evolved during this era.

291 El Almirante . . . renamed Cherouka: Ibid., 225.

291 these were his "pet" ships: Ibid., 227.

291 didn't reveal them to the Admiralty: Grindal, Opposing the Slavers, chap. 11.

292 brightest star over four difficult years: Ibid.

293 something so clearly worth saving: Peter Leonard, Records of a Voyage to the Western Coast of Africa (Edinburgh: William Tait, 1833).

293 deliberately set the Black Joke ablaze: Grindal, Opposing the Slavers, chap. 11, and Lubbock, Cruisers, 226–27.

293 lest they face the same fate: Grindal, Opposing the Slavers, chap. 11.

293 Jamaica and Nantes, Bahia and Ouidah: Leonard, Records of a Voyage.

294 more streamlined command structure: Lubbock, Cruisers.

294 the settlement finally failed two years later: Robert T. Brown, "Fernando Po and the Anti-Sierra Leonean Campaign," International Journal of African Historical Studies 6, no. 2 (1973): 249–64.

294 technologically and as an organization: Lubbock, Cruisers.

294 gradualist approach in most . . . colonies: William Law Mathieson, British Slavery and Its Abolition, 1823–1838 (London: Longmans, Green and Co., 1929).

295 abolished slavery for a second time in 1848: Kielstra, The Politics of Slave Trade Suppression.

295 economic losses slaveholders sustained with broader abolition: Slave Compensation Act 1837, 1 & 2 Vict. c. 3.

295 point of contention . . . for years to come: Richard Anderson, "The Diaspora of Sierra Leone's Liberated Africans," African Economic History 41 (2013): 101–38, and Coupland, The British Anti-Slavery Movement.

# NOTES

295 *decades before anyone would call the battle for suppression won*: Suzanne Miers, *Britain and the Ending of the Slave Trade* (London: Longman Group, 1975).

### Valediction

300 *Fair Rosamond . . . anywhere in the world . . . how a slaver was built*: Dinizulu Gene Tinnie, "In Search of the Cuban Slave Ship *Dos Amigos*," *ISLAS* 1, no. 4 (2006): 22–30.

300 *Slave Compensation Act . . . 2015, when it was finally paid off*: Kris Manjapra, "When Will Britain Face Up to Its Crimes Against Humanity?," *Guardian*, March 29, 2018, https://www.theguardian.com/news/2018/mar/29/slavery-abolition-compensation -when-will-britain-face-up-to-its-crimes-against-humanity.

# SOURCES

Act for the Abolition of the Slave Trade, 1807, 47 Geo. III, c. 36.

Al-Qasimi, Muhammad. *The Myth of Arab Piracy in the Gulf.* London: Routledge, 1986.

Allen, Douglas W. "The British Navy Rules: Monitoring and Incompatible Incentives in the Age of Fighting Sail." *Explorations in Economic History* 39 (2002): 204–31.

Allen, Joseph. *The New Navy List and General Record and the Services of Officers of the Royal Navy and Royal Marines.* London: Parker, Furnivall, and Parker, 1850.

American Colonization Society, The. *The African Repository and Colonial Journal.* Vol. 7. Washington, DC: The American Colonization Society, 1832; New York: Kraus Reprint Corporation, 1967.

Anderson, J. L. "Piracy and World History: An Economic Perspective on Maritime Predation." *Journal of World History* 6, no. 2 (1995): 175–99.

Anderson, Richard. "The Diaspora of Sierra Leone's Liberated Africans: Enlistment, Forced Migration, and 'Liberation' at Freetown, 1808–1863." *African Economic History* 41 (2013): 101–38.

Anderson, William. *The Scottish Nation; or, the Surnames, Families, Literature, Honours, and Biographical History of the People of Scotland.* Vol. 3 (*Mac–Zet*) and Supplement. Edinburgh: A. Fullarton & Co., 1877.

Araujo, Ana Lucia. "Forgetting and Remembering the Atlantic Slave Trade: The Legacy of Brazilian Slave Merchant Francisco Felix de Souza." In *Crossing Memories: Slavery and African Diaspora,* edited by Ana Lucia Araujo, Mariana P. Candido, and Paul E. Lovejoy. Trenton, NJ: Africa World Press, 2011.

Aufderheide, P. A. "Order and Violence: Social Deviance and Social Control in Brazil, 1780–1840." PhD diss., University of Minnesota, 1976.

Austen, Ralph A. "The Metamorphoses of Middlemen: The Duala, Europeans, and the Camaroon Hinterland, ca. 1800–ca. 1960." *International Journal of African Historical Studies* 16, no. 1 (1983): 1–24.

Bandinel, James. *Some Account of the Trade in Slaves from Africa as Connected with Europe and America from the Introduction of the Trade into Modern Europe, Down to the Present Time; Especially with Reference to the Efforts Made by the British Government for Its Extinction.* London: Frank Cass & Co., 1842.

Barcia, Manuel. *The Yellow Demon of Fever: Fighting Disease in the Nineteenth-Century Transatlantic Slave Trade.* New Haven: Yale University Press, 2020.

Beales, Derek. "Canning, George (1770–1827), prime minister and parodist." In *Oxford Dictionary of National Biography.* Oxford University Press, 2004; online ed., 2011. Article published September 23, 2004; last modified September 25, 2014.

Beckert, Sven. *Empire of Cotton: A Global History.* New York: Vintage Books, 2015.

Bedhampton Historical Collection. "The Time Travellers Guide to Bedhampton Village." January 2019. Accessed July 21, 2021. https://secure.toolkitfiles.co.uk/clients/21710

/sitedata/files/Time-Travellers-Guide-to-Bedhampton-Village-2019-02–18–121
424.pdf.

———. "The Waterloo Room at The Elms: 'The Gem of Bedhampton.'" Accessed July 21,
2021. https://secure.toolkitfiles.co.uk/clients/21710/sitedata/files/The%20Water
loo%20Room%20at%20The%20Elms.pdf.

Behrendt, Stephen D. "Human Capital in the British Slave Trade." In *Liverpool and Trans-
atlantic Slavery*, edited by David Richardson, Suzanne Schwarz, and Anthony Tibbles. Liverpool, UK: Liverpool University Press, 2007.

Behrendt, Stephen D., and Peter M. Solar. "Sail on, Albion: The Usefulness of Lloyd's Registers for Maritime History, 1760–1840." *International Journal of Maritime History*
26, no. 3 (2014): 568–86.

Benjamin, Daniel K. "Golden Harvest: The British Naval Prize System, 1793–1815." Unpublished, 2009. Accessed July 18, 2021. https://www.academia.edu/14515791
/Golden_Harvest_The_British_Naval_Prize_System_1793–1815

Benjamin, Daniel K., and Christopher Thornberg. "Comment: Rules, Monitoring, and Incentives in the Age of Sail." *Explorations in Economic History* 40 (2003): 195–211.

———. "Organization and Incentives in the Age of Sail." *Explorations in Economic History*
44 (2007): 317–41.

Benjamin, Daniel K., and Anca Tifrea. "Learning by Dying: Combat Performance in the
Age of Sail." *Journal of Economic History* 67, no. 4 (2007): 968–1000.

Bergad, Laird W. *The Comparative Histories of Slavery in Brazil, Cuba, and the United States.*
Cambridge, UK: Cambridge University Press, 2007.

Berry, Daina Ramey. *The Price for Their Pound of Flesh: The Value of the Enslaved, from
Womb to Grave, in the Building of a Nation.* Boston: Beacon Press, 2017.

Bethell, Leslie. "Britain, Portugal and the Suppression of the Brazilian Slave Trade: The
Origins of Lord Palmerston's Act of 1839." *English Historical Review* 80, no. 317
(1965): 761–84.

———. "The Mixed Commissions for the Suppression of the Transatlantic Slave Trade in
the Nineteenth Century." *Journal of African History* 7, no. 1 (1966): 79–93. Accessed
July 15, 2021.

———. "The Independence of Brazil and the Abolition of the Brazilian Slave Trade: Anglo-
Brazilian Relations 1822–1826." *Journal of Latin American Studies* 1, no. 2 (1969):
115–47. https://doi.org/10.1017/S0022216X00004442.

———. *Brazil: Essays on History and Politics.* London: University of London Press, 2018.

BFASS, Proceedings of the General Anti-Slavery Convention, called by the Committee
of the British and Foreign Anti-Slavery Society, and Held in London, from Friday,
June 12th, to Tuesday, June 23rd, 1840 (London, 1841).

Black, Jeremy, and Cheryl Fury. "The Development of Sea Power, 1649–1815." In *The Social History of English Seamen, 1650–1815*, edited by Cheryl A. Fury. Suffolk, UK:
Boydell & Brewer, 2017, 5–32.

Blair, David Joseph. "All the Ships That Never Sailed: A General Model of Transnational
Illicit Market Suppression." PhD diss., Georgetown University, 2014.

Boyle, James. *A Practical Medico-Historical Account of the Western Coast of Africa Embracing
a Topographical Description of Its Shores, Rivers, and Settlements, with Their Seasons
and Comparative Healthiness; Together with the Causes Symptoms, and Treatments
of the Fevers of Western Africa; and a Similar Account Respecting the Other Diseases
Which Prevail There.* London: S. Highly, 1831.

Breitborde, L. B. "City, Countryside and Kru Ethnicity." *Africa: Journal of the International
African Institute* 61, no. 2 (1991): 186–201.

# SOURCES

*British and Foreign State Papers*, 1817–1818. London: James Ridgway and Sons, 1837.

British History Online. "House of Lords Journal Volume 33: February 1772, 21–28." In *Journal of the House of Lords Volume 33, 1770–1773*. London: His Majesty's Stationery Office (1767–1830): 259–70. Accessed July 12, 2021. http://www.british-history.ac.uk/lords-jrnl/vol33/pp259-270.

———. "House of Lords Journal Volume 33: March 1772, 1–10." In *Journal of the House of Lords Volume 33, 1770–1773*. London: His Majesty's Stationery Office (1767–1830): 270–92. Accessed July 12, 2021. http://www.british-history.ac.uk/lords-jrnl/vol33/pp270-292.

———. "House of Lords Journal Volume 33: March 1772, 11–20." In *Journal of the House of Lords Volume 33, 1770–1773*. London: His Majesty's Stationery Office (1767–1830): 292–310. Accessed July 12, 2021. http://www.british-history.ac.uk/lords-jrnl/vol33/pp292-310.

———. "House of Lords Journal Volume 33: March 1772, 21–31." In *Journal of the House of Lords Volume 33, 1770–1773*. London: His Majesty's Stationery Office (1767–1830): 310–30. Accessed July 12, 2021. http://www.british-history.ac.uk/lords-jrnl/vol33/pp310-330.

———. "House of Lords Journal Volume 33: April 1772, 21–30." In *Journal of the House of Lords Volume 33, 1770–1773*. London: His Majesty's Stationery Office (1767–1830): 373–77. Accessed July 12, 2021. http://www.british-history.ac.uk/lords-jrnl/vol33/pp373-377.

British Parliamentary Papers, Volume 26. 1828.

Brooks, G. E. *The Kru Mariner in the Nineteenth Century: An Historical Compendium.* Newark, DE: Liberian Studies Association in America, 1972.

Brown, Robert T. "Fernando Po and the Anti-Sierra Leonean Campaign: 1826–1834." *International Journal of African Historical Studies* 6, no. 2 (1973): 249–64.

Brunsman, Denver. *The Evil Necessity: British Naval Impressment in the Eighteenth-Century Atlantic World.* Charlottesville: University of Virginia Press, 2013.

Burg, Barry Richard. *Boys at Sea: Sodomy, Indecency, and Courts Martial in Nelson's Navy.* New York: Palgrave Macmillan, 2007.

———. "The HMS *African* Revisited: The Royal Navy and the Homosexual Community." *Journal of Homosexuality* 56 (2009): 173–94.

———. "Officers, Shipboard Boys and Courts Martial for Sodomy and Indecency in the Georgian Navy." In *The Social History of English Seamen, 1650–1815*, edited by Cheryl A. Fury. New York: Boydell & Brewer, 2017.

Burroughs, Robert. "Eyes on the Prize: Journeys in Slave Ships Taken as Prizes by the Royal Navy." *Slavery and Abolition* 31, no. 1 (2010): 99–115.

———. "Slave-Trade Suppression and the Culture of Anti-Slavery in Nineteenth-Century Britain." In *The Suppression of the Atlantic Slave Trade: British Policies, Practices and Representations of Naval Coercion*, edited by Robert M. Burroughs and Richard Huzzey. Manchester, UK: Manchester University Press, 2016, 125–45.

Burton, E. J. "Observations on the Climate, Topography, and Diseases of the British Colonies in Africa." *Provincial Medical & Surgical Journal* (1840–1842) 3, no. 13 (1841): 249–51.

Carse, Robert. *The Twilight of Sailing Ships.* New York: Galahad Books, 1965.

Cave, Edward. *The Gentleman's Magazine and Historical Review, Volume 220* (January–June 1866). London: Bradbury, Evans, & Co., 1866.

Chapelle, Howard I. *The Baltimore Clipper: Its Origin and Development.* New York: Bonanza Books, 1930.

# SOURCES

———. *The History of American Sailing Ships*. New York: W. W. Norton; New York: Bonanza Books, 1935.

Chappell, David A. "Kru and Kanaka: Participation by African and Pacific Island Sailors in Euroamerican Maritime Frontiers." *International Journal of Maritime History* 6, no. 2 (1994): 83–114.

Christopher, Emma. "Slave Ship Sailors: A Roundtable Response." *International Journal of Maritime History* 19, no. 1 (June 2007): 333–41.

———. "'Tis Enough That We Give Them Liberty?': Liberated Africans at Sierra Leone in the Early Era of Slave-Trade Suppression." In *The Suppression of the Atlantic Slave Trade: British Policies, Practices and Representations of Naval Coercion*, edited by Robert M. Burroughs and Richard Huzzey. Manchester, UK: Manchester University Press, 2016, 55–72.

Clapham, J. H. "The Last Years of the Navigation Acts." *English Historical Review* 25, no. 99 (1910): 480–501.

Clark-Pujara, Christy. *Dark Work: The Business of Slavery in Rhode Island*. New York: New York University Press, 2016.

Clowes, William Laird. *The Royal Navy: A History from the Earliest Times to the Present*. Vol. 6. London: Sampson Low, Marston and Company, 1901.

Cochrane, Thomas. *Narrative of Services in the Liberation of Chile, Peru and Brazil, from Spanish and Portuguese Domination* (2 vols.). London: James Ridgway, 1858–59

*Colonies and Slaves, One Volume: Relating to Colonies; Africans Captured; Jamaica; Slave Emancipation; Slave Trade. Session 14 June–20 October 1831*. Vol. 19. 1831.

Cornell, Paul G. "Owen, William Fitzwilliam." In *Dictionary of Canadian Biography*, vol. 4. University of Toronto/Université Laval (revised 1979). http://www.biographi.ca /en/bio/owen_william_fitz_william_8E.html.

Correspondence with British Coms. at Sierra Leone, Havana, Rio de Janeiro and Surinam on Slave Trade, 1827 (Class A). 1838, Pre–1833 Command Paper.

Correspondence with British Coms. at Sierra Leone, Havana, Rio de Janeiro and Surinam on Slave Trade, 1828 (Class A). 1828, Pre–1833 Command Paper.

Correspondence with British Coms. at Sierra Leone, Havana, Rio de Janeiro and Surinam on Slave Trade, 1829 (Class A). 1829, Pre–1833 Command Paper.

Correspondence with British Coms. at Sierra Leone, Havana, Rio de Janeiro and Surinam on Slave Trade, 1830 (Class A & B). 1830, Pre–1833 Command Paper.

Correspondence with British Coms. at Sierra Leone, Havana, Rio de Janeiro and Surinam on Slave Trade, 1831 (Class A & B). 1831, Pre–1833 Command Paper.

Correspondence with Foreign Powers Relating to the Slave Trade (Class B), 1827. 1827, Pre–1833 Command Paper.

Correspondence with Foreign Powers Relating to the Slave Trade (Class B), 1829. 1829, Pre–1833 Command Paper.

Correspondence with Foreign Powers Relating to the Slave Trade (Class B), 1830. 1830, Pre–1833 Command Paper.

Costa, E. Viotti da. *The Brazilian Empire: Myths and Histories*. Rev. ed. Chapel Hill: University of North Carolina Press, 2000.

Costello, Ray. *Black Salt: Seafarers of African Descent on British Ships*. Liverpool, UK: Liverpool University Press, 2012.

Coupland, Reginald. *The British Anti-Slavery Movement*. 2nd ed. London: Frank Cass & Co., 1964.

Daly, Gavin. "Napoleon and the 'City of Smugglers,' 1810–1814." *Historical Journal* 50, no. 2 (2007): 333–52.

Dancy, J. Ross. *The Myth of the Press Gang: Volunteers, Impressment and the Naval Manpower Problem in the Late Eighteenth Century.* Suffolk: Boydell & Brewer, 2015.

Dawson, Kevin. "Enslaved Watermen in the Atlantic World, 1444–1888." PhD diss. University of South Carolina, 2005.

———. "Enslaved Swimmers and Divers in the Atlantic World." *Journal of American History* 92, no. 4 (2006): 1327–55.

———. "Swimming, Surfing and Underwater Diving in Early Modern Atlantic Africa and the African Diaspora." In *Navigating African Maritime History*, edited by Carina E. Ray and Jeremy Rich. Liverpool, UK: Liverpool University Press, 2009, 81–116.

Dean, Britten. "British Informal Empire: The Case of China." *Journal of Commonwealth & Comparative Politics* 14, no. 1 (January 1976): 64–81.

Desmond, Adrian, and James Moore. *Darwin's Sacred Cause: How a Hatred of Slavery Shaped Darwin's Views on Human Evolution.* New York: Houghton Mifflin Harcourt, 2009.

Domingues da Silva, Daniel. "The Atlantic Slave Trade from Angola: A Port-by-Port Estimate of Slaves Embarked, 1701–1867." *International Journal of African Historical Studies* 46, no. 1 (2013): 105–22.

———. *The Atlantic Slave Trade from West Central Africa, 1780–1867.* New York: Cambridge University Press, 2017.

Downes, Henry. Logbook of HMS SYBILLE and HMS BLACK JOKE 1827–1829 (LOG/N/41). National Maritime Museum, Greenwich, London.

Drescher, Seymour. "The Ending of the Slave Trade and the Evolution of European Scientific Racism." *Social Science History* 14, no. 3 (1990): 415–50.

———. *Abolition: A History of Slavery and Antislavery.* New York: Cambridge University Press, 2009.

Dubois, W. E. B. *The Suppression of the African Slave-Trade to the United States of America, 1638–1870.* Williamstown, MA: Corner House Publishers, 1970.

Edwards, Bernard. *Royal Navy Versus the Slave Traders: Enforcing Abolition at Sea, 1808–1898.* Barnsley, UK: Pen & Sword Books, 2008.

Egan, Pierce, and Francis Grose. *Grose's Classical Dictionary of the Vulgar Tongue: Revised and Corrected with the Addition of Numerous Slang Phrases Collected from Tried Authorities.* London: Pierce Egan, 1823.

Elbourne, Elizabeth. "The Bannisters and Their Colonial World: Family Networks and Colonialism in the Early Nineteenth Century." In *Within and Without the Nation: Canadian History as Transnational History*, edited by Karen Dubunsky, Adele Perry, and Henry Yu. Toronto; Buffalo; London: University of Toronto Press, 2015, 49–75.

Eltis, David. "The British Contribution to the Nineteenth Century Trans-Atlantic Slave Trade." *Economic History Review* 32, no. 2 (1979): 221–27.

———. *Economic Growth and the Ending of the Transatlantic Slave Trade.* Oxford, UK: Oxford University Press, 1987.

———. *The Rise of African Slavery in the Americas.* New York: Cambridge University Press, 2000.

Eltis, David., D. Richardson, D. Davis, and D. Blight. *Atlas of the Transatlantic Slave Trade.* New Haven: Yale University Press, 2010.

Engerman, Stanley L., Seymour Drescher, and Robert L. Paquette. *Slavery.* Oxford: Oxford University Press, 2001.

Falconbridge, Anna Maria. *Two Voyages to Sierra Leone, During the Years 1791—2—3, in a Series of Letters.* London: Anna Maria Falconbridge, 1794.

Ferguson, Niall. *Empire: The Rise and Demise of the British World Order and the Lessons for Global Power.* New York: Basic Books, 2004.

Fletcher, Robert S. G. "'Returning Kindness Received'? Missionaries, Empire and the Royal Navy in Okinawa, 1846–57." *English Historical Review* 125, no. 514 (2010): 599–641.

Follett, Richard. "'Lives of Living Death': The Reproductive Lives of Slave Women in the Cane World of Louisiana." *Slavery & Abolition* 26, no. 2 (2005): 289–304.

———. *The Sugar Masters: Planters and Slaves in Louisiana's Cane World, 1820–1860.* Baton Rouge: Louisiana State University Press, 2005.

Footner, Geoffrey Marsh. *Tidewater Triumph: The Development and Worldwide Success of the Chesapeake Bay Pilot Schooner.* Centreville, MD: Tidewater Publishers, 1998.

Force, William Q. *Army and Navy Chronicle, and Scientific Repository: Being a Continuation of Homans' "Army and Navy Chronicle."* Volumes 1–3. Washington, DC: Wm. Q. Force, 1843.

Foreign and Commonwealth Office Historians. "Slavery in Diplomacy: The Foreign Office and the Suppression of the Transatlantic Slave Trade." *History Notes* 17. Britain: The Foreign, Commonwealth, and Development Office, 2013. https://issuu.com /fcohistorians/docs/history_notes_cover_hphn_17.

*Foreign Slave Trade, a Brief Account of Its State, of the Treaties Which Have Been Entered Into, and of the Laws Enacted for Its Suppression, from the Date of the English Abolition Act to the Present Time.* London: John Hatchard and Son, 1837.

Foy, Charles R. "Eighteenth Century 'Prize Negroes': From Britain to America." *Slavery and Abolition* 31, no. 3 (2010): 379–93.

———. "The Royal Navy's Employment of Black Mariners and Maritime Works, 1754–1783." *International Journal of Maritime History* 28, no. 1 (2016): 6–35.

Franses, Philip Hans, and Wilco van den Heuvel. "Aggregate Statistics on Trafficker-Destination Relations in the Atlantic Slave Trade." *International Journal of Maritime History* 31, no. 3 (August 2019): 624–33.

Frost, Diane. "Diasporan West African Communities: The Kru in Freetown & Liverpool." *Review of African Political Economy* 29, no. 92 (2002): 285–300.

Fyfe, Christopher. *A History of Sierra Leone,* 3rd ed. London: Oxford University Press, 1968.

*Gentleman's Magazine, and Historical Chronicle, for the Year [ . . . ]* United Kingdom: Edw. Cave, 1736–[1868], 1866.

Goldenberg, Joseph. "Shipbuilding." In *The Historical Encyclopedia of World Slavery,* Volume II: *L–Z,* edited by Junius P. Rodriguez. Santa Barbara: ABC-CLIO, 1997, 583–84.

Gragg, Larry. "Middle Passage." In *The Historical Encyclopedia of World Slavery,* Volume II: *L–Z,* edited by Junius P. Rodriguez. Santa Barbara: ABC-CLIO, 1997, 434–36.

Graham, Gerald S. *Empire of the North Atlantic: The Maritime Struggle for North America.* Toronto: University of Toronto Press, 1950.

Great Britain. British and Foreign State Papers 1826–1827. London H.M.S.O.

Greg, W. R. *Past and Present Efforts for the Extinction of the African Slave Trade.* London: Ridgway, 1840.

Griffith, T. R. "On the Races Inhabiting Sierra Leone." *Journal of the Anthropological Institute of Great Britain and Ireland* 16 (1887): 300–10.

Griffiths, John W. *The Progressive Shipbuilder,* Volume 2. New York: John W. Griffiths, 1876.

Grindal, Peter. *Opposing the Slavers: The Royal Navy's Campaign against the Atlantic Slave Trade.* London: I.B. Tauris, 2016.

# SOURCES

Gwyn, Julian. "Collier, Sir George." In *Dictionary of Canadian Biography*, Volume 4. University of Toronto/Université Laval (revised 1979). http://www.biographi.ca/en/bio/collier_george_4E.html.

Haggard, John. *Reports of Cases Argued and Determined in the High Court of Admiralty, During the Time of the Right Hon. Lord Stowell*, Volume 2, 1825–1832, edited by George Minot. Boston: Little, Brown and Company, 1853.

Hair, P. E. H. "Aspects of the Prehistory of Freetown and Creoledom." *History in Africa* 25 (1998): 111–18.

Harmon, Judd Scott. "Suppress and Protect: The United States Navy, the African Slave Trade, and Maritime Commerce, 1794–1862." PhD diss., College of William and Mary, 1977.

Haslam, Emily. "Redemption, Colonialism and International Criminal Law: The Nineteenth Century Slave-Trading Trials of Samo and Peters." In *Past Law, Present Histories*, edited by Diane Kirkby. Canberra, Australia: ANU Press, 2012, 7–22.

Hattendorf, John B. "Maritime Conflict." In *The Laws of War: Constraints on Warfare in the Western World*, edited by Michael Howard, George J. Andreopoulos, and Mark R. Shulman. New Haven: Yale University Press, 1994, 98–115.

Hill, Pascoe Grenfell. *Fifty Days on Board a Slave-Vessel in the Mozambique Channel*. London: Charles Gilpin, 1848; Baltimore, MD: Black Classics Press, 1993.

Holman, James. *A Voyage round the World, including Travels in Africa, Asia, Australasia, America, etc., etc., from 1827 to 1832*. London: Smith, Elder, and Co., 1834.

Hudson, Paul. "Slavery, the Slave Trade and Economic Growth: A Contribution to the Debate." In *Emancipation and the Remaking of the British Imperial World*, edited by C. Hall, N. Draper, and K. McClelland. Manchester, UK: Manchester University Press, 2014, 36–59.

Huntley, Henry. *Seven Years' Service on the Slave Coast of Western Africa*, Volume 1. London: Thomas Cautley Newby, 1850.

Hurwitz, Edith F. *Politics and the Public Conscience: Slave Emancipation and the Abolitionist Movement in Britain*. London: George Allen & Unwin, 1973.

Huzzey, Richard. "The Politics of Slave-Trade Suppression." In *The Suppression of the Atlantic Slave Trade: British Policies, Practices and Representations of Naval Coercion*, edited by Robert M. Burroughs and Richard Huzzey. Manchester, UK: Manchester University Press, 2016, 17–52.

James, Douglas. "Parliamentary Divorce, 1700–1857." *Parliamentary History*, 31 (2012): 169–89.

James, William. *The Naval History of Great Britain: From the Declaration of War by France in 1793, to the Accession of George IV* (6 vol.). London: Richard Bently, 1837.

Keene, Edward. "A Case Study of the Construction of International Hierarchy: British Treaty-Making against the Slave Trade in the Early Nineteenth Century." *International Organization* 61, no. 2 (April 1, 2007): 311–39.

Kennedy, Paul M. *The Rise and Fall of British Naval Mastery*. New York: Penguin, 2017.

Kielstra, Paul Michael. *The Politics of Slave Trade Suppression in Britain and France, 1814–48: Diplomacy, Morality and Economics*. London: Palgrave Macmillan UK, 2000.

Klein, Herbert S., Stanley L. Engerman, Robin Haines, and Ralph Shlomowitz. "Transoceanic Mortality: The Slave Trade in Comparative Perspective." *William and Mary Quarterly* 58, no. 1 (2001): 93–118.

Laird, Macgregor. *Remedies for the Slave Trade*. London, 1842.

Lambert, Andrew. "Introducing William IV: A 'Sailor King'?" *Georgian Papers Programme*

*Blog*, Accessed April 30, 2021. https://georgianpapers.com/2018/02/20/introducing-william-iv-sailor-king/.

Lambert, David. "Sierra Leone and Other Sites in the War of Representation over Slavery." *History Workshop Journal* 64 (2007): 103–32.

Land, Isaac. *War, Nationalism, and the British Sailor, 1750–1850.* New York: Palgrave Macmillan, 2009.

Landers, Sharon. "Sugar Cultivation and Trade." In *The Historical Encyclopedia of World Slavery*, Volume II: *L–Z*, edited by Junius P. Rodriguez. Santa Barbara: ABC-CLIO, 1997, 618–19.

Landler, Mark. "Britain Grapples with Its Racist Past, from the Town Square to the Boardroom." *New York Times*, June 18, 2020, https://www.nytimes.com/2020/06/18/world/europe/uk-slavery-trade-lloyds-greene-king.html.

Laughton, J. K. "Collier, Sir George (1738–1795)." *Dictionary of National Biography*, Volume XI: *Clater–Condell*. London: Smith, Elder, & Co, 1887, 339–41.

Laughton, J. K., and Michael Duffy. "Yeo, Sir James Lucas (1782–1818), Naval Officer." *Oxford Dictionary of National Biography*. September 23, 2004; accessed July 23, 2021.

Laughton, J. K., and Andrew Lambert. "Collier, Sir Francis Augustus (1785–1849), Naval Officer." *Oxford Dictionary of National Biography*. September 23, 2004; accessed June 21, 2021.

———. "Warren, Frederick (1775–1848), Naval Officer." *Oxford Dictionary of National Biography*. September 23, 2004; accessed June 21, 2021.

Laughton, J. K., and Roger Morriss. "Bullen, Sir Charles (1769–1853), Naval Officer." *Oxford Dictionary of National Biography*. September 23, 2004; accessed July 17, 2021.

———. "Hayes, John (1775–1838), Naval Officer." *Oxford Dictionary of National Biography*. September 23, 2004; accessed July 17, 2021.

Laughton, J. K., and Nicholas Tracy. "Collier, Sir George (1738–1795), Naval Officer." *Oxford Dictionary of National Biography*. September 23, 2004; accessed July 12, 2021.

Lavery, Brian. *Life in Nelson's Navy.* Stroud, UK: The History Press, 2007.

———. *Royal Tars: The Lower Deck of the Royal Navy, 875–1850.* London: Conway Publishing; Annapolis, MD: Naval Institute Press, 2010.

Law, Robin. *Ouidah: The Social History of a West African Slaving Port, 1727–1892.* Oxford: Boydell & Brewer, 2005.

Law, Robin, and Kristin Mann. "West Africa in the Atlantic Community: The Case of the Slave Coast." *William and Mary Quarterly* 56, no. 2 (1999): 307–34.

Lawrance, Benjamin N. *Amistad's Orphans: An Atlantic Story of Children, Slavery, and Smuggling.* New Haven: Yale University Press, 2014.

Lawrence, William Beach. *Visitation and Search: or, An Historical Sketch of the British Claim to Exercise a Maritime Police over the Vessels of All Nations, in Peace as Well as in War.* Boston: Little, Brown and Company, 1858.

Leonard, Peter. *Records of a Voyage to the Western Coast of Africa, in His Majesty's Ship Dryad, and of the Service on That Station for the Suppression of the Slave Trade, in the Years 1830, 1831, and 1832.* Edinburgh: William Tait, 1833.

———. *The Western Coast of Africa: Journal of an Officer Under Captain Owen. Records of a Voyage in the Ship Dryad in 1830, 1831, and 1832.* Philadelphia: E. C. Mielke, 1833.

*Letter to the Committee of the London Anti-Slavery Society, on the Present State of the African Slave-Trade, Particularly that which Exists in the Colony of Sierra Leone: With Copious Extracts from the Documents Lately Printed by Order of the House of Commons, Under the Head of "Slave-Trade—Sierra Leone. 6th April 1832."* London, 1832.

Lewis, Michael. *The Navy in Transition, 1814–1864: A Social History*. London: Hodder and Stoughton, 1965.

Linebaugh, Peter, and Marcus Rediker. *The Many-Headed Hydra: Sailors, Slaves, Commoners, and the Hidden History of the Revolutionary Atlantic*. Boston: Beacon Press, 2000.

Lloyd, Christopher. *The Navy and the Slave Trade: The Suppression of the African Slave Trade in the Nineteenth Century*. New York, Routledge, 2012.

Lodge, Edmund. *Portraits of Illustrious Personages of Great Britain: Engraved from Authentic Pictures in the Galleries of the Nobility and the Public Collections of the Country with Biographical and Historical Memoirs of Their Lives and Actions*, Volume 11. London: Harding and Lepard, 1835.

Lowenheim, Oded. "'Do Ourselves Credit and Render a Lasting Service to Mankind': British Moral Prestige, Humanitarian Intervention, and the Barbary Pirates." *International Studies Quarterly* 47 (2003): 23–48.

Lubbock, Basil. *Cruisers, Corsairs & Slavers: An Account of the Suppression of the Picaroon, Pirate & Slaver by the Royal Navy during the 19th Century*. Glasgow: Brown, Son & Ferguson, 1993.

Lynn, Martin. "British Policy, Trade, and Informal Empire in the Mid-Nineteenth Century." In *The Oxford History of the British Empire, Volume III: The Nineteenth Century, by Andrew Porter and Wm Roger Louis*, edited by Andrew Porter. Oxford, UK: Oxford University Press, 1999. Oxford Scholarship Online, 2011.

Macaulay, Kenneth. *The Colony of Sierra Leone Vindicated from the Misrepresentations of Mr. Macqueen of Glasgow*. London: J. Hatchard and Son, 1827.

Malcomson, Thomas. *Order and Disorder in the British Navy, 1793–1815: Control, Resistance, Flogging and Hanging*. Woodbridge, Suffolk, UK; Rochester, NY: Boydell & Brewer, 2016.

Mannix, Daniel P. *Black Cargoes: A History of the Atlantic Slave Trade, 1518–1865*. New York: Viking Press, 1962.

Marcus, Geoffrey J. *Heart of Oak: A Survey of British Sea Power in the Georgian Era*. London: Oxford University Press, 1975.

Marshall, John. *Royal Naval Biography; or Memoirs of the Services of All the Flag-Officers, Superannuated Rear-Admirals, Retired-Captains, Post-Captains, and Commanders, Whose Names Appeared on the Admiralty List of Sea-Officers at the Commencement of the Year 1823, or Who Have Since Been Promoted; Illustrated by a Series of Historical and Explanatory Notes, Which Will Be Found to Contain an Account of All the Naval Actions, and Other Important Events, from the Commencement of the Late Reign, in 1760, to the Present Period, with Copious Addenda*, Volume 2. London: Longman, Rees, Orme, Brown, and Green, 1824.

———. *Royal Naval Biography; or Memoirs of the Services of All the Flag-Officers, Superannuated Rear-Admirals, Retired-Captains, Post-Captains, and Commanders, Whose Names Appeared on the Admiralty List of Sea-Officers at the Commencement of the Year 1823, or Who Have Since Been Promoted; Illustrated by a Series of Historical and Explanatory Notes, Which Will Be Found to Contain an Account of All the Naval Actions, and Other Important Events, from the Commencement of the Late Reign, in 1760, to the Present Period, with Copious Addenda*, Volume 2, Part 2. London: Longman, Rees, Orme, Brown, and Green, 1825.

———. *Royal Naval Biography; or Memoirs of the Services of All the Flag-Officers, Superannuated Rear-Admirals, Retired-Captains, Post-Captains, and Commanders, Whose Names Appeared on the Admiralty List of Sea-Officers at the Commencement of the Year 1823, or Who Have Since Been Promoted; Illustrated by a Series of Historical and*

*Explanatory Notes, Which Will Be Found to Contain an Account of All the Naval Actions, and Other Important Events, from the Commencement of the Late Reign, in 1760, to the Present Period, with Copious Addenda, Supplement,* Part 3. London: Longman, Rees, Orme, Brown, and Green, 1829.

———. *Royal Naval Biography; or Memoirs of the Services of All the Flag-Officers, Superannuated Rear-Admirals, Retired-Captains, Post-Captains, and Commanders, Whose Names Appeared on the Admiralty List of Sea-Officers at the Commencement of the Year 1823, or Who Have Since Been Promoted; Illustrated by a Series of Historical and Explanatory Notes, Which Will Be Found to Contain an Account of All the Naval Actions, and Other Important Events, from the Commencement of the Late Reign, in 1760, to the Present Period, with Copious Addenda,* Volume 3, Part 1. London: Longman, Rees, Orme, Brown, and Green, 1831.

Martin, Jane. "Krumen 'Down the Coast': Liberian Migrants on the West African Coast in the 19th and Early 20th Centuries." *International Journal of African Historical Studies* 18, no. 3 (1985): 401–23.

Martinez, Jenny S. *The Slave Trade and the Origins of International Human Rights Law.* Oxford, UK: Oxford University Press, 2011.

Mathieson, William Law. *England in Transition, 1789–1832.* London: Longmans, Green and Co., 1920.

———. *British Slavery and Its Abolition, 1823–1838.* London: Longmans, Green and Co., 1926.

———. *Great Britain and the Slave Trade, 1839–1865.* London: Longmans, Green and Co., 1929.

McManus, Natalie Jane. "The Pirate Pathway: The Trajectory of the Pirate Figure in Peninsular Spanish Literature from the Nineteenth to the Twenty-First Century." PhD diss., University of Virginia, 2012.

*Memoir of Admiral Sir Francis Augustus Collier.* London: G. Myers, 1850.

Miers, Suzanne. *Britain and the Ending of the Slave Trade.* London: Longman Group, 1975.

Mintz, Sidney Wilfred. *Sweetness and Power: The Place of Sugar in Modern History.* London: Penguin Books, 1985.

Morgan, Edmund S. *American Slavery, American Freedom: The Ordeal of Colonial Virginia.* New York: W. W. Norton , 1975.

Morris, Thomas D. *Southern Slavery and the Law, 1619–1860.* Chapel Hill: University of North Carolina Press, 1996.

Muddiman, J. G. "H. M. S. the Black Joke." *Notes and Queries* 172, no. 12 (March 1937): 200–201.

Mulhern, Joseph Martin. "After 1833: British Entanglement with Brazilian Slavery." PhD diss., Durham University, 2018.

Mustakeem, Sowande M. *Slavery at Sea: Terror, Sex, and Sickness in the Middle Passage.* Urbana: University of Illinois Press, 2016.

*Nautical Magazine, The,* vol. 1. London, 1832.

*Naval Chronicle, for 1805: Containing a General and Biographical History of the Royal Navy of the United Kingdom; with a Variety of Original Papers on Nautical Subjects,* Volume 14 *(from July to December).* London: Joyce Gold, 1805.

*Naval Chronicle, for 1814: Containing a General and Biographical History of the Royal Navy of the United Kingdom; with a Variety of Original Papers on Nautical Subjects,* Volume 32 *(from July to December).* London: Joyce Gold, 1814.

*Navy List, The. Corrected to the 25th of September, 1828.* London: John Murray, 1828.

# SOURCES

*Navy List, The. Corrected to the 20th of June, 1834.* London: John Murray, 1834.

Northrup, David. "African Mortality in the Suppression of the Slave Trade: The Case of the Bight of Biafra." *Journal of Interdisciplinary History* 9, no. 1 (1978): 47–64. https://doi.org/10.2307/203668.

O'Byrne, William Richard. *A Naval Biographical Dictionary.* London: John Murray, Albemarle Street, 1849.

Oldfield, John. "Afterword." In *Britain's History and Memory of Transatlantic Slavery: Local Nuances of a "National Sin,"* edited by Katie Donington, Ryan Hanley, and Jessica Moody. Liverpool, UK: Liverpool University Press, 2016, 237–46.

Olson, Sherry H. *Baltimore: The Building of an American City.* Baltimore: Johns Hopkins University Press, 1997.

Onley, James. "Britain's Informal Empire in the Gulf, 1820–1971." *Journal of Social Affairs* 22, no. 87 (2005): 29–45.

———. *The Arabian Frontier of the British Raj: Merchants, Rulers, and the British in the Nineteenth-Century Gulf.* Oxford, UK: Oxford University Press, 2007.

Painter, Nell Irvin. *The History of White People.* New York: W. W. Norton, 2010.

Parissian, Steven. "George IV: The Royal Joke?" *BBC History.* Last updated February 2, 2011. https://www.bbc.co.uk/history/british/empire_seapower/george_fourth _01.shtml.

Pearson, Andrew. *Distant Freedom: St Helena and the Abolition of the Slave Trade, 1840– 1872.* Liverpool, UK: Liverpool University Press, 2016.

Phillips, Christopher. *Freedom's Port: The African American Community of Baltimore, 1790– 1860.* Urbana: University of Illinois Press, 1997.

Postma, Johannes. *The Dutch in the Atlantic Slave Trade 1600–1815.* Cambridge, UK: Cambridge University Press, 1990.

Prince, Howard M. "Slave Rebellion in Bahia, 1807–1835." PhD diss., Columbia University, 1972.

Rankin, F. Harrison. *The White Man's Grave,* Volume 2. London: Richard Bentley, 1836.

Rankin, John. "Nineteenth-Century Royal Navy Sailors from Africa and the African Diaspora: Research Methodology." *African Diaspora* 6, no. 2 (2014): 179–95.

———. "British and African Health in the Anti-slave-trade Squadron." In *The Suppression of the Atlantic Slave Trade: British Policies, Practices and Representations of Naval Coercion,* edited by Robert M. Burroughs and Richard Huzzey. Manchester, UK: Manchester University Press, 2016, 95–121.

Rediker, Marcus. *Villains of All Nations: Atlantic Pirates in the Golden Age.* Boston: Beacon Press, 2004.

———. "Toward a People's History of the Sea." In *Maritime Empires: British Imperial Maritime Trade in the Nineteenth Century,* edited by David Killingray, Margarette Linclon, and Nigel Rigby. Woodbridge, Suffolk, UK; Rochester, NY: Boydell & Brewer, 2004.

———. *The Slave Ship: A Human History.* New York: Penguin Publishing Group, 2007.

Rees, Siân. *Sweet Water and Bitter: The Ships That Stopped the Slave Trade.* Durham: University of New Hampshire Press, 2009.

Reis, J. J. *Death Is a Festival: Funeral Rites and Rebellion in Nineteenth-Century Brazil.* Chapel Hill: University of North Carolina Press, 2003.

Ribeiro, Alexandre Vieira. "The Transatlantic Slave Trade to Bahia, 1582–1851." In *Extending the Frontiers: Essays on the New Transatlantic Slave Trade Database,* edited by David Eltis and David Richardson. New Haven: Yale University Press, 2008.

Riley, R. C., and Philip Eley. *Public Houses and Beerhouses in Nineteenth Century Ports-*

*mouth.* Portsmouth, UK: Libraries, Museums and Arts Historical Publications Sub-Committee of the Portsmouth, 1983.

Rodger, Nicholas A. M. *The Admiralty.* Suffolk, UK: Terence Dalton, 1979.

———. *The Wooden World: Anatomy of the Georgian Navy.* Glasgow: William Collins Sons & Co., 1986.

———. *Naval Records for Genealogists.* London: Her Majesty's Stationery Office, 1988.

———. *The Command of the Ocean: A Naval History of Britain 1649–1815.* New York: W. W. Norton, 2005.

Rothman, Joshua D. *The Ledger and the Chain: How Domestic Slave Traders Shaped America.* New York: Basic Books, 2021.

Ryan, Michael. "Lord Nelson: Hero and . . . Cad!" *Smithsonian Magazine,* February 2004. https://www.smithsonianmag.com/history/lord-nelson-hero-andcad–10581 1218/.

Scanlan, Padraic Xavier. "The Rewards of Their Exertions: Prize Money and British Abolitionism in Sierra Leone, 1808–1823." *Past & Present* 225 (2014): 113–42.

———. *Freedom's Debtors: British Antislavery in Sierra Leone in the Age of Revolution.* New Haven: Yale University Press, 2017.

Semmel, Bernard. *Liberalism and Naval Strategy: Ideology, Interest, and Sea Power During the Pax Britannica.* Boston: Allen & Unwin, 1986.

SIPRI. "Trends in World Military Expenditure, 2019." Information from the Stockholm International Peace Research Institute (SIPRI). Accessed July 21, 2021, https://www.sipri.org/sites/default/files/2020-04/fs_2020_04_milex_0.pdf.

Skelton, Constance Oliver, and John Malcolm Bulloch. *Gordons Under Arms: A Biographical Muster Roll of Officers Named Gordon in the Navies and Armies of Britain, Europe, America and in the Jacobite Risings.* Aberdeen, Scotland: University Press, 1912.

Slave Compensation Act 1837, 1 & 2 Vict. c. 3.

*State Papers Presented by Command of His Majesty Relating to the Slave Population in the West Indies, on the Continent of South America, and at the Cape of Good Hope: Also, Correspondence with the British Commissioners at Sierra Leone, the Havannah, Rio de Janeiro, Surinam, and Foreign Powers, Relating to the Slave Trade Volume XXVI,* Volume 2 (Session 21 November 1826–2 July 1827). Pre–1833 Command Paper, 1827.

Steffy, J. Richard. "Illustrated Glossary of Ship and Boat Terms." In *The Oxford Handbook of Maritime Archaeology,* edited by Ben Ford, Donny L. Hamilton, and Alexis Catsambis, 2012. https://www.oxfordhandbooks.com/view/10.1093/ox fordhb/9780199336005.001.0001/oxfordhb-9780199336005-e-48.

Stevenson, Robert L. "Jumping Overboard: Examining Suicide, Resistance, and West African Cosmologies During the Middle Passage." PhD diss., Michigan State University, 2018.

Strickrodt, Silke. *Afro-European Trade in the Atlantic World: The Western Slave Coast, c.1550–c.1885.* Woodbridge, Suffolk, UK; Rochester, NY: Boydell & Brewer, 2015.

Sullivan, Anthony. *Britain's War Against the Slave Trade: The Operations of the Royal Navy's West Africa Squadron 1807–1867.* Barnsley, UK: Pen & Sword Books, 2020.

Sundiata, Ibrahim K. *From Slaving to Neoslavery: The Bight of Biafra and Fernando Po in the Era of Abolition, 1827–1930.* Madison: University of Wisconsin Press, 1996.

Taylor, Eric Robert. *If We Must Die: Shipboard Insurrections in the Era of the Atlantic Slave Trade.* Baton Rouge: Louisiana State University Press, 2006.

Taylor, Stephen. *Sons of the Waves: The Common Seaman in the Heroic Age of Sail, 1740–1840.* New Haven: Yale University Press, 2020.

# SOURCES

Thomas, Hugh. *The Slave Trade: The Story of the Atlantic Slave Trade: 1440–1870*. New York: Simon & Schuster 1997.

Tinnie, Dinizulu Gene. "In Search of the Cuban Slave Ship *Dos Amigos*." *ISLAS* 1, no. 4 (2006): 22–30.

———. "The Slaving Brig *Henriqueta* and Her Evil Sisters: A Case Study in the 19th-Century Illegal Slave Trade to Brazil." *Journal of African American History* 93 (2008): 509–31.

Traditional Tune Archive. "Annotation: Black Joke (1) (The)." Accessed July 21, 2021, https://tunearch.org/wiki/Annotation:Black_Joke_(1)_(The).

Trans-Atlantic Slave Trade Database, The. Slave Voyages. 2019. Accessed June 7, 2021, https://www.slavevoyages.org/voyage/database.

Tucker, Louis L. "'To My Inexpressible Astonishment': Admiral Sir George Collier's Observations on the Battle of Long Island." *New-York Historical Society Quarterly* 48, no. 4 (1964): 293–305.

Vale, Brian. *Independence or Death! British Sailors and Brazilian Independence 1822–25*. London: I.B. Tauris, 1996.

———. *The Audacious Admiral Cochrane: The True Life of a Naval Legend*. London: Conway Maritime Press, 2004.

Van Niekerk, J. P. "British, Portuguese, and American Judges in Adderley Street: The International Legal Background to and Some Judicial Aspects of the Cape Town Mixed Commissions for the Suppression of the Transatlantic Slave Trade in the Nineteenth Century (Part 1)." *Comparative and International Law Journal of Southern Africa* 37, no. 1 (2004): 1–39.

Verger, P. *Flux et reflux de la traite des nègres entre le Golfe de Bénin et Bahia de Todos os Santos: du XVIIe au XIXe siècle*. Paris: Mouton, 1968.

Vick, Brian E. *The Congress of Vienna: Power and Politics after Napoleon*. Cambridge: Harvard University Press, 2014.

Waddell, D. A. G. "British Neutrality and Spanish-American Independence: The Problem of Foreign Enlistment." *Journal of Latin American Studies* 19, no. 1 (1987): 1–18.

Walker, James W. St. G. *The Black Loyalists: The Search for a Promised Land in Nova Scotia and Sierra Leone, 1783–1870*. Toronto; Buffalo; London: University of Toronto Press, 1992.

Walsh, Rev. Robert. *Notices of Brazil in 1828 and 1829*, Volume 2. London: Frederick Westley and A. H. Davis, 1830.

Ward, William Ernest Frank. *The Royal Navy and the Slavers: The Suppression of the Atlantic Slave Trade*. New York: Schocken Books, 1970.

Watt, James. "Some Forgotten Contributions of Naval Surgeons." *Journal of the Royal Society of Medicine* 78 (1985): 753–62.

Watts, Sheldon. *Epidemics and History*. New Haven: Yale University Press, 1997.

Wills, Mary. "A 'Most Miserable Business': Naval Officers' Experiences of Slave-Trade Suppression." In *The Suppression of the Atlantic Slave Trade: British Policies, Practices and Representations of Naval Coercion*, edited by Robert M. Burroughs and Richard Huzzey. Manchester, UK: Manchester University Press, 2016, 73–94.

———. *Envoys of Abolition: British Naval Officers and the Campaign Against the Slave Trade in West Africa*. Liverpool, UK: Liverpool University Press, 2019.

Winfield, Rif. *British Warships in the Age of Sail, 1793–1817: Design, Construction, Careers and Fates*. Yorkshire, UK: Seaforth Publishing, 2008.

———. *British Warships in the Age of Sail, 1817–1863: Design, Construction, Careers and Fates*. Yorkshire, UK: Seaforth Publishing, 2014.

# SOURCES

Winterbottom, Thomas. "Account of the Native Africans in the Neighbourhood of Sierra Leone (September 1825)." In *The African Repository and Colonial Journal*, Volume 1, edited by the American Colonization Society. Washington City: 1826; New York: Kraus Reprint Corporation, 1967.

Wolfram, Sybil. "Divorce in England, 1700–1857." *Oxford Journal of Legal Studies* 5, no. 2 (1985): 155–86.

Wright, Denis. *The English amongst the Persians: During the Qajar Period, 1787–1921.* London: Heinemann, 1977.

## Other References

Britannica Academic, s.v. "Revolutions of 1830."

Encyclopaedia Britannica Online. "Cameroon." *Encyclopedia Britannica.* https://www.britannica.com/place/Cameroon.

Encyclopaedia Britannica Online. "Industrial Revolution." *Encyclopedia Britannica.* Accessed May 21, 2021. https://www.britannica.com/event/Industrial-Revolution.

House of Gordon: https://www.houseofgordon.org/history/.

National Archives. "Britain and the Slave Trade," http://www.nationalarchives.gov.uk/slavery/pdf/britain-and-the-trade.pdf.

"Prize Medal." https://collections.rmg.co.uk/collections/objects/379924.html.

# INDEX

Page numbers beginning with 305 refer to notes.

# INDEX

369

INDEX

# INDEX

# INDEX

# INDEX

## ABOUT THE AUTHOR

A. E. Rooks hopes to always be a student of history, though that hasn't stopped her from studying everything else. She is a two-time *Jeopardy!* champion with completed degrees in theater, law, and library and information science, currently at work on a PhD in human sexuality that incorporates aspects of the legal history of sex in the United States. Ultimately, her intellectual passions are united by what the past can teach us about the present, how history shapes our future, and above all, really interesting stories.